THE WILL TO PREDICT

THE WILL TO PREDICT

Orchestrating the Future
through Science

Eglė Rindzevičiūtė

CORNELL UNIVERSITY PRESS ITHACA AND LONDON

Copyright © 2023 by Cornell University

All rights reserved. Except for brief quotations in a review, this book, or parts thereof, must not be reproduced in any form without permission in writing from the publisher. For information, address Cornell University Press, Sage House, 512 East State Street, Ithaca, New York 14850. Visit our website at cornellpress.cornell.edu.

First published 2023 by Cornell University Press

Library of Congress Cataloging-in-Publication Data

Names: Rindzevičiūtė, Eglė, author.
Title: The will to predict : orchestrating the future through science / Eglė Rindzevičiūtė.
Description: Ithaca : Cornell University Press, 2023. | Includes bibliographical references and index.
Identifiers: LCCN 2022036261 (print) | LCCN 2022036262 (ebook) | ISBN 9781501769771 (hardcover) | ISBN 9781501769788 (pdf) | ISBN 9781501769795 (epub)
Subjects: LCSH: Forecasting—History—20th century. | Science—Soviet Union—History.
Classification: LCC CB161 .R56 2023 (print) | LCC CB161 (ebook) | DDC 303.4947—dc23/eng/20220923
LC record available at https://lccn.loc.gov/2022036261
LC ebook record available at https://lccn.loc.gov/2022036262

To Francis

Contents

Acknowledgments	ix
List of Abbreviations	xiii
Note on Translation and Transliteration	xv
Introduction	1
1. What Is Scientific Prediction?	15
2. Visibility, Transparency, and Prediction	38
3. Cybernetic Prediction and Late Modern Governance	58
4. Forecasting and the Cybernetic Sensibility	72
5. Prediction and the Opaque: Prospective Reflexivity	102
6. Reflexive Control	122
7. Global Prediction: From Targeting to Orchestration	150
Conclusion	183
Notes	195
Bibliography	249
Index	277

Acknowledgments

This book grew out of a research agenda that I began to develop in my previous book entitled *The Power of Systems: How Policy Sciences Opened Up the Cold War World* (Cornell University Press, 2016), which explored interactions between East and West policy scientists as they used system-cybernetic approaches to coproduce the concept of global governance. Writing this book made me realize that many questions regarding the logic of scientific expertise cannot be answered without a proper understanding of the conceptual and institutional history of scientific prediction: a key element of both system-cybernetic thinking and the politics of scientific expertise as it was developed in both liberal and authoritarian regimes. This work is an extension of research initiated as part of the research project Futurepol, directed by Jenny Andersson, whose pioneering work on the history of the future and scientific prediction has informed this book in many ways.

This book would not have been possible without the generosity of many people who invited me to test my ideas in seminars and presentations. The idea to embark on this journey crystallized during my visiting stay at the Reppy Institute of Peace and Conflict Studies in Cornell University by invitation from Matthew Evangelista in 2018. At Cornell, I was not only woken up by the bell duly ringing from campus library tower early every morning, but I also had a splendid opportunity to have the brightest minds to scrutinize *The Power of Systems*. I would like to thank the brilliant postgraduates, who did not leave a stone unturned when discussing this book, and the faculty, especially Ronald Kline, Rebecca Slayton, and Judith V. Reppy for their questions and suggestions. I was able to take these inspirations forward thanks to Richard Staley, who hosted me as Visiting Scholar at the Department for History and Philosophy of Science in the University of Cambridge in Spring 2019, where I could dedicate two terms for writing up the first drafts while discussing the ideas with the faculty and postgraduates. While at Cambridge, I am particularly grateful to Robert Northcott and Anna Alexandrova for the conversations about the epistemology of scientific prediction and positivism. At a later stage Tony Bennett, Ivan Boldyrev, Barbara Czarniawska, Francis Dodsworth, and Irina Sandomirskaja offered their insightful comments on the manuscript and its parts. Earlier versions of chapters were presented in too many academic contexts to be listed here, but I would like to particularly thank the colleagues for their support and encouragement

x ACKNOWLEDGMENTS

at Kingston University London, the Centre for Research in the Arts, Social Sciences and Humanities at the University of Cambridge, the School of Public Administration in Gothenburg University, and the Department of Technology and Social Change in Linköping University. I would also like to thank the organizers and participants of the international conference "Worlds of Management," organized by the Institute of Contemporary History, Vienna, Austria, April 14–16, 2021, which provided an invaluable forum to discuss the global circulation of scientific governance at the crucial stage of writing.

Risking to miss many names, I want to thank Carina Abrahamson Löfström, Anna Alexandrova, S. M. Amadae, Jenny Andersson, Dmitry Arzyutov, Stefan Aykut, Lukas Becht, Daniel Bessner, Christophe Bonneuil, Jochen Böhler, Camilo Castillo, Felicity Colman, Ettore Costa, Grégory Dufaud, Till Duppe, Emma Ek Österberg, Linus Ekman Burgman, Marc Elie, Giulia Galli, Nicolas Guilhot, Alexandra Kapeller, Sandra Kemp, Roman Khandozhko, Olessia Kirtchik, Gary Kokk, Michal Kopeček, Katharina Kreuder-Sonnen, John Krige, Andres Kurg, Cristian Lagström, Robin Andersson Malmros, Andrew McKenzy McHarg, Jonathan Oldfield, Poornima Paidaipaty, Jürgen Renn, Klaus Richter, David Runciman, Elke Seefried, Johanna Selin, Clifford Siskin, Mark Solovey, Vítězslav Sommer, Anna Storm, James Sumner, Ksenia Tatarchenko, Aaro Velmet, Andreas Wenger, Steve Woolgar, and Vladislav Zubok for creating opportunities to air my ideas to interdisciplinary academic audiences and/or for your comments.

An indispensable force in organizing research on the history of transnational flows of scientific knowledge was Larissa Zakharova, who died tragically too early. Larissa's input was indispensable for this work especially as she acted as the most effective bridge-builder between French and Russian academic communities.

I would like to thank separately Maria Jose Zapata Campos and Patrik Zapata for engaging discussions about rationalities and lived realities of organization and planning in Nicaragua, Kenya, and Zanzibar. Their insights derived from active engagement with some of world's poorest communities drove me to reconsider the Soviet developmental experience. Also, I am indebted to Tatiana Kasperski and Paul Josephson for their academic friendship and unfalteringly humorous engagement with my ponderings on scientific prediction.

At Cornell University Press Roger Haydon supported the idea of this book from the very beginning and Jim Lance steered the publication process with exemplary efficacy. I also want to thank the two anonymous readers as well as Faculty Board members at Cornell for their constructive comments that helped to improve the manuscript. Michael Durnin, Andrew Lockett, and Anne Jones did fabulous proof reading and copy editing of the manuscript.

Parts of this book draw on my earlier published work. Chapter 3 draws on ideas first presented in my article "The Cybernetic Prediction: Orchestrating the

Future," in *Futures*, edited by Jenny Andersson and Sandra Kemp (Oxford: Oxford University Press, 2021). I used the research that informed my article "A Struggle for the Soviet Future: The Birth of Scientific Forecasting in the Soviet Union," *Slavic Review* 75, no. 1 (2016): 52–76, to conceptually widen and chronologically extend the survey of the development of Soviet forecasting to situate it in the context of the nineteenth century's government by numbers and early debates on planning and prediction. Elements of this article were worked into chapters 2 and 4. Chapter 5 is based on my article "The Future as an Intellectual Technology in the Soviet Union: From Centralised Planning to Reflexive Management," *Cahiers du monde Russe* 56, no. 1 (2015): 111–134 offering an extended discussion of the notion of prediction in Georgii Shchedrovitskii's thought and practice. Chapter 7 draws on my article "Soviet Policy Sciences and Earth System Governmentality," *Modern Intellectual History* 17, no. 1 (2020): 179–208, which served as an incubator for the principal idea and the argument of this present book.

This book was finalized in London during a series of lockdowns in response to the Covid-19 pandemic in 2020–2021, the time when many scholars struggled to balance work and life obligations. Francis, thanks to you this time was not just productive but also bright and full of life. The least I can do is to dedicate this book to you.

Abbreviations

ANT	Actor-Network-Theory
ARAN	Archives of the Russian Academy of Sciences
ASAI	Automated System of Analysis of Social Information
CPSU	Communist Party of the Soviet Union
GCM	General Circulation Model
GKNT	State Committee for Science and Technology
GOELRO	State Commission for Electrification of Russia
Gosplan	All-Union State Planning Committee
ICBM	Intercontinental ballistic missile
IIASA	International Institute of Applied Systems Analysis
IKSI	All-Union Institute of Concrete Social Research
IMRD	Institute for the International Labor Movement
ISA	International Sociology Association
ISA	Institute of Systems Research
KGB	State Security Committee (*komitet gosudarstvennoi bezopasnosti*)
MAD	Mutually assured destruction
MGU	Moscow State University
MIFI	National Nuclear Research University
NBER	US National Bureau of Economic Research
NEP	New Economic Policy
NIEI	Scientific Research Institute of Economics at Gosplan
NIIAA	Scientific Research Institute of Automatic Machinery
NOT	Scientific Organization of Labor (*nauchnaia organizatsiia truda*)
OECD	Organisation for Economic Co-operation and Development
OGAS	National Automated System for Computation and Information Processing
OR	Operations research
RGAE	Russian State Archives of Economics
SAS	Soviet Association of Sociology
SSF	Society for Scientific Forecasting
STP	Scientific-technical progress
STR	Scientific-technical revolution
STS	Science and technology studies

xiv **ABBREVIATIONS**

TsEMI	Central Institute of Mathematical Economics at the All-Union Academy of Sciences
TsIRKON	Centre for Intellectual Resources and Cooperation in Societal Sciences
UNECE	United Nations Economic Commission for Europe
UNEP	United Nations Environment Program
UNESCO	United Nations Educational, Scientific, and Cultural Organization
VNIISI	All-Union Institute for Systems Research
VNIITE	All-Union Institute for Technical Aesthetics
Znanie	All-Union Association for Popularization of Science
WFSF	World Future Studies Federation

Note on Translation and Transliteration

All translation from Russian is done by the author unless indicated otherwise. In transcribing Russian, the Congress Library transliteration table was followed without using the diacritic signs. The original transliteration was retained in texts quoted in English.

THE WILL TO PREDICT

INTRODUCTION

The ability to predict is a form of power. The capacity to form a judgment about what is to come, to infer the consequences of actions, and the ability to use those predictions to act, amplifies power by making it appear willful and strategic. Prediction is also central to the status of modern science and its partial displacement of other regimes of future knowledge—religious revelation, divination, astrology—from the governmental imagination. Deploying scientific predictions in planning for the long term, whether that takes the form of the Soviet Union's infamous five-year plans, capitalist industrial strategies, or global attempts to regulate the climate, is central to the legitimacy and power of government itself. And yet, the power of scientific prediction is not a given, nor is the process of prediction a straightforward case of input translated mechanically into output, prediction feeding into action. Scientific prediction is at once technical, political, social, and institutional.

In his philosophy of the will to power (*der Wille zur Macht*), Friedrich Nietzsche argued that people experience themselves as having "power" only when they are aware of their actions, when they issue "cognizant commands." However, as Linda Williams put it, for Nietzsche this cognizant will is not a "single entity," not "a capacity humans have that enables them to effect change according to their wishes," but "a complex struggle of drives," a struggle for superiority both inside and outside the subject's mind.[1] No one can freely will either oneself or others to action. Even when the will is enacted, it is rarely enacted perfectly.[2] The will to predict and to do this scientifically, as I suggest in this book, resonates with the Nietzschean struggle between the drives, but it is less about domination and

INTRODUCTION

more about navigating complexity. Nowhere else can this struggle be seen better than in the history of the efforts to predict scientifically.

This book examines the history of scientific prediction as both a concept and a form of practice as it developed in the quintessentially future-oriented country of Soviet Russia. It argues that the Russian experience of creating and using scientific predictions to transform and govern society, the economy, and nature, was not unique, but part of the wider landscape of late modern governance, offering a particularly helpful insight into the ways in which scientific prediction became a key part of the orchestration (I will return to this term later) of knowledge and power. The main purpose of this study, therefore, is more general than a history of Russian scientific thought on prediction: I use the Russian case to demonstrate that the meaning of scientific prediction changed and diversified over time as different notions of prediction were articulated in different areas of science. Few are aware, however, of this rich diversity, which tends to get lost in public debate, where scientific prediction is commonly understood as an estimate made by presumably best-informed experts and which can be confidently evaluated as either right or wrong. In turn, the success of scientific predictions is judged in a somewhat naive way: when scientific predictions appear to be right, they are taken as proof of the power of science to deliver knowledge and certainty. When scientific predictions are not confirmed by the actual turn of the events, they are dismissed, perhaps undermining the status of the organizations or individuals involved, or perhaps undermining the power and legitimacy of science more generally. This simplistic sense of scientific prediction as future-telling, which always proves to be either correct or incorrect, is pervasive. For instance, in 2013 the *New Yorker* carried an article stating that "we are now able to prophesy impending cataclysms with a specificity that would have been inconceivable just several years ago."[3] Scientists, however, continued reminding the public that "mathematicians will be the first to tell you that the output of their models are 'projections' predicated on their assumptions, not 'predictions' to be viewed with certainty."[4] Particularly instructive is public debate about the global climate crisis revealing that the complexity of scientific predictions can baffle politicians, journalists, and society, because it is clear that scientific predictions of the climate future do not offer certainty, it can be difficult to compare predictions based on different methodologies, and, finally, different policymakers and the public respond differently to them. Moreover, scientific predictions can be used to manipulate and mislead.[5] In all, it appears that instead of simplifying reality, scientific predictions make it more complex.

The idea for this study emerged in response to a range of influential research into predictive expertise in capitalist economics and politics from the nineteenth century to present.[6] Much of this work focuses on scientific prediction as an expert practice in the fields of economics, finance, and politics, approaching prediction as a positivist concept and mounting a critique of elitist, top-down uses of prediction as a device of control. The growing ambition to use scientific predictions in government, accordingly, is criticized as an alarming development toward authoritarianism expressed, for instance, in expert technocracies and police states, and particularly in the context of the so-called digital transformation of public services where the boundaries of the public and private government get blurred in the process of datafication and algorithmic decision support systems, creating new forms of exploitation.[7] In this way scientific prediction is said to be performative, not merely a representation of the world, but a way of reorganizing the world. Critiquing the Cold War uses of scientific prediction as a form of societal control, the historian Jenny Andersson proposed that "prediction . . . should be understood as a technology of future making and world crafting, a social and political technology in the Foucauldian sense."[8] Andersson draws attention to the internal diversity of these predictive technologies, which she classifies into rationalist and humanist, the former being quantitative approaches to decision techniques and the latter qualitative cultural and political critique and the imagination of alternative futures.[9] Having posited that the study of future visions and planning must involve a study of future-making techniques, including scientific prediction, Andersson and others addressed the political and societal impact of prediction in the context of the development of a particular field of expertise—future studies—a set of social and natural scientific approaches explicitly focused on producing knowledge about future events.[10] For instance, Elke Seefried charts the transnational travels of future studies and system-cybernetic decision sciences East–West and North–South, regarding the history of prediction as a development of estimates about future political, social, and economic conditions.[11] Christian Dayé explores the development of the Delphi method in forecasting in the postwar United States. In addition to these Cold War uses of scientific prediction, historians have scrutinized the related areas of scientific epistemology, environmental and climate science, and the politics of security as well as everyday knowledge. An important insight generated in this strand of scholarship is that the will to predict scientifically generated not only conceptual models, but also institutional cultures based on different attitudes to uncertainty and a range of practices forging trust in data. For instance, Ann Johnson offers a very useful discussion of what she described as empirical and rational cultures of prediction among engineers. The empirical culture of prediction was based on testing the actual performance of materials, a process that is reliable but demanding in terms of the number of tests. The rational culture of prediction was based on mathematical methods, where equations appeared to save time for the engineers but then the predictions were less reliable

4 INTRODUCTION

and prone to failure.[12] The environmental historians Matthias Heymann, Gabriele Gramelsberger, and Martin Mahony, arguing that prediction is "an intrinsic part of today's society, economy and science" and inseparable from "deference to the authority and expertise of others," show that the environmental computer modeling community formed a culture of prediction, creating influential techniques, which were then transferred to other scientific and policy communities.[13] Seeking to identify distinct cultures of prediction, these scholars helpfully point out a wide range of social and institutional resources that are required for creating and legitimizing scientific predictions in the scientific and public policy communities, demonstrating that the meaning of the term "scientific prediction" is not universally shared among scientists. The pluralism of approaches to prediction has also been addressed in security studies: for instance, in their important volume, Andreas Wenger, Ursula Jasper, and Myriam Dunn Cavelty explore scientific prediction in the late modern policy context. They use terms such as "forward reasoning" and "prevision" to delineate the study of diverse predictive techniques of data analysis and decision-making, such as futurology, scenario planning, game theory, forecasting, and risk assessment.[14] Finally, historians such as Jamie Pietruska detailed the ways in which statistical forecasting cohabited with premodern forms of prevision in the nineteenth century United States. Extending this work, Caley Horan's ongoing research explores the overlaps between astrological predictions and financial forecasting.[15]

These works form a valuable resource for understanding the social importance, historical development, and conceptual complexity of scientific prediction. However, these studies rarely explore differentiation of the notions of scientific prediction beyond indicating the transition from premodern divination and mantic knowledge to modern science; although there is a consensus that these two forms of knowledge can coexist and overlap in the practice of both experts and lay public. Moreover, the development of scientific prediction in non-Western and non-liberal governmental contexts remains insufficiently known. This gap in knowledge reflects the common presumption that understanding the history of modern science, technology, and governance requires a focus on the crucible of modernization: Western countries and institutions, where the rest of the world performed a passive role as recipients of "Western" science and are, accordingly, nonessential for the study of modern scientific prediction. Although this view has been challenged in the work on anticipatory knowledge regimes in ancient China as well as the emergent research on Cold War transnational knowledge, there is still much to be done to decolonize the Eurocentric narrative of modernization.[16] This book, I hope, will make it clear that the Soviet Russian trajectory of prediction's epistemologies cannot be reduced to a mere diffusion of Western science, as Russian debates about scientific prediction have coevolved with those of the rest of the world through exchanges, creative adaptations, and innovation since at least the eighteenth century.

Furthermore, despite differences in the political design of communist systems, particularly the pervasive use of state violence and repression, Soviet institutions faced what could be described as the typical problems of modern bureaucracies and the political and social use of scientific expertise. In this respect they resembled their Western counterparts, perhaps just constrained additionally by political restrictions and economic shortages.[17] This becomes particularly clear by expanding the scope of the study of scientific prediction beyond social and political control to the wider orchestration of knowledge, the social, and the material. For example, following a stereotypical rendering of authoritarian prediction, one might expect that scientific prediction in the Soviet Union would be used to boost the power of the Communist Party, express a utopian belief in human reason, and, in its applications, reinforce the repressive apparatus that sought to know and control the population and master the economy. Historical analysis of the course of events could then be used to argue that the Soviet belief in scientific prediction was part of the delusion and failure of the technocratic communist bureaucracy, as the system lost its political legitimacy by not being able to deliver the promised state socialist cornucopian future. At the same time as the police state exhausted and fragmented society, the economy, being based on false statistics, nonviable schemes of industrialization, and ridden with mismanagement and corruption, was run down to collapse. Ergo, the lesson learned is that governmental uses of scientific prediction are expressions of technocratic naivety and dangerous utopianism of the kind critiqued by James C. Scott.[18] This, however, would be a sadly impoverished account of both the intellectual history and historical sociology of scientific prediction in Soviet Russia and elsewhere.

Focusing on developments in late modern Soviet Russia, this book complicates this standard narrative and seeks to fill the gap by introducing a set of Russian thinkers who developed influential concepts of scientific prediction, concepts that they deemed necessary to both advance scientific knowledge and shape new governmental approaches to cope with uncertainty. These concepts were interrelated with Western intellectual developments, but they were not just an example of secondary modernization, of East–West transfer. In contrast, Soviet Russian debates about scientific prediction were informed by local intellectual tradition and emerged in response to the local institutional and political challenges faced by the Soviet state and society. These debates arose in response

6   INTRODUCTION

to social and economic reforms in the post-revolutionary period and were informed by similar discussions about the predictive power of social science and the uses of statistical prediction in management and planning in Germany, France, and the United States. This was a very complex discursive field where different institutional actors relied on a range of the notions of order, control, and prediction: for instance, approaches to prediction migrated between mathematical statistics, biology, neurophysiology, social research and economic planning, rocket science, control engineering, and war mobilization plans. While some of these fields suffered harsh ideological constraints and repression during the heights of Stalinism from the late 1920s to the early 1950s, the conceptual and institutional landscape of scientific prediction began to diversify vigorously from the 1950s. Prediction (*prognozirovanie, predvidenie*) became a key category in official Soviet discourses on governance in the 1960s. In the last decades of the Soviet regime, the 1970s to 1980s, debates about scientific prediction evolved and diversified further to address the problem of global complexity and what was seen as a need to devise a new governmental framework in response to global environmental changes. This book seeks to capture this fascinating diversity of the concepts of prediction, exploring the ways in which Soviet actors engaged with premodern notions of mantic practice, modern prognosis, and positivist prevision, statistical forecasting and explanation, behavioral adaptation, and sense-making in pattern processing.

By focusing on scientific prediction this book also develops the research agenda of the emerging scholarship on the Soviet risk society: the history of Soviet policy approaches to anticipation of global risks, disaster governance, and emergency response.[19] I propose that we must study the conceptual, social, and political architecture of scientific prediction in the way that earlier scholarship did in relation to risk. As Mary Douglas and Aaron Wildavsky put it succinctly, the term "risk" encapsulates both knowledge about the future and consent about desirable outcomes.[20] But the notion of prediction, either common sense or scientific, is part of this knowledge, even if it is not always explicitly considered. In order to understand how risk governance shapes society, we need to understand scientific prediction better, particularly its diverse forms. For this, however, the existing lens of risk studies is not enough: the organization of uncertainty through risk, influentially outlined by Michael Power, overlaps with the organization of prediction, but is not equivalent to it.[21] As I show, the social and institutional impacts of scientific prediction are different from risk: the will to predict scientifically can work as a socially integrating force, creating new types of collectives and alliances, enabling joint action. Indeed, a successful scientific prediction requires a particular kind of orchestration.

Orchestration

This book primarily concerns the forms of scientific prediction that are meant to inform governance, where the notion of governance refers to both public policy and strategic management. A common fallacy is to understand policy action as a linear model of input and output, where scientific expertise (predictions) informs policy decisions which are then implemented by the executive. This linear model has been widely criticized.[22] It is particularly unsuitable for understanding how scientific predictions originate and function. In this book I show how scientists required organizational and institutional reforms to facilitate both the making of predictions and their use in governmental practice: these prediction-makers were reflexive reformers, who argued that predictions could only be scientific when particular organizational conditions were in place. In this way, prediction-makers coproduced scientific approaches and social and organizational settings for their production and use. While coproduction of scientific knowledge and social and political practice has been widely theorized and explored in science and technology studies, I argue that the case of scientific prediction points to a particular form of coproduction, one that is based on recognizing different levels of complexity allocating appropriate types of epistemology and action to each level.

The coordination of the complex social and governmental processes and structures required for the creation and use of scientific prediction I term "orchestration," borrowing a term that was used in the 1940s by the father of cybernetics, Norbert Wiener, to describe the complex conditions of organizing observations of natural phenomena and filtering them into the abstract models of scientific prediction.[23] The term "orchestration" has also proved useful in organization studies, analysis of policy processes and science and technology studies. I suggest that orchestration can serve as a conceptual orientation because it can bridge the concerns of social constructionist approaches to science and technology and process-oriented studies of organizations and organizational behavior. The term "orchestration" describes the process through which scientific knowledge, social order, and political government are coproduced through the creation of data-gathering apparatuses, design of new research objects and subjects, and enactment of new models of order, both behavioral and institutional.[24]

Moreover, the term orchestration offers a particularly useful link to the long-standing academic interest in temporalities and organizational behavior.[25] Max Weber's influential analysis of the rationalization of time through administrative bureaucracy is commonly seen as a defining feature of Western modernity.[26] However, empirically oriented organization studies have found equal measures of chaos as well as order in modern organizations. In the 1970s the prominent

INTRODUCTION

organization scholars Michael Cohen, James March, and Johan Olsen proposed the influential "garbage can" model to explain what appeared to them as illogical allocation of priorities and unsystematic problem-solving in organizations. According to this theory, the key factor that influences what is being done in an organization is timing and synchronization: it is not the "intrinsic" meaning or logic of the problem that shifts it to priority status, or how the problem fits with the organizational structure, but the problem's position in the temporal framework of organizational activities.[27] The key insight from the garbage can model was that to make an organization more effective one has to address the problem of synchronization.

Fast forward several decades and organization and policy scholars have embraced the study of process as no less important than organizational structure (bureaucratic forms, norms, and values). Synchronization of intraorganizational and interorganizational activities has been a central task for managers and policymakers, particularly in the context of the internationalization of business and governance. Whereas the garbage can model suggests a high degree of ad hoc action and therefore can only serve as a descriptive (but, understandably, not a normative) concept, the term orchestration began to gain popularity as it suggests purposiveness and harmony. In the management literature, resource orchestration has become an established approach which puts the emphasis on management processes, particularly the diverse forms of mediation inside and between organizations.[28] However, it is in the research on policy design and policy processes, an increasingly significant area of research in political studies, that the model of orchestration as a form of governance has been rising to prominence. This rise is motivated by both conceptual development and actual reforms in governance, particularly the introduction of the open method of coordination of policy processes, formally initiated by the European Union in 2000, which was then theorized as orchestration by Kenneth Abbott and colleagues.[29] They defined orchestration as both a descriptive and normative term applicable to global, international, and multilevel governance. Here orchestration refers to a form of indirect governance, where action is coordinated between different territorial-administrative units: local, regional, national, and international.[30] There is a distinct orchestrator (a political authority) that acts through intermediaries (lower-level authorities) to achieve clear targets or outputs. Orchestration underscores "voluntary agency" (of local-level authorities), "indirect governance" through intermediaries (institutions and other actors), mobilization of resources, and establishing and achieving shared targets.[31] The key challenges are coherence and coordination, where the governor may lack operational capacity, regulatory competence, or legitimate authority.[32]

INTRODUCTION   9

Note that the model of indirect, mediated political orchestration echoes cybernetic steering, the idea imported from electronic engineering into management and policy thinking in the 1950s to 1960s.[33] The term cybernetics, proposed by the American mathematician Norbert Wiener in 1948, was derived from the Greek word *kubernētēs*, which means the steersman of a ship. I discuss Wiener's theory of prediction and control in chapters 1 and 2; here it is enough to note that the cybernetic model of steering was conceived to address the problem of effective behavioral response to changing environments. In its most simple version, the control center (the steersman) processes information flows by observing the environment and issues commands through signals. In more complex versions, several layers of control centers can be combined, they can also be hierarchically organized, as in second-order cybernetics. Note that the task of the steersman is both more challenging and, at the same time, narrower than that of an orchestrator. The steersman needs to direct and balance the ship, avoiding getting lost and capsizing. The orchestrator's task is more complex: they need to secure coherent action between many human and nonhuman actors, aligning their intentions and interactions. (Luckily for the orchestrator, nobody rocks the stage, although some human participants might "rock the boat" sometimes.) It is clear that the orchestration and cybernetic steermanship models are not opposite, they overlap in many ways, but they deal with different temporalities. The orchestration model of governance, scholars argue, will compensate for the failures of linear control in complex, uncertain, and long-term situations, where the use of simplistic administrative management based on short-term predictions and error corrections (which are the basis of cybernetic steering) is limited.[34] Furthermore, the model of orchestration does not replace, but develops the model of liberal governance at a distance that is based on self-regulation, a version of what I described as system-cybernetic governmentality in my earlier work.[35]

In this book, I use the term orchestration in a wider sense to describe the organization of different forms of agencies (i.e., not only governmental administrations, but also behaviors and materialities) in a synchronized manner. The metaphor of orchestration is, indeed, very suitable for the study of scientific prediction: an orchestra is not a solo, and, as Martin Carrier noted, "prediction is a great team player but a lousy soloist."[36] In this way, I approach the history of scientific prediction not as a trajectory of attempts to control future outcomes, doomed to fail, but as an open epistemological experimentation that feeds into the orchestration of the future, which is productive of new subjectivities and modes of action. However, by suggesting that different predictions have to be orchestrated in order to meet the criterion of scientificity, in turn, orchestrating

10   INTRODUCTION

the future in different ways, I do not suggest that either science or the future are produced in a consensual and consistent way. This would be an unhelpful simplification that the term orchestration helps avoid. The analytical usefulness of the term orchestration has already been indicated, for instance, in actor–network theory, where orchestration was used synonymously alongside terms such as assembling, arranging, and coordinating, which described the process of mobilizing and integrating different agencies and materials (these verbs were famously turned into nouns, for instance, "assemblage" and "agencement").[37] The very etymology of the term reveals the imperative to recognize the centrality of plural agencies and materialities: losing this plurality an orchestra will stop being orchestral.

The meaning of the word "orchestra" is derived from the Greek word *orkhēstra*, which originally referred to a section of the stage where dance performance took place and was adopted to describe a group of musicians performing a piece of music. There are very interesting studies in the history of music which examine orchestration as both a social and material process. It is fascinating that the great shift in orchestral practice took place as a result of Joseph Haydn's late eighteenth-century innovation in reorienting orchestration away from singers' voices to give equal importance to instruments; accordingly, the quality of the instruments became increasingly important. New materialities, in the form of improved instruments, in combination with the coordination of their diverse human manipulators, were to create new forms of music.[38] I find this shift away from the embodied, human voice (singing) to embrace the polyphony of music instrumentation helpful for thinking about the historical trajectory of scientific prediction, where the "voices" of instruments, such as mathematical equations, algorithms, and formal cognitive models come to the fore.

The story of modern scientific prediction, as I show in this book, started as a drive for orchestration of data production and representation practices: attempts to map, chart, and read the signs in what appeared as mute objects, planets, and events. The importance of the voice of the reader—the predictor—grew with the development of the method of continuous observation (diagnosis) and prediction that was continuously adjusted in line with the changing symptoms (prognosis). Orchestration of observation and prediction became central for the sciences of fleeting phenomena, such as meteorology, public health, and the economy. The more macro these phenomena became, the more pertinent was the process of orchestration, especially with the introduction of statistics and mathematical methods of prediction in governance. Starting in the 1950s and 1960s, computerized automation technologies began to churn out what appeared to be machine-produced predictions. By the second decade of the twenty-first century many residents of the plugged-in world turn to Amazon's virtual assistant Alexa for the latest weather forecasts. However, as I show in this book, computer data and digital voices are not soloists: they are but some of many elements orchestrated to produce a scientific prediction. Computer technology is not separable from other material, social, and institutional resources. The father of cybernetics, the informational theory of control, Norbert Wiener, saw this in the 1940s, and so did Nikita Moiseev, the patron of global environmental modelling and governance in the Soviet Union in the late 1980s.

The Structure of the Book

There are several different notions of prediction that circulate in the language of policymakers, scientists, and members of the public. The roots of some of these notions, as I show in chapter 1, go back to the premodern era, whereas other notions are more recent and fundamentally different from the former ones. Chapter 1 explores three types of scientific prediction: premodern prediction, modern positivist prediction, and late modern prediction based on the cybernetic sensibility, showing how different notions of prediction were created to understand and explain fleeting, ephemeral social and political phenomena.

Chapter 2 traces the first debates on scientific prediction in the postrevolutionary Russia of the 1920s and 1930s. Focusing on the Russian pioneer of economic forecasting, Nikolai Kondrat'ev, I situate the early Soviet approach to scientific prediction in the context of the long nineteenth century and French positivism. I show that some of the early positivist thinkers involved in making social and economic predictions were aware of the limitations of the approach and the link between scientific epistemology and institutional practice. They recognized that statistical numbers can create an illusion of control, especially when governance at a distance is at stake: large-scale and long-term governmental imagination operates with maps and numbers.[39] Such visibility came at the cost of distortion and disregard of the local.[40] When applied to future developments, the meaning of numerical prediction becomes even more complicated.

Once these differences are clarified, it is easier to understand the distinctiveness of the cybernetic notion of prediction, which is presented in chapter 3. Proposed by Norbert Wiener in the 1940s, the model of cybernetic prediction played a key role in informing policy and management thinking and underpinned advances in robotics, neuroscience, genetics, and climate science. Indeed, although such different communities as climate modelers, neoliberal thinkers of the Geneva school, and state socialist planners deployed very different notions of prediction, they shared a fascination with cybernetics, which inspired them to use scientific prediction to conceptualize, inform, and organize the governance of the social

12   INTRODUCTION

and natural worlds.[41] Wiener's cybernetics has been foundational for a whole range of scientific and engineering fields, particularly neuroscience, physiology, psychology, and artificial intelligence (AI).[42] His work on servomechanisms is seen as an important predecessor to Cold War cybernetic totalitarianism, leading to the emergence of what Paul Edwards termed "closed worlds," ruled by surveillance and military technology.[43] Wiener's take on cybernetic prediction, therefore, is crucially important, and is presented and analyzed in this chapter. The central argument is that Wiener understood prediction as a relational concept: not as a disembodied, boundless control loop, but as an organizational principle that relies on information and materiality and is bounded by complexity. The aim of cybernetic prediction was quite narrow, but it was inseparable from a wider effort to orchestrate knowledge production and feed it into action.

Wiener's model of the informational loops of prediction and behavioral control, as shown in the subsequent chapters, was selectively adopted and adapted in attempts to make sense of governmental problems in the economy, the management of organizations, public policy, Cold War strategy, and Earth system science. This wide-ranging fascination with cybernetics posed challenges: some areas of scientific prediction, such as statistical forecasting (defined as statistical techniques of interpolation or extrapolation of data), were expected to serve as cybernetic prediction, but this was not achievable because of different conceptual demands.

In the context of Soviet authoritarianism, however, quantification increased visibility and limited the informal and insulating power of the Communist Party. To quantify amorphous practices one needs to collect data, which, in turn, requires interinstitutional cooperation and exchange. In chapter 4, I discuss the reintroduction of the statistical forecasting of the Soviet economy and society in the 1960s as part of what I call a "cybernetic sensibility," which led to institutional reforms to the politicized, bureaucratic system. Although these reforms failed, they did so in a productive way, creating a particular "culture of forecasting," which combined the positivist notion of prediction as generation of reliable scientific knowledge with a cybernetic notion of prediction as pattern recognition and adaptation. This culture of forecasting was transnational and took shape in the institutional context of late state socialism and East–West knowledge transfer.

Both positivist and cybernetic theories of prediction were meant to be instrumental, to help decision-makers achieve their goals. But who—and how—decides the goals? In chapter 5, I present attempts to marry the informal, nontransparent social practice of goal-setting with scientific prediction in a remarkable phenomenon of post-Stalinist Russian science, the Moscow Methodological Circle. The Circle's leader, Georgii Shchedrovitskii, devised a formalist, cognitive method of reflexive goal-setting and used it to create informal collectives of scientific, cultural, and managerial elites. Prospective reflexivity is neither an inference from empirical data nor an explanation, it is about collective sense making and action. In contrast to the input–output method of statistical forecasting, prospective reflexivity envisions a future course of action where the behavior and perceptions of the actors are part of the plan. In the Soviet context, its political effects were highly ambivalent: prospective reflexivity empowered bottom-up decision-makers, enabling them to bypass bureaucratic compartmentalization. However, it also legitimized informality, creating opaque spaces for decision-making outside of institutional accountability, all of which mattered during the professionalization of management in Russia after 1990.

The orchestration of scientific prediction in secretive and securitized contexts is analyzed in chapter 6. According to classical cybernetic theories by Wiener and W. Ross Ashby, the loops of prediction as pattern recognition help organisms adapt to their environments. In the social and military context, however, some predictions are used to destabilize the situation and deceive the opponent. This chapter presents the case of Russian reflexive control, a Cold War strategic framework for decisions that sought to make the opponent—the West—more predictable and deceivable. Created by Vladimir Lefebvre in the 1960s, reflexive control theory became a fundamental component of Russian military strategic and operational action. This chapter details the trajectory of reflexive control as an epistemological attempt to tackle the problem of reflexivity that has been associated with unpredictability, ungovernability, and uncertainty. While harnessing reflexivity proved to be utopian from the cognitive science perspective, reflexive control theory survived as a conceptual tool to legitimize deception, used, for instance, by the Russian authorities during the annexation of Crimea and the war in Ukraine.

The final chapter 7 explores the changing understanding of the role of scientific predictions of global processes, where human activities transform the Earth. The notion of cybernetic prediction describes goal-seeking behavior. However, the language of goals and targets has proven to be inadequate when facing long-term and large-scale processes. Decision scientists have shown that it is very difficult and sometimes quite impossible to establish collective preferences.[44] However, AI scientists maintain that individual and collective preferences must be worked into goal-setting systems.[45] Climate change must also be mitigated by taking into consideration collective preferences to avoid green authoritarianism.[46] The question is whether the cybernetic model of predictive behavior and goal-setting is suitable for addressing large-scale and long-term problems. In this chapter I present a case study of a historical context in which this problem was addressed and the conceptual innovation of the idea of "government through milieu" and thinking from the limits. The central argument is that cybernetic prediction and government through milieu do not necessarily oppose each other but represent different stages in decision-making and governmental orchestration. The case study explores 1970s and 1980s Russian thought about the "algorithms of global development" that emerged from a debate among East and West climate scientists in the 1980s and 1990s and which paved the path for the later idea of the Anthropocene as a governmental problem.

My story ends in the late 1980s, when the will to predict scientifically gathered momentum as the center of the global political economy was shifting away from the Western advanced industrial democracies to China and Southeast Asia and when the capacity of digital technology and algorithmic governance was becoming not an expectation, but an everyday reality. For better or worse, the age that has followed promises to be the age of prediction and this book sketches a few paths that led to it.

1

WHAT IS SCIENTIFIC PREDICTION?

In this chapter I outline three distinct types of prediction: the premodern notion of prediction as conjecture, the modern notion of prediction articulated in positivism and logical empiricism, and the late modern notion of prediction anchored in cybernetic sensibility. By proposing these three types of prediction I am not suggesting that this categorization is either precise or complete but rather that it is useful to indicate the historical and conceptual differences that characterize the concept of scientific prediction.[1] These loose types will also help understand the evolution of the Soviet will to predict scientifically as it embraced all of these forms of scientific prediction. Focusing on the conceptual differences can also help understand a more general problem of a somewhat naive approach to scientific prediction in government and management. For instance, policy decision-makers tend to assume that scientific prediction is just another estimate made by scientists or experts who happen to be "better informed" and able to process larger amounts of data.

While one can find many different notions of scientific prediction in the academic literature, these notions are compartmentalized in respective disciplines, which define or use the term prediction in different ways. In the 2018 edition of the *Encyclopaedia Britannica*, for instance, prediction is considered in the articles on criminology (predicting reoffending) but the most extensive discussion of prediction is presented in relation to probability theory (the problem of control), and automata theory (servomechanisms).[2] Indeed, many historians reproduce similar notions of scientific prediction as an element derived from automation and machine control that is transferred to the models of economic planning and

16   CHAPTER 1

governance.[3] However, as I show, prediction has a much broader conceptual mandate as a central component within established "scientific knowledge" in the Western tradition, as well as part of sense-making in both Western and non-Western contexts. Contrary to common sense, scientific prediction is not always about guessing the future.[4] Contrary to the histories of the Cold War scientific expertise, scientific prediction is not always about control.

The Premodern Notion of Prediction as Conjecture

In the early twenty-first century, historians of science have turned to explore the epistemological, social, and political uses of prediction in premodern eras. Their interest was guided by two overarching questions: first, how societies in the past coped with the future and, second, the role of prediction in the development of modern Western science. Historians studied philosophical debates but also social practices in ancient Greece, the Roman republic, and China. As their studies identified a fascinating range of concepts that were deployed to organize the knowledge of the unknown, the unknown being situated along a temporal axis in the future, there is no space to do full justice to this research. I limit my discussion to a few key aspects of prediction that will matter for my subsequent analysis of late modern scientific prediction.

In the Western context, the first extensive philosophical debates about the types of knowledge of unknowns situated in the future took place in ancient Rome, where Roman philosophers drew on the Greek tradition. As Federico Santangelo shows in his extensive study of the late Roman republican debates about the limits of human knowledge, the first systematic discussion of the key notions that were used to organize thinking about the unknown was produced by Cicero (106–143 BC). According to Santangelo, Cicero introduced the notion of divination, a version of the Greek term *mantike*, from which the notion of mantic science was later derived; examples of mantic science are, for instance, chiromancy, hydromancy, and astrology. To practice *mantike* meant to identify and read constellations of signs in order to reveal the meaning and the order of the events that were to happen. Like *mantike*, the practice of divination also entailed reading signs. However, unlike *mantike*, divination sought to produce not just a reading of fleeting signs, but a form of structured knowledge (*scientia*) that was reaching out to the fundamental unknown, the area of the gods.[5] Divination was conducted as part of a ritual, performed to access the divine knowledge. For instance, augurs would interpret birds' flights and oracles would engage in different practices to survey land and prevent disasters.[6]

These different knowledge practices were tied to the view of the world that was split into areas of which some were knowable to humans while others were less knowable. In the ancient Greek tradition, the whole universe, including human lives and events, was considered finite and in principle knowable, but only from the gods' point of view. In contrast, in ancient China, the notion of the world was more open to uncertainty: the universe of things and events was seen as evolving and changeable. The Chinese version of mantic knowledge was used to help people anticipate changes and adjust their course of action in the most beneficiary way, without providing complete certainty.[7] Although the ancient Greek worldview was more static than the ancient Chinese, even this relatively static world was understood as consisting of two domains, one being more predictable than another. Cicero, according to Santangelo, proposed that some areas of life could be subject to prudent techniques of reason and judgment (*mantike*). Others could hardly be known, being subject to divine fate:

> [A]rs and *prudentia* may be useful for the prediction of fortuitous events: sailors, doctors and generals face these kinds of events at all times and use their knowledge to anticipate, or face them. Predicting someone's death is tantamount to reading what is 'in the domain of *fortuna*' (*quae in fortuna positae sunt*); such prediction is not based on any practice (*ars*) or knowledge (*sapientia*).[8]

For Cicero, as for the ancient Chinese, to be prudent meant to foresee events and take action before they happened. Action and moral judgment were deemed inseparable from different forms of knowledge of the unknowns as well as the future. But prudent predictions could be reliably made only in the areas that are in principle knowable to men and which could be acted on with a degree of certainty: such as sailing the seas, treating a patient, or commanding an army. However, many areas were outside the scope of prudent predictions: existential events, such as death or securing a political victory, belonged to the realm of the gods. Nevertheless, Greeks and Romans believed that some knowledge could be obtained even about these areas with the help of divination: partaking in the divine knowledge that can be accessed by reading the signs that reveal future events.[9] This constituted the classical notion of prediction: reading the signs in order to identify events, the knowledge of which was necessary for taking prudent action. This knowledge was regarded as a domain of specialists, it was far removed from a common guess. Without a qualified prediction (mantic or divination), there could be no prudent action. Mantic knowledge and divination were strongly associated with a temporal axis, but only interested in the future events, not in the past.[10] This formula was adopted and further developed in the medieval period.

18   CHAPTER 1

In the European Middle Ages, according to the historian Alexander Fidora, there was a shift from divination and mantic knowledge to *prognosis*, a type of knowledge that emerged in medical theory and shared many features with what later would become the modern notion of scientific prediction. In the medieval texts, divination was discussed in the context of writings on magic. For instance, in the seventh century AD the Spanish scholar and theologian Isidore of Seville wrote that "augurs and astrologers claim for their predictions a status of knowledge that, they allege, partakes knowledge of God, which elevates it above the limits of natural knowledge."[11] Other texts presented ancient Greek and Roman typologies of mantic sciences, such as chiromancy, pyromancy, geomancy, and hydromancy, but also astrology and, initially, medicine. These types of knowledge, as Fidora observed, was grouped together under one category because it was primarily interested in signs (*signa*) and not causes (*causae*). Mantic knowledge was locational, topological, concerned with logistical relations: situating events on the temporal and spatial axis. To separate the mantic knowledges from natural sciences they were classified as *sciencia coniecturalis*, conjectural science.

Conjectural science was deemed hierarchically inferior to natural sciences, particularly mathematics and physics, because conjectural science offered less certainty. Moreover, conjectural science was considered less reliable than the empirical sciences or even opinions. This is because conjectural science studied signs that either were changing or could be changed: for instance, the moving constellations of stars or evolving symptoms of an illness. In contrast, empirical sciences were based on universal laws. Similarly, opinions were also considered based on equally universal morals. Therefore, both empirical sciences and opinions were regarded more reliable and truthful.[12]

Nevertheless, although unreliable, conjectures were deemed necessary because they informed decisions and guided behavior in the changing, uncertain context. Conjectures did not explain the order of things, but they required a skillful semiological reading and the ability to bridge conjectural knowledge and practice. To give a contemporary example, originally suggested by the philosopher Nicholas Denyer, having a railway timetable and identifying arrival and departure times does not cause the train to arrive. However, reading the timetable helps a traveler to get on the right train.[13] What Denyer presents is the case of a very loose coupling between the reading of signs (the timetable) and the course of action (the arrival of the train), where signs and material infrastructures appear to "rule" human behavior. This phenomenon has fascinated social scientists since the late twentieth century. For instance, scholars representing the actor–network theory (ANT) would argue that the railway timetable does "cause" the train to arrive to a particular spot at a particular time, although not in a physical way. The timetable is the central element in an actor network, a locus which enables accountability and control of the trains that might be otherwise early or late or go to the wrong destination.[14] Organization scholars, like the social psychologist Karl Weick, would argue that the timetable is an element of a "causal loop," a sequence of expectations, explanations, and actions which result in what may appear as a self-fulfilling prophecy, the arrival of the train.[15] In line with Weick, I suggest that conjectural knowledges help orchestrate, especially synchronize, reality. As I will show in the last section of this chapter, this performative strive is characteristic of both premodern conjectures and late modern predictions infused with cybernetic sensibility.

Conjectural knowledge was an important step in the history of modern science as an attempt to create and systematize knowledge that could account for volatile and changing aspects of reality. The human body was one instance of such a reality: whereas key events of human future, such as life and death, belonged to the god's knowledge and action, health and illness were understood as cumulative processes that could be both known by humans and acted on. It was in the medieval medical treatises that, according to Fidora, the epistemological roots of modern scientific prediction can be found.[16] When it came to health and illness, the practice of divination was eventually replaced with "prognostication." The term prognostication was derived from the Greek physician Hippocrates's treatise *Prognôstikon* (Book of Prognosis), written in *ca.* 370 BC.[17] Hippocrates wrote that a physician "will the better be able to effect a cure if he can foretell, from the present symptoms, the future course of the disease." Foretelling, as Lisa Raphals noted, is a continuous process, because the course of the disease cannot be wholly foretold from its beginning. As symptoms change and evolve, they can create new courses of development and must be constantly monitored.[18]

In medical practice, conjectural semiology (the reading of symptoms as they are expressed in a given constellation of signs) foregrounded the development of diagnostic methods and what is today understood as medical prognosis. A new prognostic model was articulated in the late twelfth century, when the conjectural model of "if . . . then . . ." became widely used to structure prognosis in medical treatises. According to Fidora, this type of prognostic knowledge was increasingly specialized to increase precision in answering specific questions. An influential expression of this specialization of prognosis was decision trees, which were drawn to guide the medical judgment.[19] In medicine, as well as in meteorology, precision became a key criterion for conjectural knowledge. The difference from the ancient mantic practice was the growing importance of temporal relations between signs: a good prognosis was guided not only by structural relations, as in a decision tree, but also by chronologies of temporal relations. Not

20   CHAPTER 1

only forms of symptoms, but also the sequence and rate of change had to be identified, charted, and interpreted. This gave rise to the notion of prognosis as "a cumulative interpretation of consecutive events."[20]

The crucial epistemological breakthrough, according to Fidora, was the understanding that the course of events itself has an effect on the final outcome. This idea served as a basis for what would become modern scientific prediction, which, in turn, would form a key component of the epistemological apparatus of modern science. Indeed, Fidora suggested, it was precisely this understanding of prediction that would later separate "proper," modern sciences from nonscientific knowledges: medicine, based on the prognostic method, was accepted into the canon of modern science, whereas astrology and other mantic sciences, such as chiromancy and hydromancy, were not. Astrology was deemed nonscientific because astrologers were completely uninterested in the actual course of events. Instead, astrologers offered what were described as "global" predictions, where future events were entirely determined by a priori constellations of signs, which were removed both in terms of distance and time from the person or event in question. Unlike physicians, astrologers ignored the role of the mediated, processual, and cumulative character of reality.[21] It is interesting that the difference between medicine and astrology was not principal, but gradual, based on the distance in time and space: in medical knowledge signs, the symptoms of illness, were present more immediately, whereas astrology dealt with signs that were distant both in time and space, for instance, the planet constellation at the moment of birth.[22] However, because conjecture was closely associated with the mantic knowledges, its status was questioned in the early modern and modern periods. As the historian Mary Poovey shows in her influential study of eighteenth- and nineteenth-century Britain, critics of conjectural knowledge associated it with "self-interest, irresponsible speculation, and partisanship."[23] In its extreme version, conjectural knowledge was derided for not being based on systematic records or empirically observable facts. The more moderate version of critique pointed to the absence of interest in the mediating phenomena that linked the facts.

To summarize, modern scientific prediction, in this way, developed as a result of the rejection of divination as partaking in the gods' knowledge. It also rejected mantic conjectures, particularly astrology, because they ignored the mediating processes that linked signs and the final outcomes. However, operating with conjectures and exercising prudence remained central for the modern notions of scientific prediction that tackled the issues posed by fast-changing, obscure reality, such as sailing rough seas, commanding a battle, or curing a patient. However, as I show in the next section, an additional notion of scientific prediction was formed in philosophy, where prediction was dissociated from both conjecture and prudent action; it was placed at the very heart of modern scientific knowledge and practice.

Towards the Modern Notion of Prediction in Positivism and Logical Empiricism

The philosophical debate that zooms in on prediction (of the future) as an epistemological problem of science (what can be known with high degree of certainty) and not so much a problem of action, as in mantic knowledge (what could be done to ensure a beneficial course of events), is traditionally traced to Francis Bacon's skepticism about the possibility of coalescing particular observations into general abstractions or "universals" and David Hume's problem of induction.[24] In his *An Enquiry Concerning Human Understanding* (1748) Hume proposed that there is neither logical nor empirical basis to make reliable statements on future occurrences. According to Hume's famous example, it does not matter how many times one saw the sun rise in the morning; the regularity of observation alone is not enough to claim with certainty that the sun will rise tomorrow. Accordingly, the future course of events cannot be scientifically known if science consists of empirical observation only. According to Poovey, this statement, known as Hume's problem of induction, challenged the status of conjecture as a scientific form of knowledge. Nevertheless, some proposed that even Hume admitted that regularity still matters and that scientific prediction somehow "accords with past regularity."[25] Just what exactly is required to bridge the gap between knowledge of the known event with the unknown one, as indicated by Hume, would become a central question in the philosophy of knowledge and science, particularly in the applied domains.[26] In what follows and in subsequent chapters I show that scientific prediction works as a relational concept that is used to bridge "the Humean gap"—the problem of induction linking the observer and observed phenomena into chronological chains. Poovey, drawing on Peter Dear, offers an accessible definition of induction that is helpful here: "induction is the method Bacon recommended for moving gradually from observed particulars to the generalizations that constituted systematic knowledge." For my argument the procedure of "moving gradually" is centrally significant and prediction can be regarded as a key part of this process.[27]

One of the most influential ways of bridging the Humean gap was proposed by the French positivist philosophers who argued that it is precisely the power to predict the future that confers scientific status on knowledge. This definition of science is said to have been first proposed by Auguste Comte in his *Course de philosophie positive* (1830–1842). Comte used the term *prevoyance* (prevision) to describe a fundamental component of both scientific knowledge and the transformative application of science to the improvement of the human condition: "from science comes Prevision, from Prevision comes action" (*Course*, 1830).[28]

The power to predict, to leap from the known to the unknown, is what separates scientific knowledge from lay knowledge:

> Till the rising of the sun or of some star could be accurately predicted, as to time and place, there was no astronomical science. Its whole process since has been by introducing more and more certainty and precision into its predictions, and in using smaller and smaller data from direct observation for a more and more distant prevision. No part of natural philosophy manifests more strikingly the truth of the axiom that all science has prevision for its end: an axiom that separates science from erudition, which relates the events of the past, without any regard to the future (*Course*, 1835).[29]

Furthermore, "the punctual arrival of comets and eclipses" as they are predicted by science, for Comte disproves the existence of supernatural forces. The great precision that Comte posits as a normative standard, separates science from what he described as "vague" prophecies.[30] Accordingly, Comte ranked sciences differently according to their ability to predict precisely and to express those predictions mathematically. In this ranking, astronomy was at the top, while physics and chemistry were classed as less precise. The knowledge of such highly volatile and varied phenomena as tides was classed low in scientific status because it lacked precision.[31] Indeed, as historians noted, Comte strongly disliked probabilistic thinking, unlike other philosophers of his time who were not that much invested in the search for precision.[32] The absence of precision, particularly in statistics, was tolerated when the overall contribution of knowledge was valued. A good case in point is what Poovey described as the rise of belief in "general effects" as opposed to individual, and more concrete, experiences that took place in the nineteenth century Britain. As Poovey puts it, because the ability to see "general effects," such as "national prosperity" that might not be related to individual well-being, was increasingly valued, the missing chain of evidence or unaccounted data could be tolerated.[33] Similarly, while Comte's take on scientific prediction had a deep influence on the French school of "social science," social scientists were torn between a striving for precision and attempts to accommodate precision with probability and a less rigid approach to general laws. For instance, at the end of the century, in his *Rules of Sociological Method* (1895), Émile Durkheim posited that the approximate certainty of scientific knowledge is sufficient: "science knows no first causes, in the absolute sense of the term. For science a fact is primary simply when it is general enough to explain a great number of other facts."[34] Furthermore, much more attuned to statistics than Comte, Durkheim suggests that general laws can be deduced from a full data set if it contains enough variation.[35]

Alongside the problem of precision as a desirable though not always possible quality of scientific prediction of fleeting phenomena, modern scientists examined the problem of the future asking whether prediction must be associated with the future. The next key conceptual move in elevating the status of conjectural knowledge to that of proper, modern science was to destabilize the link between scientific prediction and the future. In the first half of the twentieth century logical empiricists proposed that prediction in fact equals explanation, and its main task is to produce novel, robustly scientific knowledge. In what follows, I briefly present an influential discussion of scientific prediction as explanation, explicated by the German-born philosophers, Carl Hempel and Paul Oppenheim, both of whom fled from Nazi Germany in the 1930s. Hempel was briefly exposed to logical positivism of the Vienna Circle, which he critiqued later in his work, but he inherited a strong interest in prediction as a criterion of scientificity.

For Hempel and Oppenheim, to put it simply, scientific knowledge is constituted by two principal building blocks: classification and explanation. Classification entails sorting observations according to different categories. Scientific explanation, as they put it, is at work when an event can be "explained by subsuming it under general laws, i.e., by showing that it occurred in accordance with those laws, by virtue of the realisation of certain antecedent conditions."[36] An important condition here is that the procedure of explanation (which could be expressed either in words or in mathematical equations) should not contradict the principles of formal logic. As Douglas usefully summarized, "The explanandum (the statement explained) should be logically deducible from a set of statements (the explanans) that included general laws."[37] For medieval physicians it was extremely important to collect cumulative observations of the actual course of developing symptoms in order to produce what they considered a good prognosis. The focus on the process and rate of change is what makes knowledge prognostic for them. Hempel and Oppenheim turn their attention to the way in which observations are described and explained, to the medium of language and particularly the logical apparatus of explanation. I suggest, however, that both medieval physicians and Hempel and Oppenheim shared the will to bridge the Humean gap between observed and unobserved facts with the help of prediction.

For Hempel and Oppenheim scientific prediction and explanation are symmetrical, but this does not mean that they are identical, because prediction is an explanation that is made before the event has been observed. The unobserved

24   **CHAPTER 1**

event in question can be situated either in the future or in the past, it does not matter. It could even exist outside of the historical chronology, as a piece of completely unknown data. Prediction is the explanation that helps detect previously unknown data. What would make a scientific explanation/prediction rigorous? It must be based on the observation of an empirical event. Then it should offer a logically consistent description of the reasons explaining why this event has occurred. The explanation must refer to both "antecedent conditions" (the empirical structure of the event) and "general laws" (that are drawn from relevant scientific theories):

> If E is given, i.e. if we know that the phenomenon described by E has occurred, and a suitable set of statements $C_1, C_2, \ldots, L_1$ is provided afterwards, we speak of an explanation of the phenomenon in question. If the latter statements are given and E is derived prior to the occurrence of the phenomenon it describes, we speak of a prediction.[38]

Thus, for Hempel and Oppenheim prediction is an explanation that allows finding a (previously unobserved) fact. This take on prediction has been presented as a core feature of science, which separates it from commonsense knowledge, in the works of many science writers, particularly those covering the fields of evolutionary science, quantum physics, and complexity. According to Hempel and Oppenheim, the possibility of using the "explanans," the combination of the characterization of antecedent conditions and general laws to describe the empirical phenomenon that has not been yet observed, is necessary: without the capacity to predict, explanation "is not fully adequate":[39]

> Only to the extent that we are able to explain empirical facts can we attain the major objective of scientific research, namely, not merely to record the phenomena of our experience, but to learn from them, by basing upon them theoretical generalizations which enable us to anticipate new occurrences and to control, at least to some extent, the changes in our environment.[40]

For example, the explanation that a car turned over on a road because of a blown tire is considered unscientific. It is a commonsense explanation because, according to Hempel and Oppenheim, the statement contains no generalization and no description of antecedent conditions. Such commonsense explanations are weak scientifically because they are useless as a basis for prediction. They do not allow identifying conditions where cars turned over on roads in the past or will in the future.[41]

Explanations can also be "incomplete": they might refer to general laws and antecedent conditions, but still fail to predict. An example of an incomplete ex-

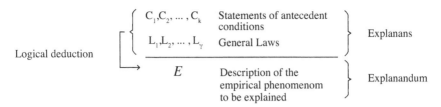

FIGURE 1. The structure of scientific explanation. Reprinted from Carl G. Hempel and Paul Oppenheim, "Studies in the Logic of Explanation," *Philosophy of Science* 15, no. 2 (1948), 138. Courtesy of University of Chicago Press.

planation would be stating that there is a link between a particular style of an artwork and the artist's illness, for instance an expressionist painting and depression or schizophrenia.[42] However, according to Hempel and Oppenheim, also the incomplete explanations that lack predictive power are not necessarily wrong. Rather, they are hypotheses which can be developed into scientific explanations with predictive power through further research.[43]

An important question is whether the symmetry thesis is valid in social sciences, which differ from natural sciences because they deal with behavioral phenomena that are influenced by such factors as intentions. According to Hempel and Oppenheim, there are no reasons why this could not be the case. Their argument goes as follows. Critics claim that social behavior is purposive, driven by goals and not so much by "antecedent conditions," like, for instance, physical conditions that lead to a blown tire. Social behavior should therefore be explained by "teleological" and not "causal" analysis.[44] Such a teleological analysis of social behavior must include goals that are pursued in the situation in question, because "the future appears to affect the present in a manner which is not found in the causal explanations of the physical sciences."[45] Hempel and Oppenheim dismiss this criticism:

> But, clearly, when the action of a person is motivated, say, by the desire to reach a certain objective, then it is not the yet unrealized future event of attaining that goal which can be said to determine his present behaviour, for indeed the goal may never be actually reached; rather—to put it in crude terms—it is (a) his desire, present before the action, to attain that particular objective, and (b) his belief, likewise present before the action, that such and such a course of action is most likely to have the desired effect. The determining motives and beliefs, therefore, have to be classified among the antecedent conditions of a motivational explanation, and there is no formal difference on this account between motivational and causal explanation.[46]

26   CHAPTER 1

For my argument it is important to understand the way in which the so-called positivist approach that considers prediction as a necessary criterion of scientificity of knowledge interacts with the notion of purposive behavior, because much of the late twentieth-century debate will be centered on this particular problem as a problem of scientific knowledge and governance. Indeed, Hempel and Oppenheim's model resonates with the early behaviorist approach developed by the much-criticized American psychologist B. F. Skinner in the 1950s to 1970s. Skinner suggested a flat, empirical epistemology where decisions and goals can be grouped together with the material "antecedent conditions" as equally "present" factors that shape behavior. Cognition, from Skinner's perspective, is nothing more than just another form of behavior, in humans or animals.[47] Skinner's approach was extremely simplistic and much criticized as it appeared to deny the notion of individual capacity to think, choose, and act; moreover, it tainted other, more sophisticated takes on incorporating cognitive goals in behavioral systems and prediction such as cybernetics, which I discuss in the next chapter.[48]

Hempel and Oppenheim's theory of scientific knowledge was further criticized by philosophers of science who deemed it incomplete, because it did not provide a procedure to explain and evaluate general laws. How can general laws be established with scientific certainty? What are their antecedent conditions? Can general laws be predicted? Logical empiricism could not answer these questions. Furthermore, postmodern theorists challenged the very ambition to explain, arguing that the most social sciences and humanities could do was to interpret.[49] Interest in prediction would regularly resurface in social sciences as part of the ever-widening introduction of quantitative methods as well as a growing demand for expert scientific advice in public policy. However, those branches of social science that claimed to be predictive were criticized as a form of astrology or, worse, expression of a mindless positivist authoritarianism, and the concept became unfashionable.[50] It was not until the first decade of the twenty-first century that philosophers, such as Heather Douglas, returned to logical empiricism to reassess the notion of scientific prediction as a productive device:

> Explanations help us to organize the complex world we encounter, making it cognitively manageable (which may be why they also give us a sense of understanding). However, . . . the sense of understanding is no good indicator of the accuracy of the explanation. It is the ability of an explanation to generate new predictions, which then serve as a check on the explanation, that improves the accuracy of our scientific explanations.[51]

For Douglas and Robert Northcott it is important to maintain the criterion of prediction and accuracy because they make scientific knowledge more robust. According to these philosophers, it is not a problem if predictions fail; in fact, it is important that scientific predictions do fail, because failing is a fundamental part of testing a scientific method. Northcott argued that, for instance, erroneous predictions can reveal weak theories, point to the insufficiency of existing explanations, and help undermine excessive certainty in the existing beliefs or understanding. In this sense, scientific prediction as explanation is understood as the engine of the heuristic, open epistemology that is required to produce ever-evolving knowledge of complex, changing reality. Northcott emphasized the value of accurate scientific prediction keeps dogmatism in check, because it requires more accuracy and accountability of theoretical postulates.[52] In a similar vein, as I will show in subsequent chapters on Soviet statistical forecasting, the criteria of prediction and precision were instrumental for those Soviet actors who desired to reform the authoritarian and failing governmental policy and institutions.

The Late Modern Notion of Prediction and Cybernetic Sensibility

The modern notion of prediction as explanation is not concerned with the flow of time in the sense that it does not care if the data in question already exist or do not exist yet. It demands well-tested knowledge: according to the philosopher Karl Popper, only those theories that have not been falsified should be used to make predictive statements.[53] However, our everyday lives are continuously shaped by predictions that are not necessarily based on logically consistent and theoretically anchored explanations. Indeed, a great many of those predictions are not even made by people but by machines that perform billions of predictions without knowing any single theory or having a logically consistent explanation ready. The word processor that autocorrects my text as I type, the ad that pops up on the wall of my Facebook profile, the Google search suggestions, the self-driving car—all these technologies are based on probabilistic predictions of what is most likely to happen next. Note that the examples I listed here refer to digital software. Like medieval physicians, software algorithms intently observe symptoms (relations between words that I sequence in a sentence or my earlier clicks) trying to discern the next move. Unlike the ancient mantic experts or contemporary astrologers, algorithms do not use "global" predictions, where the initial event fully determines the final outcome: algorithmic predictions are blind to the end result of their guesses.[54] In a peculiar way these process-tracking-based predictions are closer to the medieval notion of cumulative prognosis than to Comtean positivism emphasizing precision and certainty.

The notion of prediction as pattern recognition is used in scientific literature in a dual way, both as a component of scientific knowledge and as a natural process, a part of what is considered the natural order of things that enables cognition in general. For instance, prediction as pattern recognition in statistics and engineering can be referred to as a "scientific prediction," a cognitive operation that is based on a set of scientific methods and theories. However, in other areas of research, such as genetics and neuroscience, but also some fields of computer science and engineering, prediction as pattern recognition is approached as an empirical phenomenon that needs be explored, can be modeled and engineered. The concepts of prediction as hypothesis and explanation, and prediction as process tracing, have similarities in that they address phenomena that are possible but not yet evident (see figure 2).

Historians of science would link prediction as pattern recognition with another long-standing philosophical problem of deduction, an approach which traditionally favored the use of logic and numbers. The history of pattern recognition long predates computer modeling, and it can be tracked back to the debate whether numbers could be used to describe society and economy in the early nineteenth century. As Poovey showed in her influential study of the modern fact, eighteenth-century thinkers were rather indifferent to numeric descriptions, because numbers were deemed not as reliable as "principles" and therefore useless for scientific explanations. Numbers were considered neither "true" nor "valuable." According

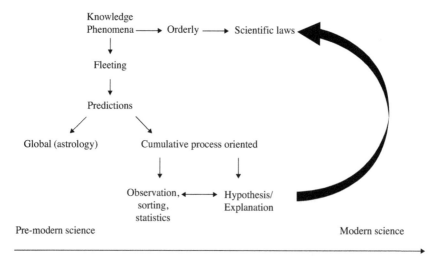

FIGURE 2. Prediction in knowledge. Source: Eglė Rindzevičiūtė.

to Poovey, a preference for the quantitative expression of facts was undermined with the declining scientific status of mantic and conjectural knowledges in the early modern period. Numerical representation had to be purged of supernatural powers.[55] The mastery of numbers and the legitimation of the numerical language was eventually established with the rise of statistical surveys and related techniques forecasting the weather, population, and economy in the nineteenth century (to which I return in the chapters examining the statistical forecasting in imperial and Soviet Russia).[56]

The difficulty with unpacking the notion of prediction as pattern recognition is that it relies on various statistical methods where the term prediction is used to describe what can be quite different operations.[57] Without going into excessive technical details, I would like to illustrate this diversity by drawing on the lucid discussion of the types of statistical prediction offered by Andrew Ehrenberg and John Bound. According to Ehrenberg and Bound, the classical definition of statistical prediction as a technique of making inference from a sample to a population, offered by the British statistician Ronald Fisher in 1935, in fact does not reflect what statisticians always do when facing large sets of data.[58] Trying to go beyond what they call the blind belief in the least square regression technique as the gold standard of statistical prediction where probabilities were used to measure errors, Ehrenberg and Bound distinguish two key types of statistical prediction. The least squares technique refers to curve fitting "that minimizes the sum of the squares of deviations of the curve from the data," an approach developed by nineteenth-century astronomers to measure planetary orbits. [59]

The first type of statistical prediction is *interpolative*. It can be inductive, deductive, or theoretical. Arguing that interpolative prediction requires absence of unusual events or controversial data, Ehrenberg and Bound note that interpolation refers to an inference from observed phenomena which happens as part of "routine deductions of a well-established finding." For instance, the statement that the sun will rise tomorrow, criticized by Hume, is one such example of a valid interpolation simply because it is based on routine observations which register a fact which is considered uncontroversial. Interpolative predictions, according to Ehrenberg and Bound, do not have to be based on large-scale observations; they can include the so-called individual interpolations, based on small sets of data. For example, a doctor's estimate made on the basis of their own routine observations of a particular patient or a group of patients is an example of interpolative prediction. Statistical interpolation can also include "now-casting," where inference is done from the same population of data and is not about the future events. For example, looking through a window, seeing that it is raining and saying "it's raining now" is an example of now-casting or, to put in a statistical language, "predicting y from x for the data to which the model has actually been fitted."[60]

30   CHAPTER 1

The second type of statistical predictions is *extrapolatory*, which is used where routine observations are not readily available. Examples include forecasting, which Ehrenberg and Bound define as "assertions about the future . . . when even the past patterns are unclear." Extrapolation can also refer to discoveries where theory points to novel data (which is consistent with Hempel and Oppenheim's notion of symmetry between prediction and explanation). Another example of extrapolation is the "what if . . . ?" reasoning, where the outcome depends on varying the input assumptions.[61]

In addition to this internal conceptual diversity, statistical prediction is part of messy social and institutional practice, as sociologists of science and technology have shown. To borrow Erving Goffman's term of frontstage and backstage, at the backstage statistical prediction is characterized by the mess caused by misbehaving numbers and machines.[62] Computer programs have bugs, they make mistakes. Very large sets of numbers do not follow the same mathematical rules as small sets of numbers.[63] At the frontstage, statistical prediction is entangled with social, political, and institutional rationales and practices that can depart significantly from the philosophical criteria of logic and accuracy.[64] This does not mean however that statistical prediction is a somehow fake or utopian science. Instead, I would argue that this internal conceptual diversity and complexity means that the practice of statistical prediction requires a complex orchestration of different conceptual, social, and material agencies. For instance, in their insightful and very timely call to explore the internal complexity of statistical "prediction cultures," Matthias Heymann, Gabriele Gramelsberger, and Martin Mahony argue that in making statistical predictions different actors seek to balance accuracy and uncertainty.[65] The stakes for this balance can be high, as statistical predictions, as outlined by Comte, are used to guide managerial and governmental actions that can be damaging for society if applied wrongly. This is important for my argument that the will to predict scientifically entailed balancing different types of predictions. Debates on what constitutes a method and practice that would qualify as a properly scientific prediction can be understood as part of this balancing act. In the remaining section, I discuss the movement away from the Comtean linear model of prediction → action, to a heuristically open approach to prediction that tolerated lack of precision by compensating with prudent action.

Coping with Uncertainty

In his influential treatise on risk and uncertainty published in 1921, Frank H. Knight reflected on what he described as "the problems of life." This problem for him was the issue of the lack of routine observations enabling accurate inferences, for, as he put it, "we know so little." Knowing more, according to Knight, is imperative, because this enables a person or an organism to have a "forward-looking" mentality. To be able to infer is also a question of identity: for Knight "to see things coming," "to react to a situation before it materializes," is what separates an unconscious vegetable and an advanced cognitive being such as a human. Not only prudence but also pragmatics is important: the adjustments that must be made when looking forward "require time, and the farther ahead the organism can 'see,' the more adequately it can adapt itself, to more fully and competently it can live."[66] However, according to Knight, prediction as inference is central for perception and behavior: he suggests that "we *perceive* the world before we react to it, and we react not to what we perceive, but always to what we *infer*." This inference concerns possible futures: for instance, considering the way in which the situation would turn out without intervention or the consequences of intervention. Inferences can be riddled with errors and they are often probabilistic estimates.[67] In the 1940s, two decades after the publication of Knight's treatise, a similar proposition, but formulated at the lower level of organization, was articulated by cyberneticians and neuroscientists studying brain and neural networks.

The idea that human and animal behavior, as well as self-regulatory processes inside organisms and the processes linking organisms to their environment, cannot be explained (and predicted) by mechanical models of linear causality was posited as a challenge for a radically new research agenda, which, as Ronald Kline showed in his history of cybernetics, would pave the way for information sciences in the 1940s (in what follows I rely heavily on Kline's account). At the heart of the problem was that the task was pattern recognition in fast-changing phenomena rather than a description of change in relatively stable phenomena by outlining the antecedent conditions and applying general laws to explain change. The idea that linear causality must be replaced with circular causality, or control through feedback loops, was proposed in a set of conferences in New York in 1946 to 1953.[68] These conferences gathered influential scholars from natural science, engineering, and social science disciplines and were organized by the Macy Foundation, originally established in 1938 to fund medical research. One of the leading applications of these ideas was in brain research, which overlapped with the work of creating the first digital computer. As Kline detailed in his study, the American neurophysiologist Warren McCulloch and the mathematician Walter Pitts modeled the brain as a system of digital neurons that could be either on or off. Their work inspired John von Neumann and Julian Bigelow to design the first electronic computer at Princeton in 1946.[69]

The digital model of the brain as an equivalent of computer processing was an important, albeit insufficient, step in the understanding of neural networks. The concept that bridged neurological and cybernetic research was "information." As

32 **CHAPTER 1**

Norbert Wiener put it in 1949, information "is a concept that can go over directly from the study of the nervous system to the study of the machine; it is a perfectly good physical notion, and it is a perfectly good biological notion."[70] The scientific discussion of cybernetic control spilled over into the public debate following the publication of Norbert Wiener's *Cybernetics: Or Control and Communication in the Animal and the Machine* (1948), an unexpected international bestseller that found itself a target of the Cold War as the very term "cybernetics" was banned in the Soviet Union in the early 1950s. One of the reasons for this controversy was the US media reports on Wiener's ideas, which were linked with what then was an ongoing topic of social anxiety about the dominance of "thinking machines," the societal detriments of the automation of labor, and the destabilizing onset of robots.[71] Wiener's cybernetics was critiqued as a capitalist attempt to dehumanize people by turning them into automatic cognitive machines.[72] This line of critique has been continued since, for instance in the discussions of the political economy of cybernetics and the digitization of labor by Seb Franklin and, somewhat unfairly paired with Skinner's behaviorism, in Shoshana Zuboff's attack against cybercapitalism.[73]

These media debates of the 1950s and the 1960s conferred on cybernetics, as Kline put it, the status of "science of robot brains." This was an unfortunate misrepresentation of very diverse research that was done under the umbrella term of cybernetics. Indeed, strands of cybernetic research argued the very opposite, that the process of cognition and behavior are so complex that they cannot be appropriately simulated in the computer because of its limited architecture.[74] The cybernetic notion of information and feedback loops influenced neurophysiology, genetics, and what would be defined as behavioral sciences in response to the Ford Foundation's use of the term in 1949.[75] Cybernetics also influenced the artificial intelligence (AI) field, the founding date of which is considered to be a conference funded by the Rockefeller Foundation at Dartmouth College in the United States in 1956, which led to a split between the strictly symbolic AI and neurophysiological modeling.[76] The rapprochement between neurophysiology and the so-called AI would happen only about half a century later. Until then, attempts to understand how the brain makes predictions and controls behavior and to create computer systems that can process information and automatically steer machines would develop in parallel. However, prediction remained a central problem and category for both streams of research.

In cyber sciences the key problem was complexity, and the term prediction was used to draw the distinction between order and chaos. In the 1970s, Chilean neurobiologists Francisco Varela and Humberto Maturana proposed the term "autopoiesis" drawing on the 1960s' idea of a second-order cybernetics. The key principle of second-order cybernetics is the idea of multilevel control, where each controlling system is controlled by another system. The interaction between them is hierarchically organized and takes place through information exchange via feedback loops. Varela and Maturana argued that such multilayered systems can inflict change on themselves and regulate themselves so that they stay balanced and viable; hence the term autopoiesis. The notion of autopoiesis and informational self-regulation widely resonated in social theories (particularly the work of Niklas Luhmann), in part in poststructuralism (Gilles Deleuze and Félix Guattari), and in art theory and practice (including contemporary art installations by the cybernetic psychologist Gordon Pask, presented in *Cybernetic Serendipity*, an exhibition organized at the Institute of Contemporary London in 1968). Since the 1940s, the role of informational self-regulation and prediction was part of many groundbreaking research agendas in the fast-growing environmental sciences, particularly computer modeling, policy sciences, AI, and neuroscience, all of which wanted to crack the problem of coordination and the integration of different orders of complexity.

With the advance of genetics, digital monitoring technologies, and computer processing power, neuroscientists gained unprecedented access to observational data on neural networks and simulation, a process that began in the 1950s and took off in the late 1990s. The key insight was formulated: the brain does not really work like Neumann's and Bigelow's digital computer, an information-processing machine that receives input via sensors from the outside, processes them, and produces output via impulses that produce behavior. However tempting this simple and elegant model might be, the brain is not equipped to do all this work, because the informational volume of the outside is enormously vast and beyond the physical abilities of the brain to sort. The question was, how do people manage to make sense of the world, even on a basic perceptual level? As Andrew Pickering demonstrates in his history of cybernetic approaches to biological cognition, as early as 1948 the British cybernetician W. Ross Ashby warned that "To some, the critical test of whether a machine is or is not a 'brain' would be whether it can or cannot 'think.' But to the biologist the brain is not a thinking machine, it is an *acting* machine; it gets information and then it does something about it."[77] Ashby insightfully described the brain as an acting machine, but his suggestion that the brain acts on the received information was still insufficient because it did not specify the cascade of mediators involved in the actual process.

Writing in the 1920s, Knight argued that humans make decisions not on the basis of perception, but on the basis of inference. Two decades later, Wiener hypothesized that the brain was essentially predictive. Since then, neuroscientists embraced this argument.[78] In the second half of the twentieth century a consensus emerged that brain activity is "data-driven," captured in the notion of bottom-up

34   **CHAPTER 1**

processing.[79] However, how exactly this bottom-up processing is organized is far from clear. It has been proposed that instead of gathering all perceptual data and analyzing it, the brain starts with estimating the most likely pattern, compares it with signals that it is receiving via perception organs, and corrects errors if its estimate deviates from the incoming signals. Indeed, the Humean gap between observation and inference does not seem to bother the brain at all. The sequence, therefore, is not

> input → prediction → output
>
> but
>
> prediction → input → output.

From the brain's perspective, everything is continuously anticipated and what Hume described as "empirical observations" are not a source of proof, but a convenient source for correction of error. Neuroscientists have proposed that this predictive power of the brain can be related to the evolutionary need to adapt to a fast-changing environment, which can need reactions in milliseconds while the limited brain capacity to process information does not allow processing inputs and issuing a signal to behave quickly enough.[80]

However, it is important to note that the notion of prediction as pattern processing is restricted to the lower levels of information processing. It does not scale up to the level of cognition that deals with abstractions. A useful explanation of this process has been presented by the British philosopher Andy Clark who draws on cognitive psychology and neurophysiology to conceptualize the predictive brain.[81] Like the earlier quoted cybernetician Ashby, Clark considers the brain a black box, a machine that sorts out its sensorial states. The process of sorting out is not like having on and off positions, as in a thermostat. It is organized into a multilevel system of information transmission as "a predictive cascade," where each level of a neural network tries to predict the patterns that are assembled at the level below. In this heuristic process of prediction and error correction the sensorial reality is an output of the brain, not an input into the brain. How does the brain know that its predictions are correct? Clark writes that the predictive success is achieved when a stable pattern that could be integrated with patterns at a higher level is established; that is, that there is a consistency between predictions as they get integrated at higher levels of abstraction. On the basis of these patterns, the brain can generate a model of the causal relations that exist behind sensory inputs, the world out there, and issue appropriate signals for the body to respond to the external environment through behavior.[82] This neurophysiological behaviorism is very different from Skinner's behaviorism, because Skinner greatly simplified the internal architecture of cognition and was not aware of the complex cascades of predictions that link information processing and behavior.

Therefore the notion of prediction as the best estimate of a pattern can only apply well to understand lower levels of complexity, where a lot of simple and diverse sensorial signals are sorted: for instance, touching a rough surface without looking at it and recognizing that it is a sheet of paper as opposed to the smooth surface of the desk on which it is lying. The sorting could go wrong and result in a predictive error: seeing a cat in a shadowy corner, where in fact there is no cat (but the brain is desperate to find a cat, so it mismatches a projection of cat-like patterns with what it actually sees). However, how this kind of sorting is integrated with abstract concepts and systems of concepts at higher levels remains unknown.[83]

Another important aspect of the model of predictive brain is that the prediction cascades operate by eliminating errors rather than by looking for proof. According to Clark, "the task of the perceiving brain is to account for (to 'explain away') the incoming or 'driving' sensory signal by means of a matching top-down prediction. The better the match, the less prediction error then propagates up the hierarchy."[84] Higher-level (model) predictions "explain away"—sort or dismiss—lower-level prediction errors and this is a continuous process that never ceases.[85] This continuous flow of prediction as pattern recognition orchestrates "environmental awareness." The predictive brain, argues Clark, actively shapes an understandable environment by coordinating neural cognition with action: "Working together, perception and action serve to selectively sample and actively sculpt the stimulus array."[86] It can be suggested that at a higher abstraction level this need for the brain to explain away irrelevant signals has informed the architectures of informational environments that seek to make them brain friendly through clear markers, like road signs and price tags in shops, and selection of colors, like, for instance, high visibility or camouflage.

Critics like Zuboff are concerned that B. F. Skinner's reductionist ideas are returning via neuroscience and digital technology. However, predictive processing of pattern recognition refers to much more complex phenomena than those described in Skinner's work. In neuroscience, the ontological status of "ideas" or "information," which for Skinner are simply "behaviors," is more nuanced, because it recognizes more clearly the different levels of complexity at which the chains of information processing take place, are integrated, and give rise to both conceptual abstractions and action. According to Clark, "First, they suggest that probabilistic generative models underlie both sensory classification and motor response. And second, they suggest that the forward flow of sensory data is replaced by the forward flow of prediction error."[87] Clark calls this "action-oriented prediction processing," which seeks to integrate a theoretical framework embracing mind, brain, and action. Some cognitive scientists claim that forward-prediction is a fundamental model that can operate without "goals," merely through comparison of sensory flows with expectations.[88] This is a model that modifies the cybernetic

36   CHAPTER 1

paradigm, a goal-driven teleological action that is based on having a clear set target, which is approached via error correction by using negative feedback loops, as outlined by Rosenblueth and Wiener. Clark, however, suggests that not all feedback-based predictions need a set target to operate. Drawing on Clark, I suggest that forward-prediction does not have to be part of teleological behavior, in the sense that it does not need a preset target to operate as it is already part of neurophysiological architecture. Nevertheless, forward-predictions form a basis from which teleological behavior can emerge and operate on the basis of other types of prediction at a higher level of abstraction. In other words, prediction cascade as a difference—or error-sorting—engine works at the sensory level, but it does not automatically scale up to the higher cognitive level. I return to this in chapter 6, where I introduce the attempts to formalize strategic deception in reflexivity theory. In chapter 7, I engage with the question of orchestrating target-based, teleological predictions to match appropriate levels of complexity in a global governance model.

In many scientific fields pattern recognition was made into an engineering problem, particularly in cases where a great volume of data has already been accumulated, where strong explanatory frameworks exist, and where categories for searching and sorting are readily available. Prediction as pattern recognition is a fundamental principle in research and design in genetics and biotechnologies, AI and algorithmically controlled markets of future behavior, and parametric architecture. Regarding the latter, architecture and design theorists have begun to address prediction (as explanation) as a thing of the past, hailing pattern recognition as the future modus operandi of design systems.[89] However, the discrepancy between low-level sensory prediction as pattern recognition and high-level cognitive prediction as manipulation with complex abstractions remains to be bridged.

Conclusion

The notion of prediction as pattern recognition is so different from Hempel and Oppenheim's notion of prediction as explanation, identified with modern scientific epistemology, that it led Andrew Pickering to go as far as declaring that cybernetic sciences are a case of nonmodern science. Pickering offered the following discussion of scientific prediction

> One could crudely say that the modern sciences are sciences of pushes and pulls: something already identifiably present *causes* things to happen this way or that in the natural or social world. Less crudely, perhaps, the ambition is one of *prediction*—the achievement of general knowledge

that will enable us to calculate (or, retrospectively, explain) why things in the world go this way or another. . . . [T]he cybernetic vision was not one of pushes and pulls; it was, instead, one of forward-looking search.[90]

Accordingly, reality, from a cybernetic point of view, is not out there as an assembly of causes and effects, but is unfolding, always in the making. Just like the medieval mantic sciences, late modern cybernetic sensibility is part of "groping in the dark," a heuristic attempt to cope with fleeting reality as described by Donella Meadows, John Richardson, and Gerhart Bruckmann in their 1982 report on the progress of computer simulation.[91] Perhaps what Pickering calls a "non-modern adaptation" is a predictive process that so far has been observed to operate at particular levels, such as micro (neural sensorial networks) but also macro (global biosphere systems). In this book, I offer a historically anchored discussion which shows just how much was at stake, socially, politically, and institutionally in the effort to define and bridge these levels of scientific prediction.

2

VISIBILITY, TRANSPARENCY, AND PREDICTION

When Peter the Great embarked on the project of modernizing Russian society at the end of the seventeenth century, he set off to import not only the ship-building technologies, bureaucracy, and architecture styles, but also to translate German and Polish almanacs containing prognostication of the weather and astrological readings of the future.[1] In the following century, however, astrology had to move aside to make place for a new form of modern science that was shaped through growing demands to develop reliable methods of prediction. And, from the ruler's point of view, what was more important to predict if not the economy and society? In this and the following chapter, I map the evolution of statistical forecasting in Russian science and governance from the nineteenth century to the 1980s as an orchestration of people, institutions, data, and ideas of what can be visible and knowable.[2] Without this wider orchestration, the practice of statistical forecasting would lose its scientificity. As Vaclav Smil puts it, statistical forecasting was created to describe mathematically those physical and immaterial changes in society and the biosphere that appear to be regular. Its primary purpose was to measure growth, progress, and decline.[3] I show that in doing this, the epistemology of modern scientific forecasting in many ways continues to draw on the medieval ideas of prognosis, the reading of signs and closely following the course of change. Like medieval prognosis, forecasting seeks to construct a conjecture that situated a particular constellation of signs on the axis of time, in the future.[4]

My other purpose is to explore positivist statistical forecasting as it developed in Soviet Russia. Many social scientists and historians use the term positivism as a derogatory term. Accordingly, they criticize the deployment of statistical forecasting in policy as a positivist and reductionist approach that disregards the fluid and heterogeneous character of social reality and is used to legitimize top-down decisions, leading to technocracy. However, as I show in this chapter, many pioneers of statistical forecasting debated positivism and scientific prediction and were reflective about their limitations. In Russia, positivism developed alongside mathematics and statistics in a symbiosis with what would become a modern state apparatus and industrial economy, although the Russian imperial authorities banned Auguste Comte's writings on positive knowledge and prevision briefly in 1848 and 1849.[5] In the early twentieth century Soviet scholars, who were fascinated with what appeared to be regularities in chaos such as population growth, epidemiology, and business cycles, delved into statistical forecasting and engaged with the Comtean positivist tradition critically. At the same time, the very process of creating forecasts alerted them to persistent uncertainties both in the method and the phenomena observed. I argue that for these Russian scientists the "scientific" component of forecasting did not always refer to certainty and blind belief in statistical data. Indeed, forecasts were considered "scientific" because they were part of asking a question rather than giving an answer. Scientific prediction was understood as an ultimate test of both method and data.

Numbers, Visibility, and Transparency

Statistical forecasting promised to enhance both visibility and transparency, inform policy decisions, make governance more effective, and, accordingly, augment its power. Policy planners, investors, insurers, meteorologists, marketing managers, educators, and traders desired to have a firmer basis for their decisions in the context of shifting and unstable realities, such as weather, crops, natural resources, and consumer choices. Statistical forecasting answered this need, supplying graphs and curves to decision-makers seeking, as the popular organizational jargon went, to "future-proof" their decisions. However, forecasts are rarely perfect; they often fail to deliver reliable knowledge as to what will happen in the future, particularly in the long term. Furthermore, knowing the likelihood of an event happening is not necessarily useful for a decision-maker if the information is not accompanied with transparency, the knowledge of the mechanism by which this event happens, so that it could be amenable to intervention and management.[6] What makes statistical forecasting a scientific prediction? What kind of politics is associated with this type of knowledge? I examine these questions through three cases central to the history of Soviet forecasting: the 1920s discussions of the limits of social and economic forecasting in the first communist state plans; the 1960s reform that established prognoses

40   CHAPTER 2

as part of long-term economic planning; and, in chapter 4, the emergence of social forecasting as a subfield of sociology in the 1960s and 1970s.

I argue that although the communist planners expected statistical forecasting to be a neutral method of gathering data that would indicate social and economic trends, statistical forecasting was more than that. Statistical forecasting had important social and political effects because it pointed to the failures of the Soviet organization of science and governmental apparatus, and, ultimately, to the intractable nature of social change. In theory, statistical forecasting was meant to help the state authorities "to see," to map, diagnose, and govern complexity. In practice, the making of statistical forecasts was not even possible without a more liberal institutional design, because, as I will show, this is a prerequisite of the production and use of reliable data. The authoritarian framework churned out flawed statistical data. This was criticized as early as the 1920s. Later, in the 1960s, scientists demanded transparency or *glasnost'* in the circulation of data, which they saw as a necessary condition for scientific forecasting.[7] Economists were not alone there: in 1966, for instance, researchers at the history institute demanded access to the archives documenting the Stalinist period.[8] However, economists were uniquely positioned to be trusted with development of new techniques, such as scientific forecasting, to help tame the chaos of the economy and social change. In effect, the institutional and epistemological requirements of forecasting began to act as constraints on communist policymakers and managers. Some of them expected that computerization of decision-making would neutralize what they saw as "grassroots Stalinism," communist party informers.[9] But the expected effect was also conceptual and fundamental: by outlining the negative economic, social, and environmental consequences of "positive" programs of development, forecasts influenced the political process of Soviet economic planning.

The Soviet experience of forecasting that is discussed in this chapter has implications that apply to all modern policy contexts, be they authoritarian, liberal democratic, or hybrid: statistical forecasting not only challenges the mechanistic, linear notions of governance and creates new forms of visibility of transient phenomena, but it also requires a particular social organization of scientific expertise. Furthermore, statistical forecasting is about building trust in data and data producing networks and institutions by enhancing transparency, a process theorized by Theodore Porter that was not limited to Western liberal democracies and that characterized the development of Soviet expert governance.[10] The latter element, transparency, is particularly interesting because of its ambivalence. Transparency, as Stefano Geroulanos showed in his extensive study, was first criticized in French cultural debates as being part of the repertoire of authoritarian regimes and their striving for control. Only later, in the 1980s, did transparency become a desirable feature of governance.[11] The Soviet debate about statistical conjectures of the future and the role of *glasnost'* must be understood in this context of shifting understanding of transparency.

Statistical Forecasting in Russia

The foundations of Soviet social and economic forecasting were laid in the transnational development of modern European science in the eighteenth century, when the first Russian scientific institutions were established, and in the nineteenth century in the context of the social and administrative reforms of the Russian empire. In Western Europe, the first efforts to collect quantitative data describing population, natural resources, and the economy started in parallel with the first scientific revolution and the expansion and institutionalization of the modern state in the seventeenth and eighteenth centuries. At the same time, research was extended from individual sick bodies to the health of populations, in relation first to nutrition and food and then hygiene. However, until the 1830s, these studies were pursued by individual scholars and social improvers rather than governmental institutions (which, one should remember, at that time were either very "thin" or did not exist at all).[12] In Western Europe, the first half of the nineteenth century saw a slow institutionalization of the emerging governance by numbers, often in response to what were perceived as social problems. For instance, in Britain the first statistical societies, formed in the 1830s, sought to capture the composition of the "social body." They were interested principally in the poor urban populations and the emerging figure of the "modern man," which was understood as a symptom of decline and social malaise.[13] This interest in reading symptoms of what is to come echoed the prognostications of the medieval physicians, but this time the reading of signs as symptoms and the monitoring of the course of their change were applied not just to individual biological bodies but to social groups and populations as a whole. In this process, the trajectories of mathematical sciences, governance, and social and political reform began to intertwine. It could be suggested that clear parallels between the emergent science of social change and the medical epistemology of prediction were not a coincidence. The scientific knowledge of the social body had to combine the knowledge of the initial state of the organism and of the course of events, that is, the development of symptoms. To meet the criteria of modern science, as defined by Comte and other thinkers of the Enlightenment, the readings and conjectures of symptoms had to be explained with reference to general laws. Establishing those general laws for populations and society, however, became a great challenge. To do this, Victorian scholars of the economy and the social drew on physics, on the Darwinian theory of evolution, the notion of stage-driven development, and

42   CHAPTER 2

eventually mathematical laws, particularly those pertaining to the S-curve, a logistical growth function which allowed a mathematical description of the process of change. It is important to note that the role of mathematics in statistical calculations increased only toward the end of the nineteenth century, when larger data sets became available. This is a very simplified portrayal of what was a very diverse and turbulent period of scientific ideas and public debates, but it sets the context for Soviet scientific forecasting.

In the Russian empire, the first mathematics research department was founded by a prominent Swiss scholar, Leonhard Euler, who was invited to St. Petersburg in 1727 and who made a breakthrough in what would become one of key techniques of forecasting, the logistical curve, a calculation device that allows data to be plotted on the axes of time and rate of change—a way to smooth disparate data that represents change by fitting it into a simple trajectory. In the beginning, mathematical statistics described the changes that had occurred in the past. It is important to understand that at this early stage, governance by numbers was mainly involved with mapping out the historical and the present condition of population. An exercise in statistical forecasting—establishing regularities and values of the data in the future—requires not only a lot of data on past regularities but also sophisticated methods of calculation. Both elements were developed during the 1800s. The key strand of modern scientific prediction was mathematical methods to work out chains of values and the rate of their change. As Smil showed in his helpful overview of the history of the logistical curve, the foundations for this theory were laid by Euler in his *Introduction to Analysis of the Infinite* (1748). This calculative device was further developed into what became known as a sigmoid curve (or S-curve) by the French mathematician Pierre Francois Verhulst, who applied the S-curve to measure population growth in 1838. Whereas the S-curve was largely disregarded until the early twentieth century, mainly because of the lack of large sets of data that is required, it became the workhorse of global trends forecasters in the 1960s, when S-curves were fitted to virtually any statistically measurable phenomenon.[14]

To put it in a greatly simplified manner, a statistical forecast offers a hypothesis, a systematic, mathematical method to approximate the reality. The statistical technicalities of this approximation seek to capture the observed regularities in a faithful manner and to offer a glimpse into the unobserved. This glimpse, a jump into the unknown, happens through extrapolation or interpolation of data on the basis of past patterns, where the explanation (a full account of causes and impacts) might be absent (at the moment of analysis, though it could be found, ideally, at the later stage). The gap between the past data and the future (forecasted) data is bridged with a beautiful mathematical invention—the logistic curve or an S-curve. Mathematical curves, as Smil put it, helped to quantify the process of "growth" as a cumulative rate of change.[15] Applied to economic and social development, growth became an explanatory and normative framework for the understanding of social change in the nineteenth century.[16] In scientific forecasting, the theory of "quantifiable" growth served as a general law in Hempel and Oppenheim's sense, enabling explaining (predicting) relevant facts.

In the 1820s, scientists began to apply the calculations of statistical probability to demographic and actuarial data (both still extremely scarce at that time). A growing number of Russian scientists received their education in Paris and brought back the ideas of Pierre-Simon Laplace, Siméon Poisson, Joseph Fourier, André-Marie Ampère, and French positivists.[17] One of those Paris-trained scholars was the prominent mathematician Viktor Buniakovskii, who absorbed both the methods and the politics of the emerging field of social statistics. Like his contemporaries in Western Europe, Buniakovskii first applied probabilistic methods to work out more precise and "morally justified" insurance premiums. He also studied Russian demography and economy.[18] Just like Laplace, who gifted his book on probability to Napoleon, Buniakovskii presented a luxuriously bound copy of his influential treatise *Foundations of the Mathematical Theory of Probabilities* (1846) to Alexander II, who succeeded the throne in February 1855.[19] In that same year the devastating loss of the Crimean War shook up the Russian empire and marked the start of extensive modernization reforms, such as building transport infrastructure and, eventually, abolishing serfdom in the 1860s.

In response to these changes, the Russian social hygiene movement became more expansive. Its members began to apply statistical theory to discern regularities and governing laws from the ebb and flow of births, deaths, profits, and losses, all of which were becoming visible thanks to the growing body of data. In doing this, Russian social reformers and demographers were relying on the positivist ideas. Starting in the 1840s, Auguste Comte's ideas were introduced in Russia and protosociological research began to emerge after the 1860s reforms.[20] The small educated social circles were receptive to the Enlightenment ideas of the parallel technical and moral progress of humankind, espoused by Comte, Turgot, and Condorcet.[21] Social reform and demographic research was, even more so than in Western Europe, an elite minority pursuit: the literacy rates in the Russian empire remained very low until the end of the century: only 45.3 percent of inhabitants in urban Russia could read, according to the 1897 census.[22]

Russian reformers and social thinkers also faced great difficulties in bridging ideas, mathematical methods, and empirical data. Imperial governance by numbers was still at the embryonic stage: population statistics were gathered in a patchy way, dispersed across different administrations and research institutions. Numbers were not trusted: it was widely recognized that those few statistics that were available were often false; for instance, pervasive fiscal obscurity worried tax collectors.[23] The prevailing mode of governmental engagement with the providers of numbers was through inspections and revisions, the spirit of which was profoundly captured in Nikolai Gogol's *The Government Inspector* (1836). Mathematical competence that would be greater than simple accounting skills was also lacking. Indeed, the shortage of mathematically trained statisticians would plague Russia for another century, until the 1950s.[24] This said, the available statistical data sets were growing, albeit slowly. The first "medico-topographic surveys," which characterized the public health of the population, were assembled in the early nineteenth century; the majority of medical research took place in military hospitals.[25] In the 1840s, following the establishment of the Imperial Russian Geographical Society, the first attempts to classify and map ethnic populations were introduced.[26] This was a particularly important development; it was where the study of the future economic use of natural resources was conducted alongside mapping indigenous peoples and assessing their role in the future society. In this process the Russian empire saw an incremental birth of its own version of the Humboldtian systems science.[27] The modernization of the empire, the need to account for its natural treasures and peoples, drove the institutionalization of modern science. In the 1850s and 1860s, a plethora of scientific societies was established in Russia; scientific knowledge was promoted in the public through their publications.[28]

The scoping of natural resources, monitoring of the weather, and the health of the social body were becoming part of the imperial governmental imagination. A department of social hygiene was established at the Ministry of Internal Affairs in 1863, large-scale medical research was launched in military hospitals, local statistics were gathered by new regional governmental administrations (*zemstva*) from 1864.[29] However, the imperial Russian social body was not scrutinized to the same extent as in Western Europe, not only because of the shortage of scholars but also because of the structurally different social reality: Russians did not have the Western problem of "the modern man," there was a lack of rural–urban movement and Russia remained an agrarian society.[30] In turn, the social hygiene movement, led by physicians, focused on the introduction of basic medical services rather than solving acute public health problems faced by the intensively urbanized Western European societies.

The emerging fields of public health could enjoy the status of proper science only if general laws, characterizing patterns of growth and change, were available to justify the gathering and interpretation of the data. Attempts to formulate those general laws abounded: as Nikolai Krementsov showed in his study of Russian eugenic thought, scholars widely borrowed from Western thought on social improvement, particularly from the newly established fields of research into human physiology and psychology. The Russian intelligentsia sought to discover a scientific way to assess "progress" and plan the future society, inspired by Darwinian ideas of evolution, environmental ethnogenesis, and Marxist dialectics. They also worried about decline and degeneration.[31] As a writer Shelgunov put it in 1863, "history—the physiology and pathology of the collective man—defines those inescapable laws that regulate the healthy development of a social organism."[32] This health, however, was no longer written in the stars, as Boris Kurakin, the prominent Russian diplomat and writer on astrology of the early eighteenth century would have believed, but to be found with the modern instruments of empirical research and carefully considered insights from statistics.[33]

If human nature, however amenable for intervention, changes slowly, nothing changes faster than weather and economic fortunes. As Jamie Pietruska showed in her fascinating study, the first statistical forecasts in the United States were developed in the nineteenth century to inform farmers and traders about future crops. The early US forecasters made calculations using data from locally observed weather and estimates of the productivity of soils. These forecasts soon came to be regarded as a valuable commodity in their own right. They were bought and sold and constituted an important part of the grain market.[34] In the Russian empire, weather monitoring began under Peter the Great in the first half of the eighteenth century. The first meteorological observation stations were established in Siberia in the 1700s. The first systematic attempts to prospect for natural resources and predict weather dated to 1849, when the Central Physical Laboratory was established in St. Petersburg. Starting in 1872, this laboratory began to publish weather forecasts. However, at that time Russian social hygienists, biologists, meteorologists, and other natural scientists just did not have the same kind of data to draw on about population, crop yields, and natural resources as US forecasters.[35] The surveys were fragmented: the widespread censorship did not encourage production and distribution of data. The situation did not improve until the first (and the last) population census was held in the Russian empire in 1897.[36]

Russian society was becoming intensively alert to anticipated changes, particularly as the nineteenth century was coming to end. The emerging late imperial "prediction culture" did not yet feature what would be known as a statistical forecast.[37] The subjects of the Russian empire, as Yuri Slezkine showed, turned either to "prophets, soothsayers and itinerant preachers" or to Marxian "prediction" of the future, emplotted in the drama of universal decline, which spoke to the millenarian sensibility.[38] The nascent communist movement could be situated in the context of this greatly diverse population of future-tellers. As Slezkine put it, "A conversion to socialism was a conversion to the intelligentsia, to a fusion of millenarian faith and lifelong learning."[39] Even in the 1920s, as Richard Stites discussed, peasants were targeted by propaganda encouraging them to trust what were perceived as "godless," scientific forecasting rather than their own instinct.[40] Russian

46   CHAPTER 2

peasants had their own approach to the economy, their key spokesman being the prominent economist Aleksandr Chayanov (1888–1937), who situated the peasant economy in a material and social space that was different from the one envisioned by imperial and state planners and which was not captured in a statistical form.[41] In this respect Russian peasants were not an exception: as Beckert suggested, drawing on Pierre Bourdieu's study of Algerian peasants' approach to the future, the statistically mediated economic vision did not fit easily with the agrarian prediction culture.[42]

The diagnostic and prognostic lenses developed by physicians to cure an individual body were eventually applied to monitor and, later, predict the health of society and the national economy.[43] Forecasting was informed by a modern scientific sensibility, acutely aware of the cumulative character of physical and social phenomena. For instance, ethnography, a science that developed alongside geology and geography—initially, in the context of museum collections—theorized and localized the cumulative change of human cultures in relation to the geological knowledge of the Earth's layers.[44] The will to predict and to do this "scientifically" was fueled by the belief that future dynamics could be made both visible and transparent, and amenable to change. Once the cumulative past was charted and theorized, once providence was revealed by the emerging discipline of professional history, once quantitative data became increasingly available, the institutional and political foundations for scientific forecasting could be laid.[45] The next section presents the institutionalization of forecasting and its use for state planning purposes in what became Soviet Russia.

Prediction and Early Soviet Planning

While the nineteenth-century social improvers gathered quantifiable snapshots of populations, in the early twentieth century their interest shifted to the study of complex interactions of societal and economic systems and the predictive use of statistical data. A growing governmental apparatus facilitated this interest. In this section I present at length the ideas of Nikolai Kondrat'ev (1892–1938), the pioneering Russian economic forecaster, positivist thinker, and theorist of prediction. Kondrat'ev was a student of Mikhail Kovalevskii, known as the first Russian sociologist, president of the Imperial Free Economic Society (1915–1916), and founder of the first sociology department at Vladimir Bekhterev's Institute of Psychoneurology in St. Petersburg. Kovalevskii also authored a study on economic growth in Europe (1898–1903). During his studies at Bekhterev's institute, Kondrat'ev became close friends with Pitirim Sorokin, who was influenced by Emile Durkheim's sociology (and would later leave Russia to become established at Harvard).[46] Kondrat'ev excelled in mathematical statistics and was interested in sociological approaches and economic history. In the wake of the communist revolution in 1917, experts in any fields of scientific and technical knowledge were rare, because the rates of literacy and higher education were extremely low across the peasant and worker estates, hence many of the graduates hailing from upper strata of society were directly enrolled in the Soviet state-building project.[47]

As mentioned earlier, Russian imperial population statistics had been systematically gathered in regional governmental agencies (*zemstva*) since 1864. This task was centralized under the Central Statistical Agency, which was created by the Bolshevik government in 1918 and which remained the primary number cruncher until the Soviet Union collapsed in 1991.[48] However, the agency lacked competence to analyze this data; many of its staff had only basic mathematical education, often in accounting.[49] To fill this gap of expertise, at the age of twenty-eight Kondrat'ev created the Conjuncture Institute at the former Imperial Agricultural Academy in Moscow in 1920. The institute pioneered the development of economic indicators to forecast the economic development of Russia (*prognozirovanie*).[50] Kondrat'ev's Conjuncture Institute was one of the first of its kind. Its rationale was inspired by the US National Bureau of Economic Research (NBER), which was also established in 1920 by a group of business and progressive politicians, and directed by the Columbia economist Wesley Mitchell, who was known for his work on business cycles. Like Kondrat'ev's institute, NBER also developed economic indicators, a field of research that had emerged in the United States in the 1890s and which was gaining an increasing prominence, largely thanks to the work of Russian-American economist Simon Kuznets, who joined NBER in 1927.[51] Similar institutes for macroeconomic forecasting were established in Cambridge (UK), Paris (1921), and Germany (1925).[52] At that time it was considered that both capitalist and communist economies had similar informational needs to be served by statistics. In postrevolutionary Russia it was hoped that economic indicators would help operationalize the Soviet theory of economic growth. Based on Karl Marx's distinction between producer goods and consumer goods, the Soviet theory of growth received its canonical expression in the writings of Grigorii Feldman, who offered a conceptual separation of the productive (industrial) and nonproductive (services) sectors of the economy in 1928. Growth, it was believed, could be achieved only by directing capital investments to the productive sector, particularly the heavy industries.[53] However, translating this theory into policy posed a difficult if not impossible task for planners. Regardless of the centralized statistical agency, collection of statistical data was extremely fragmented. It was hoped that this could be ameliorated by

48   CHAPTER 2

the Conjuncture Institute, which joined the ranks of the many 1920s agencies that turned to amassing quantifiable data on the economy, labor, and society.[54]

The problem with the economy was that it was demonstrably unstable. The question was whether these instabilities were a pathology, which could be corrected by returning the economy to its equilibrium state, or whether they were a defining characteristic of the system.[55] A chain of painful recessions, as historians showed, created the demand for economic forecasting in the nineteenth-century United States.[56] Kondrat'ev, like his Western counterparts, was interested in both predicting and taming business cycles of boom and bust. Indeed, his name would become internationally known in relation to his theory of "long waves"—business cycles lasting forty-five to sixty years, called by the Austrian economist Joseph Schumpeter "Kondrat'ev cycles."[57] For us it is important that Kondrat'ev was also interested in the scientific status of economic knowledge, particularly forecasting: What made statistical forecasting a science and not a mere guess or estimate?

In 1926, Kondrat'ev published an essay "On the Problem of Foresight" (*predvidenie*), to my knowledge the first extended piece of writing on scientific prediction in Russia. In this essay, Kondrat'ev, who read English, German, and French, drew on what was an established canon of the philosophy of science at that time, mainly the positivism of Auguste Comte, Ernst Mach, and Emile Durkheim. He also engaged with the contemporary writings on the methodology of statistical forecasting, as well as French sociological debates on prediction (*prévision*) in social research. The latter interest was shaped by his tutor Kovalevskii who, during his exile in France, founded what was considered to be the first French school of sociology, the Russian School of Advanced Social Studies in Paris (1901–1906).[58] The footnotes of Kondrat'ev's "On the Problem of Foresight" contain references to much French positivist thought, including articles in the *Revue international de sociologie*, a publication of the Paris Sociology Society, established by René Worms, whom Kondrat'ev met at Bekhterev's institute.[59] Kondrat'ev drew extensively on a positivist argument on prediction, presented in the *Revue* by Pericles Grimanelli, a proponent of positivism in social research who also served as a director general of prisons in several French *départements*. Kondrat'ev expanded Grimanelli's ideas on prediction with insights from statistical theory adding a greater emphasis on the uncertain character of the phenomena in the context of both social research and socioeconomic governance.[60]

In his writing, Kondrat'ev used several synonyms for prediction: *predskazanie* (prediction), *predvidenie* (foresight, prevision), and *prognoz* (prognosis, also used for what in English is termed forecast). He opens his argumentation with the Comtean postulate that all proper science is based on prediction and that prediction is necessary for governmental action. According to Kondrat'ev, planning is possible only on the basis of "scientific knowledge and foresight."[61] But by writing this Kondrat'ev does not suggest that such knowledge is readily available and perfect foresight is achievable; he rather develops this statement as a criticism of the problematic statistical and administrative realities in postrevolutionary Russia. Initially, his discussion of prediction follows a typical positivist argument. Prevision, writes Kondrat'ev, can be defined as knowledge of two types of events, the ones that are not yet known and the ones that have not yet happened. The relations and transition between the known and the unknown events must be scientifically explained. These relations can also be quantifiable and described mathematically. It is precisely this focus on the relations and transition between the known and unknown that makes prediction scientific, different from common sense, from a mere guess.[62] Like Comte, Kondrat'ev differentiates between scientific prediction and "prophecy," the latter being based on a belief in supernatural forces that govern these transitions between known and unknown events.[63]

However, unlike Comte, and like later positivists, Kondrat'ev is particularly alert to the difficulty of knowing these transitions between events. This type of knowledge, which is the basis of forecasting, is hardest to achieve. At the same time, it is imperative. Kondrat'ev draws heavily on Durkheim, particularly his *Rules of the Sociological Method*, to argue that the study of the evolutionary character of social events and the transition between them is at the core of social research. As Durkheim puts it, "The stages through which humanity successively passes do not engender each other. We can well understand how the progress realized in a given era in the fields of law, economics and politics, etc., makes fresh progress possible, but how does the one predetermine the other?"[64] Durkheim continues: "We can certainly say how things have succeeded each other up the present, but not in what order they will follow subsequently, because the cause on which they supposedly depend is not scientifically determined, nor can it be so determined."[65] Facing economic science, a field that was just coming into being and in which the basic characteristic data were very scarce, Kondrat'ev did not share Durkheim's optimism about knowing even the "present events," not to mention the future.[66] Kondrat'ev's skepticism was rooted in the evolutionary and biological concept of cumulative reality, according to which every given position (or data) is not exchangeable with the other positions. As he put it, economic and social "events" are strongly individual and the links between them are difficult to capture with existing methods. Here Kondrat'ev is leaving the domain of Laplacian social physics, which, as Philip Mirowski showed, would become a preferred epistemological accommodation for neoclassical economists.[67] Instead, Kondrat'ev's conceptual architecture allows for greater complexity, where the whole and individual parts are understood as interconnected, evolving systems rather than static, physical positions, an approach that resonated

50 CHAPTER 2

with the insights that were articulated in Soviet Russian and Western neurophysiology at that time.[68]

If for Comte the ability to predict was an ultimate criterion of the scientificity of knowledge, for Kondrat'ev prognosis (*prognoz*) means "a working hypothesis" rather than a statement of certain facts.[69] Kondrat'ev's argument is as follows. Some phenomena are more predictable than others. For instance, astronomic events appear to be quite regular and can be scientifically predicted, unlike weather and human behavior, which are highly complex and volatile. Prediction is possible only when the transition between events (from A to B) follows a law that could be discovered by science. Now, these laws could be very simple (static) or very complex (dynamic). However, even in the case of static laws, a model of individual causalities, such as the initial state and primary constellations, may not be fully known. Even if individual causalities are known, they might not be sufficient: one cannot simply add up causalities that may apply to a singular event to predict a long and complex course of events. In the end this means that the combination of both empirical knowledge of causality and knowledge of general laws is necessary for scientific prediction. However, even if these criteria are satisfied, scientific predictions are only approximations, they do not offer full certainty.

Kondrat'ev also considers existing methods for making scientific judgment, such as induction, deduction, a historical-comparative method, and statistics (of which he is particularly fond) and concludes that they all have their uses but also significant limitations.[70] He ends his essay listing different types of limitations that scientific prediction can face. These include the lack of richness of data, the long term, the factor of human intervention, and what he describes as the lack of the autonomy of the field (by this he means the level of complexity).[71] Kondrat'ev is also very critical of his very own field of research, namely the statistical modeling of business cycles and economic growth. This method, he writes, is highly imperfect, it remains to be developed. Economic prevision, argues Kondrat'ev, could be considered a good scientific prediction if it could localize a particular event in space and time, estimating the event's "intensity."[72] But to think that this was achievable was nothing short of utopian. Such skepticism was not uncommon in Kondrat'ev's intellectual milieu. For instance, in 1927, Kondrat'ev's close friend Sorokin entirely dismissed the predictive claims of the theories of business cycles because Sorokin did not believe that these theories could be scientifically proven. However, Sorokin admitted that regularity of events is what makes social science possible at all; the perceptions of trends and tendencies can serve a heuristic function, helping uncover causalities and formulate general laws.[73]

In his pioneering essay, Kondrat'ev addressed the key issues of the epistemology of scientific prediction that would go on to define the debate for the remainder of the twentieth century. One of the key problems that forecasters have been trying to bridge is the trade-off between the precision of prediction (its empirical content) and its location on the time and space axes (telling what exactly is going to happen at a particular time and place—or point forecasts). Although he did not suggest that it is fundamentally impossible to achieve this sort of prediction in fields such as meteorology, "socioeconomic disciplines," and "psychology sciences," he could not see this happening in a near future.[74] Kondrat'ev judged the existing work on business cycles as indicative at best, lacking concreteness, ergo useless for decision-making.

Kondrat'ev also addressed the performative and pragmatic character of scientific prediction. He wrote that the scientific status and usefulness of prediction's outcomes depended on its "purpose," by which he meant its context of use, the link with governmental or managerial practice. Scientific prediction, in this way, is deeply relational—both in terms of its epistemology and its social context.[75] I suggest that Kondrat'ev's notion of prediction contains seeds of thinking about scientific prognosis as a component of adaptive behavior. This emphasis is not surprising, because it is very likely that Kondrat'ev was exposed to the theories of coevolution of the environment and organisms as they were developed by Bekhterev in his work on reflexology.[76] Indeed, I would situate Kondrat'ev's understanding of the social and economic dynamic in the context of the emerging nonmechanistic approach to order. For instance, the restrictive positivist reductionism, based on the material models of physics, was criticized in Soviet neuropsychology by the prominent scholar and the founder of the field Alexander Luria. According to Luria, the mechanistically deterministic neurological theory failed to explain the way in which brain, organism, and behavior interact: "the conception of 'organization' is to a certain degree opposed to a mechanical conception of the organism [understood] as an equilibrium of its component parts, in that it is adequate for an analysis of some of the more complicated processes of human behavior."[77] Like Luria, Kondrat'ev questioned deterministic models of the economy. One could not simply proceed from parts to the whole; neither the organism nor the economy was "a mosaic," but rather "the complex interweaving of superimposed systems," as Geroulanos and Meyers put it.[78]

In 1926, the first Soviet census was taken. The dizzying number of calculations of future prices, industrial outputs, and crop yields formed the basis for the first Five-Year Plan. These calculations were not, Kondrat'ev wrote clearly and repeatedly, scientific forecasts. Indeed, the Five-Year Plan was more like an astrological conjecture than a scientific prognosis because it ignored the actual course of events. Tracking the actual course of events and adjusting the plan to it was actually proposed by the first Planning Committee. However, as I show in the remainder of this chapter, the interwar approach to planning that was endorsed by the party remained a mixture of simplistic positivism and what

52   CHAPTER 2

I would call astrological conjectures. There was no room for hypothesis testing, falsification, and adjustment. The practice of planning paid little heed to the complex and cumulative character of the economy and the social.

Prediction between Astrological Conjecture and Management

The building of the new Soviet state entailed building new infrastructures and their construction inevitably led to what Chris Otter described as a modern "growth of government" by enrolling vast numbers of experts, a phenomenon that had emerged in the liberal Britain of the 1840s and that characterized the first Soviet government in the 1920s.[79] As Stephen Collier noted, the first proper infrastructural project in Russia that went beyond local and regional "works" was the building of the national electric grid. In 1920, a body of experts, the State Commission for Electrification of Russia (GOELRO) was launched to develop a fifteen-year state plan for the development of electrical infrastructure. GOELRO planners and engineers became aware that the costly and large-scale infrastructure of the electricity grid could not be developed without very precise knowledge of the types and locations of the future industries to be served by it. Furthermore, as the horizon of the implementation of the plan extended to at least fifteen years, the planning had to anticipate future technology changes.[80] This, in turn, led to the understanding that planning should be informed by the history of science and technology, which was expected to give insight in the "laws of development" of the nascent industrial society.[81]

The GOELRO project led to the institutionalization of centralized national planning in Soviet Russia and the establishment of a central planning commission (Gosplan). At Gosplan methods of long-term planning were developed by many scholars, including Vladimir Bazarov, born Rudnev (1874–1939). A childhood friend of the pioneering systems theorist Aleksander Malinovskii-Bogdanov, Bazarov was interested in measuring economic growth. He contributed methodological guidelines for the Five-Year Plan, which was the first perspective plan (*perspektyvnyi plan*) in 1921–1929. Convinced that technoscientific development was a continuous process that could not be wholly determined beforehand, Bazarov published articles claiming that Soviet plans should avoid specifying the means and ends in minute detail. Instead the plans should be open-ended "plan-prognoses." Indicating that policy measures would be adjusted as the need arose, this approach stated the need for an open and flexible framework to govern the future.[82]

Kondrat'ev was highly critical of the system of Soviet planning and, although he was sympathetic with Bazarov's attempt to bring some conceptual discipline to what he described as a chaos of "mass planning," he critiqued even Bazarov's approach for being confused and insufficiently scientifically grounded. In his essay "Plan and Foresight" (1927), Kondrat'ev presented a carefully argued and devastating critique of the first planners' claim for scientificity and will to forecast. His verdict was merciless: he called the Five-Year Plan "bad and illusory," "built on sand," and an example of "autohypnosis" by numbers.[83] The key problem with the perspective plan, according to Kondrat'ev, was that Soviet planners set out to complete an impossible task: to specify all goals and objectives, as well as the measures to achieve them in great detail. This approach to planning, also criticized by Bazarov, could not be implemented because all the available calculations were wrong: they were based on insufficient data and established without a proper understanding of underlying processes. Most detrimentally, the plan required accuracy in identifying what would happen at the set location and time in the long term. It can be useful to remind the reader that the early Soviet planning used three types of plans: operational plans for one year, perspective plans for three to five years, and general plans for ten to fifteen years.[84] Kondrat'ev called the five-year plans "five-year hypotheses," although he was not against planning itself.[85] In his discussion, he invoked Comte's statement that "plan without prevision is nothing."[86] How to plan then if scientific possibilities for prevision are extremely limited?

Kondrat'ev proposed what was essentially a separation of operational and strategic planning. In this he drew on what was an established practice in major Western infrastructure companies, which, for instance, built railways and gas and oil rigs and used a rudimentary economic prevision in their planning. These infrastructure projects, wrote Kondrat'ev, were based on a "deep analysis" of economic and market trends. However, this well-founded expertise did not seek to *predict* those trends with great accuracy and certainty. Instead, it sought to establish the parameters of the minimum rentability of the planned infrastructure. This general positioning in the wider economic, political, and social context (a strategy) was completely missing from the Soviet five-year plans. Minimum rentability was not considered. Plans, for Kondrat'ev, had to be reasonably practical and "realistic." Unfortunately, as he showed in his essay, this is not what happened in Soviet planning, although enormous volumes of numbers and graphs were produced, describing in detail the sectors that were planned and depicting their state in the future. Calculations of separate components of the economy, the balance method, were mechanistically glued together. They could give some insight into the regularities that occurred in the past but were not suitable to scientifically forecast the future. For Kondrat'ev, these plans manifested "excessive courage" to make an accurate and detailed long-term prediction.[87] This, argued Kondrat'ev, was not scientifically possible in the field of society and

54   CHAPTER 2

economy. Moreover, this gargantuan task was duplicated by a great many different agencies, thus wasting institutional resources.[88]

To rectify the situation, Kondrat'ev wanted to see a "summary orientation" of control figures, which would give "confidence" to policymakers and managers to run their enterprises and sectors skillfully. In these orientations, the uncertainties of understanding society and the economy should not be hidden but made visible. Genuinely scientific planning, according to Kondrat'ev, would be based on forecasts as "hypotheses," which would not be masked as truths. Hypotheses would inform operational and perspective plans, where the plans would not be "official directives" (*kazennaia direktiva*), but "guiding directives," the implementation of which would require "maximal creative flexibility."[89] This approach to scientific governance as guidance would return in the 1970s and 1980s in the work of the mathematician Nikita Moiseev, which I discuss in chapter 7. However, in the 1920s and 1930s, planning remained dominated by ad hoc production of numbers that had little relation to reality and, as Kondrat'ev put it, in some fortunate cases, little impact on practice. Kondrat'ev's approach was strongly resisted by other planning thinkers. His most prominent opponent was Stanislav Strumilin, who advocated what was called a teleological approach to planning (completely unrelated to the flexible goal-steering teleology, theorized later by Norbert Wiener).[90]

The autohypnosis by numbers and the quasi-religious search for certainty in the 1920s and 1930s does stand out starkly as overcompensation in the context of the dearth of statistics in the preceding century. The communist state builders were determined to use science to modernize the state and society: mathematical methods were promoted in life sciences and social sciences in publications like *Statistical Method in Scientific Investigation* (1925).[91] Alongside economic planning, scientific management was introduced as a priority expertise area that was expected to lift the Soviet population out of poverty by increasing efficiency and the productivity of labor. Inspired by American Taylorism and Fordism, the movement *nauchnaia organizatsiia truda* (NOT) emerged in the 1910s and 1920s to develop "scientific" methods of labor. The relation between management, economic planning, and prediction was performative: scientific management was to reduce the chaos of the economy by making economic activities more regular and routine and, accordingly, more predictable (in the sense of being amenable to interpolation). At the same time, management thinkers engaged with epistemological questions of chronology and synchronization. Their principal interest was, of course, efficiency of labor and the use of resources. However, like their Western counterparts, Soviet management thinkers wrestled with complex questions about the epistemology of order and the nature of cognitive and behavioral communication and control.[92] One of the first systematic Russian thinkers about the role of time in management was the French-educated Valerian Murav'ev, a research secretary at the Central Institute for Labor, founded by Aleksei Gastev in Moscow, 1920.[93] Murav'ev's essay "The Mastery of Time as the Key Task in the Organization of Work" (1924) elaborated the Einsteinian notion of time and relativity, formulated in 1905. For Murav'ev, if time were understood as an expression of the material relations between things, it would be possible to know the future by studying these abstracted sequences of material relations. As he put it, time is "nothing else but change and movement." In the same way as Laplace, for Murav'ev to scientifically predict the future meant accumulating knowledge about possible configurations of things and their relations, and then sequencing these configurations. Murav'ev reflected on the systematicity of those multiple relationships. However, his writing belongs to idealist philosophy; he does not engage with positivist debates, but rather with Hegel and Bergson, contrasting the "blind and stupid" natural time with time as a result of rational human activity.[94] Unlike Kondrat'ev, Murav'ev did not address the problem of data, complexity, scale, and policy intervention as part of the project of the knowing the future.

The positivist striving for precision was expressed in the behaviorist methods of time control, developed in Russian time and motion studies. Gastev, together with Platon Kerzhentsev, a journalist and member of the communist government, founded what was called the League of Time, a group that, between 1923 to 1925, sought to "systematize time" through planning, aiming to transform what they perceived as inefficient and backward practices of Soviet industries and administration by introducing precision: "Instead of 'maybe,' an exact calculation; instead of 'in some way,' a well thought-through plan; instead of 'somehow,' a scientific method; instead of 'in some time,' at 20 hours 35 minutes on the 15th of October."[95] Time, wrote Kerzhentsev, is "a material value" and therefore must be budgeted and accounted for.[96] It was once again a simplistic Laplacian approach: when future configurations are sequenced properly, they can be controlled, and controlled precisely.[97] However, not all forms of managerial control were conceived as a linear process that could be described logistically and rationalized. For instance, in the same institute at the same time, a prominent Russian neurophysiologist Nikolai Bernshtein (1896–1966) formulated a notion of biomechanics as a cycle constituting of actions and corrections, which, later in the 1940s, he called a "reflex circle."[98] Many more examples could be invoked to support my case, but my point is that in postrevolutionary Russia there were diverging approaches to what is a proper scientific prediction in state governance. On the one hand, there was understanding of great complexity of social and economic phenomena which constrained the reach of scientific prediction. On the

56   CHAPTER 2

other hand, the urgency of economic development, the logic of political bureau-cracy, and the positivist thrust of management science propagated "illusory" pre-dictions which did not meet even the positivist epistemological criteria as science, but which nonetheless were legitimized as scientific. The notion of scientific prediction as a crucial part of scientific hypothesis-making was maintained by a wide range of innovative scholars. The criterion of predictability served as a test of knowledge, demanding better quality data, better models of dynamic relations, and, in the economy, strategic planning and flexible management. However, the very attempt to predict scientifically challenged the mechanistic contention that governed objects—be they human bodies, firms, or large-scale technical systems—were fundamentally knowable. Soviet Russian neurophysiologists, economists, and sociologists argued just that.[99] At the same time, they insisted that proper governance should be based on heuristic, scientific forecasting.

In the 1930s, macroeconomic statistics would become of great interest to govern-ments seeking to understand and cope with the Great Depression. Although, as Matthias Schmelzer noted, extensive quantitative descriptions of national econo-mies came to full existence only in the 1950s, for the interwar period there was a sense of urgency of making the workings of a failing economy visible and finding a remedy.[100] Some of those pioneering efforts in producing such visibility by num-bers belonged to Russian émigrés, such as Simon Kuznets, who was asked to esti-mate the US national income in 1934, a joint effort that led to the establishment of the notion of gross domestic product (GDP) as a measurement following the Bret-ton Woods agreement (1944), and Wassily Leontief, who directed the production of an input–output table to calculate the US postwar economy at Harvard in the 1940s.[101]

In parallel to this growth of governmental demand for numbers, in Stalin's Soviet Union the intellectual problem of making economic and social complex-ity visible, predictable, and governable was largely replaced with a political strug-gle for power: the great purges. Shortly after Kondrat'ev published his *The Long Wave Cycle* (1928), in which he argued that the ongoing decline of capitalist econ-omies could be explained as a stage in a long cycle, thus indirectly suggesting that capitalism's decline was not an expression of "internal contradictions," as Marx and Lenin would have it, the Conjuncture Institute was shut down. Some of Kondrat'ev's researchers were lucky to change their field of application, mov-ing to meteorological studies or the pure mathematical development of time se-ries methods, and survived the purges.[102] Kondrat'ev himself was not that lucky and was executed.

Soviet planning processes, as detailed by Peter Rutland and then Paul Gregory, remained conceptually confused and disorganized. Only five-year plans provided some general guidelines, albeit in a highly aggregated manner.[103] Many Soviet workers remained unskilled and their living conditions were often worse than before the revolution.[104] Soviet management scientists lacked basic equipment to conduct their experiments or to train managers.[105] That many time and motion studies could not be empirically conducted for a lack of stopwatches was one of the lesser concerns: the changing political climate would soon claim the very lives of the scientific time managers. Gosplan itself was purged in 1937, Murav'ev was sentenced to death on political grounds but died from disease before the execution. Like Kondrat'ev, Gastev and Kerzhentsev were executed between 1938 and 1940. Access to their work was forbidden to the public and specialists. The work of Gastev and Kerzhentsev would be republished in the mid-1960s, but the work by Murav'ev and Bazarov would become available in Russian only in the 1990s. Although Kondrat'ev's work on long waves was discussed in specialist circles, such as the International Institute of Applied Systems Analysis (IIASA) in Austria in the late 1970s and 1980s, his writings would be first made available to Soviet audiences in 1984.[106] The development of mathematical methods to describe and predict complex dynamics would be retained in the applied fields of electronics, mechanics, and logistics, particularly the methods of linear programming. However, the development of Soviet policy sciences would resume after the war in dialogue with American and Western European scholarship, in particular technology assessment. As I show in the next chapter, a fundamental role in opening up a space for this dialogue was played by cybernetics.

3

CYBERNETIC PREDICTION AND LATE MODERN GOVERNANCE

Whereas the first half of the twentieth century was characterized by the wish to make the economy and society more regular and predictable, the postwar period saw the rise of concern with predictability and particularly the scientific and technical applications that were created with the purpose of prediction in mind. The humanities' suspicion of scientific prediction was part of an academic culture that was critical of positivism, the roots of which go back to nineteenth century Germany.[1] It did not help that prediction and predictability formed part of the social changes described by Max Weber as the rationalization and bureaucratization of the social, expressed in the dehumanizing and mechanizing effects of Fordist and Taylorist methods of management and organization science, programs of social engineering, and the rise of technocracy, that is rule by technically educated elites. The tragedy of the Second World War amplified these concerns, evidencing the mass destructive power of "scientific" authoritarianisms.[2] After the war, the two great powers, the communist Soviet Union and the liberal democratic United States, emerged from the conflict armed with new, unprecedented technologies of computerized servomechanisms. The emerging Cold War culture of surveillance and long-range warfare further challenged the compatibility of scientific prediction and humanist values.

However, it was precisely in the postwar years that scientific prediction became more prominent than ever, thanks to its centrality in the new theory of cybernetics created by the US mathematician Norbert Wiener between the 1940s and the 1960s. In 1948, Wiener outlined a new theoretical agenda for understanding control mechanisms in complex, dynamic systems. He called this theory or approach "cybernetics," a term which he derived from the Greek word *kubernētēs*, meaning "steersman" or "governor."[3] In his cybernetics, Wiener defined the problem of control as a problem of communication and information processing, based on probabilistic prediction. Like the medieval mantic and conjectural knowledge, cybernetics paid attention to fleeting, irregular phenomena. It sought to discern regular patterns in what appeared as highly irregular or chaotic phenomena. The key difference between those modern science disciplines that seek to find "order in chaos," such as population statistics or natural evolution, and cybernetics is that cybernetics is interested in goal-oriented processes. These processes characterize conscious organisms, such as animals and humans, but they also could be part of the operation of unconscious machines or systems, such as thermostats, neural networks, and self-regulating ecological systems. Wiener's impact in conceptualizing behavioral prediction has been deep and lasting, particularly in the field of artificial intelligence (AI).[4]

Cybernetics addressed a wide field of natural and man-made phenomena. Its insights and terminology have been widely applied to analyze, model, and engineer automated technologies and social organization systems.[5] As early as the 1950s, humanities scholars questioned the applications of cybernetic control theory—as applied, for example, in the computer, electronic, and automation technologies and genetics—to understand individuals and society. Critics were particularly concerned about the contention that cybernetic prediction through feedback loops could help explain neural and behavioral coordination in biological organisms, as well as their interactions with the environment. They saw this as a threat of biological determinism that could lead to new forms of racism and subjugation of individuals. In the main, cultural critics identified cybernetics with technocracy and saw it as a new source of authoritarianism, this time founded on belief in digital technology and rationality.

From the 1950s to the 1960s, these lines of critique were advocated by some of the most prominent thinkers on both sides of the Atlantic. In France, as Stefanos Geroulanos details in his extensive history of transparency as an epistemological and political idea, cybernetics was criticized by Georges Canguilhem and Jacques Derrida.[6] Similarly, Martin Heidegger and Hannah Arendt argued that cybernetics threatened dehumanizing and depoliticizing social action, because cybernetics rendered social action as a purely technical problem. Heidegger, for instance, stated that "cybernetics is the form of technology replacing philosophy."[7] Although Arendt rarely used the very term cybernetics, she widely critiqued automation that was based on cybernetics, for instance, in *The Human Condition* (1958).[8] In these and similar critiques, as Debora Hammond puts it, "cybernetics

60   CHAPTER 3

tends to be seen as primarily mechanistic and deterministic in its approach, despite its rootedness in the recognition of contingency and indeterminacy that came out of nineteenth-century work on statistics and probabilistic systems."[9]

This chapter presents Norbert Wiener's approach to cybernetic prediction. It demonstrates that Wiener's theory of prediction was embedded in an epistemology friendly to uncertainty, as expressed in the idea of limited determinism. It is important to clarify Wiener's understanding of cybernetic prediction because his writings form an important basis to manifold theoretical developments though they themselves became objects of criticism, misunderstanding, and rehabilitation. This chapter, however, does not only provide an important background for the cases and argument developed in the rest of this book, it is also important in its own right. As John Johnston has noted, cybernetics emerged not just as a historical curiosity, but "a moment that should now be considered essential to the history of our present," a "historical nexus" out of which developed the late modern epistemology and technology of governance.[10] Indeed, the understanding of the complex epistemological legacy of cybernetics is manifest in the growing scholarship on the heterogeneous legacy of cybernetics. For example, historians have examined how the cybernetic notion of predictive control based on feedback loops—transferred from the field of electronic engineering to managerial, public policy, and cultural discourses—has been employed to enhance certainty, rationalization, and centralist direction in different political contexts.[11] Although the term cybernetics went out of common use in the 1970s as it was replaced with informatics (a term that designated a much more narrow field), the cybernetic model of predictive control has continued to underpin understanding of behavioral systems, leading to the development of what Peter Galison described as *Manichean sciences*, or sciences that seek to extend control of societies in the name of rationality and efficiency, as well as the Cold War struggle between the great powers and, later, neoliberal competition.[12] Clarifying the cybernetic notion of prediction is particularly important for understanding the history of Soviet scientific expertise and its impacts on governance and wider public culture.

Cybernetic Prediction Beyond Militarized Cold War Culture

Because Norbert Wiener's cybernetics grew out of the Second World War defense effort, it acquired a lasting reputation as a military technology. Wiener's key contribution to control science was the smoothing of statistical time series theory which he developed to improve the automated tracking and targeting functions in an antiaircraft predictor, although Wiener's work was never applied to the actual predictor at that time, because weapons technology lagged behind his mathematics.[13] However, this research laid the ground for what would become Wiener's cybernetics theory. Wiener broadened his theory of predictive control process into a wider philosophical undertaking thanks to the interactions with different scientists at the famous Macy conferences on cybernetics in New York (1946–1953). Extending his scientific engagement to a wider philosophy about the changing character of control in the thermodynamic world and its societal impacts, Wiener drew on Josiah Willard Gibbs's statistical physics, which pointed to the contingent character of the universe, where "order is least probable and chaos is most probable."[14] In such a universe, one could not rely on stationary laws of Newtonian mechanics. New types of mechanisms for the understanding of emerging order and adjustment to it had to be developed. Cybernetic theory of feedback-based control was one of the answers to this call; the other key components were fast-developing radar and computer technology.[15] Computer-powered cybernetic prediction could make knowledge work: it could fly and shoot down planes, and schedule transport logistics, but also operate electronic prosthetic limbs and machine translation systems.

What does it mean to predict cybernetically? For Wiener, prediction has a very particular meaning that builds on statistical extrapolation, where inferences about the unknown data are made on the basis of the incomplete data in the past, but is not limited to a statistical technique.[16] What makes statistical extrapolation a cybernetic prediction is its area of application as logistic knowledge that enables action: it is the estimation of a precise phenomenon's position in a given time and space, before this location actually takes place. To predict cybernetically means to gather real-time information about the observed change in a phenomenon and extrapolate a most likely trajectory of this change in the (very immediate) future. In servomechanism theory, prediction is about the extreme short-term situation of a given phenomenon in time and space. It requires quantifiable empirical data supplied through a sensor.

Cybernetic prediction is not just an intellectual exercise but a core part of steering action or behavior. It can be directed externally, as when a radar tracks an incoming missile and positions antimissile guns to shoot it down. It can also be directed internally, as when a thermostat regulates the internal temperature of a body or a room. Cybernetic prediction observes the changes in the phenomenon and in the behavior of the predictor itself, seeking to align them. As Wiener put it, these observations circulate through feedback loops which govern the predictive machine on the basis of its "actual performance" rather than "expected performance." A well-known example of a feedback mechanism is an automatic elevator, which will not let the doors open if the cabin is not in place.[17] In this way, the feedback mechanism is about simultaneity and effective adaptation to the

62   CHAPTER 3

environment. In computer engineering, feedback functions as a method of control, but Wiener expanded the concept and described feedback as a form of learning. Wiener defined learning as a process in which feedback can change "the general method and pattern of performance."[18] Even in the engineering context, cybernetic prediction can have a transformative effect, able to track and feed back the actual data and initiate learning, such as in a machine translation system.[19]

It is also important to consider Wiener's view of information. For Wiener, information is not a mechanical sorting of number values, as in a classical statistical device, but rather a probabilistic detection of patterns. Cybernetic prediction is an informational process, which takes place through decoding an order of what Wiener calls "events" or "messages": "The message is a discrete or continuous sequence of measurable events distributed in time—precisely what is called a time series by the statisticians. The prediction of the future of a message is done by some sort of operator on its past, whether this operator is realized by a scheme of mathematical computation, or by mechanical or electrical apparatus."[20] In this passage Wiener emphasizes that prediction is not based on the explanation of a phenomenon in relation to stationary laws. Prediction happens when data on the events are detected and collected (input). The next step is to conjure these data so that they shape a pattern and to project a most likely sequence of these events (patterns). Wiener notes that the world that is subject to prediction is changing and changeable: as the world is evolving, it cannot be completely foreknown. To be able to predict, in turn, is to adapt and change alongside the world or the environment. Cybernetic prediction, in this way, is principally part of an open, evolving system.

While the probabilistic and statistical functions of prediction have antecedents in eighteenth- and nineteenth-century mathematics, perhaps the most original and powerful part of Wiener's cybernetics is that it placed feedback-based prediction as the driver of open-ended, adaptive behavior rather than the deterministic mechanism of an automaton (as nineteenth-century statisticians would have had it). In this way, Wiener's model of prediction introduces an additional epistemological layer to statistical forecasting by aligning a statistical predictor with goal steering. For Wiener statistical prediction is but a part of what was described as a circular causality, where causes are placed in the future and not in the past. In the seminal article "Behavior, Purpose and Teleology," cowritten with Arturo Rosenblueth and Julian Bigelow in 1943, Wiener defined teleological behavior as "directed to the attainment of the goal—i.e. to a final condition in which the behaving object reaches a definite correlation in time or in space with respect to another object or event."[21] They distinguished predictive and nonpredictive purposeful behavior. For example, a bloodhound following a trail merely tracks the record of traces without predicting the trail, while a cat chasing a mouse must predict the

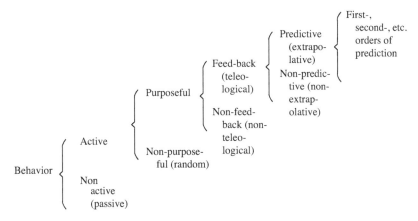

FIGURE 3. The types of behavior. Reprinted from Arturo Rosenblueth, Norbert Wiener, and Julian Bigelow, "Behavior, Purpose and Teleology," *Philosophy of Science* 10, no. 1 (1943): 18–24, 21. Courtesy of University of Chicago Press.

future moves of its prey. Predictive behavior of a higher order can anticipate the target's anticipations and act upon them.[22] It was precisely this teleological aspect of cybernetic prediction that worried positivist scientists, because the model of cybernetic control claimed to include something that materially did not yet exist.[23] However, for Wiener, Rosenblueth, and Bigelow this was not a problem, because a study of teleology was concerned not with linear, functional causality in physics, but with the mechanisms of emergent behavior.[24] As Andrew Pickering put it, cybernetic ontology readily embraced the unknown and nonexistent.

Another important point argued by Wiener is that predictive teleological behavior could be automated: a man-made device could trace, register, and analyze the patterns of behavior as "sequences of events." This aspect of Wiener's cybernetics has been widely commented on by critics fearing that cybernetic prediction-based technology would lead to a society governed by servomechanisms and AI machines. Wiener himself, however, did not think that cybernetic totalitarianism was encroaching on society. He did not consider the "automated government machines" dangerous, simply because they were "far too crude and imperfect to exhibit a one-thousandth part of the purposive independent behavior of the human being."[25] The real danger, according to Wiener, is in people themselves who may adopt the idea of cybernetic prediction to dominate others. For Wiener, an example of this misuse of prediction was von Neumann's game theory of Cold War strategy.[26] Wiener argued against using cybernetic terminology to express models of social and political governance as undesirable and dangerous, not only because it is ethically problematic but also because cybernetic language can be

64   CHAPTER 3

subjugated to political promises of certainty. Wiener alerted that any predictor, human or machine, is beset by errors "of a roughly antagonistic nature" because no predictor is exempt from the laws of thermodynamics, where any form of order is subject to entropy.[27] Incorporating fundamental uncertainty is part of the cybernetic culture of prediction.

However, this does not mean that cybernetic prediction could not be used for social governance. Quite the opposite. Wiener's notion of cybernetic prediction as an adaptive, informational, and goal-oriented process invites a particular model of future-oriented behavior. In order to make prediction theory work, it is necessary to imitate naturally occurring purposeful behavior. Animals and humans can display predictive behavior without being aware of its physics and mechanics, but the actual engineering of teleological machines or organizations requires appropriate understanding of the underlying physical and cognitive mechanisms.[28] In Wiener's cybernetics, therefore, prediction is the beginning not the end of the process in scientific understanding.

Here it is worthwhile to pause and briefly consider servomechanism theory, because it exemplifies the symmetrical notion of prediction as explanation, which may resemble the logical empiricist take on prediction, presented in chapter 1, but which is substantially different in its performative effect. Servomechanism theory conceptualizes control processes, which are used to create automated weapon systems such as antiaircraft missiles. The engineering problem is how to shoot down an enemy aircraft that tries to evade targeting. The missile's trajectory has to be set in such a way that it tracks the moving target. The trajectory is based on calculations that are themselves based on a more general physical theory of movement. The radar that does the tracking feeds the information to the computer, which identifies (statistically extrapolates) the most probable location of the aircraft on the space and time axes. This prediction is not a pure guess but is based on the time series analysis and parameters of possible trajectory, which are established by aerodynamics, which, in turn, was developed and tested through physical modeling. This engineering model of automated control can operate on prediction under the condition that its operational environment is sufficiently known, that it can be explained with reference to general laws. Moreover, the predictor inside the antiaircraft missile system must be "aware" of the positioning of guns and their ability to perform in response to the calculated results. This is a very simple model of what could be described as "self-reflexivity," a form of information processing that shapes behavior. As I show in the remaining part of this chapter, the integration of predictive scientific calculations (which are "estimates" accompanied by "explanations" or references to general laws) with actual behavior is what complicates the positivist model of scientific prediction. This is an important point, because the wider applications of cybernetics have been driven by a positivist culture of science and, in turn, cybernetic prediction-based control has been labeled as an expression of technocratic positivism.

From the 1940s to the 1960s, mathematicians, engineers, economists, and nascent management scientists from East and West, and also the global South, pursued the idea that cybernetic prediction could be applied to any purposive, change-bound system, for example, urban, social, and economic planning.[29] However, Wiener argued very clearly that social statistical forecasting is a poor technique for predicting social phenomena for two reasons. First, according to Wiener, in order to be reliable, predictions of complex systems require statistical extrapolation from very long runs of data reflecting the sequence of events in question. Second, these runs need to take place "under essentially constant conditions."[30] This means that in order to be predictable scientifically, social phenomena must be homogeneous and unfold in a smooth manner. But, unlike Comte and the positivists, Wiener did not believe that societal development is lawful. Societies, wrote Wiener, evolve disruptively and are uneven from the data point of view, particularly because of changing norms and values. This means that the same material phenomenon might mean completely different things at different times and therefore have a different social effect. For instance, as Eric Wolf showed, beaver fur was highly valued in the seventeenth and eighteenth centuries in Europe, driving colonial expansion of the British empire.[31] It would be, however, a great mistake to attribute the same economic value to beaver fur in the late twentieth century, because the context is entirely different. The differences of this nature, the value of which depends on the context and is changeable, are notoriously difficult to integrate in statistical models. Even when some societal or economic systems might appear to be predictable at one particular moment in time they have the capacity to become unpredictable at another: for instance, in econometric models, the data on steel change their significance and meaning with every new invention that may modify the overall demand for steel.[32] In all, Wiener warned the enthusiasts of social and economic cybernetics that the advantage of long runs in social statistics, even when available, is "specious and spurious" at best. Using cybernetic methods for predicting societies—and economies—for Wiener was simply bad science.[33]

Another important area of the application of cybernetic prediction is the environment. Unlike social and economic systems, environmental systems could be regarded as relatively well described and explained by physical sciences. By the mid-twentieth century considerably long statistical data runs on the aspects of physical environment had been accumulated. The quality of this data was consistently improved by establishing new, global networks to monitor the land, the ocean, and the atmosphere.[34] However, many environmental applications of cybernetic prediction were restricted by high sensitivity to both scale and time. Wiener illustrates this point with a well-known example of the difference in predicting the future of astronomical and meteorological systems (an example which was favored by the nineteenth- and early twentieth-century positivist scholars).[35] Astronomical systems comprise a relatively small number of very large particles (planets), which can differ a lot in size among themselves. By contrast, meteorological systems have a very large number of particles which are of similar size and are constantly interacting.[36] While accurate recording of initial positions and velocity of large particles (planets) in astronomy can be done with a high degree of certainty, in meteorology this is impossible:

> If all the readings of all the meteorological stations on earth were simultaneously taken, they would not give a billionth part of the data necessary to characterize the actual state of the atmosphere from a Newtonian point of view. They would only give certain constants consistent with an infinity of different atmospheres, and at most, together with certain a priori assumptions, capable of giving, as a probability distribution, a measure over the set of possible atmospheres.[37]

Here Wiener makes a strong point that the principle of linear causality has a limited role in predictive epistemology when applied to small scales and the long term. In highly complex systems even known causal relations can become unstable as a result of new, unprecedented interactions. As Wiener put it, using the Newtonian or any causal laws, "all that we can predict at any future time is a probability distribution of the constants of the system, and even this predictability fades out with the increase of time."[38] Timescale, in this way, imposes important epistemological limits on scientific prediction. For this reason Wiener's work on cybernetic prediction was predominantly concerned with very short-term loops of information processing and behavior.

Finally, an important question for Wiener and his critics was whether scientific prediction was purely cognitive and informational or material. This question particularly bothered humanists, who were concerned that the separation of future-oriented control and human body would lead to a society dominated by the values, embodied not in living beings but in the informational, automated, and authoritarian machine.[39] Indeed, Wiener famously declared that "the mechanical brain does not secrete thought as 'the liver does the bile,'" claiming that "information is information, not matter or energy."[40] It appears that information for Wiener is part of the physical constitution of the universe. Today this epistemological stance corresponds with the quantum information theory as advocated by David Deutsch. However, Wiener's own thoughts were forgotten in what would become a conversation lasting half a century on the conceptual split between information and matter. For instance, responding to computer science and telecommunications theory, which equated information with binary computer logic, Katherine Hayles developed her influential argument on the posthumanist effect of cybernetics. According to Hayles, the notion of nonmaterial information leads to an erroneous conceptual divide of materiality/body and information/mind, in this way perpetuating old Western cultural hierarchies where material, embodied, noncognitive activities were deemed to be existentially and socially inferior to cognitive and abstract operations.[41] A popular example of such a divide, for instance, was seen in the organization of the early AI research. AI researchers regarded the chess-playing computer as a model of human brain. This led many to believe that computers may replace humans in tasks that require thinking. However, later work on AI showed the reverse—that the game of chess requires only a partial cognitive function of the human brain.[42] Indeed, even the author of the first computer chess program, organizational theorist Herbert Simon, argued that human rationality is influenced by social and organizational contexts, and thus is not entirely disembodied. It is true, as Kline demonstrated in 2015, that influential forms of information theory place an extraordinary emphasis on decontextualization and disembodying of information. However, a close reading of Wiener's writing shows that his views on materiality and information were more complex and materiality friendly.[43] In what follows, I review these ideas, because the questions of materiality and cognition are very important for the notion of cybernetic prediction.

The question of materiality emerges in Wiener's discussion of scientific prediction as a model of agency. As mentioned earlier, in cybernetics, prediction is not a discrete function of a structure but rather a feature of an emergent behavior. In other words, prediction makes behavior possible and it is part of it. What prediction is not is a clockwork-like mechanism that ensures the same type of response to the same situation. Clocks can make complex and unstable behaviors of other people predictable. Cybernetics is interested in those sorts of behaviors that incorporate a form of prediction to cope with uncertain changes.

To put it in other words, the cybernetic notion of prediction does not refer to single logical operation. Wiener described prediction as the *orchestration* of different agencies: a predicting system, an observed system, and a process of interaction between the two. It is important to note here that all these agencies are not only dynamic (changing) but also materially mediated. Wiener wrote that all scientific predictions are made possible only through "observations" of particular "agencies." Stars, for instance, are observed thanks to the agency of light, what physics describes as a flow of photons.[44] In this way, there can be no direct observation and, accordingly, no purely "informational" prediction. Instead, the world must be materially mediated in a particular way in order to become "predictable."

68   CHAPTER 3

Wiener noted that the human ability to orchestrate material systems is quite amazing but still limited. It is the material and conceptual limits to orchestration that constitute the boundaries to scientific predictability. Indeed, this is where Wiener's notion of a cybernetically predictable universe departs from the positivist view. Scientific epistemology, for Wiener, is ultimately humbling: as he put it, "the direction of time is uniform" where the human role is quite limited. This means that we can see the stars thanks to the energy that has been sent, we can see the stars as the energy is arriving, but we cannot see it outgoing, because of the irreversibility of the process.[45]

To predict the future cybernetically, for Wiener, is not to employ abstract reason to master the world and time. It is rather to build predictive collectives that combine human and nonhuman actors, people and machines. For Wiener, these predictive collectives should be guided not only by the questions of feasibility (know-how) but also by desirability (know-what), that is, ethics. Scientific prediction thus conceived welcomes the incremental arrival of a new form of the universe.[46]

In organizational terms, cybernetic prediction as the orchestration of different material agencies requires creating particular techniques of recording, measuring, and interpreting data, as well as the coordination of the many actors who are in charge of them. Cybernetic prediction is materially mediated and social, bound to physics, devices, scientific epistemologies, and social institutions.

As Henning Schmidgen argued, for Wiener "the human brain, cybernetically speaking, was nothing more than a precision timer controlling the organ's processing of information."[47] This is a very helpful observation, but one should not rush and equate this notion of the brain as a synchronization device with a mechanical clock. As Schmidgen shows, Wiener extends this argument to suggest that the existence of entire cultures and societies in fact depends on the synchronized activities of people. In doing this, Wiener relied on research into neurophysiology, the origins of which dated to the early nineteenth century. Prediction plays an important part in this process of synchronization. Schmidgen refers to Kenneth Craik, a British proto-cybernetician, who described humans as "prediction machines" in 1947, hence before the publication of Wiener's *Cybernetics*. According to Craik, people engage in prediction not by choice but by necessity, as human decisions and responses lag due to their slow physiology: "Since [the human operator] is always subject to this lag, in attempting to keep up with the present he is always in fact being a prophet and extrapolating from past data."[48] The challenge for the predictive mind is to integrate discrete observations into a meaningful whole without losing their chronological dimension (what comes before and what comes after). As Schmidgen shows very clearly in his article, synchronization of cognition, behavior, and interagential action are central for cybernetic prediction.

Wiener's own writings and Schmidgen's contextualization of cybernetic prediction in the history of neurophysiology and psychology make it clear that the societal implications of Wiener's cybernetic prediction are significantly different from Knightian risk calculation. In the spirit of cybernetics, society predicts itself into being. Social action is based on individuals and collectives being able to mutually predict each other and synchronize their multiple activities. This synchronization is made possible via feedback loops and corrective self-regulation as well as by a high level of integration of incoming signals. If risk society, as Michael Power put it, is about accounting and establishing networks of trust and security via mutual observation, a society based on cybernetic prediction is about the orchestration of synchronicity, building collectives and collective behavior.[49]

Cybernetic Prediction and Its Critics

It should be clear by now that Wiener's version of cybernetic prediction has much more to offer than has been hitherto recognized. The genealogy of cybernetic epistemology as a source for a militarized, control-seeking governmental framework that overspilled from servomechanical theory into public policy and management addresses only one side of the story.[50] While Wiener adopted a fierce, if not always consistent, antimilitaristic stance, a strong case has been made by later historians who have begun mapping the internal heterogeneity of cybernetic epistemology, as it is conducive to countercultural movements, and also ideas of transparency and transnational cooperation in contrast to the militarized tracking of an enemy.[51] Most importantly, the intellectual and organizational impact of Wiener's cybernetics and cybernetic prediction has been partially obscured by an excessive focus on the digital and computer sides of this approach. Revisions like Schmidgen's and Pickering's show that cybernetic prediction is an extension of a much more complex epistemology of order and evolution, one that was formulated in neurophysiological and psychological sciences.

This epistemological and political complexity of cybernetic prediction must be taken seriously as prediction devices are becoming a central object of analysis in social and political histories. Whereas historians have long referred to machines as metaphors of social order, science and technology studies scholars have proposed a stronger theoretical program suggesting that machines are performative mechanisms generating social order. However, different types of machines do not correspond directly with different sociopolitical orders. For instance, Otto

70   CHAPTER 3

Mayr proposed that adaptive, feedback-guided systems that are open to the environment historically emerged as both metaphors and models for a liberal social and political order. Mayr contrasted liberal machines, such as steam engines, with closed systems, such as mechanical clocks, which, according to him, embodied the idea of a rule-bound and completely predictable order.[52] However, as Peter Galison demonstrated, actual mechanical clocks were, in fact, a continuous source of frustration, because they rarely ran as they were supposed to, lacked precision, and, most importantly, were notoriously hard to coordinate. The chaotic character of the mechanical clock, as Galison shows, inspired Einstein to develop his theory of relativity.[53] Perhaps Mayr's proposition could be inverted to suggest that authoritarian regimes end up being like clocks in the sense that they are chaotic. After all, a clock mechanism is but part of a wider system of synchronization and orchestration of information processing and behavior.

In a similar vein, as a metaphor and mechanism of government, cybernetic prediction has become the target of cultural criticism as inadequate for describing social relations and possibly dangerous if deployed in policy and management. This association of cybernetic prediction with at best technical terminology and at worst a politically bankrupt ambition toward authoritarian control of information can be attributed to the legacy of Cold War governmentality.[54] Cold War future visions were formulated by experts and increasingly removed from public debate, as the future of industrial development, social planning, and foreign policy began to increasingly rely on extensive statistical data and forecasts.[55] Those cases that criticize the uses of prediction in governance tend to draw on a particular linear notion of prediction as a statistical extrapolation. This linear prediction was contrasted with alternative forms of engaging with the future, such as diagnosis, scenario, and normative planning.[56] One could speculate that Wiener would have agreed with these criticisms in the sense that statistical extrapolation is of only limited use in the organization of society, because it draws on short runs of imperfect data. But it should not be forgotten that Wiener himself tried to overcome this limitation by pointing to the complex epistemological role of prediction as adaptive behavior that extended beyond calculation and control.

Louise Amoore has contrasted what she describes as "the poverty of probabilistic prediction" with new strategies for dealing with future uncertainty through the preemption of possibilities. Amoore's study of the emerging field of risk consultancy enumerated an entire list of practices that risk-assessment experts themselves claim to use instead of probabilistic prediction: "consulting, screening, remote tracking, biometric identifying, and algorithmic profiling."[57] These types of activities fit well with what Michael Power described as an organizational repertoire of risk and accounting society. However, these practices could be seen as lower-level components of cybernetic steering via predictive feedback; they are parts of a whole that is more than just a sum of its parts. Identification, tracking, surveilling could be parts of a mechanically conceived bureaucracy, but they could also be orchestrated into a wider cybernetic epistemology. I propose that notions of preemption and preparedness can be better understood as new forms of what Wiener described as "orchestration of prediction." Cybernetic prediction still feeds into preemption and preparedness at lower scales of complexity through the need to acknowledge the necessity of pattern recognition and conjecture.

Conclusion

In 1959, C. P. Snow wrote about the emergence of two distinct cultures of exact mathematical sciences and humanities, which are characterized by a deep misunderstanding of each other that constructs obstacles to more productive development of both types of knowledge.[58] In this chapter I have proposed a case for a cybernetic culture of prediction that differs in its treatment of uncertainty from the commonsense use of prediction. One culture of prediction seeks to eliminate uncertainty by formalizing the process of conjecture and seeking for greater precision in foretelling the unknown events. The key method is linear statistical forecasting and algorithmic trees. The other culture of prediction places uncertainty at the heart of estimating the unknown, calling for a reflexive orchestration of the many material and conceptual mediators to enable detection of patterns and empower adaptive action. In Wiener's cybernetics, prediction is not the end but the beginning of purposeful behavior.

Half a century ago, Wiener wrote that humans need more foresight in the age of automation, where goal-seeking machines will multiply and where the possibility of machine production of goals is very real.[59] However, one should be cautious of "merchants of certainty" who trade in probabilistic predictions as if they are astrological prognoses or mechanistic models.[60] In this context, and in line with Naomi Oreskes's argument that uncertain knowledge opens up new vulnerabilities in existing institutional practices, cybernetic prediction makes a case for vulnerabilities that in the end could bridge existing political divides.[61] The following chapters present moments from this kind of history as it unfolded in the Soviet Union, where different forms of scientific prediction were articulated in a conversation with cybernetics to orchestrate new forms of the social.

4

FORECASTING AND THE CYBERNETIC SENSIBILITY

Between the 1940s and 1960s, the cultural expectation that science should supply a continuous flow of predictions of such fleeting phenomena as weather, economy, and social changes became entrenched in what I call a cybernetic sensibility: an idea that individual and organizational behavior should be based on informational processing, predictions, and feedback. Slava Gerovitch called cybernetics a movement, not a theory: there was not a particular, well-defined theory of cybernetics that could be applied in different areas. Instead, the cybernetic notion that control is a performative adjustment via predictive processing was adopted in a loose manner, sometimes as a metaphor (in management and semiotics, for instance) and sometimes as a rigorous science (applied to servomechanisms, automation, and neurophysiology).[1] The cybernetic sensibility spread in the global North and South in a great variety of forms, ranging from postpositivist, relational, and posthumanist approaches to technocratic utopian projects.[2] Different scientists, engineers, consultants, and artists adopted selectively the elements of cybernetics to match their own worldviews and organizational needs.[3] Such was the fate of cybernetics in the Soviet Union as well.

As I showed in the previous chapter, cybernetics, a science of communication and control, became an object of boundless enthusiasm and criticism. As part of the early Cold War attack on "bourgeois pseudosciences," the Soviet ideologues banned cybernetics in 1948 without really understanding what cybernetics was about, as Gerovitch showed. Soviet cybernetics was rehabilitated in the magic year of 1956, to be declared *the* science of governance in the 1960s.[4] I will not rehearse the story, which is well covered in the many excellent histories of cyber-

FORECASTING AND THE CYBERNETIC SENSIBILITY   73

netics that the reader can turn to.[5] This chapter presents some of key moments in the history of postwar scientific forecasting as it was reintroduced into Soviet social research and economic planning. It cannot do justice to the complexity and diversity of the ways forecasting was applied in different branches and administrative territories, such as regions and Soviet republics. The key purpose here is to demonstrate how the two different logics of prediction, positivist and cybernetic, intertwined and informed the epistemological and institutional work that was pursued by Soviet social forecasters from the 1960s to the 1980s. The study of cybernetics—research into communication and control through information loops—shares the ambition to discern and understand regular patterns and describe them mathematically so as to be able to forecast scientifically. In the Soviet Union after the Second World War, cybernetics served as an icebreaker, a new governmental epistemology that facilitated the return of scientific forecasting to planning.[6] The notion of a cybernetic governance of society, economy, and nature required a flow of information about past, current, and future states.[7] Enter scientific forecasting (*nauchnoe prognozirovanie*, which includes but is not limited to statistical forecasting; from here on I will use the term scientific forecasting and will specify statistical forecasts where relevant), a method that promised data about possible future states of society, technology, and economy.

Now, as I showed earlier, the cybernetic notion of prediction is performative: it is based on process tracking which is plugged into feedback loops enabling an organism or machine to adjust to its environment. Cybernetic prediction is very different from the positivist prediction. The epistemology of cybernetic prediction is not about testing a hypothesis (and improving knowledge), but about getting on with the unknown by developing viable coping strategies via trial and error. It is about information processing and goal-seeking. The link between what was described as cybernetic technology—servomechanisms and automated systems—and scientific or statistical forecasting is very intimate. In engineering, a cybernetic system can be built as a servomechanism, containing a radar, and a calculator, able to process predictive statistical data, time series analysis. So statistical forecasting can be part of cybernetic engineering. However, to think that every use of scientific forecasting leads directly to "cybernetization" of management or policymaking is at best metaphorical and at worst misleading. Of course, the power of metaphors to shape governmental expectations should not be underestimated: eventually in the Soviet Union the notion of a mechanical universe was replaced with a cybernetic one. The metaphor of workers as cogs in the machine (scientific Taylorism and in the movement of scientific organization of labor, *nauchnaia organizatsiia truda* (NOT)) was replaced in Soviet governmental discourses by the metaphor of people as carriers and conductors of information (cybernetic governance).[8] However, as I show in this chapter, for a management or

74   CHAPTER 4

policy practice to become cybernetic, a number of organizational conditions must be met. This was acutely perceived by Soviet reformist scientists who argued for the introduction of proper scientific forecasting in planning *and* the reforming of the institution of planning and scientific expertise to accommodate a more cybernetic, responsive model of organization. In turn, scientific forecasting is not limited to the method of sorting statistical data: what makes scientific forecasts "predictions" in a logical empiricist sense is their task of testing the quality of data and explanations by succeeding (or failing) to generate novel facts.

Forecasting the Soviet Economy

The period from the Stalinist terror of the 1930s to the thaw in the late 1950s was not entirely void of efforts to apply predictive science to organizational and policy decisions. Although lofty epistemological debates on prediction were absent, important fundamental research into predictive methods was continued, which would provide an important basis for the postwar boom of forecasting. During the period, however, this work was no longer hosted in universities or the Academy of Science's institutes but moved to the military and state security sector. A good example of this is research into resource allocation techniques that underpinned the war plan prepared by the famous Soviet Russian reformer of the army, Mikhail Tukhachevskii. In this plan known resources were allocated to known organizational units. This framework of war planning required both complete knowledge of available and required resources and precise logistical distribution of activities, in this respect very similar to the principles of economic planning criticized by Kondrat'ev in the 1920s. In 1926, Abram Vol'pe, an instructor at the Military Academy, advocated "a precise plan of industrial mobilization" in the event of war.[9] Vol'pe, however, was accused of plotting a coup and executed in 1937. At the same time Soviet military planners understood that preparation for the future war included some efforts to anticipate technological innovations in weapon systems, something that became very clear during the war, when, for instance the Soviet engineers raced to develop tanks that would be faster and less susceptible to damage from firing.[10]

Another strand of research into prediction was developed by Russian mathematicians working on time series techniques in statistics.[11] Some of the most important advances in applied mathematics were made by the future Nobel Prize winner Leonid Kantorovich, who began to experiment with statistical methods to improve the efficiency and productivity of management during his internship at the water board in Tashkent, Uzbekistan, in 1929. This kind of expertise was welcomed in principle, but its practical applications were extremely limited because actual management practices in the context of shortage and technological constraints were primitive and did not extend beyond basic organization of the presence of workers.[12] However, in 1939, Kantorovich developed an algorithm for linear programming to optimize the process of production, a method that he saw as applicable at both enterprise and national levels. He informed the State Planning Committee about this potentially useful method but the proposal was rejected (in 1942 and again in 1954). The rejection referred to an old issue, one faced by the imperial administrators and Kondrat'ev: the application of Kantorovich's algorithm required gathering "too much information," which was recognized as not feasible.[13] Kantorovich and his colleagues did not give up and submitted the proposal again in 1956.

Prediction as a problem of science and engineering resurfaced in the 1950s, when the Soviet economy began to recover and the political balance of powers had shifted with the death of Stalin and the rise of Nikita Khrushchev. There was also "something in the air": the year 1956 was described by Hunter Heyck as an annus mirabilis for the development of new ideas about governability and control in the United States. Around this date a whole array of foundational texts was published in the Western world, declaring the birth of new policy sciences, such as decision analysis, operations research (OR), and systems analysis.[14] These studies also alerted Western governments to rapidly emerging technical and social changes, which could not be dealt with without richer, more reliable anticipatory knowledge. The Soviet government was also increasingly conscious of the growing complexity of its industries and economy. This was boosted by the Cold War competition: the West that Nikita Khrushchev sought "to catch up and surpass" was about to embrace a new way of thinking about the knowability of both nature and society and the uses of this knowledge for governmental purposes. Many Western governments and a growing number of postwar international organizations explored the avenues of using scientific expertise for planning.[15] Although to rehabilitate Kondrat'ev, who suggested that the decline of capitalist economies was just a moment in a cycle, was still unthinkable, the ideas of Kantorovich no longer looked so out of place.

In the wake of the Twentieth Congress in 1956, Soviet planners turned their attention back to the Western experience of economic governance, but this was a protracted and guarded process. The Soviet Union relied on its own national accounting system, the System of Balances of the National Economy, also called the Material Product System, which was used to measure and project growth. This meant that the Soviets hoped to rely on their own statistics and methods. However, from the 1960s, they also engaged in partnerships to secure access to internationally produced economic data and methods of statistical analysis, forecasting, and modeling.[16] During postwar reconstruction, but even more so in

76   CHAPTER 4

response to the slowing growth of the initial industrial burst of the Soviet economy that became evident by the late 1950s, the All-Union State Planning Committee (Gosplan) grew and professionalized.[17] An important innovation was the establishment in 1955 of a Scientific Research Institute of Economics (NIEI), dedicated to macroeconomic problems and the development of normative conceptual foundations for perspective planning.[18] One of the tasks of NIEI was to learn from similar governmental bodies in the West. To this purpose, high-level meetings were organized. In May 1958, a delegation of French planners traveled to Moscow hoping to learn about what they considered "an alternative approach": the French government put a premium on large-scale and rather centralized planning and, under Pierre Massé, new methods of planning based on long-term forecasting were developed.[19] However, in their report the French wrote that they had discovered a vast gap between the "logic of planning" and the reality of paused factory lines, the black market, and poverty.[20] The French visit was reciprocated in November 1958, when NIEI's director and prominent economist Anatolii Efimov, together with six colleagues, embarked on a two-week trip to France. Soviet economists visited factories and learned about Jean Monnet's plans and the work of the Commissariat Général du Plan. They were also disappointed with what they found. Back in Moscow, Efimov wrote in his report that "[French] planning organs naturally need to satisfy themselves with merely making a kind of 'program-prognosis,' which is made on the most general level and does not command anyone. It is in this sense that the term 'planning' is used in relation to the French economy."[21] Having labeled this kind of planning as "indicative," Efimov continued: "it is clear that under the indicative system of planning, even the most perfect method of making the branches of the economy proportionate cannot guarantee a lawful development of economics."[22] This Soviet encounter with French practices of central planning was crucial, because it shows that Soviet economists considered scientific forecasting inseparable from the organizational design and political authority. They understood the French system of integrating forecasting with decision-making as an inevitable compensation for "failed planning," a compromise, an informational tool that a weak state planning agency used to coordinate a free-market economy. Soviet economists, therefore, did not consider forecasting necessary in central directive-based planning. Kondrat'ev's insights into the epistemological limitations of scientific prediction of the economy and the value of indicative, hypothetical forecasts for decision-making appeared to be completely lost.

Just as in the 1920s, in the 1940s and 1950s Soviet long-term plans were made without forecasting. The first long-term plan (for fifteen years) was put together by Gosplan just before the Nazi invasion in 1941. In the late 1950s, Gosplan produced a twenty-year plan, the "general perspective," for the period 1961 to 1980.[23]

Both plans claimed to be based on interbranch balances, which perhaps could be classified as a type of forecasting, because they contained statistical projections of the future economy. But these balances were deeply flawed. The 1941 plan was mainly a conceptual exercise devoid of mathematical methods for calculating interbranch balances. The 1950s plan was no better. The talented economist Emil' Ershov, who would leave later NIEI to become the director of the Central Institute of Mathematical Economics (TsEMI) recalled a complete absence of any methodological literature when he was asked to develop interbranch balances in the late 1950s.[24] The calculations done for the 1961 to 1980 plan were criticized both by Westerners, most famously Wassily Leontief, but also by some Soviet economists themselves.[25]

This slow and painstaking search for improvement of economic planning methods began to converge with the military-industrial research into statistical series extrapolation methods, as well as other methods of decision sciences in the 1940s and 1950s.[26] While few archival documents are available to offer a detailed discussion of this rapprochement, the primacy of the military research is suggested by the fact that some of the first Soviet publications on forecasting focused on research and development (R&D) and technology assessment, all part of military planning. For instance, in 1964 an influential academic journal, *Voprosy filosofii* (The Issues of Philosophy), published the first article about methods of forecasting in organizing scientific research, authored by Genadii Dobrov, a Ukrainian scientist who participated in pioneering projects for the development of computers in Kyiv, Ukraine, and later established himself as the leading authority on research policy.[27] The many memoirs written by the Soviet mathematicians hint that the spread of forecasting in the Soviet Union resembled that of the United States, where the military studies at the RAND military think-tank were extended to the civil sector, although Russian historiography remains opaque about this.[28]

The transfer of scientific forecasting from the military to the civil sector was stimulated by large-scale industrial infrastructure development projects. A particularly important breakthrough can be dated to the Soviet government's decision to develop Siberian oil and gas fields and build a pipeline to Europe, a project that in its significance equaled the State Commission for Electrification of Russia (GOELRO). In the capacity of a vice chairman of the Council of Ministers and of the chairman from 1964, Aleksei Kosygin personally supported this project and was aware that the new technological structure required a longer-term outlook. I do not know if Kosygin read Kondrat'ev, but he was certainly receptive to the ideas of the prominent computer scientists Germogen Pospelov and Viktor Glushkov, who offered to computerize planning and reorient it to incorporate different methods of forecasting.[29] Furthermore, Kosygin worked in tandem with his son-in-law, the influential Westernizer of Soviet management and the mediator of

78   CHAPTER 4

many large East–West trade deals, Dzhermen Gvishiani. The Soviet version of Taylorism from the 1920s was revived, but in a significantly upgraded form that incorporated cybernetic insights and the science of ergonomics. Gvishiani in 1963 authoritatively announced that "governance was first and foremost a science."[30] Once Khrushchev was ousted in 1964 (his failed projections of Soviet economic growth were listed as evidence of the incapacity of his leadership) and Kosygin climbed up the political hierarchy to become second only to Brezhnev, the future of Soviet scientific forecasting studies was sealed. Planning was to be optimal, scientific, and based on a wide array of short- and long-term predictions.[31] Calls for flexibility that resonated with Kondrat'ev's ideas began to appear in the press.[32] In his 1965 speeches at both Gosplan and the Plenum of the Central Committee, Kosygin proclaimed that scientific forecasting was the key component of planning. Gosplan from then on should supply the republics' governments and companies with scientific forecasts, to be revised and sent back to the central planners.[33] Kosygin's notion of the role of forecasting in planning would remain set for the next twenty-five years: "Discussions of scientific forecasts need to precede the development of plans for the branches of the national economy. . . . We need to forecast scientifically the development of every branch of industry to be able to give way in time to the most advanced and progressive developments."[34] These are, for sure, general phrases, typical of political discourse. However, it is important that forecasting is presented here as part of policy practice, following Comte's formulation, according to which a scientific prediction must foreground rational action. It also resonates with the cybernetic model of a viable system, where prediction is also fundamental for any teleological, goal-oriented behavior. However, positivist prediction, cybernetic prediction, and goal orientation in interwar and postwar planning should not be considered as equivalent. There are important conceptual differences. First, Wiener's idea of cybernetic teleology should not be confused with the Soviet concept of *tselevoe planirovanie*, created in the 1920s and translated into English as "teleological planning," because these are two different approaches that invoke different types of governmentality. According to Stephen Collier, the Soviet *tselevoe planirovanie* put a premium on the internal consistency of the plan, preferably expressed numerically, and thus gave the illusion of total control of planning instruments and targets.[35] In this way, *tselevoe planirovanie* did not allow for the flexibility of a real-time feedback system as conceptualized by Wiener, geared to respond to the ever-changing environment in order to stay on its course. Second, it appears that Kosygin's call for integrating scientific forecasting and planning, and Gvishiani's call for scientific, cybernetic management, did not anticipate the clash between the mechanistic, positivist prediction and the performative, cybernetic prediction. I doubt that they expected such subversive consequences in the entire institutional organizaton of science and policy that the cybernetic approach to data collection and processing would require.

And so, following the slogan of putting "cybernetics in the service of communism," starting in 1965, Gosplan began to develop what they saw as properly scientific, long-term forecasts for economic development.[36] The Academy of Sciences institutes also embarked on this task.[37] The academic community embraced the political will to make social and economic forecasts because many scholars saw this as a window of opportunity to reform the whole estate of science, ridden with ideological censorship, ineffective organizational compartmentalization, and secrecy. This was made very clear in December 1966, when the first open academic meeting dedicated to the conceptual development of long-term planning on the basis of forecasting was organized in Moscow.[38] Arranged at NIEI, this meeting was stormed by enthusiastic crowds of scholars. According to Efimov, the novelty and importance of scientific future studies was "illustrated by the energy with which many comrades attempted to enter this hall. Such *Anschlag* is normally seen only in grand theater premieres. This is understandable, because the question of long-term prognosis is so exciting for us."[39] This was forty years after the publication of Kondrat'ev's essay on prevision. Although about 250 participants registered to attend a session on the forecasting of the national economy, more than 450 showed up; another session on mathematical forecasting was attended by 100 persons.[40] The transcript of the discussion reveals that obligatory propaganda dues were paid to the superiority of the Soviet system: the Soviet Union was called "the motherland of planning." Conveniently forgetting about Comte and the nineteenth century's reformers, the old-timer of Gosplan Shamai Turetskii claimed that French planners borrowed the "very essence of forecasting" from Russia.[41] In these pronouncements, the narrative that the GOELRO project was the source of scientific forecasting was cemented. The speakers repeatedly argued for the importance of cross-branch forecasting to estimate the future demand for energy, referring to the 1920s' "achievements" in Soviet long-term planning and the debates about the long-term prognoses as if self-evident and well known to all. However, the 1920s criticisms by Kondrat'ev and Bazarov were conveniently bypassed.[42] All this was probably both ideological and pragmatic. Many speakers were accomplished scholars and it is difficult to imagine that they were not aware of the flawed ways in which the economic data was collected in the 1920s and 1930s, as well as the limitations of the methodology of the plans, which required excessive levels of detail, even if they had never read Kondrat'ev. It is likely that in their statements they sought to establish the precedence of a Soviet tradition in forecasting, on which basis the Soviet government could legitimize establishing cooperation with the capitalist forecasters from the position of scientific parity.[43]

80   CHAPTER 4

The payment of political dues aside, the archival records of these discussions show that Soviet economists hoped to use this official orientation to promote forecasting as a tool to change practices in hitherto ad hoc and nonsystematic Soviet planning. Gosplan, they argued, did not so much develop the plans as mechanically glue them together, using proposals submitted by separate branches.[44] Proper scientific forecasting was expected to discipline the collection of data and methodology of planning as well as to expand the intellectual scope of Gosplan. The meeting discarded the 1950s idea of forecasting as an informational compensation for failed state planning. Whereas Gvishiani proclaimed that governance was first a science, a young economist, Boris Breev, insisted that "governance is not possible without prognosis."[45] In his lengthy talk, Abel Aganbegian, who was then in his mid-thirties and who later rose to become an economic advisor to Mikhail Gorbachev, pronounced that prognoses were not "a step back from planning," a possible interpretation of Kosygin's formula of forecasting as a stage of preplanning, but "a move deeper."[46] In Kondrat'ev's spirit, Aleksandr Anchishkin argued that the effort toward mathematical modeling should first be directed at understanding the current situation of the Soviet economy and only then at creating previsions (*predvidenie*).[47]

The goal of forecasting was to explore several alternative directions of development, which implied that the Soviet future was open to different trajectories.[48] To this, Leonid Kantorovich, the creator of the input–output methodology of linear planning, added that the plans should be understood as probabilistic and not deterministic. The economy, argued Kantorovich, "could not be expected to develop according to the plan," and hence multiple possibilities need always be considered.[49] This view of the fleeting character of the economy was shared by many leading mathematical economists. Years later, Ershov recalled agreeing that it would have been the utmost nonsense to expect the five-year plans to be implemented to the detail; however, this could not be suggested in public.[50]

The visibility of alternatives was accompanied by a strong emphasis on transparency (*glasnost'*). *Glasnost'* was perhaps the most striking aspect of these discussions in 1966. This was the most important difference between Kondrat'ev's time, when there was a dearth of data, and the 1960s, when historical statistics had already been accumulated and the key perceived issue was scholars' access to data. Transparency, economists argued, was part of the method that would make forecasting truly scientific. Like Kondrat'ev, at the 1966 meeting, an economist argued that the existing forecasts of separate branches, such as carbon fuels, were simply absurd and incorrect, because future development of a particular sector was being extrapolated without regard to the changes happening in related sectors. Scientific forecasting for him required sharing the data horizontally across academic and governmental organizations. Furthermore, the methodology of forecasting, it was

FORECASTING AND THE CYBERNETIC SENSIBILITY   81

argued, demanded that Soviet planners openly face some inconvenient facts. Breev insisted that the current practice of grounding the plans exclusively on "achievements" was gravely misleading. Calling for an "analytical history of national economic planning," Breev added somewhat realistically that this requirement was not expected "to be fulfilled soon."[51]

The economists' calls for *glasnost'* did not stop at the data issue. The 1966 meeting went as far as to insist on public discussion of forecasts. They did not go as far as the Austrian futurologist and the democratizer of future studies Robert Jungk, who called for grassroots involvement in the making of forecasts: the public for these Soviet economists was not the general public, but academic experts.[52] Gosplan economists trod carefully in this treacherous zone of permissibility, giving assurances that the method of forecasting did not challenge the existing power concentration because it was limited to a "small circle of specialists" at the top of government.[53] It would be easy to criticize this approach as yet another technocratic grabbing for power, but one should not forget the context, where scholars fought to get minimal conditions of institutional autonomy and access to actual data, challenging the Party's organizational monopoly on information.[54]

Looking back, it is quite clear that these arguments alone did not translate into institutional reform. *Glasnost'* did not liberalize the centralized, censored, and compartmentalized data flows within Gosplan. Although the Academy of Sciences and branch institutes were commissioned to prepare forecasts pertaining to their respective sectors, they sometimes were not given access to the key statistical data held by the branch ministries and Gosplan, not to mention other, crucially relevant sectors. The resulting forecasts remained methodologically flawed, what Kondrat'ev would have seen as the continuation of the practice of "auto-hypnosis with numbers." In the Western context, intellectual historians criticized scientific forecasting as a technocratic activity. However, even the most technical and narrow forecasting required a considerable degree of open information flow, robust and testable data, and a set of falsifiable theories explaining the transitions between events. The Soviet system was not prepared to allow for this as it would have required institutional and epistemological reform of statistical agencies, research institutes, and the political bureaucracy of planning at all levels. In practice, Gosplan resembled a medieval fiefdom where branch decisions continued to be taken without any regard to cross-branch effects.[55] Like in astrological conjecture, statistics that populated long-term plans did not reflect the actual and cumulative development of the economy.

If scientific forecasting was methodologically dissonant with the Soviet power structure, the question is, why was it encouraged? A possible answer, as I show in the next section, can be found in the wider shift of Soviet governmentality, as it called for scientific governance of an increasingly complex society. The imperative

82   CHAPTER 4

of technoscience was taken seriously. This was bolstered by the theory of the scientific-technical revolution (STR), which revised the Marxist–Leninist dogmas of ideological and materialist change to accommodate the view that science and technology were no longer a superstructure, but a direct driver of social transformation. As new sciences and technologies were being introduced, the development of Soviet society became opaque again and Marxian predictions were no longer sufficient. Scientific forecasting was called forth to map the trends of Soviet social development, not only in regard to resource planning to ensure effective implementation of large-scale infrastructures, but also to the rates and trends in education and labor participation to staff the growing industrial enterprises. Enter social forecasting, a branch of applied sociology.

Social Forecasting

The 1920s and 1930s saw multiple efforts to gather quantitative information that would help to make the Soviet society visible, the most prominent of which were the censuses run in 1937 and 1939. These were the only censuses conducted under Stalin, who refused to take stock of the Soviet population changes after the Second World War. However, the results of the 1937 census were never published and only aggregate numbers of the 1939 census were made available.[56] Although Stalin's purges ended the life of Soviet Russian sociology as an academic discipline, this did not mean that social data were not collected at all. On the contrary, data were amassed by demographers, labor institutes, and statistics departments of different ministries as the administrators and planners required knowledge about the presence of the social classes, workers, students, consumers, and cultural audiences of political enlightenment.[57] The Soviet population had to be employed, educated, fed, housed, and kept warm, and so its labor capacity and basic needs had to be known.[58] Patchy as they were and fragmented across the archipelago of the ever-growing bureaucracy, imperfect and often simply made up, statistical data on Soviet society were coming into being. In the 1960s, when all-union and regional planners became concerned with social aspects of growth, demographic research and sociology became reinstated.[59]

Soviet sociology was fully rehabilitated at about the same time as scientific forecasting in the context of incremental opening up to the West. In 1956, when the chairman of the Council of Ministers Nikolai Bulganin announced the arrival of the STR in the Soviet Union, a delegation of Soviet academicians was invited to participate in the Third Sociology Congress in Amsterdam to discuss the social consequences of technoscientific innovations.[60] In 1957, a group of Western sociologists came to Moscow. The Soviet Association of Sociology (SAS) was established in 1958 as a Cold War instrument, conceived to project a positive image of Soviet science and to make its presence felt at the International Sociology Association (ISA), established under the auspices of the United Nations Educational, Scientific and Cultural Organization (UNESCO).[61] Institutions and individuals could become members of the SAS for an annual fee of forty and five rubles, respectively.[62] As a public organization, the powers of the SAS were limited.

The research agenda of social forecasting was placed under the umbrella of the studies of the STR and scientific-technical progress (STP). Announced in 1956, the idea of the STR was integral to Khrushchev's declaration that the Soviet Union would catch up with and surpass the United States, foreseeing the building of communism in two decades.[63] The STR, the genealogy of which I have discussed elsewhere, extended Grigorii Feldman's theory of growth. As mentioned earlier in chapter 2, according to Feldman, the driver of growth was investment in heavy industries and industrial goods.[64] This now would include fundamental and applied science, R&D, and, particularly, the new information and digital technologies.

In the early 1960s, Soviet scholars strategically positioned the STR as a state socialist alternative to modernization theory; the STR was expected to have a global reach and justify Soviet aid projects in developing countries. I date the beginning of this process to Walt Rostow's visit to Moscow in 1960, where he gave a talk on disarmament to the sixth Pugwash conference. In the same year he published his *The Stages of Economic Growth: A Non-Communist Manifesto*.[65] Two years later, in 1962, Soviet social researchers fully encountered the growing impact of Rostow's modernization theory in the Fifth World Congress of Sociology in Washington, DC. From 1963 onward, Soviet academic journals began publishing criticisms of modernization theory contrasting it with what was presented as a socialist "scientific-technical revolution." One of those critics was Anatolii Zvorykin (1901–1988), a prominent historian of science and technology who survived Stalin's purges and who was tasked to coordinate the Soviet participation in UNESCO's History of Mankind project from 1956 to the early 1960s. As Elena Aronova showed, Zvorykin was fascinated with the multidisciplinary effort to write a universal history of human evolution embracing the global North and South addressing the process of decolonization, and mobilized Soviet researchers from different institutes in humanities and public health to contribute to the study.[66] At the same time Zvorykin had been interested in the ways in which changing technology was shaping the social, going beyond primitive Marxist determinism.[67] In Washington, Zvorykin debated these issues with Talcott Parsons and Robert Merton. The debate was published in the Soviet Union, but Merton refused to have it covered in *Sociological Abstracts*.[68]

Studying the STR and forecasting the future Soviet society were important mandates of the newly established Institute of Concrete Social Research (IKSI,

1968), which became, as Elena Zdravomyslova put it, "the institutional symbol of separation of sociology from Marxist philosophy."[69] The explanatory power of social forecasting was ideologically limited to the application of the official "general laws," an obligatory theoretical framework of historical materialism and scientific communism (the application of historical materialism to the analysis of Soviet society). However, the mid-range theories of urban or cultural sociology, as well as "concrete empirical analysis," provided legitimate analytical frameworks.[70] According to Titarenko and Zdravomyslova, Soviet social research of the 1960s and 1970s embraced a structural functionalist approach that was supposedly based on positivist principles.[71]

It was difficult to practice prediction in its positivist or logical empirical sense in Soviet social statistical research. The recollections of mathematically apt sociologists, such as Boris Grushin, who pioneered public opinion surveys, and Vladimir Shlapentokh, show this clearly. There was little room for critical examination of facts and rigorous testing of predictions. In practice, social forecasting was mainly limited to simplistic statistical analysis of cross-sectional data, for instance of the changing structure of labor markets and related education patterns.[72] However, the principle of monitoring the cumulative character of reality and tracing symptoms was expressed in regular surveys.

The greatest issue was integrating statistical forecasts that were principally heuristic instruments, as Kondrat'ev put it back in 1920, with policy and management practice. Indeed, such an integration was expected from Soviet sociology as an applied science, considered, as Liah Greenfeld noted, somewhat surprised, "a branch of social technology."[73] However, the use of prediction as social technology was limited: researchers were mainly interested in the process of stability and reproduction rather than change, not symptoms of social pathology and deviance, like the nineteenth-century public health reformers. As I show in the remainder of this chapter, changes and uncertainties were studied as part of the research agenda into social consequences of the STR, exploring disruptions generated by techno-scientific innovation. In terms of the sociological method, IKSI sociologists mainly applied micro analysis of individual enterprises.[74] Macro social trends were forecasted, but, as I show in chapter 7, not in sociology departments, but in the emerging systems research institutions and this work was done by OR and computer scientists.

According to the official definition, social forecasting (*sotsialnoe prognozirovanie*) was "the most advanced form of governing social relations and processes, which makes it possible to scientifically predict and solve social problems."[75] Social forecasting was, to paraphrase Comte (and Bruno Latour), science in action. The problems of Soviet society, in other words, could be anticipated and prevented. This emphasis on governability and control was contrasted with the epistemology of forecasting, according to which societal development was probabilistic. If society was governed by a game of chance, one had to acknowledge that at least some of the aspects of the future of Soviet society were beyond knowledge and control.[76] It was this gray zone between the promise of control and the openness of uncertainty that attracted scholars wishing to escape the straitjacket of Marxist–Leninist development theory.

This subversive effect of uncertainty, inherent in social forecasting, was explicitly addressed, and measures were taken to rein it in. First, the access to scientific forecasts was reserved to selected institutes and party authorities. Second, sociologists were restricted to exploring and forecasting only those social volatilities that were deemed relevant for economic planning. Economists were mainly interested in the forecasts of living standards. This was driven by the concern that the discrepancy between the income of peasants, workers, and the professionals' income was growing, a process that was exacerbated by access to private allotments. As N. Lagutin of Gosplan put it in 1966, a possibility that people will grow only flowers and not, for instance, root vegetables that could be used for food or sold on the market in allotments was "very remote."[77] The problem with private sources of income was that these were classified as a "nonproductive" sphere according to Feldman's model. However, Soviet economists understood clearly that this was a mistake. They resolved this absurd inconsistency by delegating to sociologists research into what they defined as economically profitable social activities.[78]

A study of deviance, political, and security matters was reserved for the State Security Committee (KGB) and not sociologists, although IKSI was sometimes commissioned to write reports on "social problems of defense."[79] For instance, in 1972, Fedor Burlatskii and Aleksandr Galkin's monograph "Sociology and Politics" was denied publication, because it "transgressed the remit of the IKSI."[80] Furthermore, forecasting social value change was a contradiction in terms: technically, what were the correct norms and should values be allowed to develop spontaneously? Both values and norms were fixed in the ideological discourse by the party institutions that set the desirable future norms and values. To keep the lid on the knowledge about social change, forecasting, like censuses and any large-scale data sets, was subject to censorship. The role of sociologists—the intellectual workers—was not to improvise creatively in heuristic research, but to harvest social data deemed relevant for economic performance indicators, for instance, labor productivity and consumption needs. Explorative forecasting was allowed within certain limits, as it was recognized that the government should be aware of possible divergence from ideologically approved values.[81] However, the interpretation of social forecasts was a minefield of responsibility: no researcher wanted to be accused of uncovering undesirable features of Soviet society, because this could be regarded as a criticism of the Party's failure. This was the key difference between late state socialist scholars of the social body and social reformers in the nineteenth century: in the late state socialist context, numbers were expected to speak for themselves and in only very limited contexts.

Nevertheless, sociology's subordination to economic planning entailed a constant demand for social statistics and provided the institutional rationale for the organization of social forecasting as a subdiscipline of sociology. There were many different applied fields in which sociological survey and (limited) attempts at forecasting emerged in the 1960s. These included public opinion surveys and demographic forecasts, linked to labor and urban planning, and time budget forecasts, linked to social provision of leisure.[82] However, social forecasting never became a priority science, on a par with cybernetic and systems modeling and the analysis of natural resources. The first generation of sociologists were mainly trained in humanities and had little or no experience of quantitative methods.[83] Large in terms of staff, IKSI was not as badly underequipped as the NOT institute in the 1920s, but they still lacked access to technology. At the beginning, Soviet sociologists lacked enough calculators to work out the effects of the STR, although they eventually received a Minsk-32 computer, staffed with forty-one personnel. In 1972 and 1973, an Automated System of Analysis of Social Information (ASAI) was put in place, but it was used only for basic statistical analysis and image recognition. There was no capacity for computer simulation and modeling. IKSI researchers were to receive training in quantitative methods. It is difficult to tell what the uptake was, but the reports contain many complaints about "noise and paper dust" coming from the perforation hall that processed 400,000–500,000 punch cards annually. Complaints about the staff's general absenteeism from offices and being late were made in the 1970s.[84]

Just like NOT in the 1920s, IKSI was shaken by severe, although not as violent, political turbulence soon after its establishment.[85] An important part of this was an attempt to create a subdiscipline of social forecasting on the all-union scale. This attempt, as I show in the remaining part of this chapter, was of a very different character from Kondrat'ev's work, as the energies were directed more to "action" rather than the "prediction" and "explanation" of the Comtean model.

The history of this attempt revolves a great deal around the personality of Igor' Bestuzhev-Lada, who was the face of Soviet forecasting in the international future studies community.[86] It is important to explore Bestuzhev-Lada's case in detail, because he is often referred to as key promoter of East-West cooperation in future studies. However, as I show, Bestuzhev-Lada should not be regarded as representative of the Soviet field of forecasting, because he had very particular institutional and intellectual interests that do not encapsulate the diversity of the field. Born in

1927 into a peasant family in a small village called Lada (hence his pen name) in Mordovia, about three hundred miles from Moscow, Bestuzhev-Lada began his academic career as a military historian of the Crimean war in the 1950s. He was a loyal communist, a sympathizer of collectivist decisions: for instance, in 1951 he sent a letter to Stalin suggesting taking away by force those children who were inappropriately reared by their parents in order to educate them as communist citizens in orphanages. This was, Bestuzhev-Lada wrote in his memoir, an expression of his desire to be useful and serve the central power organs.[87]

The many writings by Bestuzhev-Lada explicitly acknowledge his ambition to become a leader of future studies—but not futurology—in Soviet Russia.[88] In his memoir, he recalled wishing to write a science fiction story on moral communist citizenship. Having consulted the library catalog section on "Utopian socialism," he found H.G. Wells's *Forecast* (1901) and K. E. Tsiolkovskii's *The Future of Humanity and the Earth* (1928). These works, wrote Bestuzhev-Lada, gave him the idea that the future could be studied scientifically in the same way as the past; this idea is similar to the suggestion of Hempel and Oppenheim that scientific prediction is a logical operation that can be equally applied to phenomena in the past and in the future, although I do not know if Bestuzhev-Lada had a chance to read Hempel and Oppenheim. In any case, Bestuzhev-Lada claimed having coined the term "futurology" in 1956, completely independently of Ossip Flechtheim, the German futurist, who first suggested the term in Western literature.[89] It is, however, uncertain to what extent he pioneered the field in the Soviet Union: Bestuzhev-Lada's first publications in the future studies field appeared in 1967; hence they postdated Genadii Dobrov's work in technology assessment and Kosygin's call for forecasting.[90]

After the Second World War, scientific forecasting was one of many innovative scientific approaches that explicitly sought to make the future visible and transparent. This ambition worried the Western critics of governmental rationalism and authoritarianism, who identified opaqueness not as an enemy, but as a vital resource for individual autonomy and the functioning of civil society. In his history of the French thought on transparency, Geroulanos detailed the arguments that individual citizens had a right to remain invisible and nontransparent to the state, but the state and its experts, in contrast, had to be transparent to the citizens.[91] To diminish the negative impacts of what was perceived as asymmetrical transparency where the population could be scrutinized by the state but not the other way around, public participation and engagement were increasingly debated in relation to the production and use of scientific knowledge of future development. This led, as historians have shown, to the proliferation of future studies methods, as they diversified into embracing qualitative, participatory approaches in addition to the positivist and statistical methods.[92]

88   CHAPTER 4

For instance, the Austrian writer Robert Jungk established his Institute of the Future in 1954 with the aim of promoting future studies as a participatory, democratic process of creating grassroots expertise. In contrast, other experts worked to increase transparency of the volatile social, economic, and political realities by refining the tools for decision-makers in the governmental departments. The US operations researcher Herman Kahn founded his think tank, the Hudson Institute, to supply what he presented as impartial cost–benefit scenarios of the demographic and economic consequences of nuclear war. Kahn also sought to change the terms of public debate in his controversial *On Thermonuclear War* (1960). In the 1940s and 1950s, US future studies frequently sprang from the military-industrial complex, most notably the RAND Corporation, where Kahn began his career. At RAND, Olaf Helmer and his team developed the Delphi method, an influential technique based on an anonymous expert opinion survey conducted over several rounds to bring expert views close to consensus. This method was first publicized in 1964.[93] In Europe, large-scale infrastructure planning demanded statistical data and predictive expertise; this demand was met by international organizations such as the United Nations Economic Commission for Europe (UNECE) and the Organisation for Economic Co-operation and Development (OECD), for which the prominent representative of technoscientific forecasting, Erich Jantsch, conceptualized explorative and normative forecasting techniques in 1967.[94] As the richer data sets were becoming increasingly available, scientific forecasting branched out into more technical, statistical approaches, which combined time series analysis and complex modeling and more normative approaches, integrated with organizational processes of goal-setting and decision-making.

In many cases, Hempel and Oppenheim's notion of scientific prediction as a heuristic search for possible explanations prevailed over the Comtean notion of prediction as inference based on certain knowledge. To predict in statistical forecasting meant to correlate data points, aiming to replicate the dynamic of change that is observed in reality as faithfully as possible. A theoretical explanation about why some correlations held was not always considered necessary. At this stage, the making of statistical forecasts entailed a great national and international effort to orchestrate data, particularly the organizational practices that produced the data, the techniques—including the mathematical apparatus and computer technology—and the culture of interpretation of the results in the decision-making context. The postwar pioneers of forecasting experimented with all components of this process.[95]

Bestuzhev-Lada quickly realized that if governmental decisions had to be grounded in prognostic research, a new institutional and social landscape would need to emerge. In the summer of 1966 a Russian publicist and thinker Edvard Arab-Ogly—a former editor of the influential publications *Voprosy filosofii* (The

Issues of Philosophy) and *Problemy mira i sotsializma* (World Marxist Review), then the head of the concrete social research department at the Institute for the International Labor Movement (IMRD)—offered Bestuzhev-Lada a position as head of a unit (in Russian, *sektor*) for forecasting the socioeconomic consequences of STR.[96] In the mid-1960s IMRD provided a pocket of relative liberty for highly heterogeneous scholarship, united by a search for ways to bypass communist dogma.[97] Arab-Ogly was personally interested in forecasting, especially in the field of demography.[98]

To get this higher administrative position Bestuzhev-Lada was ready to sacrifice his academic prestige: at that time IMRD belonged to the trade union organization (it became an Academy of Sciences institute later) and had a lower status than the Institute of History.[99] Nevertheless, for Bestuzhev-Lada to head a unit was a step toward establishing himself as the authority in the field of Soviet forecasting. At the IMRD, he was not keen on competitors. For instance, Bestuzhev-Lada is said to have prevented the publication of a book on approaches to prediction authored by several colleagues at IMRD, such as Merab Mamardashvili, Aleksandr Zinov'ev, and Oleg Genisaretskii.[100] Bestuzhev-Lada's ambition ran high and he dreamt about creating a scientific council for forecasting at the Academy of Sciences.[101] Therefore, when two years later academician Aleksei Rumiantsev invited Bestuzhev-Lada to join the newly established IKSI as a head of department (in Russian, *otdel*) with a promise of about seventy staff, he immediately agreed (and cunningly planned to remain at his IMRD unit as a vice-chairman).[102]

In February 1969 Bestuzhev-Lada joined IKSI but found out that things did not work out as expected. He did not get to chair the promised department with a staff of seventy, but only a unit with four or five people. There was no office space either: in the beginning the unit held meetings in an apartment in the science town Dubna, outside Moscow. Then, it turned out that Bestuzhev-Lada had to share his research agenda with Zvorykin, the head of a unit for studying the social consequences of the STR, who oversaw the collaboration with the ISA and research programs at UNESCO, and who prepared reports on the STR for high-level Soviet representations abroad, such as at the Council of Europe. Zvorykin also led social forecasting studies of labor and leisure, and corresponded with leading researchers, such as Radovan Richta in Czechoslovakia.[103] Indeed, the Soviet report on cultural policy for UNESCO contained a detailed account of forecasting in the cultural sector, which was no longer perceived as serving solely as ideological education but rather as a postindustrial economic sector. Thus, Zvorykin wrote:

> For the purpose of forecasting the development of culture and working out a long-term cultural policy, increasing use is now being made

90   CHAPTER 4

> of the methods of structural and system analysis. By these means it is
> possible to make forecasts by smoothing the statistical curve obtained
> by the observation of recent processes, expressing it in analytical terms,
> and then extrapolating to the future. . . . The first question of interest . . .
> was how the ratio between scientific and artistic culture in the U.S.S.R.
> is changing. We compared the numbers of scientists—doctors and mas-
> ters [*kandidaty*] of science—with the number of members in the main
> unions of creative artists. . . . We took the statistical data for the period
> 1950–1967, worked out the extrapolation formulae by smoothing the
> statistical curve obtained, and then, using these formulae, calculated
> the number of scientific workers and creative artists for the years 1970,
> 1980, 1990, and 2000. As a check, the corresponding figures for 1950
> and 1960 were also calculated by the same method. Comparison of the
> actual and calculated figures for 1950 and 1960 indicated that our
> method of forecasting was sufficiently accurate.[104]

According to this forecast, the membership of unions of creative artists would
increase by *ca.* 400 percent and by 2000 would reach a total of 128,600. As the
number of scientists was expected to grow by about 600 percent to 383,100,
the number of artists in relation to the number of scientists would decrease from
30.4 percent in 1950 to 25.1 percent in 2000. The report was an expression of a
postindustrial optimism, indicating increases in creative professions. The only
anticipated decline concerned cinema-goers, who were expected to be watching
television at home.[105] This forecast, typically, did not anticipate a new type of
technology driving social chance. For instance, VCR recorders would boom in
the late 1980s, creating a black market of illegal home recordings and their sales,
and bringing into existence unlicensed "video salons"—cinema halls where
people would pay to see a poor-quality copy of *Rambo*.[106]

When it was not commissioned by international organizations, IKSI research
was fundamentally subordinated to the needs of Gosplan, which required it to develop statistical methods for social indicators to inform industrial planning, particularly regarding the siting of factories and the availability of labor, as well as the
population's education and consumption needs.[107] Unlike Zvorykin, Bestuzhev-
Lada was not interested in statistics; his preferred method was expert surveys.[108] In
contrast, Zvorykin was more comfortable with the functionalist view of the STR
and well equipped for conducting (at least simple) statistical trend surveys.[109]

It is difficult to pinpoint the substance of Bestuzhev-Lada's contribution to
social forecasting. The intellectual content of his writing was mainly derivative
of Western publications, and his sociological surveys were methodologically
flawed. It could be fair to say that his role was that of an organizer, seeking both

FORECASTING AND THE CYBERNETIC SENSIBILITY   91

to consolidate Soviet forecasting as an autonomous field and to establish links with Western future studies.[110] His international contacts dated back to the IMRD times. In 1967 the prominent institutional entrepreneurs of future studies Robert Jungk and Fritz Baade, who would later be involved in Soviet energy forecasts, visited Moscow and met Bestuzhev-Lada at Ivan Efremov's apartment. Efremov was a scientist and author of the famous novel *Andromeda Nebula* (1957), which describes a global communist society set several thousand years in the future.[111] At this meeting the idea of the World Future Studies Federation was discussed. Inspired by this discussion, Bestuzhev-Lada initiated a forecasting section at the SAS. Reportedly, not all members of the board welcomed this suggestion.[112] Nevertheless, Bestuzhev-Lada was included in Soviet delegations to the World Future conferences in Oslo (1967) and Tokyo (1970), but could not go: according to archival documents, for bureaucratic reasons the Soviet delegation was late and did not participate.[113] In 1969, on the invitation of Johan Galtung, a pro-Soviet thinker, founder of peace and conflict studies, and, indeed, the World Future Studies Federation, Bestuzhev-Lada visited the Peace Research Institute in Oslo.[114] Further international contacts were developed through the ISA. Bestuzhev-Lada was first elected as the head of the STR section of the ISA Congress in Varna (1970) and later as a vice-chairman, alongside the prominent French futurist Bertrand de Jouvenel, of ISA's committee for future studies, and he was included as a founding member of the World Future Studies Federation (1973). He described retrospectively the year 1970 as the high point in his international career and, indeed, Bestuzhev-Lada established himself as gatekeeper for Soviet–West interaction on social forecasting.[115] Furthermore, unlike some of his colleagues, he emerged unscathed through the political overhaul of IKSI in 1970 and 1971. Bestuzhev-Lada got entangled in this process because he participated in the unsanctioned Society for Scientific Forecasting (SSF).

The story of the SSF is all smoke and mirrors. Facts are scarce and can only be drawn from conflicting personal memoirs and the few archival documents, which are essentially accusations and therefore very likely heavily biased.[116] Established in 1968, but never formally registered, the society stemmed from the Committee for All-Union Symposia in Scientific Forecasting (established in February 1967) at the SAS. This committee was chaired by Bestuzhev-Lada.[117] Although it was supported by the top leaders of the Academy of Sciences and included members of Gosplan, apparently no formal permission from the Central Committee was sought. Such informal arrangements were not unusual: even large construction projects such as museums, sports stadiums, and even science cities were built without formal permissions in the Soviet Union.[118]

The society was headed by the academician Vasilii Parin, a prominent biophysicist, who specialized in space research and conducted several studies about

92   CHAPTER 4

future medical developments.[119] In the documents Bestuzhev-Lada is named as co-organizer of SSF, although he denied having this role and, in line with the prosecutors of SSF, claimed that this organization was used as a vehicle for extending the personal influence of the engineer Boris N. Tardov of the Research Institute of the Metallurgical Ministry.[120] In 1969 Tardov, acting as a vice-president, attempted to formally register the SSF as a public all-union organization, governed by an assembly and able to confer academic degrees. In 1970, the SSF planned to organize 1,600 events involving 200,000 participants. The problem with the SSF, it seems, was not so much the content but the form and scale of its activities: the SSF emerged from the bottom up and organized its activities horizontally across the industrial branches and academic institutes.

In June 1971, an investigation was launched and the outcomes were severe, although not for everyone. Consumed with anxiety, Parin had a stroke and died before being summoned for questioning. Tardov was penalized and had to move to Latvia.[121] However, Bestuzhev-Lada made an informal agreement with prosecutors to serve as scapegoat; in his words, they needed to symbolically punish someone who had a doctor's degree, and therefore he was given a reprimand (*vygovor*). To say that he got off lightly is an understatement: Bestuzhev-Lada wrote in his memoir that by way of compensation he received two holiday trips abroad and was then requested to suspend his academic activities for one year, mainly staying in his summer house. Bestuzhev-Lada kept his position as head of unit at IKSI (renamed the ISI in 1972). In June 1972 he was back at work, included in a group to provide expertise for the national complex program of social development.[122] In September 1972 Bestuzhev-Lada traveled to Bucharest to participate in the Third Future Studies Conference, organized with the personal support of Nicolae Ceaușescu.[123] Following this conference, the Presidium of the Soviet Academy of Sciences decided not to formally support the organization of the World Futures Studies Federation (WFSF), but instead to consider Soviet participation in future meetings case by case.[124] This gave the opportunity for Bestuzhev-Lada to attend the WFSF meetings, but without the formal status of Soviet participation, although he was named as a founding member of WFSF.

It is difficult to tell if the problem was the method (statistical forecasting of social developments) or the horizontal, interorganizational, and international activities that provoked the crackdown. I could not find much substantive research that emanated from the SSF. In terms of chronology, the purge of the SSF coincided with purges at IKSI but it is difficult to say if they were directly related.[125] It is possible that these attacks were of a personal nature, using ideology as a rhetorical tool to legitimize decisions.[126] In spring 1972, IKSI's director Rumiantsev was replaced by Mikhail Rutkevich, a hard-line communist but also someone who promoted sociology at Urals University.[127] Lurii Levada and Grushin were transferred to

TsEMI. Under the wing of Gvishiani, an influential promoter of East-West cooperation in policy science, some IKSI employees found shelter in the State Committee for Science and Technology (GKNT) Institute of Management Problems and, after 1976, in the All-Union Institute for Systems Research (VNIISI). Social forecasting was retained as a unit at the reorganized IKSI/ISI and in 1972 a commission for forecasting was organized under the All-Union Council of Scientific Societies, a lower-rank structure which mainly engaged in retraining academics.[128]

One thing is clear though, the epistemology of social prediction interested very many different scholars and this interest led to novel forms of research organization, even if they were short lived. The epistemological questions were not addressed explicitly: unlike the NIEI economists, Bestuzhev-Lada was not concerned with *glasnost'* or transparency, data flow, and trust in data. Rather, he dreamt of social forecasters having the central role in government. In the late 1960s, Bestuzhev-Lada contacted several aides of Politburo members suggesting a secret commission for social forecasting, which would analyze the social consequences of political decisions taken by the Politburo. This commission, wrote Bestuzhev-Lada, would work in partnership with the military-industrial complex as the Academy of Sciences.[129] If Bestuzhev-Lada was keen to help the security apparatus, what kind of society did his future methods envision?

Soviet Future Society Forecasted

The early work of Bestuzhev-Lada shared many visions with Efremov's *Andromeda Nebula*, particularly a global orientation and a belief in inexhaustible resources. Bestuzhev-Lada's turn from historical research to current affairs was documented in his book *If the World Disarms* (1961), written as a propaganda commentary for peace talks between Khrushchev and Kennedy that took place in Vienna, June 1961. Outlining several alternatives for societal development which could be boosted by redirecting the expenditure on armament, *If the World Disarms* engaged with themes that were becoming central in future studies: the consequences of nuclear war and societal and industrial futures. Bestuzhev-Lada's notions of the future were extractive and exploitative: he detailed the progress that would be achieved by transforming natural systems and did not consider ecological consequences.[130] He wrote about, for instance, industrial megaprojects in the far north, such as the construction of "new Leningrads" and "new Stockholms" by removing the permafrost in Siberia and by warming up the Arctic Ocean by redirecting the Gulf Stream to create a "British climate" in the Far East.[131] Interest in climate engineering was indeed developed by the Soviet atmosphere sciences, particularly Mikhail Budyko.[132] As the world population growth was welcomed, in

94   CHAPTER 4

line with the Soviet humanist ideas, Bestuzhev-Lada found it "unacceptable" that such a large surface area of the Earth was occupied by the ocean. This major natural restructuring could start, for example, with draining the Mediterranean Sea and creating picturesque islands, a process which, according to Bestuzhev-Lada, "would not be costly at all."[133] The book is filled with similar utopian stories, which, regardless of Bestuzhev-Lada's self-presentation as a rigorous scholar, are not substantiated with research findings or even basic environmental forecasts. The tropes were also clichéd, widely used in the genre of social utopian writing since Wells's *Forecast*.

At the same time the environmental costs of economic development increasingly worried Soviet economic modelers. For instance, in an international meeting on technology assessment, organized in Warsaw in 1970 (hence before the publication of *The Limits to Growth*), Soviet scholars argued for the inclusion of climate change in technology assessment, as well as for the need to study negative outcomes of the "scientific-technical progress," such as pollution.[134] Bestuzhev-Lada, however, did not engage with the policy agenda in a substantive manner. His publications became less empirical, restricted to methodological reviews, and based on secondary sources. During the IKSI's overhaul Bestuzhev-Lada probably learned the lesson that it was safest to say nothing of substance. Even *A Window to the Future: The Contemporary Problems of Social Prognosis* (1970), his key work done at IMRD was little more than a superficial introduction to Western future studies containing no Soviet data. He does, however, offer an interesting linguistic discussion of scientific and nonscientific forms of prediction. The Russian words describing statements about what is to come are *prorochestvo, proritsanie, predugadovanie,* and *predskazanie*. Like Kondrat'ev, Bestuzhev-Lada considers *predvidenie* (prevision) as a suitable analytical term, while *predskazanie* (prediction) he equates with guessing. But his favorite term is *prognozirovanie* (prognosis), which he defines as a type of *predvidenie*. Bestuzhev-Lada adopted a positivist, Comtean notion of prognosis as not simply a statement about the future but a form of a systematic, scientific research into the course of change that is used to influence this change in a desirable direction.[135] Then, somewhat similarly to Hempel and Oppenheim, Bestuzhev-Lada considers prognosis scientific if the following criteria are met: "analysis and synthesis, induction and deduction, observation and scientific experiment, classification and systematization, assumption and hypothesis, analogy and extrapolation (the extension of a line of development, the lawfulness of which structure in the past and in the future are sufficiently well known, to the future by thought)."[136] These are formal qualities, wrote Bestuzhev-Lada, but the practice of prognosis entailed both less formal and less technical approaches, such as the intuition of a scientific expert, the use of analogy with already-known phenomena and processes, and, finally, direct extrapolation of processes into the future.[137] In this discussion,

Bestuzhev-Lada pools together a wide range of scientific approaches and methodologies without clear distinction of their differences and limitations. All scholarly research, it seems, can be predictive.

In the context of sociology, the public opinion survey and social attitude surveys fascinated young social scientists since the 1960s as a method allowing a glimpse into Soviet society. As noted by the historian Aro Velmet, Soviet sociologists initially saw their role as providers of self-regulatory feedback in the increasingly complex industrial society.[138] Although Bestuzhev-Lada advocated the method of expert surveys, in line with Olaf Helmer's Delphi method, he did not practice it himself. A significant issue was that "experts" were difficult to find. As his colleague at IKSI noted, "Do we have such experts? They still have to be born, finish school or university, receive scientific degree, and learn to prognose. We do not have such a quantity of experts."[139] Furthermore, Bestuzhev-Lada probably understood that to be able to elicit expert opinions, a great formal authority was required, as well as access to high-level decision-making. Expert surveys are a version of the Delphi method, in which a group of anonymous experts are asked to assess the likelihood of future developments; their answers are statistically aggregated and circulated within the group. They then revise their opinions based on this aggregated data. In 1969 two influential scientists from the military-industrial complex and promoters of information theory, Germogen Pospelov and Vitalii Maksimenko, pointed out that "the best-known method in our country" was the Delphi method, adding that although it was created at RAND, the Delphi method was equally suitable to inform decisions in a state socialist system.[140]

The deployment of the Delphi method in the Soviet Union, however, was jeopardized by the extreme lack of trust. No single Soviet expert would trust a sociologist's promise of anonymity and volunteer information that would diverge from the official discourse and expectation. Surveys were perceived as questioning and posed a risk: the KGB ran their own "expert interviews" with managers and gathered public-health data independently of research institutes, ministries, and branch agencies.[141]

The epistemological complexities of prediction, the quality of data, the intricacies of the mathematical apparatus, and what the underlying "laws" that would help identify and explain change could be did not interest Bestuzhev-Lada. When he did engage with statistical forecasting, he did it in such a simplistic way that even his colleagues could not help but criticize him. For instance, in 1972 Bestuzhev-Lada's unit developed social indicators and forecasted the future needs of young people in the 1990s. The categories for needs were established, it appears, without preliminary research and included "food, clothing, healthcare, sex, socialising, love." The report contains a shallow study that had no substantive findings.[142] A verbatim report of an internal discussion revealed that Bestuzhev-Lada

96   CHAPTER 4

had built his study on the assumption that "people in the 1990s will behave in the same way as today." As he put it, "we should not expect to discover America."[143] His colleagues disagreed, particularly the sociologist Vladimir Shlapentokh, one of the leading scholars specializing in quantitative survey methods, who suggested that should the environment that satisfied the needs disappear, the needs would disappear too. Furthermore, as Shlapentokh observed, the sociological studies of current Soviet lifestyles were flawed and insufficient, hence they could not serve as a reliable basis for forecasting. For instance, a study of time budgets, conducted at IKSI, for some reason gathered the data that registered respondents' activities during one day only.[144] Indeed, Shlapentokh suggested that a survey of what people consider as unsatisfied needs would serve as a better indication of what the future holds.[145] Further criticism pointed to the importance of industrial changes. A frustrated Vladimir Lisichkin, who defended a doctoral thesis on forecasting as a complex scientific problem in 1967, appealed to common sense, arguing that Western forecasts were predicting that there would be about 85 percent of new goods in France in 1985 and thus, quite possibly, different needs among young people.[146] Bestuzhev-Lada had little to say in defense of his forecast.[147]

This was not the individual case of an ambitious but failed scholar but part of a general phenomenon: even in the late 1980s, when social value studies were extended to include studies of deviation, particularly alcohol and drug problems, Soviet social forecasting did not indicate the coming of disruptive social change. Projecting continuity, social forecasting served as a tool for conserving the status quo.[148] Perhaps Soviet social forecasts worked as now-casts, but instead of fitting actual data to a model, they fitted the data to a normative ideological framework. Another possible reason is that like the late nineteenth-century forecasters, who studied cycles and trends with the aim of eliminating them rather than understanding their dynamic and adjusting to complexity, the late twentieth-century Soviet government sought for simplified solutions.[149] In principle, statistical forecasts of macro phenomena were expected to be plugged into feedback channels to ensure the self-regulation of the complex Soviet social system. In practice the onset of the fatigue of meaningless statistical data churned out by the growing Soviet bureaucracy lost the aura that it had in the 1920s, the times of Kondrat'ev. Statistics were not good even for "autohypnosis." In the context of informality that governed decisions at enterprise and policy levels, statistical forecasts were deemed irrelevant, a mere organizational ritual that was observed and then ignored.

IKSI did not have a monopoly in social forecasting: statistical forecasts of social, industrial, and environmental changes were developed in many other academic milieus that were closer to the heart of economic planning, industrial management, and national security. As I have demonstrated in detail elsewhere, Soviet scientific forecasting was more substantial when it was practiced in the context of international cooperation, but also in the fields of OR and computer modeling, which became alternative social sciences, offering different conceptual structures for predictions that departed from historical materialism.[150] The institutional link connecting the perestroika of the 1980s and the 1960s is found in the 1970s, when economic and technoscientific forecasting became solidly established as an area of East–West cooperation. At the VNIISI, equipped with Western computers, alternative long-term forecasts were made and submitted to the Politburo.[151]

The key point is that the very will to predict served as an important criterion of proper science. Soviet scholars were required to make predictions, but then they were prevented from doing this by the very political organization of research institutions. The will to predict thus fueled the criticism of the entire Soviet system of social and economic sciences. This was made evident when many the participants of the 1966 debate on forecasting the Soviet economy took up prominent positions after 1986, when, for instance, the economist Aganbegian became Mikhail Gorbachev's economic advisor. Although it took them two decades, economists succeeded where Bestuzhev-Lada had failed: in 1986 the Institute of Economics and Forecasting of Technoscientific Progress was formed on the basis of several departments at the TsEMI on the initiative of Aleksandr Anchishkin, Iurii Iaremenko, and Stanislav Shatalin. In the late 1980s Soviet scholars began applying their forecasts to model difference and change, outlining pathway scenarios to alternative futures. It was none other than Shatalin, in his capacity as economic advisor to Gorbachev, who masterminded joining the expertise of Eastern European and Western planners to design the restructuring of state socialist economies. The famous five hundred days program outlining the transition to a managed market economy, developed in 1989, was conceived at the International Institute of Applied Systems Analysis (IIASA) in Austria, an institute created under patronage of Kosygin and Gvishiani in 1972.[152] However, as Zubok showed, by that time it was too late to forecast and plan the Soviet economic development as the decentralization of the economic system led to chaos and collapse, which was in part caused by corruption and in part by the lack of local expertise in management and planning.[153]

The failure of Gorbachev's reforms could be seen as a failure of synchronization of activities among newly established enterprises and existing companies and bureaucracies, a process that was well visible in the field of scientific forecasting where the institutional center of gravity for predictive expertise was shifting away from central national institutions to international organizations. The head of central archives, Rudolf Pikhoia, reminisced that while it took him a few hours to find the Ribbentrop–Molotov Pact in the state archives, locating Gosplan's primary statistical data took weeks.[154] Not that these statistics would have

98   CHAPTER 4

been of much help: as Zubok showed in his detailed account of the economic reforms initiated by Gorbachev, the existing system of accounting for finance and production was quickly eroded by the privatization and liberalization of enterprise activities.[155] At the later stage, in the early 1990s, the economic data gap was hurriedly filled by the experts from the International Monetary Fund and the World Bank.[156]As perestroika accelerated, the institutional landscape of social and economic forecasting was quickly fragmenting. From 1988 to 1990, a dizzying range of nongovernmental commissions, societies, and associations was established to develop a research and policy lobby in economic, social, and environmental forecasting. Some of them claimed to have been modeled on the RAND Corporation, probably to gain a competitive edge through symbolic association with the famous Cold War think tank.[157] A case in point is the professional trajectory of Igor' Zadorin, a mathematician who began his education in the prestigious Fiztekh, the Moscow Institute of Physics and Technology, in the mid-1980s. At the same time Zadorin worked at a secret defense research institute, where he organized a biweekly seminar on sociology and forecasting. Among those who attended those seminars was Sergei Glazyev, later a member of Boris Eltsin's government, more recently economic advisor to Vladimir Putin, and said to be a possible successor to Putin's presidency.[158] Zadorin was increasingly fascinated with sociology, changed his field, and wrote a doctoral thesis under Bestuzhev-Lada's supervision in parallel to his job at the secret laboratory Almaz which developed cruise missile systems during the 1980s. Seeing potential in what was an untapped field of research into voters' behavior and attitudes, in 1989 Zadorin established the Centre for Intellectual Resources and Cooperation in Societal Sciences (TsIRKON), a non-governmental think tank specializing in applied social and political research.[159] TsIRKON conducted its first studies of political attitudes in 1990 and 1991 and continued its activities for the next three decades, positioning its activities as a "pure" research agency rather than a political consultancy.[160] To establish legitimacy, Zadorin used his ties with the Moscow Methodological Circle adopting its performative approach to scientific prediction, which is considered in the following chapters. Ironically, as Zadorin's TsIRKON emphasizes its autonomy from decision-makers, it departs from Bestuzhev-Lada's utopian dream of an in-house scientific expertise that would feed directly into the governmental loops.

Conclusion

In his *Growth* (2019), Smil forewarns the reader that the omnipresent logistic curve and the data that is fitted does not forecast but indicates the future.[161] The unknown, the missing piece of the puzzle, is indicated by the curve, but the mechanism of how this puzzle fits with the wider picture, why it is located precisely where it is, might not necessarily be clear. Statistical forecasting, from Hempel and Oppenheim's point of view, can be understood as an example of a heuristic, hypothetical science that is moving toward an explanation. When people forget the heuristic character of forecasts, wrote Smil, they are at risk of making grave errors in their decisions. Ignoring the forecasts, as the Soviet government routinely did, can be equally damaging.

It should not be forgotten that forecasting is a form of scientific prediction that is very different from predictive processing—a process that is conceptualized in the cybernetics of adaptive systems. However, in the macro models of governance, the function of an informational signal—feedback correction—was attributed to scientific forecasting. This was a major source of error because it led to the organizational culture that placed too much trust in forecasts as trackers of a reality that was presumed to be out there. Smil describes this as a "mechanistic use" of forecasting, which is based on a fundamental misunderstanding of the statistical method.[162] Philosophers of science, such as Robert Northcott, critiqued this habit of the unreflexive use of forecasts, proposing that economic forecasts should be put to the test by requiring them to provide precise "point predictions" rather than indicating wide ranges of possible outcomes. Such point predictions are more easily falsifiable, they enable a more proper scrutiny of the forecasting method. Most importantly, many, if not most, point predictions fail, reminding the users of this kind of method that these are instruments for the scientific exploration of an uncertain reality.[163]

The economic historian Paul Gregory showed that with the exception of short, quarterly plans, the exuberant Soviet planning system had little impact on actual organizational practices and the performance of the Soviet economy.[164] However, I suggest that the heuristic epistemology of scientific prediction was changing the normative understanding of what it means to govern. As revealed in the NIEI debate in 1966, leading Soviet economists expected that the methodological imperatives of forecasting would enable them to overcome the fragmentation of Soviet planning into branches. Their aims resonated with Cold War politics. The Soviet government, concerned with maintaining its image as a superpower, could not afford to lag behind in the development of predictive policy sciences. In practice, this ambition was reined in by the lack of data that could be trusted, a side effect of pervasive restrictions of circulation of raw data that could be tested.[165] The Soviet orchestration of social and economic prediction as a form of scientific knowledge was failing to support the regime. In their conceptual architecture, Soviet numerical presentations of the future were closer to medieval conjectures and astrology (although popular astrology was banned in the Soviet Union until

100 **CHAPTER 4**

1988).[166] Soviet official publications contained numbers, graphs, and curves to evidence the victorious growth of communism, which ignored transitions between the different states of the system—events or symptoms.

Just like the interwar time managers, who lacked timers to test their simple time–motion models, social and economic forecasters at the institutes of the Soviet Academy of Sciences lacked access to computers and data sets. This lack of data was acknowledged, but only in internal reports: regardless of the widely propagated technoscientific progress that was to propel the Soviet Union into the foremost ranks of advanced countries, the Gosplan statisticians complained that "statistical data on technoscientific progress in the Soviet Union is collected absolutely inadequately."[167] Or, in a discussion at the Presidium of the Soviet Academy of Sciences in 1983, the economist Shatalin stated that although TsEMI employed one thousand staff, it did not manage to construct an optimal plan for the Soviet economy during the two decades of its existence; in turn, even the twenty thousand staff of the Gosplan system had never produced a well-balanced plan.[168] Economists complained that in reality planning was fragmented and "monopolized" by the branch ministries, which were in charge of the entire process of labor, production, capital investments, construction, and social provision for their workers; a situation described as "feudalism" by the physicist Lev Landau. The complex, long-term development program, based on interbranch forecasting and developed since the early 1970s, was meant to bridge this fragmentation. By 1983 it was clear to economists that this effort was doomed to fail.[169]

For my argument it is centrally important that this gap was noticed and criticized. This criticism hinted that new governmental norms were in place, which enabled observers to view actual Soviet planning practices as structurally defective. The future of the Soviet economy was constructed as more open, probabilistic, and even uncertain. However, the ideological restriction of public discourses constrained the actual repertoire of alternative futures of Soviet society that could be forecasted. This would change only in the late 1970s and 1980s, in line with increasing awareness of the deterioration of the global biosphere and the recognition that the gas and oil resources were not boundless and would be exhausted in the foreseeable future.[170]

To conclude, Soviet scientific forecasting contributed to the development of a belief that governance without reliable information was condemned to fail. It was becoming clear that the present state of production and economic sectors could not be interpreted without some idea of their future values, and these future values could not be known without data about the past. Making this vicious loop of nonknowledge explicit, Soviet forecasting of the 1960s called for better visibility and accountability, something that paved the way for *glasnost'* and the policies which opened up Soviet society to more of a free flow of information. However, not all reformers considered the transparency of numbers a key resource for prediction. As I show in the next two chapters, no less influential notions of prediction were formulated by those who engaged with murky informality and extreme complexity of cognition and behavior. These champions of invisibility, unlike cultural critics of transparency in East and West, saw it as an important governmental resource to be harnessed and manipulated.

5

PREDICTION AND THE OPAQUE
Prospective Reflexivity

The construction of Soviet communist society was the orchestration of the future par excellence: the government assembled ideological, material, and institutional resources to propel its populations into a new state of existence, expected to be characterized by equality, prosperity, and a cornucopian vision of progress.[1] In line with the ideals of Enlightenment modernity, the communist social order was meant to be legible, transparent to the gaze of the leader, the bureaucrat, and the scientist.[2] However, at the same time the communist regime relied heavily on the asymmetry of knowledge, secrecy, and fear. The ideal of comprehensive vision and the corresponding certainty of knowledge was not equally distributed, but organized hierarchically to enable centralized, top-down control. Even those at the top of the political hierarchy could never be certain to know it all. The arbitrary application of power and terror resulting in lack of consistency and transparency of governmental actions, according to Hannah Arendt, is the preferred mode of government in totalitarian regimes, the opposite of the democratic ideal of the rule of law and effective at keeping populations in a state of permanent anxiety and submission.[3] In the Soviet Union, particularly in the late period of the 1950s to 1980s, the lack of transparency was further amplified by the continuous failure of centrally commanded, bureaucratically run institutions, which led to the emergence of a pervasive compensatory mechanism, an informal society and economy, characterized by the exchange of favors known as *blat*.[4] In this way, both the organization of the Soviet state and the lived everyday experience of the population contradicted the principles of consistency, visibility, and rationality.

PREDICTION AND THE OPAQUE   103

This chapter explores the way in which scientific prediction was used to maintain and legitimize opacity generated by informal social practices in the authoritarian society. It presents a genealogy of the idea of "prospective reflexivity" (in Russian, *vpered napravlennaia refleksiia* and *prospektivnaia refleksiia*) as it was articulated in the writings of a Soviet management thinker, Georgii Petrovich Shchedrovitskii (1929–1994). The legacy of the thought and practice of Shchedrovitskii (pronounced Shae-dro-vitsky) forms a fascinating mangle of ideas, social networks, myths, and legends that continue to animate both academic and practitioner management communities in Russia today. The magnetic power of prospective reflexivity is the promise of a scientific prediction that embraces informal practices.

Indeed, unlike scientific forecasting, discussed in chapter 4, prospective reflexivity's ambition was not to make the complex objects of governance legible and accountable, "predictable" over the long term. Prospective reflexivity was not a guess, an estimate, or an explanation. The concept of prospective reflexivity captures the performative aspect of predictive knowledge that enables integration and coordination of collective action. As I show in this chapter, prospective reflexivity sought to reconcile a formalist theory of cognition with murky depths of social informality and uncertainty, the great unknown of the Soviet social. Prospective reflexivity promised a mechanism of coping with the mess of things and people that were dysfunctional, invisible, disorderly. Scientific forecasting harbored the promise of an automated steering of large trends by providing statistical data input to computer software that could replace a human decision-maker churning out policy recommendations and issuing signals to steer production. In contrast, the concept of prospective reflexivity referred to a fundamentally embodied practice, seeking to capture the part of human subjectivity that unfolds in a collective action. Instead of making things visible, prospective reflexivity allowed them to stay invisible. Instead of modeling continuity and stability, like Soviet scientific forecasting, prospective reflexivity sought to first destabilize and deformalize managerial relations, in order to create preconditions for a new form of an interactive order.[5]

Prospective reflexivity, in this way, drew upon and amplified what was seen as informal social relations. These informal relations compensated for the dysfunction of the Soviet economy by redistributing goods and services but, as Alena Ledeneva argued, informality turned out to be a "modernization trap" in the post-Soviet context.[6] Scholars interpret the impact of Soviet informalities in different ways, depending on whether they were located in the economic sphere (the informal economy) or politics (the nascent civil society). In the post-Soviet context both forms of informality are criticized as sources of corruption: vast corruption

104   CHAPTER 5

was indeed an insurmountable problem in the Soviet economy, its destructive power was fully revealed in the collapse of the Soviet economy in the 1980s when Gorbachev's reforms unleashed the chaotic behavior of industrial and commercial enterprises.[7] However, the picture is even more complicated: sociologists and organization scholars suggest that formal rules and informal practices constitute a complex assemblage rather than opposites. Prospective reflexivity arose from a similar insight, acknowledging that cognition can be represented through a formal, scientific knowledge but it must be actively inserted into a social context in order to have an impact on practice. Whereas the proponents of scientific forecasting were mainly interested in institutional design, Shchedrovitskii was interested in personal interaction as the key context for the orchestration of the future.

It is important to understand that the concept of prospective reflexivity was consciously developed as an alternative to central planning and centrally commanded management practice. It first emerged in Shchedrovitskii's writings and lectures in the 1960s and spread widely through the practice of activity games in the late 1970s and the 1980s. Prospective reflexivity did not have an institutional home, it was born in the informal intellectual context of the Moscow Methodological Circle (first called the Moscow logical circle, 1952–1954), which evolved from a student discussion group into a network centered first on the philosopher, and later dissident, Aleksandr Zinov'ev and, from 1958, on Shchedrovitskii. The members of the circle discussed Marxism, formal logic, and social psychology, but also the systems approach and information theory. Retrospectively, Moscow methodologists described themselves as adhering to the systems approach.[8]

Shchedrovitskii's authority was derived not from technocratic neutrality or institutional position, but rather his bravado in claiming to have developed a new theory of knowledge, his unorthodox approach to intellectual discussion, and a certain disregard that he had toward ideological but also social boundaries. His contemporaries recall his aura, describing him as a mysterious, charismatic personality, a Voland, the dark character from Mikhail Bulgakov's novel *Master and Margarita*.[9] Shchedrovitskii was one of the first genuine management consultants and gurus in the Soviet Union: in the 1980s he conducted almost 100 training sessions, many of which hosted 150–200 practitioners. His legacy has become part of public culture, at least among Moscow elites.[10] Shchedrovitskii's work is quoted in thousands of research papers and dissertations published mainly by Russian researchers in the fields of management, media studies, political science, philosophy, and pedagogics.[11] However, as management writing continues to be treated as gray literature in the mainstream political science and sociology, and as management consultants have yet to find their place in the social history of governance, Shchedrovitskii's work remains little known outside Russian academia.[12]

The Shchedrovitskii legacy is not limited to the somewhat narrow niche of management theory but is directly linked with the post-Soviet business and political elites that emerged in the 1990s: many high-level government officials who shared engagement with Shchedrovitskii rose in ranks under Putin. For instance, Sergei Kirienko, the deputy chief of staff at the Kremlin and a former head of Rosatom, the Russian nuclear power corporation, responsible for nuclear weapons, appointed Georgii's son Petr Shchedrovitskii as Rosatom's head of strategy in 2008. Other influential supporters include Anton Vaino, the chief of staff (2016–2022); Viktor Khristenko, previously the minister of industry, trade, and energy, and the chairman of the board of the Eurasian Economic Commission (2012–2016); and Andrei Reus, a former director-general of Oboronprom, a Russian–Belarusian corporation specializing in the defense industry, including the production of military helicopters. Reus is chairman of the Georgii Shchedrovitskii Institute of Development.[13]

In this chapter I examine Shchedrovitskii's role in the development of Soviet management and policy sciences, analyzing his efforts as a particular attempt to harness informal practices to enhance control of the future, practices that complemented planning based on formal, scientific knowledge. By formal knowledge, I refer to the scientific expertise produced within established institutional environments, such as research institutes and laboratories, documented in publications, and fed into the governmental process through reports and statistics, the end products of science. It is on this formal scientific knowledge that the existing studies of the Soviet scientific governance tend to focus, attributing to the Soviet regime the characteristics of a high modernist state.[14] Now, high modernist states, the argument goes, have a particularly formal take on time: time is a dimension produced by knowledge instruments, such as clocks, diagrams, statistical time series, history, and, an array of future studies methods.[15] High modernist states seek to capture, understand, and control the apparent chaos of life by creating institutions and professions to mediate knowledge production, planning, and governance. This ambition increased in scale from the 1940s to the 1960s, when so-called Big Science, bringing together the military and industrial complexes and flagship infrastructural and space projects, required its combination of scientific and managerial expertise, both in the East and the West.[16] However, as I showed in the previous chapters, this process of formalization was obstructed by multiple failures and bottlenecks. These failures created a niche for Shchedrovitskii's methodology. I argue that Shchedrovitskii's methodology, in particular his notion of prospective reflexivity, challenged the input–output model of scientific forecasting (according to which the information revealed by scientific forecasting was supplied to the Soviet planning organs to assist decision-makers).[17] I detail the ways in which Shchedrovitskii developed his own model of the reflexive coproduction of

106   CHAPTER 5

the future, as revealed in his theoretical writings and the documentation of his workshops and lectures. A brief note on my sources is necessary. I mainly draw on the published primary materials, namely books, articles, and memoirs published by Shchedrovitskii and his colleagues, which reveal the conceptual importance of informality for future-oriented governance. Shchedrovitskii famously taped his workshops and transcribed them; although not all these transcripts are available, the materials that I could access contain useful examples of informal interaction.

Goal-Setting

Goal-setting is at the heart of planning. The declaration of goals works like a searchlight showing what is to come. In the organization and management theory, goal-setting is expected to make behavior and its outcomes predictable— identifiable, explainable, expectable, and accountable. In practice, organization and social psychology researchers such as Karl Weick have showed, the goals that are achieved tend to be ascribed to actions retrospectively. In other words, goal-setting can be understood as a performative fiction, written looking both forward and backward.

What is the place of scientific prediction in this context? As I showed in chapter 3, the notion of teleological behavior that was driven by future goals and not past causes was proposed by the foundational thinkers of cybernetics Wiener, Rosenblueth, and Bigelow in 1943.[18] For them, prediction is a form of heuristic information processing that supports adaptive behavior. It is a form of alignment with the changing environment, rather than an objective, formal representation of the world (as Hempel and Oppenheim would have it). The cybernetic theory defines teleological behavior as a process that seeks a particular goal and continuously evaluates the present state with regard to an anticipated, final state. The goal is reached when the current state overlaps with the anticipated state. Goal-seeking behavior, exhibited by a human, an animal, or a machine, relies on communication with the external environment, flowing through feedback loops. Goal-seeking behavior operates on the basis of perceived difference between the anticipated state and the actual state. Finally, perception of difference activates teleological behavior.[19]

In computer science and engineering, the idea of teleological prediction was applied in radar tracking and targeting systems. In physiology and neuroscience, it informed the notion of bottom-up processing, which is activated by the difference between the anticipated and the actual sensorial input to a neural network. At its highest level of engineering, the integration of informational signals, teleological behavior is about goal-setting. This hypothesis has informed many political theorists, from Karl Deutsch, who sketched an institutional skeleton of the state as an information processing system in his *The Nerves of Government* (1963), to the proponents of network governance in the 1990s and the open method of coordination, introduced in the European Union in 2000. However, the original cybernetic notion of prediction-based, teleological behavior was only applied to lower rungs of behavior, the perceptual alignment with the environment. It is about the neural networks trying to identify "what is really happening."

In the Soviet Union, the question of what was really happening was close to impossible to answer. Marxist–Leninist theory offered a clear and quite rigid model of social mobilization: what were presumed to be inert, unreflexive masses were to be activated, made conscious of their social and historical mission, and set on a course of action in achieving it. The Communist Party's role was to steer the masses by issuing programs and instructions, but the very moment this model of command was activated, the ontological and epistemological reality appeared to crumble into pieces. Paying dues to the ideology and the party power structure was not negotiable, but, at the same time, informal and personal relations shaped the everyday political and organizational decision-making.[20] Yet though these informal practices were a public secret, they were not recognized as legitimate in the Soviet Union: any divergence from the top-down organization of democratic centralism and party control was suspect and subject to the investigations of the security organs (KGB).[21] Everyone knew about the personalist approach to decision-making, but this knowledge was a source of persistent anxiety. Informality was everywhere but it was not to be seen. As I show in the following section, Shchedrovitskii's genius was to lend a formal, scientific methodology to confer an aura of legitimacy on informality, wedding it to the formal planning of the future in Soviet enterprises and administrations.

The First Soviet Management Guru

Georgii Petrovich Shchedrovitskii was born into a highly educated family in Moscow. His father was an engineer, hailing from a politically active and affluent family of Russian Jews, and his mother was a medical doctor, trained in microbiology. Like many Russian families, they lost some of their relatives in Stalin's terror, but this did not weaken their loyalty to the regime.[22] During the Second World War, Georgii's father was sent to oversee an aircraft factory in Kuibyshev (now Samara, in the southeast of European Russia). After the war, he was appointed the director of Orgaviaprom, the Research Institute for the Organization of the Aviation Industry. In his memoir, Georgii recalled meeting members of

108   **CHAPTER 5**

both the party and the military-industrial complex elites as part of a normal everyday life.[23] His was a privileged social environment of scientific and technical intelligentsia, who shared a commitment to communism and were well integrated in the Soviet elite *nomenklatura* but saw themselves as being on the periphery of the really influential circles. They led what was a comfortable life in Moscow in the 1940s and 1950s: the Shchedrovitskii family occupied two rooms in a large communal apartment, with a shared kitchen and bathroom, situated in a beautiful building on Vozdvizhenskaia Street, a stone's throw from the Kremlin. At school, Georgii excelled in mathematics and enrolled to study physics, a very popular subject, at Moscow State University (MGU) in 1946. However, in 1949, he transferred to the philosophy department, to the disappointment of both his parents and physics teacher. They worried not only about Georgii's career but also about his personal safety: philosophers were frontline "ideological workers," the first to suffer from sporadic party purges.[24] The education was limited: Karl Marx's *Capital* was virtually the only original philosophical writing on the curriculum, but Shchedrovitskii read Marx with great interest, absorbing Marx's theory of knowledge and intrigued by the notion of thinking as a social and material activity. In a different world Shchedrovitskii could have become a philosopher of science, but such a subfield, extending beyond Marxist dialectics, did not exist at that time. Feeling that rigid observance of Marxist–Leninist dogmas and "pervasive fear" among the faculty were not helping him address fundamental questions of knowledge, Georgii sought shelter in a newly established department of logic, which was relatively unaffected by ideological dogmatism (and at times heavily criticized for its "formalist," hence nonmaterialist dialectic, approach).[25] It was not a safe haven: for instance, in June 1948, philosophers of logic felt under attack and wrote a letter to Stalin dissociating themselves from what they described as excessive scholasticism and declaring their allegiance to socialism's goals. The party zealots distrusted logicians, because it was impossible to infer scholars' political views from their writing.[26] Nevertheless, it was in the departments of logic and, later, analytical philosophy that a Soviet strand of epistemology and philosophy of science would develop from the 1960s.[27]

Shchedrovitskii graduated in 1953 and, in February 1954, he launched a seminar on logic and philosophy at MGU. This seminar became the Moscow logical circle: an informal group of five or six young graduates who took long walks around the city, pausing sometimes in a bar.[28] The group included some of the future members of what would become the Moscow Methodological Circle, such as the mathematician Aleksandr Zinov'ev, the author of a famous satire of Soviet academia *The Yawning Heights* (who fell out with the group in 1958), the sociologist Boris Grushin, and a Georgian philosopher, Merab Mamardashvili.[29]

Such informal scholarly gatherings were becoming more common in the mid-1950s when, following Khrushchev's direction of "peaceful coexistence" with capitalism, the Soviet public space began to open up to the East European press and tourism, first from the state socialist countries, the so-called the third world countries, and eventually from the West.[30] The mid-1950s saw the beginning of the Soviet postwar recovery and the first results of heavy investment in science education; the first science cities were built fast to serve the Soviet military-industrial complex as well as the industrial economy.[31] In Moscow, the spirit of relative openness provided a space for the encounters among humanities and exact science scholars, particularly when these meetings were mediated with the transdisciplinary umbrella of cybernetics.[32] For instance, the first seminars on mathematical linguistics were organized by young graduates Viacheslav Ivanov and Vladimir Uspenskii at MGU in 1956, who discussed, among other things, machine translation and the parallels between neuroscience of brain and computer science.[33] In 1957, the neurophysiologist Bernshtein, who worked at Gastev's institute and survived Stalin's purges, used cybernetic concepts of system and feedback to articulate his theory of circular neurophysiological action. In his theory of reflexive action loops, Bernshtein replaced Wiener's term target with the term "a model of future event."[34] Cybernetic language was, in this way, both adopted and modified to make sense of predictive and teleological behavior. In philosophy, several informal groups sought to conceptually reform Marxism–Leninism, most famously in the circles around the philosopher Evald Il'enkov, founder of a content-genetic approach to logic.[35] Such group meetings were not without risk: they were closely scrutinized by the KGB. Shchedrovitskii's group, for instance, was questioned and reprimanded, but not prevented from meeting. After all, their intellectual interest was more than legitimate—it addressed the burning concern of how to make behavioral control more effective. The group gained reputation and recognition in Moscow's intellectual world. In 1962, together with later prominent systems theorists Vadim Sadovskii and Erik Iudin, Shchedrovitskii launched a seminar on systems analysis methods in science and technology under the auspices of the Scientific Council for Cybernetics of the Academy of Sciences; the work of this seminar continued until 1976. In this seminar young scholars discussed Western approaches to general systems theory.[36] Other systems thinkers, such as Igor Blauberg, formed a close circle of Shchedrovitskii's friends. Later in the 1960s, Shchedrovitskii would coauthor one of the first works on the systems approach in the Soviet Union.[37] In all, the Moscow Methodological Circle sought to combine the emerging systems approach with Marxist political theory and epistemology: it revisited Marx's *Capital* searching for a definition of systematic and performative knowledge.[38]

110   **CHAPTER 5**

Exposure to Marxian dialectics—according to which thought was a form of activity—formal logic, and Jean Piaget's and Lev Vygotsky's developmental psychology shaped Shchedrovitskii's intellectual agenda. He attended lectures of educational psychologist Lev Landa, who promoted algorithmic approach to learning and was increasingly interested in organizational behavior and learning.[39] His candidate of science dissertation (*kandidatskaia dissertatsia*), defended in 1964, examined cognitive reflexivity in learning as it was presented in the work of Vygotsky, a prominent psychologist who hailed from Belarus and established his school in Moscow.[40] Another important influence was his peer, a rising star scientist, Vladimir Lefebvre, who developed a theory of reflexive control in military strategy in his *Conflicting Structures*, first published in 1967.[41] According to Lefebvre, a person can influence the opponent by imposing on the opponent their own conceptual basis for decision-making.[42] Lefebvre's semiotic strategy of control, to which I return in the next chapter, would inspire Shchedrovitskii to develop psychological and system-analytical elaborations of reflexive control of collective behavior in nonmilitary settings.

In 1956, just at the beginning of de-Stalinization, known as the Thaw, Shchedrovitskii joined the Communist Party of the Soviet Union (CPSU). This was explained retrospectively by his friends as a pragmatic decision. According to them, Shchedrovitskii did not believe in changing Soviet institutions or policies. Instead, he wished to "change the people."[43] Joining the CPSU was therefore the expression of his loyalty to the Soviet government and, probably, of a hope that this would help advance his professional career.[44] In the mid-1960s, Georgii married a philologist, Galina Davydova (his third wife), whom he met at a seminar in 1963, and they settled in an apartment on Malyi Mogiltsevskii Street in a pretty neighborhood, not far from Arbat, filled with museums and theaters, a short walk from MGU's Department of Philosophy. At that time, his life was as comfortable as it could have possibly been for a young Soviet intellectual.

Following his graduation, Shchedrovitskii was affiliated with the Academy of Pedagogical Sciences, then the All-Union Institute of Technical Aesthetics (VNIITE) from 1965 to 1969, and later the Institute for the International Labor Movement (IMRD). Although Shchedrovitskii traveled abroad only once, to Bulgaria in 1991, his affiliation with these and other institutes facilitated his access to Western scholarship.[45] Both VNIITE and IMRD hosted scholars interested in novel social approaches. However, these and similar spaces of relative liberty were contracting as Khrushchev lashed out against artists and writers who tried to push the limits of permissibility of socialist realism, particularly in 1962 and 1963.[46] When Khrushchev was replaced with Leonid Brezhnev in 1964, the space for cultural expression continued to shrink, a process which accelerated after the Prague Spring in 1968.[47] The 1969 attempt to murder Brezhnev was not conducive to the culture of permissibility, but the changing context was not able to extinguish what Zubok described as a "culture of self-help," practiced by Soviet intelligentsia, which translated into political action.[48] Shchedrovitskii was not an anti-Soviet dissident in any sense, but he signed a letter in support of his former students Aleksander Ginzburg and Iurii Galanskov in the same year. Ginzburg and Galanskov were tried for engaging in underground publication, including a compilation of documents pertaining to an earlier trial of the anti-Soviet writers Andrei Siniavsky and Iulii Daniel (1966).[49] The punishment was harsh: Shchedrovitskii was expelled from both the party and the VNIITE in March 1969. His monographs on design methodology, which were already in the pipeline, were never published. Nevertheless, friends saved Shchedrovitskii from becoming an outcast, arranging for a position at the experimental workshop of the Artists' Union, which provided a modest income and enabled him to continue his work on the theory of learning. He remained actively involved in the development of the Methodological Circle.[50] Although a career in the top institutes at the Academy of Sciences was no longer possible, Shchedrovitskii was invited to give talks, participated in research seminars, and maintained informal connections with the Institute of Systems Research (VNIISI, established in 1976) and the Institute of Control Sciences, where innovative research into systems approach was concentrated.[51] His informal club was regarded with suspicion by the authorities, but his scientific approach was not.[52]

Excluded from the Soviet academic mainstream, Shchedrovitskii turned to intellectual entrepreneurship. In the late 1970s, he embarked on the increasingly popular form of management training through business or simulation games, which he used as a testing ground for his theory of reflexive thinking activity. Some compared Shchedrovitskii's games with existing approaches to critical thinking training.[53] They also resembled strategy and decision simulation games, which were developed in the military and operations research centers (more in Chapter 6), as well as the VNIISI and the Academy of National Economy in Moscow.[54] The novelty of Shchedrovitskii's approach was that he transferred this method to a lower-level managerial practice, first and foremost to regional and urban planning.

Making Reflexivity Work

Shchedrovitskii defines his methodology as an intense, reflexive formulation and coordination of group goals through the means of a highly formalized scientific method. Methodology, according to Shchedrovitskii, is first and foremost performative: "The essence of methodological work is not so much understanding

112   CHAPTER 5

but the creation of methods and projects; it does not simply reflect, but rather builds, creates anew through constructing and projecting."[55] He continues: "the principal products of methodological work, such as constructions, projects, norms, methodical prescriptions, and so on, cannot be tested and are never tested as truthful. Only their feasibility can be tested. . . . When we design a project for a city, it is meaningless to ask if our project is truthful, for this project corresponds not to a city that is, but to a city that will be; the project does not reflect a city, but the city will realize the project."[56] Shchedrovitskii posits his methodology as a value-neutral tool, a nonpolitical technology: methodology is neither truthful nor false, it either works or does not. The question to what end methodology is working is the responsibility of managers, not methodologists. The role of a methodologist, according to Shchedrovitskii, is to create conditions that would enable managers to cope with the future uncertainty through collective efforts of thinking activity, in which reflexivity plays an important role.

The original meaning of the word "reflexivity" entails looking back and not forward. Reflexivity describes "a mental action, process, etc. turned or directed back upon the mind itself; involving intelligent self-awareness or self-examination."[57] How does this fit with Shchedrovitskii's notion of "prospective reflexivity" or, as it is sometimes translated into English, reflexiveness?[58] To define prospective reflexivity, Shchedrovitskii blended Hegelian and Marxist theories which attributed a generative function to ideas, the role of conscious goal-setting for behavior and change. Also, Shchedrovitskii was inspired by the cognitive and system-cybernetic sciences, particularly their applications in operations research.[59] Shchedrovitskii's work was part of a wide movement in 1960s psychology and social science toward reflexivity and I return to this in chapter 6.[60] The way in which he sought to anchor his theory in practice is reminiscent of both French *la prospective* (indeed, he uses the term "prospective," in Russian, *prospektivnaia refleksiia*) and American business and policy simulation games. If *la prospective* was designed to facilitate strategic planning in large, bureaucratic organizations, such as the state administration in France, American business games were developed to assist in solving concrete problems in firms.[61] Both sought to establish informal relations across administrative divides, mobilizing informality to project new visions of the future and create consensus that would stabilize future activities and make them more "predictable," but by prediction they meant "coordinated anticipation."[62] Shchedrovitskii's approach was similar in spirit: he argued that his methods did not aim to offer certainty about the future, because "no one can tell beforehand what system-structural understandings are necessary" for resolving a managerial problem.[63] By this, Shchedrovitskii meant that relevant knowledge, solutions, and certainty can emerge only as a side effect of group activity thinking. According to his biogra-

PREDICTION AND THE OPAQUE   113

phers, Shchedrovitskii did not believe in the production of policy-useful knowledge in the isolated environment of a scholar's office. The future was to be discovered jointly by the group of stakeholders, and the role of the scholar, or methodologist, was to guide this discovery with the help of techniques specially developed for the training sessions.

Let us look more closely at activity games, a curious component of Russian management thinking that achieved surprising popularity in the 1980s. The origins of activity games can be traced to the period after the end of the New Economic Policy (NEP), when in 1932, Maria Birshtein (1902–1992) applied the method of war gaming to the management of the Ligovo typewriter factory with the aim of increasing production. First affiliated with the Bureau of Scientific Organization of Labor, Birshtein was later based at the Leningrad Institute of Engineering and Economics. In Leningrad, she developed a forty-eight-hour-long simulation game for a textile factory, which was said to enable managers, engineers, and administrators to establish new ways of communicating with each other across administrative divides, a practice that they later transferred to the actual working environment. Although proven successful, this method was short lived: alongside all scientific approaches to management and economics, activity games were banned by Stalin in 1938. Birshtein survived Leningrad's blockade, but her first complete work was published only in 1989 (and circulated in thirty thousand copies).[64] However, the first department of business games was established at Leningrad State University in 1972.[65] In the West, simulation games were developed after the Second World War, pioneered with the Monopolog game simulating decision-making in military logistics which was developed at the RAND corporation in the United States and widely spread through the American Management Association and McKinsey.[66] At Harvard Business School, case method of teaching students was introduced to train the students to assess management problems from different viewpoints, extending Alfred North Whitehead's idea of action-oriented learning that was originally formulated in 1933. The elements of Shchedrovitskii's technique resemble both the Harvard case study method and business games: it uses a lot the veneer of scientificity expressed in schemes, formulas, and diagrams—all of which became part of management learning repertoire in the 1970s.[67]

To tackle cognition as part of social interaction, Shchedrovitskii drew heavily on Vygotsky's theory of learning and borrowed Birshtein's idea of simulation games, which he rebranded as thinking activity (in Russian, *mysle-deiatel'nost*).[68] Unlike both the US business games and Soviet military games, which often used computer software and were based on scoring to measure the decisions' impacts and results, Shchedrovitskii's games were "open." These sessions encouraged participants to become more reflexive by considering the conceptual schemes that

114   **CHAPTER 5**

they rely on habitually in their work. Once they became more aware about their cognitive and interactional patterns, they would be asked to create new forms aligning them with the reflections of their game partners. This conceptual framework was strongly influenced by the cybernetic notion of teleological behavior, discussed earlier, according to which human behavior is a goal-directed system in which thinking is mobilized to both set the goals and regulate the behavior through feedback.[69] Shchedrovitskii's games were designed as reflexive feedback systems. Following Lev Vygotsky, and in contrast to structuralists, Shchedrovitskii contended that "the world is not structured through language . . . it is, in contrast, structured through activity [*deiatel'nost'*]."[70] Activity was more than just behavior (*povedenie*): he differed from Skinner in claiming that thoughts were not behaviors, but rather systems of thinking behaviors. Shchedrovitskii's approach was close to the second-order cybernetic notion of autopoiesis, a circular process where "a living system's organization causes certain products to be produced, . . . [and] these products in turn produce the organizational characteristics of that living system."[71] For Shchedrovitskii, collective thinking activity was precisely such a case of societal autopoiesis, fundamentally embodied, social, and enfolding through collective action. Importantly, thanks to the Kosygin reform of the mid-1960s, all Soviet enterprises that had more than one thousand staff were required to formally research and professionalize their management practices. This led to the establishment of departments specializing in applied industrial sociology which produced an endless flow of policy papers and recommendations on how to improve organizational and management practices. By the 1970s, there was a vast organizational demand for Shchedrovitskii's expertise.[72]

One of the earliest games addressed the problem of the supply of consumer goods to the Urals region and was organized in August 1979. During this game (which lasted nine days) in the village of Novaia Utka in Sverdlovsk region, it was recognized that "the ineffective supply of consumer goods" to the region could not be solved as such: this would have been utopian and impossible. However, participants came up with a different goal, to create a new "program of complex research and projects," an organizational resource which would help to organize the supply of consumer goods in the future.[73] This outcome might appear to be a trivial one. Managers who face a complex organizational dilemma tend to invest in the process, this way postponing the dealing with the dilemma to the future. However, in the context of Soviet administration, this was something of an achievement. Habituated to repetitive affirmation of commitment to the faithful implementation of the party's plan, Soviet managers struggled to shape their own understanding, goals, and projects. A participant of these first games wrote retrospectively that both local administrators and intellectuals found the idea of reflexive goal-setting and an open future mystifying: "There was a lot of different gossip spread and we whispered that this was Voland with his entourage." Georgii Shchedrovitskii, the witness wrote, "trained his team until exhaustion. . . . We were graduates from Ural universities, who did not possess either new ideas or high academic degrees; we had not been abroad, did not speak foreign languages, and did not have experience of *exploration, research, and analysis*. . . . In all, people enjoyed [Shchedrovitskii's] internal dialogue."[74] Here this participant described the seminar as a captivating performance, but it is also clear from this account just how new the idea was that management was an intellectual activity, not just following administrative rules. Shchedrovitskii himself was pleased with this game: on its basis, he prepared twenty-nine further games conducted from 1979 to 1981. The areas of application included the planning of nuclear power plants, cities, geological research, and higher education.[75]

Activity games, wrote Shchedrovitskii, were "a new, complex and systemic organizational form for team thinking activity," the outcome being a new, better, and shared understanding of the situation.[76] This form of socialized knowledge was achieved through a performative, prospective reflexivity:

> methodology was not simply a theory of the means and methods we employ in our thinking and activity, but was also a form of organization and thus a "framework" for all of people's vital activity, including thinking activity. This kind of methodology could not be transmitted, like knowledge or a set of instruments, from one person to another, but rather could only evolve, grow out of a context, as it were, through people's being brought into a sphere of methodological thinking activity that was new for them, but in which they were given the opportunity to participate in a complete and integral vital activity.[77]

That a repressed scholar was commissioned to rectify failures in such a sensitive area of Soviet industry as nuclear energy is a telling fact of the organizational demand for novel solutions. Shchedrovitskii was approached by the Institute for Staff Training of the All-Union Ministry of Energy in Moscow to design an activity game for top managers at one of the most important Soviet nuclear plants, Beloiarsk, in the closed science city Zarechnyi. This game ran from December 1980 to July 1981.[78] Beloiarsk was the first Soviet nuclear power plant to use a new fast breeder reactor, BN-600, which, in theory, could recycle spent nuclear fuel (a very unstable process). It would also produce plutonium close to weapons grade.[79] The construction of this power plant was going excruciatingly slowly, as it had started in 1969. In March and April 1980, Shchedrovitskii went to Zarechnyi to conduct an activity game, called, in the best spirit of Soviet bureaucracy, "Providing for the normal functioning and development of technologies

116   **CHAPTER 5**

and development of the Nuclear Power Plant." Unlike the exercises of *la prospective*, these activity games were not so much about anticipating the unexpected: they aimed to facilitate a shared understanding of what the "expected" or "normal" could be like.[80]

The goal was to remove the unexpected, a pervasive part of Soviet managerial reality. Workers would get drunk and not show up on the floor. The building materials would not be supplied in time. When supplied, they would be of inferior quality and a large part of them would anyway be stolen. Most of the time "management" meant dealing with last-minute emergencies. Decisions could not be taken without approval of superiors, and the process of approval would be highly bureaucratic. As the result, workers and managers would be averse to doing anything that fell outside their administrative responsibility. Their activity was a "nonthinking" one; their decisions and actions followed the administrative script, ignoring the evolving environment around them. This is, of course, a crudely simplified picture. However, it gives some idea of what sort of universe of thought and action Shchedrovitskii's "prospective reflexivity" was set to question and transform.

The hope was that the games would enable the participants to "project and program their future thinking activity" and recreate this activity in any organizational context.[81] Prediction, in this case, is an effect of social, reflexive alignment of meaning-making. Shchedrovitskii understood predictability in a particular way. He rarely used the term itself (*predskazuemost'*). He preferred traditional categories of management speak, such as planning, programming, and projecting.[82] This neutral vocabulary rendered his method familiar, it fitted well with the party planning jargon. The focus on reflexivity tapped directly into the source of real power: informal relations and networks. Prospective reflexivity promised a methodology to enable processes "here and now"; situational analysis, goal-setting, and situational problematization.[83]

According to Shchedrovitskii, "the central law and principle" of an activity game is what he described as an "organized chaos." By this he actually meant an independently active (*samodeiatel'naia*), self-organizing and self-developing system of behavior.[84] And, as I mentioned earlier, Shchedrovitskii's "thinking activity" underscored the collective and performative character of thinking: for him, thinking is never a disconnected, solitary exercise. Thinking activity could be pursued only as part of a team where a joint world (*mir*), amenable to governance, would emerge. This world would include both governors and the governed, as they align their projections of themselves and others—how each of the participants is mirrored in the mind of the others. Shchedrovitskii's approach resembled Erving Goffman's description of games as world-building activities. Thinking activity was a way to create and perpetuate an informal collective into the future.[85] The social is imagined, reflexively and collectively. To govern the social entails the orchestration of this reflexive thinking activity. In this way, Shchedrovitskii's methodology mobilized a particular notion of governance, based on an embodied, social, and reflexive mind. An individual actor for him is not a data point, a rational decision-maker who seeks to maximize utility or minimize risk; an individual actor is but an element of their own and others' projections that intersect, mirror, and shape each other. Prospectiveness is about making this mirror game last over longer or shorter time periods. It is about co-ordination, alignment, synchronization—the orchestration of the future.

This is an interesting version of technocracy. According to the traditional understanding, technocratic governance appears where individuals in charge rely on specialist knowledge to govern what they perceive as objective, lawful reality that could be in principle known and acted upon. For Shchedrovitskii, when a manager deals with objects or technical systems, they inevitably confront the cognitive schemes, intentions, and behavioral patterns of other humans associated with these objects. In this way, a managerial reality cannot be fully dominated by a particular expert knowledge. Managerial realities are heterogeneous games of mirrors. An effective manager will be one who aligns those mirrors with a desirable effect (on time).

How does prospective reflexivity fit with our classification of the scientific uses of prediction? Clearly, it is not a method to obtain new data that could be scientifically explained, in Hempel and Oppenheim's sense. It is neither a guess nor statistical extrapolation. It is a mode of aligning cognitive schemes and actions, a process similar to the behavior theorized by cyberneticians, which gives birth to a viable collective behavior able to agree on and carry out particular projects. It is a form of social engineering—but completely different from Taylorist scientific management, closer, perhaps to what Stephen Collier and Anke Gruendel described as planning by design, a radical idea that emphasized participatory methods and that emerged in Western Europe in the 1960s and the 1970s.[86] Shchedrovitskii sometimes called his activity thinking a sociotechnics (*sotsiotekhnika*), by which he meant an intellectual technology to disturb and destabilize bureaucratic patterns of organization, behavior, and thinking.[87] It should be noted here that Shchedrovitskii derived the term sociotechnics from the English term "systems engineering," applying the systems engineering approach to any organizational situation.[88] The idea was that sociotechnics dealt with hybrid objects or, as Shchedrovitskii called them, "centaurobjects," where human activities and material objects were located on the same epistemological plateau. They were both cognitive *and* material.[89]

The purpose of the games was to develop a new understanding of problems rather than to find the best solution to a very particular organizational task. The

118   CHAPTER 5

route was long and winding.[90] For example, Shchedrovitskii described an activity game dedicated to the development of societal systems, which involved 160–190 participants in Krasnoiarsk in 1986 as follows:

> So we, the gaming team, sought to "break out" from the present space of the activity into the space of history. I had really amused myself with my fellow gamers there, and took a chance to enjoy myself. Why so? The [theme of the] game was so [great] that everyone was saying, I, I, I will come! And they came.... I was saying, guys, excellent, since you are here, so get out! And they looked at me and said, we cannot see anything, it is dark and scary. I waited for a while and then suddenly pulled the carpet from underneath their feet, and they all went flying in the space of history, and it was very interesting to see how they jerked their little arms and legs.[91]

To be sure, this quote is drawn from Shchedrovitskii's retrospective narrative and tells us more about his own approach to his seminars rather than what was actually happening there. He enjoyed watching people lose the safety of conventional meaning-making, disrupting the existing templates of speaking about the past and future. One way of doing this was to position the habitual understanding of the problem in relation to a different time scale. For example, in another activity game, conducted with the municipality of Riga in Soviet Latvia (1986), the chairman of the Riga city council realized that they would never solve their managerial problems without a long-term, strategic understanding of the future of the city.[92] Using the long term to frame current problems in the context of either the past or the future, Shchedrovitskii aimed to estrange Soviet managers from their administrative scripts, the minute, day-to-day problem-solving. The long term was not a space of statistical curves, but of intersubjective reflection on the managers' roles and identities, projected into the far future.[93] Shchedrovitskii criticized scientific forecasting (having a limited understanding of the statistical method) because he presumed that forecasts merely provided knowledge about the "self-developing" "natural world," whereas reflexive thinking activity, expressed in programming and projecting, was part of human teleological behavior.[94]

Orchestrating Post-Soviet Informality

Shchedrovitskii's work has been continued by his followers to the present day, largely by his son Petr, who pioneered much of the strategy training in the public sector of the Russian Federation, established a School of Cultural Policy, and, in 2005, the Scientific Foundation of Georgii Shchedrovitskii in Moscow. Petr Shchedrovitskii himself became a highly influential management consultant and political technologist in Russia: he claims to have trained about 100,000 managers, ranging from cultural managers to diamond producers. Also, from the year 2000 he coauthored and widely disseminated the idea of the "Russian world" (*Ruskii mir*). The Russian world idea has become part of Russia's soft power arsenal, driving her cultural diplomacy by reaching out to global and transnational communities of Russian speakers and strategically mobilizing them to pursue Russia's national goals.[95] Furthermore, the intellectual legacy of Georgii Shchedrovitskii has been institutionalized through the many volumes republishing his articles, lectures, and activity-game training sessions. Histories of Russian managerial thought inevitably include Shchedrovitskii as an important phenomenon and attempts are made to introduce him in English and French, while highly positioned officials in Putin's regime pay homage to Shchedrovitskii's methodology.[96]

In the 1970s and 1980s Shchedrovitskii's notion of thinking activity constituted an important break in the governmental logic of progressive time and, in turn, the communist future, as laid out in the party's plans. Unlike the linear, input–output model of scientific forecasting of social and economic development, where specialists feed data to policymakers to help them make informed decisions, Shchedrovitskii did not separate the data, the subject, and the action. For prospective reflexivity there is no clear division between language, thinking, and behavior, subject and object. Instead, Shchedrovitskii's method underscores the reflexive and performative character of thinking in a group: he argues that ideas cannot be separated from subjects and that thinking is a form of activity. Thinking activity is an open (documented in methodological publications and transcripts) but, at the same time, opaque practice. It is a method that does not hide its manipulative power.

Conclusion

Unlike scientific forecasting, which produced detailed images of the future in graphs and maps of statistical trends, thinking activity was a performative intellectual technology, which sought to destabilize the Soviet present by overthrowing the administrative and conceptual frameworks that guided the managers who participated in Shchedrovitskii's games. The idea was to undermine the rigidly defined administrative bureaucratic roles, which were strongly linked with specific, short-term problems and enmeshed in *avral*, or last-minute

120   **CHAPTER 5**

management. The breaking down of this framework, according to Shchedrovitskii, gave an opportunity to the managers to think about the long term and develop a more holistic, systemic view of their governmental task. Yet what did the long-term future hold in Shchedrovitskii's seminars? What was the role of prospective reflexivity in coping with uncertainty?

It is difficult to give a conclusive answer, yet the methodology of Shchedrovitskii's seminars suggests the primacy of fostering a shared understanding and trust which would perpetuate relations that were informal but anchored functionally in organizations. It led to the building of new, horizontal ties in the organization that departed from administrative scripts. Prospective reflexivity was a scientific method to cope with future uncertainty, but it (1) did not produce knowledge of something before it happened, (2) did not explain the anticipated phenomenon, and (3) did not provide guesswork or estimates of probabilities and chance. What prospective reflexivity sought to accomplish was to reshape the understanding of the actorial self, making visible the way in which the self is projected into the future and is integrated in the equivalent projections of the other actorly selves. It is a method of cognitive positionality: the question is not only "Who is the I that acts and thinks?" as in a simple form of reflexivity, but "What are the versions of I that are projected in the future by others and how my I will fit best with those projections so that the projecting actors can engage in a joint activity?"

This is a fairly complicated theory. The activity game worked as a ritual: becoming part of Russian managerial culture, part of everyday. Not unlike the Americans who engaged in everyday futuring by consulting clairvoyants, fortune-tellers, and mediums, as shown in Jamie Pietruska's *Prediction in America*, Soviet and post-Soviet managers flocked to Shchedrovitskii's workshops, which had an aura of exclusive, esoteric knowledge.

Shchedrovitskii wanted to change people, not institutions. If scientific forecasters at the Gosplan Research Institute of Economics called for transparency and more open circulation of data, the sessions of organizational activity games would foster the formation of informal, nontransparent networks never aimed at reforming the system itself. Unlike economic forecasters, dismissed as elitist technocrats, Shchedrovitskii's managers remained invisible sociopolitical technologists. Although some scholars interpreted Shchedrovitskii's seminars as examples of Soviet civil society, others considered them ambivalent. His activity games sought to discover the conditions for the "normal" rather than to experiment with the conditions for radically new things. Even in the late 1980s, Georgii Shchedrovitskii emphasized that his method was different from the alarmist and critical warnings of other scientists, who sought, in the words of Aaron Wildawsky, to "speak truth to power."[97] Instead, thinking activity is geared to providing "concrete solutions," the emphasis being on coordination and self-regulation beyond formal bureaucratic structures. In Shchedrovitskii's circles, the power to shape the future became linked to the notion of an informal community, integrated through informational processes. After 1991, the reflexive methodology of Shchedrovitskii lost its alter ego, the centralized command economy, to become a powerful tool in the hands of the new Russian political technologists.

6

REFLEXIVE CONTROL

"Reflexivity is generally seen as a mixed blessing."

(Flanagan 1981, 375)

In the previous chapter, I considered how a form of prediction, the concept of prospective reflexivity, fared in Soviet and post-Soviet Russia. Prospective reflexivity was intended to establish and consolidate a new form of the nonbureaucratic social relations to empower organizational action. It helped people to interact directly, bypassing their hierarchical and compartmentalized roles to address organizational problems by projecting their actions into the future. In contrast to scientific forecasting, the principal resource was neither statistical data nor estimates of probability, but the very process of intersubjective alignment: projecting the self reflexively in the collective future.

In this chapter I turn to the theory of reflexive control (in Russian, *refleksivnoe upravlenie*), whose origin in Moscow in the 1960s overlapped with that of prospective reflexivity. While prospective reflexivity is little known outside Russia, reflexive control theory commands international interest because it is linked with security concerns: since 2014, there is hardly any mention of Russia's "hybrid" and "informational" warfare in Ukraine without reference to the principle of reflexive control.[1] Reflexive control theory is considered the first distinctive strategic concept originating in Russia, its prominence comparable with Western concepts such as the Prisoner's Dilemma, first proposed by RAND strategists in 1950 and mutual assured destruction (MAD), coined by Donald Brennan in 1962 and adopted in the US nuclear defense by Robert McNamara in 1965.[2]

Unlike prospective reflexivity, reflexive control is not meant to enhance cooperation and solve collective problems, but to support a winning strategy and make the opponent lose. To enact reflexive control means to lure the opponent into a frame of thinking that would eventually lead to the opponent's disadvantage.[3] The goal of reflexive control is to make the outcomes of manipulation and deception more predictable. The term prediction here refers not only to estimating the outcomes of manipulation by logical deduction of the opponent's course of action, but also to explanation and active intervention. It is assumed that the opponent's action is guided by an underlying cognitive scheme, which can be manipulated and replaced with a different one that is passed on to the opponent secretly, without one's knowledge. The creator of the theory, Vladimir Lefebvre (1936–2020), explained the principle of reflexive control by using a classic example of deception: "'Do with me whatever you like,' said Brer Rabbit to the Fox, 'but do not throw me into a briar patch.' The Fox throws Brer Rabbit into a bush. Brer Rabbit escapes."[4]

A scientific method of deception sounds like an oxymoron. In the Western tradition, as Robert Merton put it, science is identified with the values of truthfulness, transparency, and fairness.[5] Culturally, cheating is seen as a skill that could be admired but that is deeply problematic, as in the figure of a con artist. In what way can a "science of cheating" claim legitimacy and authority? Here it is useful to revisit Nikolai Gogol's play *The Gamblers* (1842), where Gogol laid out the gamblers' own justification of the ethical dilemma posed by professional cheating. A passionate and talented gambler, Uteshitelny, relays a story of how a group of gamblers managed to smuggle a set of marked cards into a game. This enabled them to score a big win. His interlocutor responds enthusiastically:

> *IKHAREV*: That's what I call clever! People say it is fraud and deception, but in reality it is brain work, development, finesse!
>
> *UTESHITELNY*: Those people don't understand the spirit of play. Play is impartial; it is no respecter of persons. Let my own father sit down at a game with me—I'd skin him the same as any stranger. Who tells him to play? At the card table all are equal.[6]

Gogol's gamblers justify their behavior by claiming that the rules of the game are not discriminatory, but objective. They have no relation to moral judgment. A similar reasoning, as I will show, underpins the ethical justification of reflexive control as a scientific technology of deception. However, what makes both reflexive control and Gogol's gamblers' strategy work is the asymmetry of knowledge where the objectivity of the game is a mere illusion: the lines that separate "the game" and "the reality" are obscured and known to only one contesting side. Successful deception means shaping the interpretive frames of the opponent in such a way that the opponent's reality and choices narrow down and their behavior becomes predictable.

In the context of policy or managerial strategy, deception is both ethically and socially problematic because deception influences actorial identities, particularly

124   CHAPTER 6

their social or symbolic status. Practicing deception is costly: if cheating is detected, the gambler risks punishment and will certainly be excluded from the future games. Moreover, cheating and deceptive manipulation threaten the very fabric of the social: Émile Durkheim would have classified deception as anomic behavior. Deception is particularly costly for collective actors, such as organizations. For instance, companies and governments seek to appear as trustworthy agents at all costs, even when they are caught cheating. This observation has led some commentators of international politics to classify reflexive control as part of the arsenal of "weak," typically nonstate actors facing stronger opponents.[7] Strong states and organizations, according to this line of thinking, do not need to resort to ensnaring the opponent. They have enough resources to shape the opponent's behavior via persuasion or coercion. However, other commentators argue that this is no longer the case because digital media have transformed the playing field: trustworthiness is not what it used to be because of the ubiquitous content and endless possibilities of manipulating audiovisual materials. In this context, Russia's adoption of reflexive control, which was known in the Soviet military for more than half a century, could be understood not as weakness, but as a reasonable response to the opportunities presented by information technology. Indeed, some see the use of reflexive control as an expression of Putin's decisive reorientation away from the notion of Russia as a weak regional power to a major world power.[8] As a Finnish scholar of Russian national security Katri Pynnöniemi noted, Russia's invasion in Ukraine in February 2022 was preceded by extensive rounds of diplomacy which was used as strategic deception at an unprecedented scale.[9]

In Russia, reflexive control theory has a strong purchase in both military and business thinking. It is understood as something more than mere cheating, a "science" of decision-making. Leading Russian strategy consultants regularly publish academic studies on the subject, conferences and entire research centers are organized to explore the application of reflexive control in military and civil contexts.[10] The concept of reflexive control has been established in Russian philosophy, management, public policy, and pedagogic research: research projects and training programs on reflexive governance are conducted at prestigious institutions such as the Institute of Systems Research at the Russian Academy of Sciences and the National Nuclear Research University.[11] The wide-ranging interest in reflexive control theory can be explained by a long-standing desire to predict and influence complex human cognition and behavior. Reflexive control fits well with (and is genealogically related to) the behaviorist approach, which was notoriously declared by B. F. Skinner as immune from ethical concerns.[12] Reflexive control is also driven by ongoing innovation in digital technology, because it addresses a fundamental problem faced by artificial intelligence

(AI) researchers, namely how to formalize abstract, integrative concepts and operational schemes in ways that would enable an autonomous AI.[13] In this way, reflexive control theory forms an important part of the evolution of anticipatory governance, behavioral science, and AI.

Reflexive control theory was originally developed by a Russian game theorist Vladimir A. Lefebvre (in Russian, Lefevr) in the 1960s. Lefebvre was initially trained as a mathematician, defended his *kandidatskaia* dissertation in psychology, and had extensive experience working on military applications of decision theory. In 1974 he emigrated to the United States and did not return to Russia until 1990. His work on East–West negotiation strategies informed the Reagan–Gorbachev talks on nuclear disarmament in Reykjavik in 1986. Following Lefebvre's suggestion, US and Soviet administrations used different communication strategies to report the agreement to the US and Soviet populations.[14] In Russia, Lefebvre's students have long praised reflexive control theory's significance beyond military strategy, claiming that it was a groundbreaking attempt to integrate the mathematical and psychological sciences and philosophy in order to study anticipation and behavioral control.[15] Indeed, a vigorous institutionalization of Lefebvre's intellectual legacy is currently taking place in Russian academia: some followers contend that Lefebvre deserves to be acknowledged as a central figure in social and political thought, pointing out a certain conceptual proximity between Lefebvre's ideas on reflexive control, Karl Popper's notion of imperfect knowledge, and George Soros's writing on reflexivity in finance.[16]

In what follows, I reconstruct the emergence of Lefebvre's reflexive control theory in the Soviet Union, situating it in the context of Cold War politics and intellectual thought. I then trace Lefebvre's intellectual and personal journey as he developed his approach to prediction of reflexive behavior in the 1960s and the 1970s. The chapter concludes with a discussion of the performative role of reflexive prediction as strategy.

Reflexivity

There is, of course, a very long history of the idea of reflexivity and its role in the transformation of the social. Historically, the concept of reflexivity emerged in Western philosophy to describe a human mental process of creating images of both external and internal worlds. The external world included the objects that existed outside the mindful subject, such as the sun, mountains, and other people. The idea of the internal world referred to the mind's ability to consider itself, to practice self-reflection.[17] This model of cognition was expanded to include a reflection, as in a mirror image, of the mental operations of other subjects. Visual artists

FIGURE 4. Diego Velázquez, *Las meninas o La Familia de Felipe IV* (1656) © Photographic Archive Museo Nacional del Prado. Courtesy of Museo Nacional de Prado.

have long engaged with the phenomenon of reflection and projection, drawing on it as a resource in their work. Consider Diego Velázquez's painting *Las Meninas* (1656), which has mesmerized historians and philosophers for much of the last century (see figure 4).

Michel Foucault, for instance, starts *The Order of Things* (1966) by describing *Las Meninas* as a network of gazes. According to Foucault, the viewer who is looking at Velázquez's painting is actually standing in the position where the sitter (the royal family) would have sat. This is suggested by the mirror, painted in the background, which reflects the image of the royal couple. The viewer is invited to self-identify with the royal reflection and, accordingly, to realize that they are "observing being observed by the painter."[18] Velázquez, according to Foucault, did not just paint an unusually complex portrait of the Spanish royal family (who are only seen in a mirror reflection in the background) but also produced a critical commentary on classical representation. The viewer is in the position of the sovereign. However, this position cannot be perceived directly. It is revealed by the mediation of both the gaze of the others (the painter) and the reflection (in the mirror). This, Foucault suggests, prompts a redefinition of thought itself: thought should be understood not as a simple mirror image of the world out there, but as a transformative reflection, "both knowledge and a modification of what it knows, reflection and a transformation of the mode of being of that on which it reflects."[19] The problem is, however, that, according to the art historian Joel Snyder, Foucault misunderstood the technical structure of perspective drawn by Velázquez. The viewer would not have been reflected in the mirror had the room presented in the painting been "real." Furthermore, Foucault's suggestion that the traditional representation places the individual subject at the center, suggesting a privileged point of view of the individual mind, does not apply to classical paintings, because they can be viewed successfully (appearing as "realistic") from many different positions.[20] Snyder adds that Foucault erroneously presumed that the mirror was meant to provide an objective reflection of the outside world. It did not: in the renaissance culture, the mirror reflection represented "the self that is fashioned through art" and to observe a reflection in the mirror was seen as superior to the direct physical act of gazing at "the unmediated" reality.[21] In turn, Velázquez's painting is better interpreted as a statement that reality could be improved by making it imitate its own reflection.

If there is a lesson to be learned from this debate on *Las Meninas* it is that perception, interpretation, and mobilization of reflexive images is open to different pathways of understanding, reducing these pathways is a serious challenge: as Owen Flanagan observed, "reflexivity is a mixed blessing."[22] Foucault's work was part of the long-standing sociological debate on determinism and freedom. The question was how automatic, mechanical habits and mindful, abstract reflexivity combined as building blocks of social order. Historians traced the development of the notion of the self as a composition of parts that act upon each other reflexively. For instance, Foucauldians argued that this architecture of the self was fundamental for the liberal "conduct of conduct": self-betterment, self-governance, and external influence through reflexive pedagogy.[23] However, the debate about the composite, reflexive self also concerned the factors that automatized and constrained individual behavior: neural, physical, and social systems. The answer to the question of whether individual behavior can be determined mainly internally

128 CHAPTER 6

or externally had political implications. The debate was also about disciplinary identities of social research and natural science. Since the early twentieth century, the whole social science and humanities field was shaped by a struggle between what was understood as a materialist and reductionist behavioral approach (which focused on habits), and a cultural, interpretivist approach (which focused on reflection). Following Immanuel Kant, for whom reflexivity was the key capacity of human reason and a necessary precondition for human civilization, many influential thinkers defended reflexivity as the special domain of social sciences and humanities.

In this context, reflexivity was defined as a capacity of mind to form abstractions that are dynamic and amenable to change. Anthony Giddens, for instance, classified late modern society as "reflexive modernity," exemplifying a Kantian belief in the civilizational quality of reflexivity as an advanced stage of human evolution, a stage that is characterized by a greater individual freedom.[24] Scholars of science and technology studies (STS) declared that social constructionist epistemology was inherently reflexive.[25] As Dick Pels noted, in its politically stronger version, feminists and race scholars employed reflexivity "to position" their own role in the production of knowledge, avoiding what were seen as biased abstract concepts.[26] In a similar spirit, historians called for a "more reflexive" historiography.[27]

In contrast, habit was defined as the other of reflexivity, an automatic mechanism that enslaved the individual self and reproduced existing social systems. Foucauldian scholars suggested that habit and reflexivity were socially stratified concepts that informed different forms of governance. Governmental practices that targeted habits were deemed suitable to control lower social classes. For instance, pedagogical institutions would encourage the working-class students to follow instructions and defer to authority. In contrast, the notion of reflexivity, embedded in the Kantian ideal of cultivation of the self, was reserved for elite education, where students were encouraged to think individually, critically, and creatively.[28] As sociologist Tony Bennett argued, following Dewey, making mass behavior predictable was about imposing habits, "unthinking routines."[29] In this context, habit was understood as part of the mechanization of the social, whereas reflexivity was seen as a pathway to escape the iron cage of bureaucracy and social conformism.[30]

However, the separation of habit and reflexivity did not happen in physiology, neuroscience and neuropsychology, ecology, and cybernetics, where both reflection and habit were understood as fundamental organizational components of complex, evolving systems. For instance, in the early twentieth century, the French philosopher Gabriel Tarde proposed that social change can be driven not only by reflexivity, but also by habit. However, to understand this habit's function one needs to consider the scale of complexity and the temporal horizons. According to Tarde's evolutionary approach, habits emerge as people respond to their environment. These responses might appear as automatic at the time when they happen, but in fact they are part of a long cycle of corrections. Those habits that have proven to be successful will be transmitted to the next generation. In other words, what might appear at a given moment to be the mindless habit of a given population can appear as a reflexive change, shaping the population's interaction with its environment, from the long-term perspective.[31] Habits can be cogs of change. Reflection can be a control device.[32]

The problem of understanding the relation between reflexivity and habit was addressed in the postwar cognitive and behavioral sciences, predecessors of what is now called "cybernetic behaviorism."[33] An influential model was suggested by the cybernetician Gordon Pask, who conceptualized the dialogical self and offered a model of reflexivity as multilevel information processing (see figure 5).[34]

Cybernetic thinkers linked behavior with cognitive operations of the mind, but not always conscious ones. In turn, the working of the mind was described in behaviorist terms: the brain was understood as a machine of *both* calculation and action. A participant of the Macy conferences, which mapped the agenda for the pioneering research in cybernetics in New York in the 1940s, the anthropologist Gregory Bateson theorized behavior and cognition as reflexive processes. Bateson was particularly excited by Ross Ashby's model of homeostat, which simulated learning and emerging order and applied these insights to the study of social behavior. For Bateson, the individual mind and social order emerge as they interact with the environment through perception and information loops. These loops are organized in a hierarchical system: what can be considered reflexive at one scale is automatic on another scale. This insight allowed Bateson to propose a new model of learning, which was very similar to Tarde's ideas: Bateson explained learning as a process of reflexive adaptation to contexts, which eventually "sink into habits."[35]

As I show in the next section, the Russian reflexive control theory deployed a notion of reflexivity that was similar to Tarde's and Bateson's. For Cold War strategy, reflexivity was not so much a "privileged point" of generating more reliable knowledge, but an actionable point. This action, however, had little to do with the Kantian pedagogy of enlightenment and persuasion, and everything to do with the shaping of (cognitive) behavioral environment and habituation. The key problem was how to formally represent this reflex–habit system and how to use these representations to conduct the conduct in what Foucauldian scholars refer to as a liberal governmentality.

FIGURE 5. Drawing by Gordon Pask. Reprinted from Heinz von Foerster, "On Self-Organizing Systems and Their Environments," in *Self-Organizing Systems*, eds. Marshall Clinton Yovits and Scott Cameron (London: Pergamon Press, 1960), 31–50, 34. Courtesy of Elsevier.

Reflexive Control

Since the 1960s, a Soviet version of what can be called cybernetic behaviorism emerged. The problems of adaptive and teleological behavior interested linguists working on the cybernetics of the brain (Viacheslav Ivanov), atmosphere scientists (Mikhail Budyko), and environmental scientists (Evgenii Fedorov), as well as psychologists and philosophers (Georgii Shchedrovitskii and Georgii Afanas'ev). The most fertile soil for the cybernetic notion of teleological, future-oriented behavior was in the applied, high-priority fields of operations research (OR), systems analysis, and management. They formed the basis for "scientific governance" (in Russian, *nauchnoe upravlenie*), a Soviet version of public policy science. Reflexive control theory grew from this context. As Lefebvre put it, reflexive control is not merely about prediction, but about the shaping of behavior.[36]

Born in Saint Petersburg (then Leningrad) in 1936, Lefebvre experienced the Leningrad blockade during the Second World War. The members of the Lefebvre family were lucky—they were evacuated to Alma-Aty in Kazakhstan in 1942.[37] Vladimir would grow up in Moscow and attend an elite school a short run from the Kremlin. However, the evacuation imprinted Lefebvre with traumatic memories: for instance, he described in his memoir seeing the bodies of those who had died in the overcrowded transit being thrown off the packed train car, which affected him deeply.[38] Many survivors of Soviet deportations and the Second World War witnessed similar experiences of the crumbling of social values and order. These experiences, according to Irina Sandomirskaja, had an important intellectual legacy too because they encouraged reflexivity. For instance, Sandomirskaja suggested that witnessing the extreme disruption of life during the siege of Leningrad, but also Stalinist terror, Soviet literary scholars and linguists turned instead to investigate the formalist disruptions of the symbolic order of things: when reality stops making sense, the mind turns to investigating its own structure.[39]

In 1962, before graduating in mathematics from the prestigious Mathematical Mechanics Faculty at Moscow State University, Lefebvre followed a friend's advice and applied for a research position in a secret research institute, a so-called postbox (*pochtovyi iashchik*), the Scientific Research Institute of Automatic Machinery (NIIAA), directed by Vladimir Semenikhin. NIIAA was established in 1956, with code name NII-101, under the Ministry of Radioelectronics. The institute specialized in automated missile-control systems. Lefebvre was appointed at the laboratory of engineering psychology (established in 1961 by Vladimir Zinchenko, a prominent cognitive psychologist), where he directed a group of young researchers, such as Vladimir Lepskii, Pavel Baranov, and A. Trudoliubov. Zinchenko's laboratory was part of the Theoretical Department, directed by Dmitrii Panov, "a

132 **CHAPTER 6**

very intelligent man with a pale face and hands."[40] Lefebvre and his colleagues, whom he described as "student types," shared a small corner office. Lefebvre was described as an insightful and imposing, "masculine" personality, able to formulate complex ideas in a clear way, although he expressed himself with difficulty, his speech being punctuated with pauses.[41] For Lefebvre this period of his career was particularly stimulating and creative; there was a sense of mission and mystery as the laboratory's research was instrumental in how the Soviet Union performed in the Cold War. The missile gap contributed to the sense of urgency: the United States accelerated the development of its first intercontinental ballistic missile (ICBM) Minuteman in response to the Soviet Sputnik, launched in 1957. As the Soviets rushed to catch up with this technological breakthrough, all staff had to be involved and the young researchers were given unusual tasks.[42]

Although at that time Lefebvre's research task did not have much to do with the grand strategy of Cold War communication it presented a few interesting intellectual challenges. Lefebvre worked in a team that was developing a new type of a mobile military computer system that could be deployed in a battlefield, "Beta-1."[43] Creation of this system was tasked to the Central Defense Research Institute No. 27 of the Ministry of Defense (TsINII), established by Anatolii Kitov in 1954. Its versions were also developed in the Scientific Research Institute of Electronic Mathematical Machines (NITsEVT), housed in a building that was nicknamed a horizontal skyscraper, the longest building in Moscow (720 meters). There was an urgency to this project. The United States launched its first system, Mobidic, a digital computer mounted on trucks, in 1959 so the Soviet Union had to catch up. Eventually sixteen such mobile computer systems, able to assist battlefield operations that deployed missiles and radars, were produced.[44]

Lefebvre was tasked with creating a wargame, a software simulation of battlefield operations for the purpose of training commanding officers. While working on this game, he suggested including decision-making and communication in addition to the movement of troops and deployment of weapons. The commanding officers were skeptical about this proposal. As Lefebvre wrote retrospectively, Soviet military commanders considered battlefield military decisions as a matter of art and creative improvisation and emphasized that decision-making in combat situations had to deal with deception both by issuing decisions with intention to deceive and by recognizing deceptive information. A military decision-maker not only had to process physical information (e.g., the evasive action of an enemy pilot that is being targeted), but also to judge if the received information was intentionally misleading. In turn, one also had to release deceptive information strategically. As servomechanisms could track, target, and anticipate the evasive action of a moving object very quickly, they could replace a human operator in automated antiaircraft missile defense systems.

REFLEXIVE CONTROL   133

However, a computer could not replace human decisions when it came to manipulating the opponent's understanding and recognizing being deceived by the opponent. This argument that the computer could not possibly cheat better than humans did not deter Lefebvre from the task. He began dreaming about creating a logical machine of deception.[45]

Another source of inspiration for Lefebvre was astronomy. He was fascinated with the discrepancy between the laws described in theories of astrophysics and human perception, the fact that although the natural phenomena were not like they appeared to be but sometimes the mechanisms of natural phenomena could be felt intuitively. He became particularly interested in classical proportion of the golden ratio, which suggested that humans were able to recognize perceptually mathematical structures.[46] Curiously, a similar insight led the prominent American neurophysiologist Warren McCulloch to develop an interest in studies of neuroprocesses. McCulloch studied classical proportions and went on, with Walter Pitt, to develop the pioneering mathematical models of communication and control in neural systems.[47] Like McCulloch, Lefebvre desired to develop "a proper science" of mental processes, in which "the work of a psychologist would somehow resemble the work of a theoretical physicist."[48] Lefebvre wanted to find a way in which the mind was aligned with the universe.

Pursuing this task, Lefebvre began to read all Western publications on decision science that he could obtain: as luck would have it, his highly secret research institute was fairly well provided with translations of key works and scientific journals.[49] Lefebvre's early work refers to such central authorities as Thomas Schelling, Anatol Rapoport (who later would become Lefebvre's intellectual supporter), and John von Neumann, as well as mathematical modelers such as Edward Moore, biologists and linguists, working in a cybernetic spirit, such as Lars Lofgren, and military thinkers, such as Basil Liddell Hart.[50] Furthermore, Lefebvre retrospectively wrote that Duncan Luce and Howard Raiffa's *Games and Decisions* (1957, translated into Russian in 1961) "had a great influence on everybody who worked in our 'postbox.'"[51] Based at Columbia and then at Harvard's Kennedy School, Raiffa promoted an empirically grounded approach to game theory that served as an alternative to abstract rational choice theory. Indeed, later, Raiffa's course about approaches to teaching negotiations caused controversy in the national press. In 1979, the *Wall Street Journal* wrote that students were taught "to lie" at Harvard. In fact, Raiffa taught students to analyze different bargaining strategies, including what he called "strategic misrepresentation."[52] Lefebvre sympathized with Raiffa's criticism of US rational choice theorists who attempted to eliminate the man from the decision situation, which was presented as a purely logical puzzle. Criticisms like Raiffa's were also pressed by scholars based at RAND Corporation's Social Science Division.[53] However, sensing that good decisions cannot be made without

134   CHAPTER 6

taking into consideration the human factor, Lefebvre began to explore the possibility of the mathematical modeling of reflexive processes that take place in the mind.

As early as 1968 Lefebvre wrote about the futility of construing "a strict theory of any kind of processes" in society and the economy. Human activity, according to Lefebvre, "evolved in the context of continuous clashes of activities, ideas and feelings"; the agentic structure thus conceived was a challenge to existing cybernetic thought and mathematical methods. While Lefebvre acknowledged the importance of groundbreaking work by John von Neumann and Oskar Morgenstein's *Game Theory and Economic Behavior* (1944), he wrote that game theory, while being normative and prescriptive, could not help a decision-maker understand either the different actors involved in a conflict or, sometimes, even the very character of the conflict itself. Instead, as Lefebvre put it, "[A] classical tragedy and a serious novel still remain the best source of our knowledge about human conflict."[54] Reflexive control was to do what Frederick Lanchester's equations, devised in 1914 to 1916 to identify the optimal distribution of military weapons and logistic systems and to calculate the attrition in a battle, could not do: namely, to theorize the distribution of strategic decision positions in politics and public policy. This task required a method and epistemology that sought to formalize the processes previously attributed to empathy.

The young Lefebvre's life was not confined to the postbox institute, he was active in several informal intellectual milieus in Moscow. As a university student, he attended the famous seminars of the Moscow Methodological Circle, an informal initiative of young philosophy students seeking to rejuvenate the stale discipline, which was being choked off by Marxism–Leninism. The circle was led by the philosopher Georgii Shchedrovitskii, an eccentric and charismatic thinker (see chapter 5), who taught Lefebvre a course in logic in the elite school (the one located close to the Kremlin). Shchedrovitskii, only seven years older than Lefebvre, was known as an engaging and innovative teacher who told students to ignore textbooks as he preferred to invent his own problems. However, Lefebvre found Shchedrovitskii's approach "insufficiently scientific" and was disappointed to find initially little interest in exploring reflexivity in the circle. Lefebvre left the seminar in 1963. Only later Shchedrovitskii would realize the importance of reflexivity and start exploring it in his work on prospective reflexivity in the 1970s.[55]

According to his contemporaries in the mid-1960s Lefebvre, who was still in his thirties, became something of an intellectual celebrity in Moscow. Lefebvre presented his work at seminars on game theory at Moscow State University organized by the prominent mathematician and the pioneer of Soviet game theory Iurii Germeier.[56] Lefebvre's mathematical, formalist approach to thought process promised a meaningful intellectual and scientific engagement in the desert of the ideology of dialectical materialism.[57] Lefebvre's early ideas on the formalization of reflexivity inspired others, such as Feliks Ereshko, a student of Nikita Moiseev (for Moiseev, see chapter 7; Ereshko would go on to become a prominent game theorist and operations researcher, tasked with implementing computer systems in the agricultural sector in the 1980s).[58] Lefebvre's first book, *Conflicting Structures* (*Konfliktuiushchie struktury*, 1967), was followed by a brief version, *The Algebra of Conflict* (*Algebra konflikta*, 1968), coauthored with the philosopher Georgii Smolian. Smolian, whom Lefebvre had met at NIIAA in 1966, would become a prominent systems theorist, based at the All-Union Institute of Systems Research (VNIISI). *The Algebra of Conflict* was published in a run of sixty thousand copies, which sold well being priced at twelve kopeiki by the All-Union Association for Popularization of Science (in Russian, *Znanie*).[59] Work on reflexive control was mainly developed and disseminated in the community of Soviet psychologists and military thought.[60]

In the late 1960s Lefebvre organized a research group on psychological and cybernetic approaches to reflexivity in cooperation with the computer scientist Dmitrii Pospelov, philosopher Vadim Sadovskii, and psychologist Veniamin Pushkin. This group included the mathematician and psychologist Vladimir Lepskii, the philosopher Georgii Smolian, and the electronics engineer Pavel Baranov. Lefebvre's intellectual influence was growing: his research was published in the first yearbook of the prestigious *Systems Research* (in Russian, *Sistemnye issledovanie*) of the Academy of Sciences in 1969. In 1972, Lefebvre defended a dissertation on mathematical and psychological approaches to reflexivity in conflict situations. Recognizing that advances in theorizing reflexivity and its control could have important implications for management and planning, the leading economic research center, the Central Economic and Mathematical Institute (TsEMI), invited Lefebvre and his NIIAA group to join them.[61] At TsEMI, Lefebvre ran an interdisciplinary seminar on mathematical logics, cybernetics, semiotics, and psychology, in which he sought to develop what he called "psychographics," a mathematized, formal representation of reflexivity.[62]

His theoretical work was received with great interest in the military strategy community and, what worried Lefebvre, the State Security Committee (KGB). According to Lefebvre, Dmitry Panov, the cofounder and the first director of the All-Union Institute of Scientific and Technical Information (VINITI, established 1956), was interested in the prospect of modeling reflexive systems and was known to have strong links with the KGB. In the late 1960s, Lefebvre was invited to brief KGB officers; they invited to him to "cooperate," a euphemism that referred to becoming an associate. Lefebvre wrote retrospectively that he agreed to provide the security organs with briefs about his research but declined the

KGB's offer to work for them.[63] This was not unusual: while many Soviet scientists keenly worked with the military, few agreed to work for the KGB. Scientists saw the military as a legitimate partner because they used scientific discoveries to enhance the Soviet Union's international status and to contribute to the national security. Furthermore, the culture of militarism, as David Priestland suggested, pervaded Soviet culture and society, where the values of honor, self-sacrifice, and mobilization served as a social glue. The military ethos, espoused by scholars and unskilled workers alike, helped individuals cope with their everyday hardships and justify their personal sacrifices; it served as a prosthesis of individual dignity and as such was widely exploited by the Soviet ideological and security agencies.[64] There was also a very practical reason: the military funded scientific research generously, at the same time allowing scientists considerable intellectual autonomy. There were, of course, difficulties. The link between theory and practice was not as direct in the military as there was a lag in implementation and many scientific innovations probably were never deployed. The relative autonomy was also an obstacle: like in the West, the operations research and decision scientists argued that their decision techniques could only perform well when the OR expert gets on well with the military, because key information could never be fully disembedded from interpersonal relations.[65] Hence Lefebvre's direct experience of working in a military research unit helped the transfer of his ideas to the military operational planners, but his position as an outsider prevented him from testing out his approaches in practice, as far as it can be told from the sources that are available.

The field where the young Lefebvre's ideas were readily adopted was in military strategic thought, particularly publications by Valentin V. Druzhinin, a general, a military theorist, and deputy director of the agency for automation of control and radioelectronic combat at the General Staff (Genshtab). Trained in radioelectronic science, Druzhinin contributed to the establishment of the integrated early warning radar system, which was initiated in the early 1960s and implemented in the 1970s.[66] The General Staff and the Soviet military strategy community were known as forming a somewhat surprisingly open intellectual milieu, engaging with Western thought even during the Stalinist period. Under Brezhnev, the General Staff invested in training programs in operational research, systems analysis, and other cognitive and computer-based methods, published textbooks, and research journals. The idea that war action was a systematic process that had to be studied scientifically underpinned the military's interest in Lefebvre's reflexive control. However, it is difficult to tell whether they adopted Lefebvre's ideas in practice. Lefebvre's reflexive control theory belongs to what could be described as "operational planning," a highly flexible technique to be applied in a combat situation, based on interaction with the enemy, recognition of errors, and correction. This approach is sometimes described as a cognitive behavioral technique. Operational planning, as the historian William Thomas noted, is conceptually and institutionally separate from logistics, which in the Soviet Union was embodied in Tukhachevskii's war planning. Logistical war planning was organized around the principles of linear programing, optimal resource allocation, and rational procurement, the areas, where, as Condoleezza Rice estimated, the Soviet General Staff experts had a very limited impact.[67]

Regardless of growing recognition in academia and policy circles, Lefebvre was increasingly dissatisfied because the institutional space for his work was narrowing. At the end of the 1960s, Lefebvre realized that his new work might never get published. He did not receive rejection letters, but some editors told him personally that his work was no longer publishable and a few publications that he had submitted were indefinitely delayed. The political context was becoming more tense. Following the Prague Spring of 1968, many scholars who engaged with Western approaches and who were typically located in the newly established, post-Stalinist Soviet social science institutions, were accused of disloyalty and of corrupting communist science, and they were sometimes fired. Although TsEMI was not particularly affected (in fact it has served as a shelter for many scholars), many sociologists were forced to leave the Institute of Concrete Social Research (IKSI), the key site for Soviet sociological research. The space for qualitative social science and relative academic freedom shrank. Even those Soviet scientists who applied what were considered safe and politically neutral mathematical methods in their research were at risk. In addition to this, Lefebvre worried that he might become a victim of repression for medical reasons. In his letter to Anatol Rapoport, he explained that he wanted to emigrate because of his psychological condition which he described as "a vegetative neurosis." Worried that he might be diagnosed as mentally ill, Lefebvre feared ending up in a Soviet psychiatric clinic: he knew only too well the physical consequences of overmedication. An official diagnosis could have also ruined his career.[68] As it happens, Lefebvre's wife, Victorina, was Jewish and the Lefebvre family decided to emigrate, using a window of opportunity when the government announced permission for Jews to leave the Soviet Union. From the 1960s to the mid-1990s, 1.2 million Jews, about a half of the total Soviet Jewish community, emigrated.[69] In 1972, the year Lefebvre defended his candidate thesis, Richard Nixon visited Moscow to meet Brezhnev, and the Lefebvres applied for a permission to leave the Soviet Union. They departed for the United States in 1974, in this way adding to the exodus of scientists and intellectuals who left the Soviet Union in the 1960s to 1980s.[70] Before leaving Moscow, Lefebvre received an unexpected invitation to meet with Aksel Berg, an admiral, pioneer, and a key patron of Soviet cybernetics. Berg's invitation indicates not only the significance of Lefebvre's work but also the concern there was about the brain drain that the Soviet

138   CHAPTER 6

Union had begun to experience. For instance, in 1977, a prominent linguist, Igor' Melchuk, left for Canada and the Lithuanian semiotician Tomas Venclova, who was also a member of the Soviet branch of the Helsinki Committee for Human Rights, emigrated to the United States. Departures of significant scholars were, however, still rare. The major wave of emigration of Soviet scientists would start only in the late 1980s and peak in the early 1990s, when an estimated seven thousand research scientists left. Many émigré scholars specialized in mathematics and systems modeling.[71]

The life as an emigrant in the United States was challenging in the beginning. Lefebvre did not speak English to a high standard and had to resort to working as a teaching assistant of Russian.[72] Indeed, he was dependent on his wife's linguistic competences (and analytical expertise): Viktorina Lefebvre was an accomplished linguist, a scholar in her own right. She translated her husband's main works into English and helped design experiments for his cognitive psychology research projects. Eventually, Vladimir Lefebvre obtained a researcher's position at the Institute of Mathematical Behavioral Sciences at the University of California, Irvine, where Victorina got a position teaching Russian in the languages department.

In emigration, Lefebvre became fascinated with what he saw as cultural differences that informed decision processes in the Soviet Union and the West. He began to broaden reflexive control theory aspiring to build a general theory of cognitive valuation. In the 1980s, he gained a reputation as an expert in cognitive value systems in Soviet and Western societies. There could not have been a more relevant time to explore such a theme: East–West relations had stalled with the disruption of arms control talks in 1983 and Reagan's launch of the Strategic Defense Initiative, or "Star Wars" program. The United States withdrew from several international collaboration schemes, such as the International Institute of Applied Systems Analysis. At the time when Soviet and US scientists published a warning to world governments about the global environmental impact of nuclear war, in 1983, increased efforts were put into research of negotiation processes. Many perceived the world as being on the brink of disaster, and popular media reinforced this feeling by broadcasting films on nuclear war. As a member of the Russian elite expat community, Lefebvre became known to Jack Matlock, a diplomat and later the US ambassador to the Soviet Union, who advised Ronald Reagan on Soviet and East European matters. In 1984, Matlock wrote to Robert McFarlane, Reagan's National Security Advisor, informing him about Lefebvre's work on Soviet and US approaches to conflict and suggesting that Lefebvre be included in a small group of eminent Russian expats due to meet Reagan.[73] Although this idea did not materialize, in 1985 Matlock did invite Lefebvre to the White House, where they had a lengthy conversation on the US–USSR negotiations. Following this meeting, Lefebvre sent a report to Matlock in which he recommended that US negotiators should not demand that Gorbachev make any public statements acknowledging compromise. Lefebvre wrote that acknowledging compromise was a feature of the Western model of negotiation. In contrast, the Soviet model of negotiation was based on explicit confrontation, the statement of what was not acceptable under any circumstances. This, according to Lefebvre, did not mean that the Soviets refused to compromise, but the actual compromise had to be left between the lines and not acknowledged in public. It was not only a way to preserve face by asserting autonomy, but also the expression of a cognitive model that helped sort options. The unacceptable options are stated first; this helps to scope the space for maneuvering.[74] It is difficult to tell just how much Lefebvre's ideas influenced negotiations in Reykjavik, but Matlock did send a letter thanking the scientist for the suggestions and materials.[75]

Lefebvre became engaged in what was at that time a small East–West network of scientists interested in the institutionalization of cybernetics and systems thinking.[76] These exchanges convinced Lefebvre further about the East–West cultural divide. For instance, he recalled arguing with Stafford Beer, following Lefebvre's presentation of a paper at the Seventh European Meeting on Cybernetics and Systems Research (EMCSR) at Vienna University in 1984.[77] In this conversation, Lefebvre realized that it was difficult to translate the term "self-reference" into Russian "because there is no tradition of thinking in these terms." The Western scholars of self-organization focused on examining the mechanism that enables "the image of the self to become adequate to the self." The Russian scientists, in contrast, were more interested in the ways in which the image of the self could become inadequate to the actual self. Lefebvre gave an example of the self-image of the saint: a person cannot be considered as a proper saint if she already has an image of herself as a saint. The status of sainthood can only be awarded externally, by society. Accordingly, this status is only valid where there is mismatch between the socially projected image of the self and the internally constructed image of the self.[78] Another difference, according to Lefebvre, was that the Western second-order cyberneticians were interested in the emergence of self-organizing systems, while the Soviet version of second-order cybernetics was principally developed in application to Cold War strategy, to work out the mechanisms of influencing the observer (the Cold War opponent). This, of course, was not exactly the case: Soviet second-order cybernetics was widely used to rethink the theory of learning, neuroscience, environmental science, management, public health, and linguistics.[79] Lefebvre's statement rather describes his own intellectual milieu where the premium was placed on strategic applications of reflexivity.

140   CHAPTER 6

A Reflexive Game of Deception

Whereas in the Soviet Union, reflexivity was increasingly perceived as a resource to be weaponized, in Western decision science it was posited as an insurmountable obstacle. As Isaac Joel elucidated, in Cold War United States reflexivity was understood as "a powerful, potentially dizzying, kind of mutual dependence of decision makers," where "[E]ach player knows that their best move depends on what others do; but each player also knows that the other players know this too, and they know that the other players know that they know, and so on, in a potentially infinite regress."[80] The problem of reflexivity becomes more difficult when there is no information intentionally exchanged between players. Joel uses Thomas Schelling's example of a homeowner facing a burglar, where the absence of informational exchange results, paradoxically, in an overflow of information to be processed by both parties. Neither of the parties confronting each other, the homeowner or the burglar, wishes to reveal their true intentions (both actually want to flee), because they are worried about being attacked from behind. At the same time, both opponents are aware of this. They are also aware of each other's awareness. This overflow of reflexivity, according to Schelling, results in an unstable outcome (the increased likelihood of a first strike that will escalate the conflict).[81] Information on the opponent's reflection in conflict situation, it appears, constituted excess, which decision scientists sought to reduce in order to make it controllable. According to Joel, US decision scientists bracketed away reflexivity as an unavoidable problem, which was to be tolerated and tempered.[82]

In contrast, Lefebvre approaches reflexivity as a resource, as an actionable characteristic of behavior. In his influential publications, *The Algebra of Conflict* (1968) and an article written for the influential journal *Voprosy filosofii* (1971), Lefebvre distinguished between two approaches to conflict. The first is an OR and game theory approach that seeks to establish the optimal strategy in the context of any given parameters. The second is what Lefebvre described as a new, loosely defined approach that explores the operation of human consciousness in conflict situations. Lefebvre termed this latter process as a "reflexive game," in which players reflect judgments of their opponents in their own consciousness.[83]

Lefebvre was skeptical about rational choice theories, particularly the Prisoner's Dilemma games, where no information was exchanged between players. However, this does not mean that he rejected rational choice. According to Lefebvre, experiments with such games provided "an external statistical description," which is only a first step in the exploration of internal cognitive mechanisms.[84] A formal description of consciousness could not be represented in the language of formal logic, based on fixed true and false values. This is because decisions in conflict situations necessarily operate on the basis of judgment and not a procedural search for truth.[85] However, Boolean algebra could be used to represent these cognitive operations, argued Lefebvre, helping to open up the black box of cognition, something that people do intuitively without much effort: "An escaper can escape from a persecutor only if he correctly projects on his own screen not only the activities of the persecutor, but also the way in which the persecutor is reflecting the activities of the escaper on his own screen."[86] In the reflexive game, "each opponent strives to reflect the other [and in so doing] thus gets an opportunity to outsmart him."[87] This model of reflection is partially based on formal logic as it tries to construct accurate presentations of reality, operating with "real" or "true" characteristics. But it does not stop there. The next step is to model exchange and relationality in the reflexive game, where the opponents try to consider each other's reflexive constrictions of each other, passing the values of true as false and of false as true.

In the Cold War context, this epistemological stance of mobilizing true/false values as performative rather than representational has interesting implications. In *Algebra of Conscience* Lefebvre refers to Edgar Allan Poe's story "The Purloined Letter," which describes a boy who outsmarts others. The boy's winning strategy is to identify with the opponent's intellect, assuming even the opponent's body language and emotive expressions.[88] This is an example of effective reflexivity, usefully summarized by Anatol Rapoport:

> A person experiences his feelings, beliefs, attitudes, etc. directly. Possibly a dog also experiences his feelings (e.g., hunger, rage) directly. A human being, however, has also higher orders of awareness. He can be aware of his own awareness. "This is good" is an expression of a feeling. "I know that this is good" expresses awareness of still higher order. As far as we know, only human beings are capable of "multiple-tier" awareness of this sort. Thus, a person has an "inner world" of which he is directly aware. He may also be aware of his awareness of his inner world, have an image of someone else's inner world, an image of someone else's image of his own inner world, etc.[89]

Lefebvre was not alone in positing the importance of intuition and identification with the opponent in decision situations—a similar idea was famously argued by the RAND analyst Bernard Brodie.[90] However, unlike the scholars of the RAND's Social Science Division, Lefebvre tried to find an algebraic expression of this internal game of mirrors. At the same time, he formulated a strong principle that deemed that a dialectical materialist approach and the Marxist–Leninist political criticism of Western capitalism were both deeply insufficient for a winning Cold War strategy. In the context of Soviet criticism of the idea of structural convergence of Western and state socialist economies and societies, Lefebvre claimed that some form of intellectual convergence with the opponent

142   CHAPTER 6

is absolutely necessary as a stage in strategic decision-making. Convergence, from this point of view, must be at once genuine *and* manipulative: the identification with the opponent should not lead to structural isomorphism and the adoption of the same goals and reconciliation.

The difficulty lay in making the recognition and reproduction of "the reality" (the opponent's perception of the situation) amenable to manipulation. As Lefebvre put it, there is a particular logic to reflexive games, "[O]ne cannot base this logic on the notions of 'true' and 'false'. Conflict situations are played out in a particular mode of reasoning, where, in contrast to a scientific dispute, the more sophisticated liar wins."[91] In the terms of reflexive control theory, "a more sophisticated liar" is "a player who has a greater level of reflexivity." This means that a player can articulate a whole system containing his/her own choices in relation to the opponent's choices that are also reflexively linked to his/her own choices.[92] However, in organizations or international relations, writes Lefebvre, players tend to have very similar imitational abilities. Parity in the capacity to simulate reflexive conflict situations poses a very difficult problem for reflexive control theory.[93]

The key claim of reflexive control theory is that sharing information with the opponent leads to a more predictable scenario of events. Information sharing can increase the chance of determining the opponent's future behavior. In his early publications, published in the 1960s, Lefebvre illustrated his theory with different examples, both hypothetical and borrowed from history. The arsenal of the means of deception included "provocations and intrigues," "disguise" (in Russian, *maskirovka*), "challenges," "creation of false objects," and "lies in general in all contexts."[94] Reflexive control could target different aspects of the opponent's mental world, for instance, to shape the opponent's goals. The most ambitious task of all is to shape the opponent's "doctrine," by which Lefebvre referred to "a certain algorithm, which helps to develop a solution from 'the goals' and 'the screen' [the reflexive presentation of the conflict situation]."[95] Further examples of reflexive control include passing on "the screen" to the opponent, the neutralization of the opponent's capacity to deduce the sequence of events from present situation, and identification of the opponent who is engaged in counterreflexive control.

Those actors who use game theory in their decision-making can be targeted with reflexive control. According to Lefebvre, "[G]ame theory, like any mathematical technique, can only be used when reality is schematized and reflected on 'the screen'"; therefore, a good strategist could feed the opponent with the information that will shape the preconditions of the game.[96] In this case, an interesting interplay of truthfulness and cheating emerges. A player X truthfully calculates according to a payoff matrix a result which provides X "with a sort of guarantee." This creates a strategic opportunity for the opponent Y, who "has a potential opportunity to 'pass' the information that benefits Y. On the basis of this information X will do a 'truthful' calculation, which will lead to X's loss." Lefebvre concludes that "[T]his type of 'dishonest' game is a type of an 'honest' reflexive control."[97]

In the model of reflexive control, the considerations of morality and ethics vanish. According to Lefebvre, because reflexive control "is not tainted with lies," social and moral constraints do not apply to it. This makes reflexive control an objective and universal method that can be used not only in conflict situations, but also in different areas of management.[98] However, what does it mean to apply a reflexive strategy in practice?

Reflexive Control in Practice

First of all, it is very difficult to observe and measure the impact of reflexive strategy, because it operates internally, as a semiotic projection. It is difficult to link occurring behaviors and decisions with acts of manipulation that cause them. Perhaps this is why the textbook examples of reflexive control often draw on dialogues and situations presented in fiction: in actual practice the thought process is not always expressed and documented in a conversation. However, is this not the case with any course of action that is presented as a result of strategy?

A good case in point is George Soros, an influential stock exchange speculator and global philanthropist, who claims that the awareness of reflexivity guides his investment decisions, particularly helping him to recognize the symptoms of boom and bust in financial markets. Born in Hungary in 1936, Soros emigrated to London in 1947 and studied economics at the London School of Economics (LSE). At the LSE, Soros also read philosophy with Karl Popper and adopted his ideas of the open society and the principle of falsifiability of theories as the key criterion of scientific knowledge. Following his studies, Soros worked in finance in the City of London. This experience made him realize the limitations of neoclassical models of the economy. Soros understood that stock markets do not behave like a natural world, which was presumed in economists' models, because it was expectations of financial markets that determined supply and demand, and not the other way around. As Christopher Bryant put it, Soros observed that participants in the markets respond not to the presumed fundamentals of value such as, for example, dividends and assets, but rather to the opinions of other participants. Like for the viewer of Velázquez's *Las Meninas*, the finance trader's reality is always mediated by the reflections of others, "markets can influence events they anticipate."[99] In 1956 Soros moved to New York and continued developing his interest in reflexivity in finance, when Lefebvre was grappling with reflexivity in

144   CHAPTER 6

military operations in Moscow.[100] Both Lefebvre and Soros would come to the conclusion that uncertainty that is generated by reflexivity cannot be resolved, but it can be acted upon and become an instrument of action.[101] As Soros put it, "[I]n the real world, the participants' thinking finds expression not only in statements but also, of course, in various forms of action and behavior. That makes reflexivity a much broader phenomenon than self-reference: it connects the universe of thoughts with the universe of events."[102] This connection, once known, could be profitably exploited:

> I developed my own variant of Popper's model of scientific method for use in the financial markets. I would formulate a hypothesis on the basis of which I would invest. . . . In contrast to science, a financial hypothesis does not have to be true to be profitable; it is enough that it should come to be generally accepted. But a false hypothesis cannot prevail forever. That is why I liked to invest in flawed hypotheses that had a chance of becoming generally accepted, provided I knew what the flaw was: It allowed me to sell in time. I called my flawed hypotheses fertile fallacies and I built my theory of history, as well as my success in financial markets, around them.[103]

According to Soros, strategic thinking is a reflexive practice, where subjects seek to gain adequate images of their opponents' minds in order to shape their own course of action, as well as to predict their opponents' behavior.[104] The concept of reflexivity, in this way, seeks to bridge individual cognitive processes and collective behavior. As Alex Rosenberg put it, for Soros, "reflexiveness is a relationship between strategies," that is expressed in manipulation or participation.[105] Historians and theorists of military and foreign policy strategies are principally interested in exploring the possibilities and limitations of, first, judging the situation correctly, and second, anticipating the opponents' behavior. The primary focus of such research is to help decision-makers to reduce their own misperceptions. Once correctly identified, the opponent's misperceptions can be exploited.[106]

In his memoir, Soros wrote that he took advantage of his opponents' misperceptions because thanks to those misperceptions the opponents behaved predictably. In contrast, Lefebvre wanted to find a mechanism in which the misperceptions could be planted in the opponent's mind to *make* the opponent's behavior predictable. In both cases, prediction is understood as a simple deduction of a course of action. It is not a probabilistic pattern recognition, but an inference based on the explanation provided by their theory. This is what enables both Lefebvre and Soros to claim that their approach is "scientific." The temporal horizon for both types of intervention, financial and military strategy, are generally short. The action cycle of reflexive deception (reflexive control for Lefebvre) or taking advantage of misperception (fertile fallacy for Soros) can work only once and, ideally, in a very straightforward situation where there is sufficient information. Once complex Popperian philosophy and Boolean algebra are put aside, one cannot help but notice that the reflexive practices suggested by Lefebvre and Soros are quite common sense. Why bother, then, to present these techniques of taking advantage or cheating as a scientifically grounded strategy?

The answer could be found in the symbolic meaning of the very notion of strategy. According to Luca Zan, strategy theory oscillates between two opposing poles. At one extreme, strategy is expressed in highly abstract models of mental cognition such as rational choice and other models in decision science. At the other extreme, the idea of rational decision is abandoned entirely; strategy is approached as a purely pragmatic behavior, situated in a particular context which can be observed and researched ethnographically but not from the perspective of logic or mathematics.[107]

One way of bridging the pragmatic and abstract approaches to strategy is to consider both forms of strategic thinking as social phenomena that perform a symbolic organizational function.[108] This notion posits strategy as a complex mediator that enables different actors to perform together, providing "an obligatory point of passage, whereby [strategy] enacts and connects an organization and its world."[109] Thanks to this power to connect different actors and actions, strategic thought can perform not so much as a decision tool, but as a symbol.[110] The symbolic power of strategy lies in its capacity to explicate and embody scientific rationality and modernity in an organizational context.[111]

Although modern governments and firms have always engaged in some form of planning their future, the discourse of strategy as a key governmental instrument became widespread only beginning in the mid-twentieth century. During and after the Second World War, strategic approaches were developed in large US corporations and then further advanced by the military-industrial complex. From the 1970s onward, strategy became institutionalized as an academic subject in US and West European universities, particularly in the newly founded business schools.[112] The US business school approach to strategy was based on industrial economics; however, the field was much more diverse in Europe, where sociological approaches informed strategy thought.[113] In the Soviet Union, industrial economics and sociology did not thrive as they were classified as bourgeois sciences, designed to empower managers and therefore deemed unsuitable to the egalitarian Soviet society. Soviet strategic thought, however, was mainly anchored in the so-called exact sciences, appearing in the fields of cybernetics, OR, and systems analysis, but also, as it turned out in the case of Lefebvre, cognitive psychology.

146   CHAPTER 6

As a result of the spread and proliferation of strategy as an organizational device in corporations, firms, and government departments, as well as the belief that strategy can improve performance and enable better accountability and control, many leading Western and Soviet intellectuals and policymakers came to consider strategic thought as a symbol of late modernity itself. A history of strategy's talismanic role could shed new light on strategy as the expression of a particular Cold War modernity. In line with organization scholars John W. Meyer and Brian Rowan, as well as Carter, Clegg, and Kornberger, it can be proposed that strategy has become an institutionalized myth that confers legitimacy on organizations.[114]

This is a particularly important insight when considering the deployment of reflexivity in Russia's military operations in the twenty-first century, leading to what the British journalist Edward Lucas has described as the New Cold War. Reflexive control, according to the US military analyst Timothy Thomas, informed Soviet and post-Soviet operations planning at many stages, from being aware of possible targeting by reflexive control to enacting reflexive control of the West through publishing Russian military doctrines, from nuclear deterrence to internet phishing and leaks of confidential documents.[115] The analysts listed the following events as evidence of reflexive control: covert actions of "little green men" (the obfuscated Russian forces) in Crimea, the fake footage of the escalation of the Donetsk–Luhansk conflict in 2014 (actors were employed to play the victimized East Ukrainians in footage that was broadcast on Russian news channels), and different messages sent to different audiences reporting the downing of Malaysian Airlines flight MH17 in July 2014.[116] The goal of these activities is said to replace the existing "interpretative screen" with one that would lead Western leaders to take decisions that are advantageous for Russia. For instance, cyber forces defaced Ukrainian and Polish websites by placing visuals linking the nationalist content with fascist symbols, and they hacked billboards in Kiev to display casualties and describe the leaders of the nationalist movement as war criminals.[117] It was suggested that Russia's informational warfare operations in Ukraine achieved their objective because the Russian government managed to maintain plausible denial of involvement for a considerable time, simultaneously minimizing the threshold of violence so as not to prompt an international reaction. The Russian annexation of Crimea is presented as the culmination of a decade of "cognitive operations," which solidified the Russian identity and undermined the West in the eyes of Crimean residents and in Russia proper.[118] The Russian cyber operators also targeted the West: the North Atlantic Treaty Organization (NATO) computer system, the European Union (EU) referendum campaign in the United Kingdom, and the presidential election in the United States. They bought commercials spreading divisive content and sent phishing emails in summer 2015 and spring 2016 to targets in the United States, when the presidential election campaigns were announced. An estimated 2.5 percent of receivers clicked on a malware link, enabling hackers to gain access to documents and monitor information on their computers. Only in October 2016 Russia was accused with interfering in the elections.[119]

These activities are described as symptoms of informational warfare, which was enshrined in Russia's strategic documents and in the institutions it built, for instance, establishing information operations forces, which was announced by Russia's Minister of Defense in 2017.[120] Among the outcomes of these efforts, according to the analysts, were an attempt to frame the Ukrainian democracy movement as a fascist revolution and to undermine trust in the procedures of the presidential election in the United States and the EU membership referendum in the United Kingdom. The intensity of engagement was attributed to the availability of digital means to spread information on a large scale and was compared with the propaganda exchange that used to occur during major wars in the twentieth century.[121] However, Russia's strategic deception preceding the invasion in Ukraine in February 2022 was regarded as unprecedented.

Given the range of diversity of actions in this context it is necessary to ask under what conditions a particular course of action gets recognized as a "strategic" one. Actions and events can be retrospectively described as "strategic," although they might appear as mundane or opportunistic when they are happening.[122] In a similar vein, when is manipulation a mere lie and when does it become reflexive control? Insights from organizational sociologists might be relevant here. According to Carter, Clegg, and Kornberger, strategic thought is about power garnering and self-legitimation: "Bearing the name of strategy, a particular form of rationality gets made up; one that is very good at rationalizing and sanctioning itself in the name of the 'bigger picture,' the 'mission,' 'the future' and other heroic images."[123] From this perspective, the rise of reflexive control theory in post-Soviet Russian policy discourses begins to make more sense: its mission is to offer a "bigger picture" and to legitimize existing and new constellations of power relations. When deception is not just a lie, but part of "reflexive control," the work of a policymaker, a journalist, an actor, and a soldier can acquire an aura of professionalism and legitimacy. If the symbolic power of strategy is to link different actors in a functional, pragmatic framework of action where meaning-making plays an important role, reflexive control theory can be said to work, even in the absence of a clear causal link between strategy and events.

Conclusion

Every conflict, wrote Lefebvre, is primarily "an intellectual exchange," where cognition is a special form of power.[124] Indeed, Soviet and post-Soviet Russian

148   CHAPTER 6

attempts to harness reflexivity to control behavior must be read in the context of what Bruno Latour described as the dream of governing at a distance, a form of governance that is possible only through multiple translations that may appear weak: "What we so much admire in the Greek miracle is a reversal of power relations: the weakest, that is, a tiny people holding only shadows and paper forms become stronger than the ancient and powerful Egyptians with their heavy stone pyramids."[125] These shadows and paper forms, in the cases discussed in this chapter, are the sketches of cognitive schemes of others. These sketches of reflexive systems are sorting mechanisms that help generate, group, and report the different narratives, labels, and programming codes as part of reflexive strategy. Although Russia was described as "the most advanced nation in informational warfare," reflexive control expresses a wider desire to influence and shape the behavior of others so that it becomes predictable.[126]

In the Cold War context, reflexive control theory appealed to the status of exact knowledge, even science, because it posited the strong need for knowledge of the opponent's perspective as a prerequisite for Soviet strategic advantage. To practice reflexive control meant to formulate research agendas that would go beyond ideological caricatures of the behavior of capitalist powers. It called for a nuanced empirical and psychological understanding of Soviet and Western societies. Both qualities, Lefebvre hoped, could be described and modeled in the networks of Boolean algebra. However, whereas this epistemological realism was a welcome addition to Soviet science, the control part of Lefebvre's theory of reflexivity remained deeply problematic and, ultimately, unresolved. How can one know if one's own premises are passed on successfully to the opponent? Was not Lefebvre's hope to formalize reflexive games in a mathematical language set to fail from the start?

For Popperian thinkers such as Soros, reflexivity was a source of misconceptions, leading to market failures; Soros claimed to be able to identify these misconceptions at the right moment and take advantage of them.[127] Lefebvre hoped that that unruly reflexivity, just like dark matter in physics, could be harnessed for governmental purposes, that there was a way to describe and order the reflexive chaos. However, as Lefebvre noted himself, the reflexive control principle worked best when the opponent was not aware of it being applied.[128] Once reflexive control enters a loop of intersubjective reflexivity, it soon becomes practically useless, because complexity increases. Counterreflections become unmanageable and the opponent ceases to be predictable. This insurmountable informational barrier constitutes a serious limitation of reflexive control theory. A logical outcome of the overflow of reflexivity would be, following Lefebvre's own observation, to dumb down the opponent: the greater the intellectual gap between the reflexive capacity of conflicting agents, the better the chance of outsmarting the opponent. In this respect, Russia's effort to spread false information both at home and abroad, which has intensified to the extreme during the war in Ukraine, coheres well with some of the principles of Lefebvre's reflexive strategy, where the identity of the reflecting subject is being transformed, for instance, when Putin accuses Western countries of being "the empire of lies" and his strategists argue that the spread of disinformation is nothing but "an ultra, super truth" in the context of the military conflict. During the early days of the war in Ukraine it does appear that reflexive control is being deployed at home, targeting the Russian population, as much as abroad.

It is difficult to assess the exact impacts of the deployment of reflexive control. Historians of traditional strategy can evaluate strategic principles and plans in the light of additional data describing the events. However, historians of reflexive control face the difficulty of the very identification of relevant events. Whereas grand strategy debates entail often lofty considerations of geopolitics, rationality, and history, reflexive control theory appears as a technical device empowering the deception and manipulation of individuals.

The obvious conceptual weakness of reflexive control theory is its failure to consider the opacity of language, translation, and meaning-making. It relies too heavily on the assumption that actors will think consistently and seek to make their decisions align with their actions. The Soviet Russian theorists' attempt to make reflexivity work is certainly a signal of a strong modernist hope in taming chaos and chance, this time both being located inside and not outside of the decision-maker. Decades later, in the context of Russia's war in Ukraine reflexive control appears to be used not as a rational decision-making tool, but as a justification, legitimization, and identity shaping device.

7

GLOBAL PREDICTION
From Targeting to Orchestration

This final chapter concludes the intellectual journey of scientific prediction in Russian and Cold War modernity. It presents an attempt to address what is probably the most challenging task for scientific prediction—to generate knowledge about extremely complex, large-scale, and long-term phenomena, knowledge that would be faithful to reality and, at the same time, actionable, useful for collective decision-makers. This ambition is no less bold than the Newtonian desire to discover the mechanical laws of the universe enabling us to understand and operate the physical world. It is also destined to fail. However, as I show in this chapter, the failure to make such scientific predictions could be and was productive. The iterative process of preparing large-scale, long-term predictions can bring about significant social and political impacts, for it entails an important form of orchestration of the future.

At the moment of writing, in 2022, few would disagree that the risks posed by the ongoing global climate crisis demand scientific predictions. At the same time, journalists and members of the public have been agonizing over the range of possible outcomes that scientists have been predicting, as well as the shortage of predictions that are specific in terms of time and space. In order to make predictive knowledge actionable, decision-makers will need to know what exactly the thresholds of the warming of the atmosphere and the ocean are, where will winds, rains, floods, and droughts hit, and when. These are Comtean criteria of scientific prediction, so deeply ingrained in policy thinking, but which cannot be fulfilled in the context of global changes. However, as I showed in previous chapters, the limitations of positivist prediction were questioned by the Russian economist Nikolai Kondrat'ev in the 1920s and the US mathematician Norbert Wiener in the 1950s and 1960s. They both argued that the Comtean model of scientific prediction is too simplistic and cannot cope with high complexity. While these and other thinkers agreed that not all complex phenomena could be scientifically predicted, they also pushed the conceptual reach of scientific prediction so that it could still be of use in the science of fleeting phenomena. After all, they agreed that without the will to predict there could be no science.

The very role of predictability as a criterion of the scientificity of knowledge became a central concern in the field of Earth system governmentality, an interdisciplinary area of study that combines the perspectives of environmental history, international organization, and studies of science and technology to investigate the social and political consequences of the emerging role of mankind as a geological force.[1] In the 1960s and the 1970s Earth system scientists became convinced that the rigid, positivist notion of prediction could not cross the threshold of high complexity, in terms of both knowledge and action.[2] In this chapter I trace this process by examining the intellectual contribution to the debates on scientific prediction made by a prominent Soviet Russian scientist, policy entrepreneur, and public intellectual, Nikita Moiseev (1917–2000). Moiseev's thought forms a particularly important part of the global history of scientific prediction, bridging the histories of cybernetics and systems analysis, on the one side, and the histories of authoritarian, liberal, and infrastructural governance, on the other side. Following an outline of Moiseev's intellectual biography, the main part of the chapter details how computer-based policy sciences shaped the epistemological framework of late Soviet thought on Earth systems governance (what Moiseev identified as the noosphere) and the role of predictability. The chapter concludes with a discussion of the transformation of the notion of governance from purposive control to guidance through milieus. This, I propose, constituted an important shift to embrace the collective, synchronizing role of scientific prediction as it goes beyond cognitive operation as in logical empiricism and beyond target-seeking processes of adaptation in cybernetic behaviorism.

Prediction, Milieu, and the Anthropocene

Before we proceed, it can be useful to remind the reader about the conceptual features of cybernetic prediction (presented in chapter 3), because it bridged the transition from a positivist notion of prediction as the knowledge of facts that can be explained with reference to general laws to a performative notion of

CHAPTER 7

prediction as a behavioral process that is part of the adaptation and modification of the environment. In Norbert Wiener's cybernetics, the governance of behavior or what would be called dynamic systems is an informational process, which can be characterized by the following stages. First, a desirable state of a governable system (a target) is identified. Then, a path for reaching this target is decided on the basis of observation of what is actually happening (the actual behavior of the system). This observation of what is happening must be continuous, for the environment is changing: for example, a mouse or an enemy pilot is evading the pursuer, air temperatures or market values are fluctuating. Observations of these changes are channeled to the decision-making center (the brain of the predator, the investor, or the computer powering the antiaircraft missile system), which issues signals to start the corresponding action (to anticipate the future location of the mouse in order to catch it, to estimate the future location of the enemy plane in order to shoot it, or to estimate the market value of shares to buy or sell them). This information flow that feeds into action was described by Wiener as feedback loops.

This model of cybernetic control through feedback loops was highly practical. It was applied to both the study and the engineering of integral, hybrid systems that could incorporate men, machines, and biological processes.[3] It has made possible automatic lift doors, digital prosthetics, self-driving vehicles, digital marketing on social media, telecom queuing, and medical diagnostic systems, among other things.

However, there were limits to the scalability of cybernetic control: it is one thing to create a self-driving metro line or even a car, and another to create a self-regulating urban transport system. It is possible to create a functioning thermostat for a room or even a large building, but such buildings must be strongly isolated from their environment, forming a system that is linked with their environment in a highly controlled manner (insulation, solar panels, window shades, and rain collection points, for example). Some environmental scientists initially embraced the cybernetic principle to conceptualize the self-regulation of ecological systems, such as rivers, lakes, or populations of plants and animals, while others, like James Lovelock, were even more ambitious and thought that the entire planet Earth could be characterized as such a cybernetic self-regulating system. However, as the empirical data were beginning to accumulate in the 1970s and 1980s, Earth system scientists understood that they could not rely solely on the cybernetic control theory to conceptualize and steer human intervention in global change. The problem of shooting an agile enemy bomber during the Second World War, which had given rise to cybernetics, was a very different problem from the challenge posed by the accumulation of carbon dioxide in the atmosphere and the slow melting of glacial ice. Control of long-term and large-scale processes was of a different order, as their scale exceeded the frameworks of human time. In this case, the horizons of change stretched from seconds as in the cat and mouse chase, from decades as in economic planning, to hundreds and thousands of years.

This new problem of large-scale, long-term, and complex change called for a revision of the intellectual apparatus of governance. As I show in this chapter, neither positivist nor cybernetic notions of scientific prediction were abolished as such. Instead, they were carefully orchestrated into layers of complexity. To put it in a simple way, at a low level of complexity a positivist, Comtean or logical empiricist prediction could be used, for instance in mechanical engineering and hypothesis testing. At a higher level of complexity where not only facts but also behaviors are in question and where short-term adaptation is required for achieving goals, cybernetic prediction can serve well, in, for instance, human communication and a self-driving car. The models of reflexive control and prospective reflexivity can be deployed to manage social interactions in groups. In the cases of long-term and large-scale processes, where the reach of positivist, logical empiricist and cybernetic predictions is extremely limited, the emphasis shifts to creating *milieus* in which all of these types of predictions could operate in a viable way.

Governance of the long term and large scale becomes the orchestration of decision and behavior environments: creating institutional, legal, and material limits and channels for decisions and actions that operate with these lower-level predictions. The role of milieu is to guide the behaviors and processes that are driven by mechanisms that could be "predicted."

The orientation to milieu as an epistemological and governmental approach was not meant to replace but to complement scientific prediction as a cognitive operation. Indeed, the term goes as far back as modern scientific predictions: the concept of milieu was referenced in nineteenth-century sciences that described and conceptualized relationality, such as mathematics, evolutionary biology, neurophysiology, and psychology. The idea of milieu as an epistemological device for curing organisms and shaping individual and collective behaviors has been analyzed in a range of excellent histories of medicine, science and technology. Milieu informed the late twentieth century's complexity science and resilience approach. In the early twenty-first century, governance through milieu has been addressed in the work on neoliberal governmentality and behavioral public policy.[4]

The idea that governance through milieu constitutes a distinct form of state intervention in the fields characterized by great complexity and uncertainty, such as, for instance, human population, was proposed by Michel Foucault in his lectures delivered at the Collège de France in 1978 and 1979.[5] With governance through milieu, Foucault tried to capture those forms of steering and control that did not seek to influence individuals as discrete agents, whose minds and wills were sources of action, but rather focused on their "environment." Here "environment" referred to material systems of relations, in which these individuals were embedded and upon which they were functionally dependent. Foucault's use of the concept "milieu" was significantly influenced by the writings of his doctoral examiner and mentor Georges Canguilhem.[6] According to Canguilhem, the modern scientific notion of milieu refers to relationality itself, where it is impossible to separate the object from its environment.[7] As I showed in the earlier chapters, this notion of milieu to which Canguilhem referred was developed by biologists and particularly neurophysiologists in the early twentieth century, whereas its crudely simplified and mechanistic version was adopted by B. F. Skinner and in some forms of behaviorist psychology.[8] As Skinner's behaviorism was rejected as unethical and conceptually flawed, the concepts of milieu and behavior became suspect in many critical cultural disciplines. However, the ongoing research in psychological and neurological sciences as well as social and cultural studies, especially the studies of digital culture, that embraced the cybernetic concepts of system, materiality, complexity, and informational regulation constitutes a growing field where the coproduction of the self, behavior, and milieu are analyzed beyond Skinnerian behaviorism.[9]

Since the 1980s, Foucault's idea of government through milieu has inspired several influential research agendas: Foucauldian scholars historicized colonial attempts to use different milieus, or complex material and institutional infrastructures, to control at a distance those colonial subjects who were deemed unable to reflexively govern themselves.[10] Urban sociologists and media theorists focused on infrastructural milieus' effects on social and political practices.[11] Environmental sociologists and historians created the new term environmentality to analyze the emerging global climate governance.[12] While these government through milieu studies developed in disparate fields, they share a focus on the governmental effects of different types of material milieus, be they urban architecture, roads, or digital networks, but also regulatory milieus such as the architecture of financial and economic systems.[13]

This chapter introduces the conceptual shift from target-oriented governance to government through milieu as it took shape as part of the attempts to create a new world order during the Cold War. These were attempts to reorchestrate the politics and organization of data and scientific knowledge so that they could be deployed to predict the global environmental future. These efforts, as Moiseev's example shows, led to fundamental revision of authoritarian dogmas of governability, the role of scientific expertise in global governance, and concepts of man's relationship with nature. I argue that through this process, a Soviet version of Earth system governmentality has emerged. The Soviet Earth system governmentality shared strong parallels with what has been described as a classical liberal model of negative governance (the night watch state) as well as with

Friedrich von Hayek's approach to global nongovernability. Both classical liberal and von Hayek's approaches emphasized the creation of institutional and informational milieus that would guide individual and collective behaviors by preventing and limiting their consequences, rather than by establishing policy and management targets. The liberal notion of limited governance coupled with active intervention in orchestration of the milieu rose to prominence thanks to the advancement of computer modeling technology and the attempts to manage Cold War tensions through East–West intellectual transfer. Rethinking the epistemology of scientific prediction was key to this process.

In previous chapters I detailed the ways in which Soviet scientists approached scientific prediction in the economy and management. This chapter concerns the Soviet contribution to Earth system governance and its role in what was named by the Dutch atmospheric scientist Paul Crutzen as the era of the Anthropocene. Crutzen attributed his concept's intellectual origins to Russian theories of the biosphere and noosphere.[14] The origin of the concept of the biosphere, that part of the Earth's layer constituting of living matter, dates to the second half of the nineteenth century. Conversely, its sibling concept, the noosphere, was developed by the Russian geologist and natural scientist Vladimir Vernadskii (1863–1945) and French philosophers Pierre Teilhard de Chardin and Edouard Le Roy, whom Vernadskii met in Paris from 1922 to 1925.[15] Vernadskii's book *The Biosphere* (published in Russia in 1926 and first translated into English only in 1986) posited that living matter was shaped through the interaction of solar energy and biogeophysical processes. While Teilhard de Chardin coined the concept of the noosphere to describe the ultimate stage of human progress, where cosmos, god, reason, and the material world would unite, Vernadskii saw the noosphere as a stage of the development of living matter, the biosphere, where humankind becomes a geological force and human reason (*razum* in Russian) acquires power to drive the change.[16] A noosphere is therefore a particular stage of biospheric development, where global coevolution becomes governable.[17]

Vernadskii's legacy significantly shaped Soviet thought on global governance during the Cold War as his geophysical philosophy was extended beyond the natural sciences into the new field of decision and policy sciences, characterized by operations research (OR), economic and management cybernetics, and systems analysis.[18] Yet as I show, the unique challenges of global environmental governance required a substantive revision of the scientific concept of prediction. It was Nikita Moiseev who offered this revision, transforming Vernadskii's geophysical philosophy into an applied policy science, entrenched in the global concerns of the Cold War. For Moiseev, to govern the global biosphere required the invention of new policy sciences, which would enable humanity to step into what Vernadskii described as a stage of the noosphere.

156   CHAPTER 7

However, neither Comtean positivist nor a cybernetic notion of prediction could help to serve as a criterion of scientificity and a guiding mechanism for action. In this chapter I argue that Moiseev, in Nikolai Kondrat'ev's spirit, addressed the central problem of scientific (un)governability head on, as he pointed out that scientific prediction of global change cannot be achieved by a simple combination of statistical methods of data production and a cybernetic model of feedback-based information processing. Like Norbert Wiener, Moiseev called for a substantive reorchestration of the social and material universe so as to make the world future predictable. Scientific prediction, in other words, was a futile cognitive experiment if it was not embedded in an institutional reform. Moiseev hoped to see a new, global ecology to predict itself into being and, in that process, erode Cold War divides.

Indeed, Moiseev was a patron of global computer modeling in the Soviet Union, and in the early 1980s he cooperated with Crutzen on the famous nuclear winter study, a computer simulation of the environmental effects of nuclear war. While the legacy of the nuclear winter study can certainly be seen in Crutzen's formulation of the Anthropocene theory, Moiseev used the nuclear winter simulation to argue that the idea of governing the global biosphere was not an intellectual utopia, but a challenge for policy science. Furthermore, the Soviet political context was becoming receptive to Moiseev's ideas, because, as Vladislav Zubok detailed in his exhaustive history of the last decade of the Soviet Union, in the late 1970s and first half of the 1980s, a strong political consensus emerged to reform the system of political administration and economic planning.[19] This reformist orientation was accelerated by Mikhail Gorbachev, whom Moiseev advised both when Gorbachev was the chairman of the Stavropol region and the general secretary of the Communist Party of the Soviet Union (CPSU).[20] The area of burning concern was the failure of Soviet agriculture to deliver food to the population; Moiseev initiated the development of a computerized decision-making model for agricultural development in the Stavropol region, a project which was implemented in cooperation with the International Institute of Applied Systems Analysis (IIASA) in Laxenburg, Austria.[21] The extent of Moiseev's contribution to the late Soviet domestic and foreign policy will not be clear until his archival materials become available in the future. It is clear, however, that Moiseev worked closely with Gorbachev's aides Ivan Frolov and Vadim Zagladin in this way feeding directly to the idea of the new world order promoted by Gorbachev. This is not surprising, because, as the historian Vladislav Zubok observed, Gorbachev was deeply committed to the development of new intellectual approaches to governance.[22] Moiseev was also central to the introduction of "global problems" as a priority area in the CPSU's long-term plan in 1986; the global problems included such issues as carbon dioxide emissions, world population growth, and world energy resources, all of which could not be resolved within the boundaries of a single state. In addition to high-level policy engagement, Moiseev had a wide societal impact as a prolific popularizer of science: his books were published in runs of thousands of copies and were widely read in society and by managerial elites in the 1980s. Since Moiseev's death in 2000, his intellectual legacy has been fostered by institutes of the Russian Academy of Sciences and leading university departments.[23] In the next section I present Moiseev's intellectual biography, for his figure deserves to be included in the international cast of what Quinn Slobodian described as globalists, forgers of the new world's conceptual and institutional order to implement neoliberal, limited government.[24] However, while Western neoliberal globalists shared their background in economic and social sciences, Moiseev arrived at similar insights from mathematics and Earth system modeling.

An Institutional Entrepreneur of the Soviet Anthropocene

To trace the biography of Moiseev, a scholar who bridged different political regimes, social worlds, and scientific disciplines, is to trace central shifts in governance in the twentieth century. The story of Moiseev is the story of the communist revolution and Russian nationalism rooted in an imperial past, but also of technoscientific modernity, based on postpositivist epistemology and global thinking. It is also a story of the search for political rationality and control with the help of the instruments of technoscience, leading to fundamental revision of what it means to be rational. To do justice to the personality of Moiseev is therefore beyond the limits of this chapter; I introduce only briefly his intellectual and political trajectory.

Born in Moscow in 1917, Moiseev grew up in a noble family, the legacy of which, as he detailed in his memoirs, was expressed in his deep skepticism toward the Communist Party, although Moiseev passionately endorsed the socialist principle of social equality and regarded himself as a communist. Moiseev's maternal grandparents died in cholera epidemics and his mother was adopted by a Baltic German aristocrat Nikolai Karlovich von Meck (1863–1929), an influential railway entrepreneur and patron of the arts. The household of von Meck hosted such luminaries as Claude Debussy and Pyotr Tchaikovsky, the latter a member of the extended family. Nikita Moiseev's father, Nikolai Moiseev, graduated from the law faculty at Moscow State University (MGU), was keenly interested in economics and statistics, and studied Japanese language and economics as a diplomat in Tokyo. The Moiseev family suffered Stalin's repressions: the adoptive grandfather

158   CHAPTER 7

was shot in 1929 and Moiseev's father was killed in Butyrki prison in 1931. However, Moiseev joined the Communist Party during the Second World War, motivated by his patriotic feelings for Russia rather than to the party. In his memoir, Moiseev reflected extensively on his relationship to Soviet Russia, trying to reconcile his interest in science and service to the state with his painful family history.[25] The trajectory of the Moiseev family can be well understood through the lens of the viability of the imperial Russian social estates, which, as Tomila Lankina detailed, continued reproducing and generating social solidarity regardless of the brutal repression and bureaucratic imposition of the communist class system.[26]

The young Moiseev attended the mathematical seminars for talented children organized by the prominent mathematician Israel Gel'fand at the renowned Steklov Institute of Mathematics; he won a national competition in mathematics and passed the exams for the prestigious MGU department of mathematics and mechanics. However, Moiseev was refused a place on the course because of his bourgeois background; only thanks to Gel'fand's personal support was Moiseev eventually enrolled at the university, from where he graduated in 1941.[27] Immediately Moiseev was recruited to the army, appointed as an engineer to the air force, and sent to the frontline.

After the war, in 1948 to 1949 Moiseev was employed in the military-industrial complex specializing in rocket technology: as a senior engineer, he worked on dynamics and ballistics at the missile design institute NII-2 of the Ministry of the Aviation Industry and taught the dynamics of guided missiles at the Bauman Moscow State Technical University, where he met some of the key scientists behind the Soviet space program, such as Iurii Pobedonostsev, Sergei Korolev, and Vladimir Chelomei.[28] However, in 1949 the Moiseev family were again repressed: his elderly stepmother was arrested, Moiseev was fired, and he fled from Moscow in 1950, finding shelter in the Rostov State University in Southwestern Russia, where he taught hydromechanics. Only at the beginning of the Thaw in 1956, when Nikita Khrushchev denounced Stalin's terror and personality cult, could Moiseev return to Moscow. The influential academician Mikhail Lavrent'ev, the founder of the principal Soviet science city, Akademgorodk, in Novosibirsk, invited Moiseev to become a professor and dean at the Department of Control and Applied Mathematics (which trained specialists for the Soviet space program) at the Moscow Physics-Technical Institute (MFTI). In the same year Moiseev was appointed as a researcher at the Computer Center of the Soviet Academy of Sciences, where he would work for more than three decades.[29] In 1966 Moiseev became a corresponding member of the Soviet Academy of Sciences (full member in 1970) and was appointed as a vice-director for research of the Computer Center in 1967. Moiseev's scientific contribution to the Soviet military-industrial complex, particularly space, aviation, and nuclear programs (from 1956 he had clearance to access high-level classified data), and his unparalleled social skills propelled him into the position of research director at the Computer Center in the Soviet Academy of Sciences. The Computer Center became established as the leading research center in computer science, applied mathematics, and automation, providing support, for instance, for Pavel Sukhoi's jet-fighter design lab.

In addition to tapping into the Cold War arms race and the expansion of the Soviet military-industrial complex, Moiseev's career coincided with the opening of the Soviet system to the West and Prime Minister Kosygin's call to introduce scientific forecasting into Soviet planning and management, which I discussed in chapter 4. Here Moiseev bridged the gap between academia and government by initiating several strategically important and intellectually innovative fields: OR, the systems approach, and, from the 1970s, computer-based modeling of complex environmental and socioeconomic processes. Having established a solid reputation as an applied mathematician, Moiseev worked closely with several founding figures of innovative research institutions, such as Lavrent'ev; scholars working in diverse fields falling under the umbrella term of cybernetics, including the influential mathematician Aleksandr Lyapunov, who taught Moiseev mathematics at university in the 1930s, and with whom Moiseev had a long-lasting friendship; and Viktor Glushkov, who would launch the ambitious but unsuccessful program of the all-union computer network.[30] Fluent in French (he also read English), Moiseev traveled abroad and actively forged links with leading Western scholars. These trips inspired Moiseev to integrate Vernadskii's theory of the biosphere and noosphere with computer-based control sciences.

The Soviet 1960s were characterized by continued technoscientific optimism, but also by growing awareness of the ineffectiveness of centralized planning, stalling economic growth, concern with the environment, and increasing pollution.[31] Moiseev encountered what Sverker Sörlin and Paul Warde described as the emerging "integrative imagination" of environmental change as a mathematician specializing in control processes.[32] The idea of the environment as a system of relations which is changing and needs to be explained, and not just a context that can be used to explain changes in organisms, emerged after 1948 in the writings of William Vogt and Fairfield Osborn.[33] In 1955, a Wenner-Gren symposium, "Man Changing the Face of the Earth," consolidated what would become environmental thinking as a form of concern about global, long-term, and future-oriented changes. The term "environment" entered policy use in 1957 when the British governmental science advisor Solly Zuckerman proposed the notion of the "environmental sciences."[34] The development of Soviet scientific environmental thinking was rooted in the nineteenth century's scoping for resources and the subsequent work on the Earth's "living matter" in the spirit of Vernadskii. As Jonathan Oldfield noted, in the 1960s Russian scientists coined the concept of biogeocenose, which resembled the Western concept of ecosystem.[35] Moiseev's writings draw on this Russian scientific tradition at the same time expressing similar concerns to those of the systems scholars Donella and Dennis Meadows, the polymath James Lovelock, and the economist Kenneth Boulding, to mention but a few Earth system thinkers who crossed disciplinary boundaries to conceptualize coevolving Earth and human systems in the 1970s and 1980s. However, in contrast to the Meadows, Lovelock, and Boulding, Moiseev distinctively focused on the epistemology of governance and control, becoming in effect a philosopher of public policy.

By the 1960s the Soviet policy science community was ready to embrace the environmental turn not only because they were concerned with the pollution and preservation of nature. Soviet scholars were also attracted to the concept of the environment as a hybrid system, which integrated human and nonhuman actors. Conceived as part of the environmental system, society and human behavior could be explored scientifically outside Marxist–Leninist dogma according to which economic structures and property relations determined social and cultural forms.[36] To define the communist society as "Earth's living matter" meant to depoliticize the social in terms of the official ideology. Of course, such depoliticization was regarded as political in its own right, creating new forms of agency and institutional autonomy. The freedom it offered, however, was relative: as I showed in previous chapters, scientists experienced many institutional obstacles to accessing data and providing direct input in policymaking, despite the Soviet government's investment in the economic applications of mathematics. For instance, being a specialist in dynamic programming and optimization of decision-making in technical systems, Moiseev was enthusiastic about applying his expertise to economic planning and began to advise the State Planning Committee (Gosplan) regarding the development of social indicators of economic growth. However, having encountered the institutional reality of absent data and fragmentation, Moiseev realized that Gosplan's planning process was not based on scientific expertise, but on political bargaining among enterprises as well as what accounted as social and organizational rituals of the high-level economy of favors.[37] Even from a scientific point of view there was not much that Moiseev could have contributed: not only was the quality of the economic statistics data poor, but access to it was very limited. But this did not matter in the end, because like Friedrich von Hayek, Moiseev became convinced that the economy was too complex to be mathematized. As Moiseev put it, the very assumption of regular economic development and planning (in Russian, *planomernoe razvitie*) was conceptually erroneous. Quantitative policy science alone, argued Moiseev, could not guarantee efficient governance of the national economy, be it communist or capitalist.

In the same decade, from the 1960s to the 1970s, Hayek, an economist, encountered systems theory and the mathematician and systems theorist Moiseev approached economy as a governmental problem.[38] Hayek did not read Moiseev, but he read writings on cybernetic self-regulation, while Moiseev read Hayek, which stimulated his interest further in the role of scientific expertise in the government of complex systems. Moiseev crystallized this view during his visits as a guest professor at Yale University, where he was invited by the economist Tjalling Koopmans—who later won the Nobel Prize—in 1974 and 1976.[39] In a paper presented for the Yale faculty, Moiseev proposed the idea of the ultimate ungovernability of economics. Just like Norbert Wiener, Moiseev argued that socioeconomic processes were far too complex to be captured by existing computer modeling techniques.[40] Moiseev even suggested that the term "planned economy" was an oxymoron. He proposed to use the term "guided economy" instead of governed (or controlled) economy (*napravliaemaia ekonomika* instead of *upravliaemaia ekonomika*, in Russian). Koopmans, invested in linear programming methods, reportedly, "did not like this paper at all," which did not bother Moiseev very much, but the Russian scientist was apprehensive about the possible political consequences of his talk. Moiseev was relieved to find out later that back in Moscow "no one had even noticed it."[41]

In his memoir, Moiseev reported having lost his belief, in the late 1960s, in the capacity of positivist science and mathematical applications to make long-term economic forecasts, which could come across as ironic, because in 1968 he established what would become one of the leading centers of economic modeling in the country.[42] But in doing this, Moiseev developed a reflexive approach to computer modeling and prediction. Like Nikolai Kondrat'ev in the 1920s, Moiseev argued that macroeconomic models can give "at best" a snapshot of the present and that their capacity to produce reliable long-term forecasts is close to zero. He wrote this bluntly in his confidential letter to the head of Soviet research and development, the vice-chairman of the State Committee for Science and Technology (GKNT) in 1980.[43] Convinced that the growth of scientific expertise increases the rate of change in socioeconomic systems, because increasing availability of knowledge makes decision-making harder rather than easier, Moiseev turned to the issues of complexity, evolution, and self-organization. Considering that policy sciences could be more fruitfully applied to environmental problems than economical ones, particularly in the Soviet context, he began to develop computer-based modeling of the biosphere and to rethink the fundamentals of scientific knowability and governance.[44]

Moiseev did not develop these ideas in isolation: encounters with Vernadskiian scholars and links with Western scientists were vital. Moiseev himself wrote

162   CHAPTER 7

that his interest in global systems and biosphere emerged during his visit to a French research center dedicated to the management of large technical systems in Fontainebleau near Paris. This was a formative experience of Western intellectual culture: Moiseev stayed in the Latin Quarter, drove a small Renault, read von Hayek's *The Road to Serfdom* in French, and regularly met with Russian expatriate intellectuals, such as the Russian microbiologist Sergei Vinogradskii's daughter, who knew Vernadskii when he stayed at Sorbonne from 1922 to 1926.[45] Since then Moiseev would keenly engage in international collaboration; his interest was facilitated by the United Nations Educational, Scientific, and Cultural Organization (UNESCO) program Man and the Biosphere launched in 1971, events organized by the Club of Rome in relation to its first report, *The Limits to Growth* (1972), the IIASA (established in Laxenburg, Austria, in 1972), and the Paris Institut de la Vie, founded by the French policy activist Maurice Marois in 1971. Having initiated one of the first Soviet computer laboratories modeling geophysical and biological processes in land, ocean, and atmosphere at the Computer Center, Moiseev had contacts with climate research centers at Livermore and the University of Oregon in the United States. Finally, from 1983 to 1985, under the auspices of the International Council of Scientific Unions, Moiseev participated in the follow-up study of the environmental consequences of nuclear war.

Starting in the early 1970s Moiseev published widely on the applications of policy sciences for economic and organizational planning, drawing on theoretical advances in cybernetics and systems analysis.[46] His later work drew inspiration from Vernadskii's writings on the biosphere and noosphere, resulting in the publication of *Man, the Environment, Society* (1980), *Man and Biosphere* (1985), and *The Algorithms of Development* (1987). The last book, which was reworked into *Man and Noosphere*, and printed in a 100,000-copy run in 1990, argued that governability and control were central intellectual issues in the age of mankind as a geological force.[47]

Moiseev was by no means alone in the emerging field of Earth system governance in the Soviet Union: he drew on the work of the leading atmosphere and climate engineering scientist Mikhail Budyko, who significantly advanced biosphere thinking into what was then a nascent global environmental science.[48] The prominent geophysicist Evgenii Fedorov's writings on the interaction between man and biosphere as a social and governmental issue formed another important influence.[49] Moiseev's competence in mathematical modeling also helped him to forge interdisciplinary links: according to the historian Douglas Weiner, by the mid-1970s mathematical methods became the dominant approach in Soviet environmental and ecological science, promoted by scientists following Nikolai Timofeev-Resovskii's intellectual lineage. However, there were important political cleavages among the pioneers of mathematized environmental governance.

Some environmental scientists, such as Stanislav Shvarts and Evgenii Fedorov, were strongly committed to the centralist, scientific projects of the transformation of nature, while others, such as Nikolai Reimers and Moiseev, were deeply skeptical about it.[50] Unlike ecologists, who were interested in conservation, Moiseev sought to extend mathematical insights into self-organization to the governance of the biosphere. Initially this intellectual pursuit fell on deaf ears: Moiseev wrote that even bright mathematical biologists, like Iurii Svirezhev, and mathematical cyberneticians, like Lyapunov, did not appreciate his interest in the epistemology of the governability of the complex organization of the biosphere.[51]

Moiseev's breakthrough came during the escalation of the Cold War under Ronald Reagan in 1983, when Moiseev became widely known as the patron of the Soviet study of the environmental effects of nuclear war. In 1982 Paul Crutzen and John Birks formulated the hypothesis that a nuclear exchange would generate smoke particle emissions, a cloud causing a global darkening and cooling. This hypothesis was tested jointly by US and Soviet scientists who simulated several scenarios of the environmental consequences of nuclear war on the General Circulation Models (GCMs) of global climate in 1983. These simulations confirmed the hypothesis of nuclear winter, where the biosphere of the global North and South would be destroyed by the global cooling, and the less harsh scenario, nuclear autumn, where the biosphere in the Northern hemisphere, although badly affected, would survive. In any case, both scenarios established that nuclear war would cause irreversible climate change. Led by Moiseev, the Soviet team gathered such leading scientists as atmosphere physicists Georgii Golitsyn and Vladimir Aleksandrov, climatologist Mikhail Budyko, mathematician Georgii Stenchikov, and population biologist Iurii Svirezhev, among others.

The nuclear winter study informed nuclear strategy, disarmament, and Earth system science, but it can also be argued to have contributed to the development of Moiseev's concept of the noosphere, where the biosphere can become governable once the principle of governance through milieu is applied, and Crutzen's concept of the epochal change to the Anthropocene.[52] Indeed, both the noosphere and the Anthropocene are epochal and analytical concepts, as they indicate a historically changing relationship between mankind and the Earth. The key difference between these terms is that Crutzen's Anthropocene sought to draw attention to scientific evidence of humanity's geological impact on the planet (he was not the first to propose this), whereas Moiseev borrowed Vernadskii's concept of the noosphere to explore the potential and limit of the application of policy sciences on the global level. It is important to add, however, that both Crutzen and Moiseev called for the renewal of a global governmental agenda. For instance, in his seminal article Crutzen connected the Anthropocene with the control revolution, the rise of automation since James Watt's invention of the steam engine, writing that control is

164   **CHAPTER 7**

the key problem posed by this new era: "a daunting task lies ahead for scientists and engineers to guide society towards environmentally sustainable management during the era of the Anthropocene."[53] It is quite remarkable that Moiseev attempted to do just that some two decades earlier on the other side of the Iron Curtain.

From 1980 Moiseev began to popularize the global modeling of the biosphere and to speak up for grave environmental problems, both in the Soviet Union and in developing countries, such as Vietnam.[54] He saw these activities not only as part of being of service to society, an important part of scientific ethos in Russia, but also as a form of policy entrepreneurship. By ushering in the noosphere, where global biospheric change becomes governable in the governmental discourses, he began to engage with higher levels of politics, beyond academia and the military-industrial complex. Moiseev's publications in influential journals paved the way for the introduction of global problems in the CPSU's program in 1985. When Gorbachev began advancing his reforms to introduce *glasnost'* and international collaboration, Moiseev's globalism informed the emerging agenda of the new world order. The significant public status of Moiseev is testified by the fact that alongside the prominent Russian physicist Evgenii Velikhov, Moiseev was appointed to the commission set up to clean up Chernobyl after the explosion in 1986.[55] Later, Moiseev became the president of the Green Cross Russia, an international organization that was established by Mikhail Gorbachev in 1993 to deal with the environmental consequences of military activities. Moiseev also chaired the State Council for the Analysis of Crisis Situations and was the president of the Russian National Committee for the United Nations Environment Program (UNEP). In 1995 UNEP awarded Moiseev the Global 500 Award; Paul Crutzen would receive this prize the next year. However, by the time Moiseev's ideas found their receptive audience at the highest echelons of the Soviet power, the Soviet system began collapsing due to Gorbachev's economic reforms and strengthening nationalist movements. The 1990s saw an extreme deterioration of Russian economy, accelerating brain drain of globally oriented scientists.[56]

Unlike many Soviet science and civic activists who established societies to pursue specific issue-driven agendas, Moiseev focused on intellectual and institutional reform seeking to fundamentally transform the intellectual apparatus underlying global governance. His position toward the official government institutions could be described as that of an enterprising "reform technocrat," to borrow a phrase from David Priestland.[57] Moiseev saw his duty as enlightening policymakers and facilitating new institutional designs for governing complexity, using the noosphere theory to establish conceptual and institutional links between expanding geophysical sciences and public policy sciences.[58] Accordingly, in what follows, I focus not so much on the theory of the noosphere as an instrument to legitimize environmental protection in the Soviet Union, but as part of a new approach to governance through milieu, one that required definition of new notions of rationality and control that went beyond the idea that global processes can be steered on the basis of cybernetics.

Transnational Development of the Biosphere and Noosphere

Although the term biosphere and the name of Vernadskii occasionally surfaced in specialist writings in the West, such as Eugene Odum's influential textbook *Fundamentals of Ecology* (1953), it was only at a UNESCO conference in 1968 that the term biosphere was first used in the context of international science and policy.[59] In the same year Odum's *Fundamentals* were translated into Russian. Since then, the development and spread of the biosphere concept has been documented in many histories of the geosciences, but it is less widely known that the concept of the biosphere also entered management and policy sciences, in parallel with the rise of the systems approach, a transdisciplinary science of organization that achieved prominence in the East and West from the late 1960s.[60]

The concept of the biosphere was introduced into Soviet policy discourses and systems thinking in the late 1950s. Vernadskii's ideas inspired different scholars, ranging from climate science (Mikhail Budyko, Evgenii Fedorov), soil science (Viktor Kovda, with whom Moiseev had a close professional relation), to anthropology (Lev Gumilev, with whose interpretation of the noosphere Moiseev strongly disagreed).[61] For Moiseev the central figure was the geneticist Nikolai Timofeev-Resovskii, who was based in the closed science city of Obninsk, home to the first Soviet nuclear power plant. Timofeev-Resovskii was interested in the cross-fertilization of mathematics, genetics, and computer modeling and was among the first ones to revive Vernadskii's theory of the biosphere after the end of the Stalinist era in 1956.[62] Moiseev met Timofeev-Resovskii through the mathematical biologist Iurii Svirezhev; this encounter led to regular meetings-turned-informal-seminars in Moiseev's office, which often ran late into the evening. Discussions with Timofeev-Resovskii not only enthused Moiseev to develop computer applications for modeling interactions among geophysical and living systems, but also facilitated Moiseev's friendship with Kovda, an influential Soviet Russian scientist who was involved in the setting up of the UNESCO program "Man and the Biosphere."[63]

In addition to biologists and soil scientists, Moiseev fostered relations with scholars at the Central Geophysical Laboratory in Leningrad, the Institutes of Oceanography and Geography, and MGU. His networks did not stop at the Iron

166   CHAPTER 7

Curtain: Moiseev met Jay Forrester and Dennis Meadows at the first UNESCO Conference on Global Problems in Venice, Italy, in 1971. Capitalizing on the momentum in the wake of the Venice conference and the subsequent publication of *The Limits to Growth* (1972), Moiseev obtained a grant to create two laboratories for mathematical modeling of the biosphere, which were awarded by the chairman of the section of Earth Sciences at the Soviet Academy of Sciences, Aleksandr Sidorenko. This institutional innovation must be seen in both domestic and international political contexts: while the Soviet Union began to actively brand its foreign policy with global environmental concerns, prominent scientists such as Budyko and Fedorov began to publish specialist and popular books on the global environmental crisis. The emerging computer-based global modeling was an important nexus that bridged techno-optimism and global concerns. For instance, in his long afterword for Forrester's *World Dynamics* (published in Russian in 1978), Moiseev declared that computer simulation of complex biosphere processes could provide a scientific foundation for world government.[64] The Russian translation of *World Dynamics* resonated widely: Moiseev's name became familiar in the circles of cultural and environmental dissidents.[65]

Having borrowed Vernadskii's idea of mankind as a geological force and inspired by Vernadskii's vision of the noosphere where scientific reason would organize planetary development, Moiseev operationalized Vernadskii's geophysical philosophy to rethink the wider governmental implications of mathematical methods, drawing on insights from OR, systems theory, computer-based modeling, ecology, and climate science. In his writings, Moiseev often used the terms biosphere and noosphere interchangeably, but generally by the noosphere he meant the near future when the application of policy sciences to global planetary governance would be possible both conceptually and institutionally. First and foremost, Moiseev was interested in the applied mathematical side of rational planetary governance: here Moiseev was deeply influenced by Henri Poincaré's work on differential equations. Indeed, mathematical thinking about parameters and limits led Moiseev to define governmental rationality as thinking from the limits, rather than as a maximizing or optimizing process.[66] Moiseev also read Teilhard de Chardin's *The Phenomenon of Man* (1955) and was familiar with James Lovelock's Gaia theory, which was first formulated in the 1960s; indeed, the first computer-based modeling system of global ecology at the Computer Center was called "Gaia" in the early 1980s.[67] Moiseev certainly knew work by Paul Erlich, a US biologist and active public policy lobbyist who popularized the term "coevolution" in the West in the late 1960s; these two scientists met through the nuclear winter project in the early 1980s.[68] While coevolution was defined by Erlich and Peter Raven as a reciprocal change in the interaction of different species, Moiseev extended the definition to embrace the coevolution of living and nonliving matter.[69] In addition to the prominent geologist Vasily Dokuchaev, the theorist of tektology Aleksandr Bogdanov (Malinovsky), Vernadskii, and Teilhard de Chardin, important influences were Budyko's and Federov's writing on global climate, Kovda's writings on waste, Piotr Anokhin's work on biological cybernetics, and Ivan Schmalhausen's work on evolution, all of which Moiseev put in dialogue with ideas on changing systems and self-organizing order developed by such scientists as molecular biologist Manfred Elgen, energy dissipation theorist Lars Onsager, and, obviously, Norbert Wiener's cybernetics. Furthermore, Moiseev touched upon political economy debates by Adam Smith, David Ricardo, Vilfredo Pareto, and, at a later stage, Hayek. Although Moiseev paid dues to dialectical philosophy, making occasional references to Karl Marx and Hegel, he made it clear that Marxist approaches were insufficient to understand the complexity of global coevolution. In 1970, Moiseev argued that Marx's omniscient and mechanistic Laplacian model of the economy and society could not be applied to the complex realities of the late twentieth century.[70] His proposal echoed Hayek's idea that one can engineer components but not the wholes of national and world economies.[71] Unlike Hayek and Geneva neoliberals, Moiseev believed that computer modeling had an important role to play in global governance. This, as I will show, was due to Moiseev's intimate knowledge of the social and political effects of computer modeling as a social practice and not only as a source of numerical representation and an informational input and output in decision process.[72]

How should we interpret Moiseev's ideas in the Soviet context? Was he a Soviet version of a neoliberal globalist? As I show in the remainder of this chapter, Moiseev arrived at his views on limited governance by trying to be conceptually consistent with what was a changing notion of the scientific prediction of fleeting phenomena. It is this awareness of the uncertain but at the same time productive and performative nature of scientific prediction that forms a common denominator in Moiseev's and the Geneva neoliberals' ideas. However, Moiseev's originality was in cross-fertilizing ideas from different fields to redefine the role of scientific prediction in global environmental governance, where economy is only part of a complex whole.

From Targeting to Orchestration

In the 1980s Moiseev joined the ranks of scholars alerting governments to the fact that the coevolution of man and the biosphere could not be left ungoverned: mankind's activities had become such a significant factor in deterioration of the whole biosphere, creating the risk of nuclear war, industrial accidents, pollution,

168   CHAPTER 7

and, ultimately, carbon dioxide-induced climate change, while growing production and consumption was causing depletion of global resources.[73] But in order to govern, as Comte said, one needs to have predictions first and the paradigm for scientific prediction was a combination of the cybernetic notion of prediction as information processing and statistical forecasting, where forecasts served as a source of information to be processed. In order to address these complex issues from the perspective of cybernetic predictive rationality, one has to identify a desirable state of the global system, establish policy targets, and allocate pathways for achieving those targets by optimal control methods.

However, this conceptual model of steering based on prediction can be applied only to relatively stable and simple systems. In contrast, change in the global biosphere is driven by complex, contingent factors that affect different scales of the system differently. Causal mechanisms at the micro level are often decoupled from processes at the macro level: for instance, the individual behavior of an animal does not explain the collective behavior of a pack of animals, because the two are different systems. While the planetary system is highly regular and relatively well predictable, many subsystems of the Earth, such as the weather or human economies and societies, are not predictable in the long term.[74]

Could global Earth governance ever be rationalized in line with cybernetic prediction? According to Moiseev, it is only possible if we use a particular concept of governance and rationality. Mankind's role as a geological force, argued Moiseev, can be theorized as a process of self-organization, where living and nonliving natural components intertwine and shape each other. In this process, he wrote, the ontological distinction between man and nature becomes redundant. Accordingly, the science of the global biosphere should approach changes in society and nature not as a clash between two essentially different systems, but as the coevolution of particular organizational forms.[75] In line with the logical empiricist notion of prediction, the laws describing the interaction between society and nature as coevolving systems are required for predictions to count as scientific.

Proposing that "organization" is a fundamental concept just like "energy" and "matter," Moiseev defined organization as stabilization, a condition where variables are conservative and change slowly.[76] In other words, things that change more slowly are more "organized." Mankind's role on Earth, then, is to become a wise and responsible organizer, to slow down the global environmental changes that are spurred by human activities. This clashed with the modern notion of management, practiced by the scientific organization of labor movement in Russia in the 1920s and revived by Gvishiani in the 1960s, which aimed at speeding up production process, by assembling faster factory machines and enabling faster labor. Clearly speeding up and slowing down are strategies that apply to different levels of complexity and that need different types of predictions.

GLOBAL PREDICTION   169

Equipped with scientific data, methods, and computer technology, man could become "a master of the biosphere," but not in the sense that man would finally "conquer nature" (a popular trope of the Soviet discourse of progress). Man would become a *manager*, able to "consciously use the resources of the planet in order to guarantee the conditions for coevolution."[77] It is important to note that Moiseev's use of the term management (*upravlenie*, still better translated as "governance") resonates strongly with the original notion of scientific management, proposed by Frederic Winslow Taylor and promoted by the US president Franklin Roosevelt in the early twentieth century. Roosevelt backed Taylor hoping to introduce more efficient, scientific management techniques with the aim not to speed up production, but to "conserve" and not waste capital, labor, and machines. As management theorists argued in 2017, the original approach of scientific management was created to work against the misuse of humans and nature, albeit this original meaning of scientific management has been lost and replaced with notions emphasizing technocracy, productivity and growth.[78]

Like Roosevelt, Moiseev looked for a way to reduce damage caused by industrial development, but his concern was the global scale and high complexity. Moiseev proposed that it would be intellectually consistent to base the principles of the governance of global development not on acceleration and growth, but on slowing down the rate of change. In doing this, mankind could no longer rely on self-organization through adaptation to the changing environment, because the environment had begun to change in such a way that adaptation was not a viable strategy anymore. Therefore, adaptation, which Moiseev termed "the strategy of nature," must be replaced by "a strategy of Reason," a new mentality of governance based on a qualitatively different scientific definition of what can be considered as rational and effective control.[79]

First, in order to think meaningfully about rational governance of the global Earth system, one must go beyond the policy thinking that prevailed in the 1960s and 1970s, which was based on a model of linking information, decision, and action, utilizing the cybernetic notion of teleological control via feedback. Moiseev's argument proceeds in the following way: predictive control in cybernetic engineering systems is possible only under conditions where the purpose of the system which is being controlled is known. Consider the classical problem of the antiaircraft defense system: if the enemy pilot's intention (target) is known, the trajectory of the plane and the missile can be predicted with a high level of certainty and the enemy bomber can be hit. However, this model of control is difficult to apply to complex systems, such as human societies, which are characterized by multiple, intertwined goals, and are therefore less predictable. Different actors can evaluate the same situation differently or have contradictory goals. Even if a shared goal is

170   **CHAPTER 7**

agreed upon, there can be many different ways of achieving it.[80] Whereas this social complexity makes teleological control mechanisms, such as social policy, very difficult to translate from an intellectual program into action, the geophysical complexity of the global Earth system (the interaction of the atmosphere, the ocean, and the land) makes teleological control simply redundant. One cannot ask the Earth what is her goal.

The question of whether the global Earth system can be described as a purposive system has actually bothered many bright minds. Some thinkers, such as the British scientist James Lovelock and American biologist Lynn Margulis, considered that the Earth can be seen as teleological, proposing that all ecological systems, including the planet Earth, actively seek homeostasis, a particular state of equilibrium.[81] However, writing ten years after the original publication of the article outlining the Gaia theory, Moiseev, aware of historical examples of unpredictable and catastrophic changes to biospheric systems as well as being informed by the nuclear winter study, did not believe in naturally occurring homeostasis. According to Moiseev, the very idea of equilibrium promised a false hope of control and was dangerous, because it obscured the fact that human activities impacted geophysical processes in nonlinear ways, which could never be fully understood. The outcomes of interventions in the biosphere could never be predicted with confidence over the long term. Furthermore, Moiseev argued that it is centrally important to recognize that, in the case of the Earth system, the governing bodies are not outside but inside the system that is being governed.[82] This means that in order to predict the global biosphere policymakers will need to predict themselves—thus adding the level of reflexivity and additional complexity to what is already a highly complex system.

Drawing on systems theories of growing complexity, Moiseev posited that theoretically the controlling center coevolves with the controlled system by being part of it. Controlling interventions make the system ever more complex and uncertain.[83] There is simply no starting point, no stable Newtonian position from which the ongoing changes could be observed, levered, and steered. The Comtean positivist ideal of predictive scientific rationality was not achievable. In this context, Moiseev viewed the optimal governability of the environment significantly differently from many Soviet contemporaries who resorted to the simplistic ideological argument according to which the capitalist strive for profit was the source of imbalance. A good case in point is the influential environmental scientist Evgenii Fedorov, who used his scientific authority to criticize the irrational use of global natural resources, at the same time carefully aligning their arguments with the ideological doctrine of the political superiority of communism and the commitment to growth. Fedorov proclaimed that the long-term global goals of world governance could only be achieved by replacing the capitalist system with a socialist society, where environmental governance could be put to optimal, rational use.[84] Such arguments were not only deterministic in the sense that they attributed causes to the political and economic nature of a regime, but also simplistic in that they drew a clear dividing line between the natural world and the social and political world. Moiseev sought to show that both aspects of this argument were flawed.

The political identity of the governmental system, argued Moiseev, was irrelevant for Earth system governance. He argued that growth, in many cases, was a problem not a solution. However, the key issue for Moiseev was the understanding of control that had to be revised. In Soviet policy sciences "control" was defined as "purposive governance" (in Russian, *upravlenie*): an intellectual, interventionist activity based on information. According to the ideal model of cybernetic control, any given object of control must be thoroughly examined by scientists; its behavior must be monitored, tracked, and predicted. If the controlled object is a social collective, such as an organization, a state, or a sector of the economy, the control of its behavior must be institutionalized through a centralist bureaucracy and the political party apparatus, which sets the object's goals for the future. This cybernetic model of steering proliferated in Soviet management literature. Such diverse activities as the performative brain, the management unit in a firm, and the presumed control center of the economy—Gosplan—were described as being able to formulate goals, project them into the future, and reflexively adjust the behavior of the systems under their control according to changes in the environment.[85] It was precisely this intellectual model of informational control that formed the basis of Viktor Glushkov's project of OGAS, the all-union national automated system for computation and information processing, which was meant to provide a centrally integrated flow of information across all Soviet enterprises and institutions.[86] However, in the case of the global Earth system, wrote Moiseev, there was no certain knowledge to be had, there were too many intertwined behavioral systems to control and, importantly, there was no central authority to set the goals.[87] What can it mean to govern the Earth system, if it is unpredictable and uncontrollable?

In response to this question, Moiseev offered what can be described as theory of governance that *orchestrates predictions*, rather than operates on the basis of prediction. In this model, scientific predictions are not scientific inputs into the governmental machine where policies are outputs. Instead, the governmental machine must be organized and streamlined in such a way that scientific predictions are produced in an orchestrated manner, at an appropriate level of knowledge, and used at an appropriate level of action. Governance as guidance takes care to align epistemological and governmental practices to avoid erroneous uses of predictions. First, according to Moiseev, the institution of predictive scientific expertise remains indispensable at lower scales of the Earth system:

172   CHAPTER 7

statistical forecasting can map long- and short-term consequences of human activities that could potentially destabilize the biosphere.[88] At the global scale, these negative consequences must be prevented by establishing boundaries and thresholds to human activities, such as limits to local and aggregate levels of pollution, exploitation of resources, and the extinction of species. In this way, the lower-level predictive scientific expertise forms an important basis for managing higher levels of complexity, the global scale, and the long term. However, the gap between these two levels can be bridged only if the prevailing governmental attitude to precision and certainty is abandoned. The role of scientists in Earth system governance (what Vernadskii and Moiseev would describe as the noosphere: the biosphere plus governmental apparatus) is to identify basic, crude parameters that define the boundaries of global environmental change within which mankind's biological survival is possible. This sort of scientific knowledge can be only approximate, imperfect, and uncertain. This is a very different requirement, if compared with the epistemological grounds for cybernetic control, which seeks to make predictions as precise as possible. For Moiseev, the crudeness of knowledge is not a problem, but an asset: it is important not to eliminate uncertainty by offering false precision. To put it in other words, the cybernetic prediction is suitable for very short-term interventions in response to fast changing situations, where precision of information and intervention is desirable. To govern the global, planetary scale and the long term means to slow down and use crude, uncertain knowledge to map the limits of viability.

However, this crude, parametric knowledge of the limits must be made actionable. Positive, target-based control must be replaced with negative guidance. To govern the global biosphere, according to Moiseev, is not to govern prescriptively (do x, y, z), but to govern prohibitively (do anything except for x, y, z). Here the governor does not impose a concrete goal on the governed system, but instead imposes limits through a system of prohibitions.[89] It is easy to see how different is this model of prediction concerned with limits from the positivist notion of prediction, based on complete knowledge. Negative guidance can be reconciled with the logical empiricist notion of prediction as a hypothesis, where the criterion of precise prediction can be used to assess the quality of theories, but the overall expectation in global governance as guidance is based more on pragmatic approach, seeing what works rather than a pure theory testing. The notions of forward reflexivity and reflexive control can feed into the government of governing apparatus, but they are clearly unsuitable to address the biosphere's changes. In other words, global governance for Moiseev is inherently liberal at the large scale, long term, although this does not entail that more precise predictions and controls cannot be used at the short term and lower complexity.[90]

GLOBAL PREDICTION   173

Moiseev terms this type of control as "guided development," one that abandons the desire to set concrete goals, to measure intentions, and to exercise informational control and is therefore different from "the control of a process" (*napravliaemoe razvitie* versus *upravlenie processom*). Moiseev employs mathematical language and hydromechanics metaphors to describe such negative guidance: he writes about "algorithms" and "channels" of development, but these algorithms and channels do not guide the movement to a predefined end goal. They work as shores, as prohibitions or taboos, setting limits to those human activities which are deemed to threaten the desirable evolution of the biosphere. Mankind, in this way, is left in principle free to formulate and pursue its many different goals, as long as its actions remain within the boundaries of given parameters. Moiseev imagined human activity to be channeled like a water stream in such a way that it does not disturb the biosphere.[91] Interestingly, at about the same time, 1979, Hayek would also employ the metaphor of water stream to argue that the flow of society and economy cannot be governed in a "rational" way but must be approached as an adaptive process.[92]

Scientific articulation and institutionalization of these thresholds serve as the epistemological foundation for a global governance that moved away from cybernetic "targeting" discourse, which in turn, as Geroulanos observed, required transparency and, ideally, precise data and understanding of the underlying mechanisms, to cybernetic "orchestration," which entailed the building of scientific infrastructures and institutions and political negotiation.[93] Note that targeting and orchestration are not incompatible. I suggest that the two approaches belong to the same cybernetic spectrum, but they are situated at its opposite ends. While targeting is suitable for cybernetic control of simple behavioral or dynamic phenomena, orchestration characterizes the governance of highly complex phenomena. Orchestration, in Moiseev's writing, is mainly negative and legalistic; it is about setting the limits to damage. It is also productive, because the role of these limits is not to mechanically constrain the autonomy of individuals and social groups, but to serve as cognitive channels, a computer-mediated milieu, guiding pluralistic social self-organization. Limits, not targets, come first in policy decisions within governance as guidance. Once limits are set, the many actors are left free to make scientific predictions to guide their activities.

Debates on "critical thresholds" of climate change and the ensuing securitization and risk management abounded among Western climate scientists in the early 1990s.[94] Moiseev saw these debates not as a mere technical quibble, but as a central component of the cybernetic governmentality of the noosphere. In this respect Moiseev's view is close to what Timothy O'Riordan and Steve Rayner describe as precautionary science: government of high complexity must combine

174 **CHAPTER 7**

intuition and foresight rather than knowledge that claims certainty.[95] However, whereas O'Riordan and Rayner promote the role of scientists as persuaders, ensuring institutional pluralism, Moiseev wanted to redefine the very notion of rationality and control and educate a wide range of decision-makers about the inevitable uncertainty of scientific knowledge, the impossibility of positivist prediction at the global scale and long term, and the importance of parametric limits in considering policy options. Moiseev wanted to change the existing epistemological culture of global governance that mobilized the notions of intention, prediction, certainty, and linear control.

It is important to note that since the late 1990s, policymakers' responses to uncertainty were mapped and theorized in the influential scholarship on the politics of preparedness.[96] Particularly important is the work on the adoption and implementation of the concept of resilience, developed by C. S. Holling at the East–West think tank IIASA, with which Moiseev was also closely involved, in the 1970s and 1980s.[97] In this context, Moiseev's efforts to develop a conceptual, technical, and institutional basis for governing uncertainty at a global scale in the Soviet Union during the period when the Soviet economic system was in severe decline are quite remarkable.

Indeed, it is worthwhile to pause and consider Hayek's ideas on the nongovernability of the world economy. It may read as counterintuitive that a communist OR scientist and an Austrian economist would arrive at a similar conclusion regarding the nature of scientific expertise and world government. In what follows, I draw on the excellent study by Quinn Slobodian to demonstrate that what would become known as a neoliberal approach to limited governance was a reaction to limited predictability. In their own ways, both Moiseev and Hayek reacted against the simplistic Comtean model of scientific prediction and planning, which they deemed deeply unsuitable for the complex realities of the global economy and environment. Both trajectories extend the line of inquiry that Kondrat'ev grappled with in the 1920s and 1930s.

The parallels are striking. Hayek, together with Ludwig von Mises, established the Business Cycle Research Institute in Vienna in 1927. As Slobodian put it, "neoliberalism was born out of projects of world observation, global statistics gathering, and international investigations of the business cycle."[98] Hayek was initially enthused with the promise of "great predictions," which he discovered at the National Bureau of Economic Research in the United States.[99] However, his enthusiasm waned. Neoliberal epistemology was founded on the insight that the accumulating data remained insufficient for "forecasting"; the apparent expansion of numbers on the national and, starting in the 1930s and 1940s, world economies were of little use in predicting the future dynamics. According to Slobodian, the neoliberals felt that the avalanche of numbers posed a risk of false belief and even worse decisions, thus voicing exactly the same concern as Nikolai Kondrat'ev, who warned the Soviet planners of "auto-hypnosis with numbers" in the 1920s.[100] As Slobodian showed, the use of business "barometers" placed economists alongside the established "esoteric" sciences, such as weather forecasters and medical doctors.[101] This is not just a metaphor or a loose parallel, as I showed in chapter 1: indeed, science's attempt to predict fleeting phenomena continued to be associated with mantic, conjectural knowledge even in the twentieth century. However, further development of knowledge was away from scientific prediction as explanation toward scientific prediction as a performative information processing, part of behavioral action.

The Geneva school of neoliberals thus turned away from the sophisticated numeric representations to think in "orders."[102] This also characterizes Moiseev's direction, when he moved away Gosplan's attempt to refine social indicators to embrace thinking in orders, inspired by complexity science as it developed in mathematics of chaos, neurophysiology, ecological dynamics, and global Earth systems theory. Both Geneva neoliberals and Moiseev placed less belief in statistical prediction as inference from a given set of numbers that are believed to reflect the reality out there, than in the design of institutions that would secure a more predictable order.[103]

Being experienced in both scientific research and policy, Moiseev harbored no naive hopes that Earth system science could provide certainty or that scientific experts could directly influence Soviet, or indeed any, policy decisions. He therefore never offered any "optimal solutions," particularly in the long term. Instead, Moiseev cautioned against the illusion that such solutions may exist (hence his fierce criticism of the term sustainable development). Instead of long-term solutions, he called for the creation of forms of long-term engagement in the process of a continuous search for compromise, a process in which globally accessible scientific expertise would be coproduced with stakeholders. This policy interface, envisioned by Moiseev, also placed a significant emphasis on a robust legal framework, consisting of mainly negative prohibitions to regulate human activities. In this respect, Moiseev's policy thinking coheres with the stance of Geneva school neoliberals and Walter Lippmann, as described by Slobodian.[104] Like neoliberal globalists, Moiseev argued for an international legal setup. He wanted to see what he called "institutes of agreement" developed for this purpose, ideally under the auspices of the United Nations.[105]

However, this institutional change at the international level alone would not suffice: the conceptualization of governance and control must change as well. Moiseev argued that it would be impossible to define and solve the problems of the global biosphere if the underlying discourse remained based on a teleological, cybernetic notion of control and a reductionist expectation of science to

176   CHAPTER 7

supply decision-makers with a linear, deterministic analysis of complex process. Nowhere could this concern be more adequately placed than in the Soviet Union, where the party and industry leaders were blind to persuasion from below and suspicious of anybody who questioned the value of certainty and centralist leadership. Accordingly, Moiseev proposed abandoning centralist control, based on the idea (but not practice) of long-term forecasting and plans, replacing it with negative, regulatory government through taboos. Like the 1930s' globalist neoliberals, who held that "If the economy was beyond representation, then the task was to find a framework to contain and protect it," Moiseev was searching for a system of taboos to prevent global self-destruction.[106] This negative, legal framework, based on the imperative of the self-preservation of humanity was his "algorithm of governance." The program was not prescriptive, but negative, not tracking a goal like Wiener's predictive cat chasing a mouse, but avoiding danger, rather like the lift doors that would not open if the cabin is not aligned with the floor. Note that by government as algorithmic activity Moiseev did not mean a centralized computer and surveillance system, the visions of which were attempted by Stafford Beer in Allende's Chile and Viktor Glushkov in the Soviet Union. It is closer to Hayek's neurophysiological notion of knowledge as a program of rules that enable pattern recognition and steer behavior.[107]

Like the US decision scientist Kenneth Arrow, Moiseev recognized that it is impossible to reach a global agreement on the target outcomes of environmental protection because of international economic inequalities. He hoped, however, that the consensus on the limits of global environmental change could be achieved. The desirable target would be universally defined as a state of the biosphere that ensures human survival; its parameters would be set by Earth system scientists, engaged in cross-border cooperation in data collection and modeling, thus producing a cognitive, computer-mediated milieu for governance. Moiseev's model resonates with what Hayek arrived at independently in the 1970s, when, according to Slobodian, he borrowed insights and terminology from systems and cybernetic discourses. Hayek, like Moiseev, worked to find a way to get around the problem of limits. For Moiseev, the solution was a conceptual shift from targets to limits, guidance, and milieus. Hayek made a remarkably similar move, proposing to replace what for Wiener was control with cultivation: "cultivation, in the sense in which the farmer or gardener cultivates his plants, where he knows and can control only some of the determining circumstances, and in which the wise legislator or statesman will probably attempt to cultivate rather than to control the forces of the social process."[108] Although Hayek's cultivation and Moiseev's milieu may sound similar to what Zygmunt Bauman described as "a gardening state," these are very different approaches. The model of a gardening state described by Bauman is based on the Laplacian, positivist notion of the possibility of perfect knowledge, visibility, and

GLOBAL PREDICTION   177

transparency.[109] Bauman's metaphor of the gardening state, as Jacobsen and Marshman noted, extended the line of social critique of the use of positivist prediction in the government of the social originally suggested by Charles Wright Mills in the 1950s.[110] Moiseev's arguments should be seen as an extension of this criticism of simplistic scientific positivism. In contrast to the gardening state that relied on strict categorization between desirable plants and nondesirable weeds, described by Bauman, Moiseev proposed the models of cultivation and guidance through milieu recognizing self-regulation, the limitation of knowledge, and the importance of ethics, and pointing to the complex orchestration of cognitive and material means to channel preexisting energies so that they thrive and do not undermine themselves. It is about orchestrating the world into viable being where the power of scientific prediction is limited, but central. As I suggested earlier, many levels of prediction could be involved. At the level of lower complexity, predictions as explanations can help engineer robust system components. However, at higher levels of complexity, scientific prediction becomes closer to its neurophysiological meaning: Hayek, for instance, proposed in his Nobel speech that "pattern prediction" is the most that science can offer for the understanding of fleeting phenomena.[111]

Thinking from the limits would lead to different policy solutions: Moiseev made a range of such proposals, applying guidance in the areas of national security, economy, and the environment, following Mikhail Gorbachev's reforms of the Soviet economy and state after 1986.[112] For instance, instead of complicated institutional bargaining over the reduction of the nuclear arsenal, trying to identify which types of weapons should be decommissioned first, Moiseev proposed limiting the efficiency of nuclear defense by imposing new constraints on it. All nuclear nations would cooperate, creating a vast and expensive global surveillance system, enabling all members to track the activities in their nuclear sectors. A surprise launch of a nuclear missile and retaliation would become strategically impossible and nuclear weapons would eventually become obsolete.[113] In the economy, Moiseev wanted to abolish "authoritarian planning," introducing market mechanisms as conductors for negative feedback in the economy. However, this liberalization would be beneficial only if limits to the markets were established, providing guidance toward socially desirable goals.[114] As Zubok detailed in his history of the collapse of the Soviet economy, Gorbachev failed to establish precisely such limits before decentralizing economic activities.[115]

In the environmental governance, trust in data was crucial for such negative guidance, which would have to rely on global ecological information databases. The limits for global environmental planning would be set in the light of loads that local and regional social and economic systems could bear, thus ensuring the welfare of local populations.[116] For Moiseev, scientific expertise, particularly computer modeling, was vital for the establishment of such taboos or thresholds, forming a

178   CHAPTER 7

socio-informational milieu of decision-making which would socialize the governing elites into these new notions of a rationality of limits and guidance. Technical solutions have their own politics: this had been made clear in Foucauldian research on the governmental effects of material milieus, such as urban, transport, and energy infrastructure, the construction of which shapes local populations.[117] The next section proposes that Moiseev's governance through guidance was just such a political project of informational infrastructure.

The Liberal Politics of Governance through Milieu

In order to be actionable upon, the complex Earth system must be subjected to a particular form of articulation, one which Theodore Porter called a "thin description," expressed (ideally) in a mathematical language.[118] Soviet global modelers had long argued that those computer simulations that seek to represent the full complexity of geophysical and anthropogenic processes were useful only for research, not for policy decisions.[119] As O'Riordan and Rayner would later observe, the method of computer-based modeling uses a simplified system of discrete elements, which does not replicate faithfully the complex character of the biosphere.[120] The simplicity and reductionism of global models, wrote Moiseev, are not necessarily misleading, because the data are but one component of scientific expertise for policymaking. The governance of the complex, global biosphere should be based on relatively primitive models, because such models can identify the most significant causal effects and major trends. Whether this approximate information is sufficient to establish limits to guide development, it is possible to judge only on the basis of a combination of scientific, social, and pragmatic intelligence, which is fundamentally important in modeling such complex systems. This is why Moiseev did not limit his interest to mathematical modeling but sought to transform the very conceptual and institutional contexts in which modeling was used. His theoretical ambition was to bridge the so-called cultural lag between advanced scientific and technological knowledge and societal and political values.[121]

This debate on the quality and use of models and data pointed to the fact that there would have to be a change in repositioning of scientific expertise to government if governance was to guide the global biosphere: for Moiseev, Soviet global modelers were not mere advisors (providers of predictions) to politicians, but orchestrators of the entire milieu for decision-making. Furthermore, this Soviet vision of governance through milieu adds an important focus to the Foucauldian studies of negative, liberal governance, where governance through milieu is generally associated with the regulation of subjects considered unable to govern themselves. This approach enabled top-down government-at-a-distance without relying on the mechanism of self-regulation, as the capacity to self-regulate has been seen as absent in such subjects of governance as the working class, criminals, or indigenous peoples. As Tony Bennett put it, "It is particularly in relation to populations that are excluded from the forms of self-action identified with liberal forms of subjectivity that the logic of government via milieus comes into play."[122]

In Moiseev's model of the negative government of the Earth system through the milieu of computer simulation, the subjects who display a lack of what was deemed to be adequate self-regulation were the elites: Soviet Communist Party leaders, *nomenklatura*, and managers of enterprises. In his vision of the noosphere, a scientifically governed Earth system, control does not flow top down, from the central government, but bottom up, from internal, autonomous discussion among experts to the government decision-makers. This can be understood as an attempt at liberalization without full democratization: Moiseev's model of government as guidance does not consider wider public engagement in decisions but is restricted to securing a form of interaction between scientists and policymakers.

Furthermore, governance as guidance through milieu can be important in those cases where strongly polarized political ideologies are at play and where political and administrative hierarchies are very strong. For example, mathematical language and computer modeling enjoyed a unique epistemological autonomy in the Soviet context of political censorship. Whereas Soviet literary and policy discourses were tightly controlled to communicate positive images of the Soviet future and technoscientific progress, paying explicit dues to the primacy of the party in decision-making, the modeling of the global Earth system represented innovative and critical thought beyond official planning. The intellectual mission of global modeling was to enhance awareness of the limits to human knowledge and control, socializing policymakers to accept uncertainty as an inevitable condition. Here Earth system modeling formed a hybrid milieu where scientists could not be separated from the results crunched out by the computer, because the interpretation of modeling results was not accessible to a nonspecialist; tacit knowledge of how a particular mainframe computer worked was necessary to understand and evaluate the results. As global modelers held the monopoly of the production and interpretation of data about the past, current, and future state of the global biosphere, they broke down the centralist structure of party decision-making. Global modeling also transformed the Soviet governmentality by habituating policymakers into working without the notion of purposive control of individuals and societies, at least at the global level.

In this way, by developing a policy science for Earth system governance, Moiseev effectively contributed a building block for a new governmental milieu in

180   CHAPTER 7

the late Soviet Union. The political effect of this theory was establishing what can be described, paraphrasing Tony Bennett, as a new set of natural and social givens, where natural givens were the planetary boundaries, established with the help of computer-based modeling of global geophysical processes.[123] The planetary boundaries could only emerge as "natural givens" thanks to the invention of new social givens, namely, transnational scientific networks that cut across the Iron Curtain that were crucially important for the production and exchange of data describing the Earth system. Moiseev's extension of policy science to the global biosphere was not only an original intellectual experiment, but also an effort to intellectually transform existing Soviet policy practices, both institutionally and socially, in the 1970s and 1980s.[124]

Conclusion

Just like the pioneers of cybernetics in the 1940s, many Earth system scientists created their own theories of sociopolitical governance as they were searching for new models of engagement with policymaking. As Brian Wynne has repeatedly argued, climate science emerged not so much as a truth machine, but as reality-based social and policy heuristics, "an organising basis for a broader coalition of motivations, meanings, and social, ethical and political concerns."[125] Most early twenty-first century debates among Earth system scientists themselves reveal a continued search for new governmental epistemologies and practices that could bridge the intellectual and political gap between scientific expertise and government.[126] It is in this context that this chapter proposed viewing the Soviet case of Earth system governance as an instructive lesson in the politics of ideas at the changing interface between science and global governance.

Moiseev's extension of Vernadskii's ideas about the biosphere and noosphere to global governance resulted in the articulation of a liberal, negative, bottom-up mode of government through milieu. While in the West, Teilhard de Chardin's noosphere theory remained mainly a philosophical explanation of the relationship between mankind and the Earth,[127] in the Soviet Union, Vernadskii's writing about the noosphere inspired innovative policy thinking. Its legacy is still felt in twenty-first century Russia: through Moiseev's publications in the 1980s and 1990s the noosphere spread as a model of a new, global governmental imagination, inspiring a diverse range of applications.[128] Intellectually, the postcybernetic notion of control as guidance undermined several components of the very institutional identity of the Soviet system: centralized administration and branch-specific goal-setting, the belief in linear control, and, ultimately, the utopia of a bright, predictable future. This argumentation was made possible by the legitimacy that

Soviet global modelers enjoyed, having contributed to the nuclear winter forecast, but it was also related to the political agenda of Gorbachev's perestroika, where institutional reform suddenly became possible. Indeed, Gorbachev's strive to decentralize party apparatus was extended to include the Earth system as a nonhuman agent in decision-making, mediated by computer simulations. But the scale and long-term nature of planetary purposes challenged the use of scientific prediction. For Moiseev, to govern in the age of the noosphere was to create a globally integrated governmentality, based on new institutions, but also on new intellectual models of control, able to make sense of complexity, remaining reflexive over the contingent coevolution of mankind and planet Earth.

In this respect, Moiseev's theory of governance through guidance entailed an epistemological revolution in the context of Soviet modernization, where scientific expertise was traditionally allocated the role of loyal service to political leaders. Governmental use of milieu to guide societal practices posited the importance of carefully orchestrated efforts by international scientists. In the Soviet Union, one of the first such milieus was the Gaia modeling system designed at the Computer Center in Moscow, which was used to simulate the environmental effects of nuclear war, the acidification of water, soil, and forests, and the impact of carbon dioxide on climate change. This epistemological infrastructure was mobilized by scientists to lobby for different policies, ranging from nuclear disarmament to the reduction of pollution and resource use. The global biosphere, materialized through computer systems, became a medium to govern the governor, the party, and industrial elites, an instrument of bottom-up activity.

Many of the conceptual principles enshrined in Moiseev's framework of governance through guidance of the 1980s remain relevant in the second decade of the third millennium, as world climate scientists continue trying to get to grips with issues of a similar character. The idea of prohibitive regulation found its implementation in the setting of "planetary boundaries," first approved by the international climate change scientists' collective in 2009.[129] The search for "institutes of agreement" continues, most visibly in the team led by Frank Biermann, seeking to develop a viable model of international environmental governance. However, Biermann's proposal mainly focuses on organizational design, completely rejecting the management approach as a form of rigid, hierarchical steering through control.[130] In contrast, Moiseev's approach is more perceptive of the need to renew the very understanding of management as a new type of governance, to look for a new governmental imagination. The epistemological project of inquiring into the organizational forms of the coevolution of social, living, and nonliving matter is pursued in science and technology studies. While different conceptual approaches to the governance of complexity are tested by resilience scholars, it should not be forgotten that much of the vocabulary of resilience theory is derived from Cold

War policy sciences. This is particularly important, because the bridging of Earth system sciences, policy sciences, and actual governmental practice remains a great challenge. Taken seriously, Moiseev's point that the cybernetic notion of purposive governance, based on short-term prediction and feedback, is fundamentally unsuitable for large-scale and long-term aspects of Earth system governance, could open up new avenues for reconceptualizing government and control at the pragmatic level.

CONCLUSION

In this book I sought to make a case for the treatment of scientific prediction as navigation of complexity by orchestration of knowledge and action. In doing this, I sought to extend the field of risk studies into the field of prediction, because just like the term risk in the twentieth century, prediction is becoming a defining term of the twenty-first century as societies face the unprecedented uncertainties posed by the global climate crisis and the development of digital technologies. The global climate crisis posits the problem of the unpredictability of the natural environment, while digital technology is perceived to threaten people's liberty by making them more predictable. Indeed, the questions of agency, liberty, risk, and prediction are intrinsically related: societies and individuals desire to predict risks to be secure, free from worry and danger, free to pursue their goals, but then, what does it mean to predict, particularly to predict scientifically?

The mandate of scientific prediction, however, goes beyond risk management and behavior control: as I showed in this book scientific predictions can be deployed as a critical and reflexive device, requiring a constant search for new ways of orchestrating cognition and human and nonhuman agencies. I hope that the story of the Soviet Russian scientific predictions presented in this book can help us better understand the ways in which scientific prediction can operate in governance in liberal democratic contexts too. In creating new approaches to prediction, Russian thinkers were not just catching up or lagging behind the West: East–West interaction during the Cold War was multidirectional and new approaches to prediction were developed in response to local intellectual, social,

184 CONCLUSION

and institutional contexts. While both French positivism and Norbert Wiener's cybernetics constituted major intellectual influences in Russian science, the distinctive approaches developed by Russian scholars such as Nikolai Kondrat'ev's notion of limited prevision in economic planning, Georgii Shchedrovitskii's prospective reflexivity, Vladimir Lefebvre's reflexive control, and Nikita Moiseev's call to orchestrate multilevel predictions in order to create governance as guidance through milieu, represent original and timely intellectual innovations. On both sides of the Iron Curtain, diverse approaches to scientific prediction, based on the ideas of reflexivity and complexity, emerged in response not only to the epistemological criteria of science, but also the experience of organizational and social practices, particularly organizational failures of state planning, enterprise management, and international and global governance.

The distinct approaches to scientific prediction presented in this book have hopefully encouraged the reader to consider the internal diversity of predictive knowledge. But acknowledging diversity is not enough: it is also important to recognize that scientific predictions are not formal techniques of decision-making, they cannot be reduced to data, formulas, schemes, algorithms, or narratives. These Russian scientists discussed in this book emphasized that using scientific prediction in policy and management is not like following a recipe for a discrete decision or judgment in an isolated context: in contrast, the will to predict scientifically requires wide social and institutional orchestration of scientific knowledge production, synchronizing it with decision-making in organizations.[1] Scientific predictions, first and foremost, are stabilizing devices: they focus attention, mobilize agency, and synchronize collective action. However, it is the way in which predictions are bound to their context that makes predictions scientific in the modern sense: decontextualizing those predictions as mere tables, numbers, equations, or scenarios leads to a form of knowledge that I call "scientific in form, astrological in content."[2]

For instance, as I showed in chapter 2 focusing on the emergence of economic forecasting in the postrevolutionary Russia in 1917 to 1939, the positivist notion of prediction informed economic planning and social forecasting and even in its simplistic, reductionist, and overtly optimistic forms was a criterion of the scientificity of planning. For Nikolai Kondrat'ev scientific prevision was about faithful factual description and explanation of transition between two events, the known and the unknown ones, the known events being captured by statistical data on the economy and the future events being goals set in an economic development plan. As Kondrat'ev was acutely aware that knowledge about past events—especially ones characterizing economic and social development—was limited, Kondrat'ev recognized the severe limitations of economic and social statistics, deeming them unsuitable for long-term and precise planning. More-

CONCLUSION   185

over, each time scientists like Kondrat'ev examined social and economic predictions they unmasked their flawed assumptions and ideological as well as incompetent uses of statistics. The history of positivist scientific prediction in interwar Soviet Russia is therefore not only a story of centralized state control, but rather a story of criticism of the communist planning utopia and organizational behavior and a call for institutional reform to develop new organizational practices for statistical data gathering and scientific epistemologies for the economy. It is also a story of interruptions, where Russian thought on scientific prediction, devastated by Stalin's repressions and Second World War destruction, developed in bursts and jumps, rediscovering its past and forgetting it again, reassembling the elements in a strategic and pragmatic way.

As I showed in this book, following the Second World War, a wide-ranging consensus has been reached across many scientific disciplines and policy spheres that to focus on prediction scientifically is to treat the mediating processes, which link symptoms/signs and outcomes, seriously. To put it in simple words, the modern epistemology of scientific prediction led Soviet scientists to face social and organizational reality, however inconvenient it was, as it diverged from the political utopian notions of Soviet progress.[3] This led to an increasing discrepancy between political planning and expert knowledge production in the policy fields: a process that can be characterized as a dysfunctional orchestration of prediction. As I showed in chapters 2 and 4, tracing the development of Soviet economic and social forecasting from the 1920s to the 1980s, the question to what extent complex social and economic processes can be knowable, can be described in numbers, and how their change can be represented and modelled statistically, was debated in the field of social and economic prognosis. For Kondrat'ev, an economic prognosis was a working hypothesis rather than a source of reliable facts, predicting future events precisely was unlikely and the success of prediction depended on the context of its use. This critical, relational approach to economic forecasting was not welcomed by the Soviet authorities. On the one hand, Soviet authorities required economists to churn out statistical numbers as part of the organizational rituals of accounting, where the role of statistics was to politically legitimize decisions rather than to guide them. On the other hand, the view of society as a simple machine, where inputs, be they ideology, money, or violence, determined the outputs, for instance such as social behavior, prevailed. The Soviet regime produced a lot of statistical numbers, many of which claimed to be results of prognoses, but these numbers obfuscated rather than revealed the cumulative development of the economy and society.

Only during Khrushchev's thaw, as I showed in chapter 4, did the Soviet regime open up for the scientific orchestration of prediction in the Soviet Union. The path for this opening was paved by wartime mobilization during the Second

186   CONCLUSION

World War and postwar technological developments, requiring a more robust science of organization to secure logistics and battle operations, and operate the nuclear, mining, and chemical industrial complexes. Different types of scientific prediction emerged: the positivist notion of prediction as a criterion of scientific knowledge remained influential in planning and management, the statistical measurement of evolutionary change informed a range of disciplines from economics to biology, and, with the onset of cybernetics, prediction based on pattern recognition was developed in computer science. The latter became particularly influential, leading to what I call the cybernetic sensibility, an understanding that evolutionary, complex, and fleeting phenomena are structured through informational feedback and prediction and an expectation that they can be described mathematically, simulated in computers, and deployed as part of organization. The cybernetic sensibility legitimized the need to recognize divergence, difference from the policy goal being not as deviant and treacherous but as an organic part of spontaneous evolution, and to act on it. The cybernetic sensibility was adopted across East and West, requiring a processual integration of the production of predictive scientific expertise and organizational decision-making. In the Soviet Union, as I showed in the last four chapters of this book, this integration could not take place fully, in part because of the leadership's naive approach to scientific prediction as titbits of information that are instructive, to be used as astrological prognoses, in part because of the demand for nonknowledge generated in what Ledeneva described as the informal economics of favors, and, last but not the least, because of the paucity of the available data. However, despite this, the cybernetic sensibility was a source of innovation as it shaped the conceptual architecture of scientific prediction in communication, management, and governance. Some of these innovative strands were detailed in the chapters exploring what I called the late modern concepts of scientific prediction—prospective reflexivity, reflexive control, and global governance as guidance through milieu.

I would like to propose that it is these three intellectual legacies of the late modern notions of scientific prediction that paved the way for the contemporary Russian governmental imagination, enabling it to exploit the new conditions of increasingly digitally mediated and globally interconnected politics and social life. Focusing on the reflexivity and complexity of long-term and planetary scale developments, these approaches are only loosely coupled with the positivist scheme of science–prediction–action. With regards to prospective reflexivity and reflexive control, the will to predict individual cognition and group behavior and to orchestrate them poses serious ethical issues, where managers use forward-directed technologies of reflexivity to tap into social informality in organizations and the Russian government uses reflexive control to organize and justify strategic decep-

CONCLUSION   187

tion in informational wars, both at home and abroad. Both prospective reflexivity and reflexive control thrive in spheres of opacity, that is, the lack of a subject's own understanding of the self and the other, at the same time *increasing* rather than decreasing this opacity in the name of effective pursuit of organizational or strategic goals. To predict reflexively means to mobilize behavior through identity construction rather than to account for a logistics of goal-directed action. For instance, as a result of the Russian government's strategic deception deployed in the buildup to the invasion of Ukraine, Russia is said to have undermined its actorial identity as a rational state because it misused diplomacy to deliver lies.[4] However, Kremlin actors regard themselves like Dostoyevsky's players—craftsmen of warfare and performative tellers of truth bringing about a new reality.

It was not the purpose of this book to present an exhaustive discussion of the different types of scientific prediction, but rather to develop a sociological and historical study of prediction that is sensitive to plurality. As I showed, approaches to scientific prediction developed in a spontaneous, ad hoc, and lively manner, thriving on conceptual and technical transfers between different fields. What can be gleaned from the cases presented in this book is that the development of notions of scientific prediction was as turbulent as the growth of postwar technoscience. This turbulence and plurality of approaches led to multiple transfers and cross-fertilization of ideas and techniques, but it also led to somewhat mistaken use of different types of prediction, where different techniques were expected to deliver the same kind of result. For instance, the techniques of statistical forecasting of mid- and long-term social and economic development were deemed equivalent of very short-term pattern recognition used in cybernetic models of tracking and correction via feedback loops. After all, designers of servomechanisms, neurophysiologists, and geneticists used statistical methods and computers, just like economists and planners. The military planners of logistical systems used linear programming, while combat interactions, which, in Lefebvre's theory also included the enemy's cognition, used feedback loops to read and deceive the opponent. Despite these apparent technical and conceptual parallels, the techniques of linear programming as a decision aid were different from feedback-based processing of fast changing information in neurophysiological systems and servomechanisms.[5] Indeed, the epistemological differences between the statistical forecasting of macro developments and the behavioral control described by cybernetics should not be underestimated.

Attempts to combine these techniques mechanically in a policy context led to disappointment in the techniques as planning and decision aids, at best, and bad decisions at worst, where forecasts were regarded as a form of certain knowledge and acted upon. In the 1960s Karl Deutsch wrote about "the nerves of government" and Marshall McLuhan dreamt about the "cybernation" of society

188   CONCLUSION

through media technology. In the 1970s, cyberneticians such as Viktor Glushkov and Stafford Beer tried to put this idea into action by devising digitally networked command centers for the Soviet Union and Chile, OGAS and Cybersyn. All of them underestimated the many levels of complexity and the number of mediators required to produce and channel data through those "nerves." No statistical forecasting of complex human actions could be done at such high speed and quality so as to feed into real-time decisions. Today we are not short of such examples as, for instance, so-called real-time algorithmic processing in predictive policing. As researchers have shown, the algorithmic predictions of crime events do not feed directly into the police response in real time, as in a cybernetic prosthetic arm. Instead, guesses of possible crimes are screened at regular periods and used as a rationale to launch or withhold action.[6] Algorithmic predictions in policing are mediated by too many agencies and cannot be qualified as being "real-time."[7] The only situation when the policing algorithms are applied in what counts as real time, that is, immediately, is the case of "sorting" observations into predefined categories, for example in instances of ethnic profiling during stop and search at border control.[8] It can be argued that ethnic profiling and "stop and search" policing is but one component of the loop of the situational prediction process.[9]

It is clear that the will to predict scientifically requires careful balancing between levels of complexity and the ability to deploy the correct epistemological tools (predictions) in appropriate contexts. As I showed in chapter 7, focusing on the global and long-term prediction of the coevolution of mankind and the environment, Soviet complexity scientists, such as Nikita Moiseev, proposed that cybernetic target-based predictions could only perform well at a lower level of complexity. As Moiseev wrote in the 1970s and 1980s, to make sense of government at the higher level of complexity, such as the interaction of economy, demography, pollution, and the global biosphere, new terms are required, such as negative guidance, which works not through setting targets and predictive orientation of behavior, monitored by the steersman, but through boundaries that are instead channeling behavior. Today the ongoing debates about global climate governance are looking for new models integrating scientific expertise, policy decisions, markets, and implementation actions.[10] These debates are still taking place along the same conceptual lines that were articulated by systems scholars in the 1980s.[11]

Perhaps the most pressing challenge for such scholarship is shaping the public culture of coping with failure as an inevitable part and parcel of scientific predictions. For example, the experience of the Covid-19 pandemic made it evident that statistical forecasting of the rates of spread of the infection and mortality was not a window on the future, but an important heuristic tool enabling both the monitoring of the population and checking the relations between policy measures and public health.[12] That many of these forecasts failed is not so much a failure of science as such, but rather an expected part of a robust process of scientific knowledge production. However, different forms of prediction fail in different ways: the Comtean and, later, logical empiricist notion of prediction as explanation help testing the explanatory power of theories. The failure of prediction as pattern recognition helps us to notice changes in the environment and inform the organism's or machine's adaptation to it. The notions of reflexive control and prospective reflexivity address failures of collective behavior in organizations or seek to cause a failure of the opponent. Scientific prediction, in this way, requires coping with failure in ways that echo what Theodore Porter described as the politics of mechanical objectivity, a form of bureaucratic quantification that generates trust precisely because it is vulnerable to scrutiny.

Making Sense of the Failure to Predict

Cold War governments have been widely criticized for having evolved into elitist technocratic systems, blinded by the arms race and guided by a utopian idea of rationality. In this context the will to predict was added to the catastrophic portfolio of Cold War governmentality as the list of harmful uses of scientific (and scientifically engineered) predictions is a long one and growing. As I showed in this book the notions of prospective reflexivity and reflexive control constitute techniques that seek to manipulate the behavior of others, be they collaborators or opponents. A similar will to predict but, at the same time, to govern through opacity stemming from the asymmetry of power is expressed in the algorithmic governance based on tracking and modifying online user behavior and the efforts to create digital behavior markets by reducing individual people to data points, as criticized by Shoshana Zuboff.[13] Even the uses of climate change predictions to balance out the world economy and the biosphere pose the threat of environmental authoritarianism.[14] Although these are valid and very serious concerns, the problem lies, I argue, not with a particular type of scientific prediction that is either erroneous or misapplied, but with the orchestration of the entire decision and behavioral milieu where these predictions are created and used.

First, politics and societies that are "unpredictable," in the commonsense meaning of the term as having knowledge about future events, appear to cause a lot of concern. The dismantling of the bipolar Cold War order, the pluralization and changing character of social and political power with the advance of the internet and social media, is increasingly understood as a presumably new, "unpredictable" world, where even mature liberal democratic societies experience

190   CONCLUSION

fragmentation and polarization, processes that put democracies to the test. When Russian military forces invaded Ukraine in 2014, Western media repeated that Putin had become "unpredictable." A few years later, the label of unpredictability was applied to the US President Donald Trump.[15] The outcomes of the British referendum to leave the European Union in 2016 surprised even the Conservative Party who organized the referendum. The culmination of the failure of predict was the scale of Russia's war in Ukraine in February 2022 that extended beyond the already destabilized regions of Donetsk and Luhansk putting the entire country under threat. Both scholars and political commentators argue that the loss of the sense of predictability is accompanied by the rise of conspiracy theories, where neither facts, nor explanations, nor informed future guesses appear to matter any longer.[16]

Second, the tolerance for unpredictability decreases among politicians and the public when things are perceived as turning out for the worse. Scholars, on the other hand, get baffled when events stop complying with their theories even when they change for the better, as they did in the annus mirabilis of 1989. The collapse of the communist regimes in Eastern Europe followed with the dissolution of the Soviet Union in 1991 placed the entire field of East European and Soviet studies in an uncomfortable situation, because these major events were perceived as unexpected, challenging the prevailing consensus about the stability of the communist system. Area scholars were judged for failure like medieval physicians seeking to diagnose and foresee the course of illness of a patient, because they failed to predict the outcomes of the course of reform. Controversy ensued: were the particular experts to be blamed for inadequate knowledge, or did the communist collapse question the very legitimacy of social science (remember the positivist criterion of prediction as a test of scientific knowledge)? Indeed, it was neither/nor. Many scholars mounted sophisticated theoretical argumentation to explain why and when the Soviet system should collapse and this collapse was expected. According to Michael Ellman, both Bolsheviks and Trotskyists expected the communist regime to collapse in the 1920s and 1930s. Later, Soviet economists warned the communist government about the severe decline of rates of growth in the late 1970s and early 1980s. Some Western scholars also indicated that the Soviet regime was seriously threatened by different forces.[17] For instance, in 1978 the prominent Sovietologist Archie Brown suggested that Russian nationalism threatened the communist order, while other scholars, such as the French historian Hélène Carrère d'Encausse, warned about the destabilizing power of Islamic communities in the Soviet Union.[18] Similarly, in 1981, the émigré Jewish-Lithuanian political scientist Alexander Shtromas argued that the Soviet Union would inevitably collapse not only because of Russian nationalism, but also because of the internal loss of ideological legitimacy.[19]

CONCLUSION   191

In the same period, others, like Randall Collins presented a prediction that the Soviet Union would collapse, dating this collapse before a nuclear war would occur (on the basis of his theory of state power).[20] Other theories were presented as having a predictive capacity following the event: for instance, the Estonian émigré Rein Taagepera, who modeled collapses of the great empires in the 1970s and 1980s, argued that the same dynamics featured in the Soviet Union and, post factum, modeled its collapse.[21] It is true, however, that at the time when they were made, these estimates were minority views and were mainly ignored in mainstream Soviet and Cold War scholarship. What is more, although it had been established in retrospect that these scholars happened to anticipate correctly the evolution of the Soviet system, this did not make their work more influential in the field.

In the 1990s, many journals and books hosted forums debating the very scientific status of social science knowledge, which was undermined by the perceived scholars' inability to predict the end of the Soviet Union and, in turn, of the Cold War.[22] These debates, however, revolved around two meanings of scientific prediction: the logical empiricist one as hypothesis and explanation, and the logistical one, as in statistical forecasting, where an event is pinned firmly to a point in space and time. Other scholars, particularly political scientists and economic historians, examined the earlier explanatory frameworks hoping to identify the reasons that hindered their ability to foresee the collapse.[23] The significance of the wider orchestration of prediction escaped the focus of attention. Zubok's study of the Soviet collapse, for instance, presents a fascinatingly rich story of the organizational chaos unleashed by Gorbachev's economic liberalization reforms that changed the rules for production and trade without modeling the possible impact on the economy. Moreover, the *perestroika* reforms did not challenge the ineffective collection of reliable statistical data on the enterprises. The Communist Party of the Soviet Union failed to anticipate both the actions of economic actors and the problem with acquiring data on their activities. In a fabulously ironic way, Gorbachev's *glasnost'* increased opacity of the late Soviet economy instead of making its workings transparent and accountable to the actors and government.[24]

However, does this evidence of failure, where the will to predict scientifically does not live up to expectations, suggest that the will itself must be relinquished? The answer is probably not. In the 1970s the social psychologist Karl Weick wrote about the mystery of prediction, which is embedded in a particular cognitive dynamic, where people align their judgments in relation to their performance, a process that happens retrospectively. Repetitive "cause loops," wrote Weick, create a sense of predictability. These loops consist of judgments, statements, and actions; together, they constitute order, which is enacted in a way

192   CONCLUSION

that can resemble a self-fulfilling prophecy. These prophecies are not just positive feedbacks, described by Robert Merton (when gossip of a failing bank causes a bank run and results in the failure of the bank). Prediction in organizational sense-making, according to Weick, is always retrospective.[25] To extend Weick's thought, the most basic form of prediction performs the function of synchronization of organizational action, where people in organizations act "as if" they can predict (each other's behavior and the changes in the organization's environment). These "as if" actions are performative: together they enact a predictable organization. However, this condition of collective, synchronized predictability is fragile, it is good as long as the actors continue acting "as if." Once the actors give up their convention of predictability and agree that their organization and the surrounding world are "unpredictable," the order is likely to fall apart. When this happens—and it happens all the time—different notions of scientific prediction can be deployed to rebuild the stability. While many decision-makers deploy the models of scientific prediction described in this book, others, like their predecessors hundreds of years ago, resort to astrologers, clairvoyants, and witchcraft.[26] One has to be cautious to avoid rigid binaries of modern and nonmodern when analyzing these forms of predictive knowledge, for their conceptual architecture and social worlds overlap in many ways.[27]

To reset the debate about the legitimacy of the will to predict—and to do this scientifically—it is imperative to look back at the history of prediction. The key argument of this book is that the debate about scientific prediction's validity and usefulness for governance constituted an important part of Soviet Russian modernization. But this was not an exclusively Russian story: a similar study could be done on the basis of Western or Chinese materials, but the Soviet Russian case allowed me to articulate the key conflict lines and tensions that emerge where scientific and commonsense notions of prediction are confused. In the context of the centrally commanded, extremely politicized administrative governance of the Soviet system, science was both endowed with great authority (and, in some instances, limited autonomy from party politics), but was also made vulnerable to the volatile political context of its application. I believe that my argument can be extended to consider Russia's war in Ukraine as an extreme case of politics where the will to predict scientifically is virtually absent. Although at the moment of writing in March 2022, many commentators argued that Putin's decision to invade Ukraine is based on multiple miscalculations of the societal dynamics in the country and is therefore missing a viable strategy for the long term, perhaps a reference to the murky Nietzschean struggle of drives in the will to power helps better to characterize the decision-making at Kremlin, where the role of scientific expertise is far from evident. It is beyond the powers of scientific prediction to foretell the outcomes of the war in Ukraine; however, a democratic use of scientific prediction could contribute to making sure that those outcomes will benefit the Ukrainian society as much as possible.

In all cases of scientific predictions and their failures, the flows of data and behavior must be orchestrated by synchronizing the social, institutional, and material agencies of humans and non-human. Refocusing the scholarly discussion on the will to predict scientifically as democratic orchestration of different forms of knowledge and agencies, hopefully, will help us better understand the failures so that we can fail better.

Notes

INTRODUCTION

1. Linda L. Williams, *Nietzsche's Mirror: The World as Will to Power* (Lanham: Rowan & Littlefield, 2001), 26, 32.

2. Andy Clark, "Whatever Next? Predictive Brains, Situated Agents, and the Future of Cognitive Science," *Behavioral and Brain Sciences* 36 (2013): 181–253; Daniel Kahneman and Amos Tversky, "On the Psychology of Prediction," *Psychological Review* 80, no. 4 (1973): 237–251; Dan Ariely, *Predictably Irrational: The Hidden Forces That Shape Our Decisions* (New York: HarperCollins, 2008).

3. Nathaniel Rich, "The New Science of Disaster Prediction," *New Yorker*, (19 November 2013, https://www.newyorker.com/news/news-desk/the-new-science-of-disaster-prediction.

4. Kit Yates, "Why Mathematicians Sometimes Get Covid Projections Wrong," *Guardian* (UK edition), 26 January 2022.

5. Elke U. Weber and Paul Stern, "Public Understanding of Climate Change in the United States," *American Psychologist* 66, no. 4 (2011): 315–328; Retto Knutti, "Should We Believe Model Predictions of Future Climate Change?" *Philosophical Transactions of the Royal Society Series A* 366 (2008): 4647–4664. For manipulation and deception see Naomi Oreskes and Erik M. Conway, *Merchants of Doubt: How a Handful of Scientists Obscured the Truth on Issues from Tobacco Smoke to Climate Change* (London: Bloomsbury, 2011).

6. Sandra Kemp and Jenny Andersson, eds., *Futures* (Oxford: Oxford University Press, 2021); Max Saunders, *Imagined Futures: Writing, Science and Modernity in the To-Day and To-Morrow Book Series, 1923–31* (Oxford: Oxford University Press, 2019); Jenny Andersson, *The Future of the World: Futurology, Futurists, and the Struggle for the Post-Cold War Imagination* (Oxford: Oxford University Press, 2018); Jens Beckert, *Imagined Futures: Fictional Expectations and Capitalist Dynamics* (Cambridge, MA: Harvard University Press, 2016); Helga Nowotny, *The Cunning of Uncertainty* (Cambridge: Polity Press, 2016); Peter J. Bowler, *A History of the Future: Prophets of Progress from H.G. Wells to Isaac Asimov* (Cambridge: Cambridge University Press, 2017); Walt Friedman, *Fortune Tellers: The Story of America's First Forecasters* (Princeton, NJ: Princeton University Press, 2014).

7. Shoshana Zuboff, *The Age of Surveillance Capitalism: The Fight for a Human Future at the New Frontier of Power* (New York: Profile Books, 2019); Seb Franklin, *Control: Digitality as Cultural Logic* (Cambridge, MA: MIT Press, 2015).

8. Andersson, *The Future of the World*, 6, 27.

9. Andersson, *The Future of the World*.

10. This work, in turn, was an important extension of the intellectual history of the future and temporality, pioneered by Reinhart Koselleck, *Futures Past: On the Semantics of Historical Time* (New York: Columbia University Press, 2004 [1979]) and extended by Barbara Adam and Chris Groves, *Future Matters: Action, Knowledge, Ethics* (Leiden: Brill, 2007). The history of the future can include, but goes beyond, the traditional agenda of the political and cultural critique of studies of utopia, as in, for instance, the influential work by Frederic Jameson, *Archaeologies of the Future: The Desire of Utopia and Other*

NOTES TO PAGES 3–6

Science Fictions (London: Verso, 2005) or imaginaries such as in Peter Bowler, *A History of the Future*, as well as the epistemology of prediction in premodern cultures, as in Federico Santangelo, *Divination, Prediction and the End of the Roman Republic* (Cambridge: Cambridge University Press, 2013).

11. Elke Seefried, "Steering the Future: The Emergence of 'Western' Futures Research and Its Production of Expertise, 1950s to Early 1970s," *European Journal of Futures Research* 2, no. 29 (2014), https://doi.org/10.1007/s40309-013-0029-y.

12. Ann Johnson, "Rational and Empirical Cultures of Prediction," in *Mathematics as a Tool*, eds. Johannes Lenhard and Martin Carrier (Cham: Springer, 2017), 23–35.

13. Matthias Heymann, Gabriele Gramelsberger, and Martin Mahony, eds., *Cultures of Prediction in Atmospheric and Climate Science: Epistemic and Cultural Shifts in Computer-based Modelling and Simulation* (London: Routledge, 2017).

14. Andreas Wenger, Ursula Jasper, and Myriam Dunn Cavelty, eds., *The Politics and Science of Prevision: Governing and Probing the Future* (London: Routledge, 2020). See also Stefan C. Aykut, David Demortain, and Bilel Benbouzid, "The Politics of Anticipatory Expertise: Plurality and Contestation of Futures Knowledge in Governance— Introduction to the Special Issue," *Science & Technology Studies, Finnish Association for Science and Technology Studies* 32, no. 4 (2019), 2–12.

15. Jamie Pietruska, *Looking Forward: Prediction and Uncertainty in Modern America* (Chicago: University of Chicago Press, 2017); Caley Horan, "Investing in the Stars: The Astrology of Money and Markets in the Modern United States," an unpublished presentation, STS Circle at Harvard, 19 November 2018.

16. For Cold War future studies in Eastern Europe and global South see Lukas Becht, "From Euphoria to Frustration: Institutionalizing Prognostic Research in the Polish People's Republic, 1969–76," *Acta Poloniae Historica* 116 (2017): 277–299; Vítězslav Sommer, "Forecasting the Post-Socialist Future: Prognostika in Late Socialist Czechoslovakia, 1970–1989," in *The Struggle for the Long Term in Transnational Science and Politics during the Cold War*, eds. Jenny Andersson and Eglė Rindzevičiūtė (New York: Routledge, 2015), 144–168; Elke Seefried, "Globalized Science: The 1970s Futures Field," *Centaurus: An International Journal of History of Science and Its Cultural Aspects* 59, nos. 1–2 (2017): 40–57. For comparison of classical Western and Chinese approaches to prediction see Lisa Raphals, *Divination and Prediction in Early China and Ancient Greece* (Cambridge: Cambridge University Press, 2013).

17. Janos Kornai, *The Socialist System: The Political Economics of Communism* (Princeton, NJ: Princeton University Press, 1992).

18. James C. Scott, *Seeing Like a State: How Certain Schemes to Improve the Human Condition Have Failed* (New Haven, CT: Yale University Press, 1995).

19. On East–West collaboration in the governance of global risks, see Eglė Rindzevičiūtė, *The Power of Systems: How Policy Sciences Opened Up the Cold War World* (Ithaca, NY: Cornell University Press, 2016); Marc Elie, "Late Soviet Responses to Disasters, 1989–1991: A New Approach to Crisis Management or the Acme of Soviet Technocratic Thinking?" *Soviet and Post-Soviet Review* 40, no. 2 (2013): 214–238; Marc Elie, "Governing by Hazard: Controlling Mudslides and Promoting Tourism in the Mountains Above Alma-Ata (Kazakhstan), 1966–1977," in *Governing Disasters: Beyond Risk Culture*, eds. Sandrine Revet and Julien Langumier (Cham: Palgrave, 2015), 23–57. See also Sonja Schmid, "Chernobyl: Data Wars and Disaster Politics," *Nature*, 566, no. 7745 (2019): 450.

20. Douglas and Wildavsky do not consider the meaning of prediction, for instance whether it means induction, inference, or prospective reflection. They use the term prediction to describe an estimate of an unknown event occurring in the future—a common understanding of prediction in risk studies. Mary Douglas and Aaron Wildavsky, *Risk and Culture: An Essay on the Selection of Technological and Environmental Dangers*

(Berkeley: University of California Press, 1983), 5; Ulrich Beck, *Risk Society: Towards a New Modernity* (Thousand Oaks, CA: Sage, 1993).

21. Michael Power, *The Audit Society: Rituals of Verification* (Oxford: Oxford University Press, 1997); Michael Power, *Organized Uncertainty: Designing a World of Risk Management* (Oxford: Oxford University Press, 2007).

22. Key criticism was presented by Benoît Godin, "The Linear Model of Innovation: The Historical Construction of an Analytical Framework," *Science, Technology and Human Values* 31, no. 6 (2006): 639–667; see also, Silke Beck, "Moving Beyond the Linear Model of Expertise? IPCC and the Test of Adaptation," *Regional Environmental Change* 11 (2011): 297–306.

23. Norbert Wiener, *Cybernetics: Or Control and Communication in the Animal and the Machine* (1948; Cambridge, MA: MIT Press, 1965), 34–36.

24. Bruno Latour, *Reassembling the Social: An Introduction to Actor Network Theory* (Oxford: Oxford University Press, 2005). Writing on governmentality, Michel Foucault captured this simultaneous coproduction of governmental techniques and objects, although neither Foucault nor governmentality scholars paid much attention to predictive expertise, focusing instead on the classificatory effects of the politics of statistical data. See Nikolas Rose, *The Powers of Freedom: Reframing Political Thought* (Cambridge: Cambridge University Press, 1999); for an overview of the role of data in governmentality studies see Evelyn Ruppert, Engin Isin, and Didier Bigo, "Data Politics," *Big Data & Society* 4, no. 2 (2017): 1–7; for an explicit focus on prediction see Claudia Aradau and Tobias Blanke, "Politics of Prediction: Security and the Time/Space of Governmentality in the Age of Big Data," *European Journal of Social Theory* 20, no. 3 (2017): 373–391.

25. There is a wealth of research into social and cultural temporalities and notions of time, which are relevant, but go beyond the scope of this study. For a foundational ethnographic study, see Mircea Eliade, *The Myth of Eternal Return: Cosmos and History* (Oxford: Blackwell, 2018 ([1949]).

26. Paul du Gay, *In Praise of Bureaucracy: Weber–Organization–Ethics* (London: Sage, 2000).

27. Michael D. Cohen, James G. March, and Johan P. Olsen, "A Garbage Can Model of Organizational Choice," *Administrative Science Quarterly* 17, no. 1 (1972): 1–25.

28. David G. Sirmon, Michael A. Hitt, R. Duane Ireland, and Brett Anitra Gilbert, "Resource Orchestration to Create Competitive Advantage: Breadth, Depth, and Life Cycle Effects," *Journal of Management* 37, no. 5 (2011): 1390–1412; see also Nielsen Åkerstrøm Andersen and Justin Grønbaek Pors, *Public Management in Transition: The Orchestration of Potentiality* (Bristol: Policy Press, 2016).

29. Martina Prpic, "The Open Method of Coordination," European Parliamentary Research Service, PE 542.142 (2014), 1–2; Kenneth W. Abbott, Philipp Genschel, Duncan Snidal, and Bernhard Zangl, eds., *International Organizations as Orchestrators* (Cambridge: Cambridge University Press, 2015); Kenneth Wayne Abbott, Philipp Genschel, Duncan Snidal, and Bernhard Zangl, "Orchestration: Global Governance through Intermediaries" (2012) http://dx.doi.org/10.2139/ssrn.2125452; Kenneth W. Abbott, Philipp Genschel, Duncan Snidal, and Bernhard Zangl, "Two Logics of Indirect Governance: Delegation and Orchestration," *British Journal of Political Science* FirstView (2015): 1–11; Thomas Hale and Charles Roger, "Orchestration and Transnational Climate Governance," *Review International Organization* 9 (2014): 59–82.

30. This model of orchestration is derived from the management of informational systems and networks and can be found in network governance and meta-governance studies. Jonna Gjaltema, Robbert Biesbroek, and Katrien Termeer, "From Government to Governance: A Systematic Literature Review," *Public Management Review* 22, no. 12 (2020): 1760–1780.

198   NOTES TO PAGES 8–13

31. Lena Bendlin, *Orchestrating Local Climate Policy in the European Union: Inter-Municipal Coordination and the Covenant of Mayors in Germany and France* (London: Springer, 2020), 36.

32. Bendlin, *Orchestrating*, 40.

33. See, for instance, Karl W. Deutsch, *The Nerves of Government: Models of Political Communication and Control* (New York: Free Press, 1963).

34. An engineer specializing in human–computer interaction, Guy André Boy proposed the model of the orchestra to describe and organize the governance of complexity: "agents require a common frame of reference (a music theory analogue), contracts (scores) must be appropriately and formally coordinated (the role of the composer), real-time coordination must be assured (the role of the conductor), and an agent must have specific abilities to perform according to contracts (role and proficiency of the musicians). Contracts are seen as scenarios or storyboards, with an additional responsibility dimension." Guy A. Boy, *Orchestrating Human-Centred Design* (London: Springer, 2013), 9.

35. Rindzevičiūtė, *The Power of Systems*.

36. Martin Carrier, "Prediction in Context: On the Comparative Epistemic Merit of Predictive Success," *Studies in History and Philosophy of Science* 45 (2014): 100.

37. For instance, John Law occasionally used the term orchestration as a component of "translation," an STS concept created to describe and analyze arrangements of different agencies, such as human–nonhuman actions that are mediated mainly through inscriptions. John Law, *After Method: Mess in Social Science Research* (London: Routledge, 2004), 29; John Law "Notes on the Theory of the Actor-Network: Ordering, Strategy and Heterogeneity," *Systems Practice* 5 (1992): 379–393.

38. Emily Dolan, *The Orchestral Revolution: Haydn and the Technologies of Timbre* (Cambridge: Cambridge University Press, 2013).

39. Theodore Porter, *Trust in Numbers: The Pursuit of Objectivity in Science and Public Life* (Princeton, NJ: Princeton University Press, 1995).

40. Scott, *Seeing Like a State*.

41. Rindzevičiūtė, *The Power of Systems*; Heymann et al., *Cultures of Prediction*; Quinn Slobodian, *Globalists: The End of Empire and the Birth of Neoliberalism*. (Cambridge, MA: Harvard University Press, 2018).

42. Ronald Kline, *The Cybernetics Moment: Or Why We Call Our Age the Information Age* (Baltimore: Johns Hopkins University Press, 2016); Stuart Russell, *Human Compatible: Artificial Intelligence and the Problem of Control* (London: Viking, 2019).

43. Peter Galison, "The Ontology of the Enemy: Norbert Wiener and the Cybernetic Vision," *Critical Inquiry* 21, no. 1 (1994): 228–266; Paul Edwards, *The Closed World: Computers and the Politics of Discourse in Cold War America* (Cambridge, MA: MIT Press, 1996); Dominique Pestre, "Complex Systems and Total War: British Operational Research and the PM Statistical Branch at the Beginning of World War II," in *Nature Engaged: Science in Practice from the Renaissance to the Present*, eds. N. Biagoli and J. Riskin (New York: Palgrave Macmillan, 2012), 83–100.

44. Kenneth Arrow, *Social Choice and Individual Values* (New York: Wiley, 1951); Beckert, *Imagined Futures*.

45. Russell, *Human Compatible*.

46. Christophe Bonneuil and Jean Baptiste Fressoz, *The Shock of the Anthropocene: The Earth, History and Us* (London: Verso, 2016); Astrid Kirchhof and John Robert McNeill, eds., *Nature and the Iron Curtain: Environmental Policy and Social Movements in Communist and Capitalist Countries, 1945–1990* (Pittsburgh: University of Pittsburgh Press, 2019).

1. WHAT IS SCIENTIFIC PREDICTION?

1. For discussion of the term prediction see these important studies: Jens Beckert, *Imagined Futures: Fictional Expectations and Capitalist Dynamics* (Cambridge, MA: Harvard University Press, 2016); Philip Mirowski, *Machine Dreams: Economics Becomes a Cyborg Science* (Cambridge: Cambridge University Press, 2002). Particularly extensive reflections can be found in Jenny Andersson, *The Future of the World: Futurology, Futurists, and the Struggle for the Post-Cold War Imagination* (Oxford: Oxford University Press, 2018) and Louise Amoore, *The Politics of Possibility: Risk and Security Beyond Probability* (Durham, NC: Duke University Press, 2013) as well as the volume edited by Andreas Wenger, Ursula Jasper, and Myriam Dunn Cavelty, eds., *The Politics and Science Prevision: Governing and Probing the Future* (London: Routledge, 2020). These studies, however, tend to settle on one definition of scientific prediction, while I argue that it is important to recognize the plurality of different notions of prediction in science and expertise.

2. In *Britannica* the most comprehensive article on prediction is dedicated to the mathematical statistics of time series and the use of time series to solve engineering problems of information and control, theorized by a Swedish mathematician, Herman Wold, in 1938. Wold's work informed both the American Norbert Wiener and the Russian Andrei Kolmogorov, who contributed highly influential theories on the extrapolation and smoothing of time series in the 1930s and 1940s. In the next chapter I offer a detailed discussion of cybernetic prediction, which influenced different domains of scientific knowledge and organizational practice in the second half of the twentieth century. This chapter lays the groundwork for this discussion, sketching out the richness and diversity of prediction's history and epistemological scope.

3. It is worth citing this passage that defines prediction as a logical inference of value that can be applied in different fields:

> An important problem of probability theory is to predict the value of a future observation Y given knowledge of a related observation X (or, more generally, given several related observations X1, X2, . . .). Examples are to predict the future course of the national economy or the path of a rocket, given its present state. Prediction is often just one aspect of a "control" problem. For example, in guiding a rocket, measurements of the rocket's location, velocity, and so on are made almost continuously; at each reading, the rocket's future course is predicted, and a control is then used to correct its future course. The same ideas are used to steer automatically large tankers transporting crude oil, for which even slight gains in efficiency result in large financial savings.

David O. Siegmund, "Probability Theory," *Encyclopaedia Britannica* (2018), https://www.britannica.com/science/probability-theory/Conditional-expectation-and-least-squares-prediction#ref407444.

4. This commonsense understanding of prediction is presented, for instance, in the *Oxford English Dictionary*, where "to predict" is explained as "to know beforehand," to estimate the future.

5. Federico Santangelo, *Divination, Prediction and the End of the Roman Republic* (Cambridge: Cambridge University Press, 2013), 47–48. Some historians, however, refer to divination and mantic knowledge as synonymous, but this is not the place to resolve this long-standing debate. See Michael Lackner, ed., *Coping with the Future: Theories and Practices of Divination in East Asia* (Leiden: Brill, 2018); Lisa Raphals, *Divination and Prediction in Early China and Ancient Greece* (Cambridge: Cambridge University Press, 2013); and the particularly lucid study by Alexander Fidora, "Divination and Scientific

NOTES TO PAGES 16–19

Prediction: The Epistemology of Prognostic Sciences in Medieval Europe," *Early Science and Medicine*, 18 (2013): 517–535.

6. Santangelo, *Divination*, 106.

7. Raphals, *Divination and Prediction*.

8. Santangelo, *Divination*, 63. The Roman practice of divination, "the consultation of the gods with a view to establishing their will and their position on an envisaged action," according to Santangelo (p. 5), was a part of religious ritual that shaped Roman everyday life. Divination is also characterized by Lisa Raphals as the "normal" everyday activity of consulting "extrahuman" knowledge. Raphals, *Divination and Prediction*, 2.

9. Santangelo, *Divination*, 64.

10. "The problem of the future," argues Raphals, is "universal," a defining feature of European and Chinese societies (p. 6). In Chinese the interaction of time and space is called *yu zhu* (p. 10). The ancient Greeks had a notion of a fairly predetermined and therefore knowable future, in contrast, the Chinese had a pragmatic and flexible notion of the future. Raphals compares these two cultures by exploring the institutional, social, and political contexts and practices of the production of divinatory knowledge. She shows that divination was a source of "power, authority and consensus" in these societies. However, ancient "Chinese normative questions on good and ill auspicea did not seek predictions, but they were centrally concerned with regularity in cycles of time" (p. 380). For Raphals, it is not so much "prediction" as an attempt to "know the future" that is important in ancient Chinese and Greek divination, which can also be explained as a "systematizing attitude to the world" (p. 380). For a very helpful discussion on how the Chinese approach to time can be linked with modern forms of forecasting in future studies and how it can be different from the Western approach to prediction as mantic knowledge, see Dragos Simandan, "Wisdom and Foresight in Chinese Thought: Sensing the Immediate Future," *Journal of Future Studies* 22, no. 3 (2018): 35–50; and Leo Howe and Alan Wain, eds., *Predicting the Future* (Cambridge: Cambridge University Press, 1993).

11. Fidora, "Divination and Scientific Prediction," 519–521. See also Ilkka Kantola, *Probability and Moral Uncertainty in Late Medieval and Early Modern Times* (Helsinki: Luther-Agricola Society, 1994).

12. According to Mary Poovey early modern thinkers were skeptical about quantitative economic knowledge because they deemed it conjectural and therefore less reliable than solid, morally grounded opinions. Mary Poovey, *A History of the Modern Fact: Problems of Knowledge in the Sciences of Wealth and Society* (Chicago: University of Chicago Press, 1998). To fast forward, the predictive power of opinions would return to the scientific agenda in the mid-twentieth century, not because of their moral value, but because of their collective nature that could be capitalized on by polling methods. See Christian Dayé, "How to Train Your Oracle: The Delphi Method and Its Turbulent Youth in Operations Research and the Policy Sciences," *Social Studies of Science* 48, no. 6 (2018): 849–850; and Philip Tetlock and Dan Gardner, *Superforecasting: The Art and Science of Prediction* (New York: Random House, 2016).

13. Nicholas Denyer, "The Case Against Divination: An Examination of Cicero's De Divinatione," *Cambridge Classical Journal* 31 (1985): 5, cited in Raphals, *Divination and Prediction*, p. 3.

14. Michel Callon, "Some Elements of a Sociology of Translation: Domestication of the Scallops and the Fishermen of St Brieuc Bay," *Sociological Review* 32, no. 1 (1984): 196–233.

15. Karl E. Weick, *Making Sense of the Organization* (Oxford: Blackwell, 2001), 11–14.

16. Fidora, "Divination and Scientific Prediction," 526.

17. Fidora, "Divination and Scientific Prediction," 523.

NOTES TO PAGES 19–25   201

18. Lisa Raphals, "The Ethics of Prediction," in *How Should One Live? Comparing Ethics in Ancient China and Greco-Roman Antiquity*, eds. R. A. H. King and Dennis Schilling (Berlin: De Gruyter, 2011), 278–303, 284.

19. Fidora, "Divination and Scientific Prediction," 529.

20. Fidora, "Divination and Scientific Prediction," 531–532.

21. Fidora, "Divination and Scientific Prediction," 531–532.

22. Fidora, "Divination and Scientific Prediction," 524–525.

23. Poovey, *A History of the Modern Fact*, 220.

24. Poovey, *A History of the Modern Fact*, 8.

25. Poovey, *A History of the Modern Fact*, 222.

26. It is not possible to do justice to the long and vast debate on prediction in philosophy of science. For a useful overview, see Jonathan Fuller, Alex Broadbent, and Luis J. Flores, "Prediction in Epidemiology and Medicine," *Studies in History and Philosophy of Biological and Biomedical Sciences* (2015), 1–4.

27. Poovey, *A History of the Modern Fact*, 14.

28. Auguste Comte, *The Positive Philosophy* (1830–1842), trans. Harriet Martineau [1896] (Kitchener, ON: Batocher Books, 2000), 43. On the same page, "There can be no doubt that Man's study of nature must furnish the only basis of his action upon nature; for it is only by knowing the laws of phenomena, and thus able to foresee them, that we can, in active life, set them to modify one another for our advantage." For Comte, prevision is part of what he understood as an indirect modification, arranging material phenomena so that they can impact each other, because, as he put it, the "direct" power of man is very weak. This relates to Wiener's idea of orchestration as management of the "arrival" of the universe through material and sensorial inputs in organisms and machines, which I discuss in chapter 3.

29. Comte, *The Positive Philosophy*, 151–152

30. Comte, *The Positive Philosophy*, 181–182.

31. Comte, *The Positive Philosophy*, 198.

32. Gertrude Lenzer, ed., *Auguste Comte and Positivism: The Essential Writings* (London: Routledge, 1998), cited from Roy Moxley, "Ernst Mach and B. F. Skinner: Their Similarities with Two Traditions for Verbal Behavior," *Behavior Analyst* 28, no. 1 (2005): 33.

33. Poovey, *A History of the Modern Fact*, 234.

34. Emile Durkheim, *The Rules of Sociological Method*, trans. W. D. Halls (1895; New York: Free Press, 1982), 138.

35. Durkheim, *The Rules of Sociological Method*, 155.

36. Carl G. Hempel and Paul Oppenheim, "Studies in the Logic of Explanation," *Philosophy of Science* 15, no. 2 (1948): 136. I am grateful for the inspiration to revisit the writings of positivists to the postgraduates at the Department of History and Philosophy of Science at the University of Cambridge, with whom I had the privilege to discuss this study during my visit in Spring 2019.

37. Heather Douglas, "Reintroducing Prediction to Explanation," *Philosophy of Science* 76 (2009): 446.

38. Hempel and Oppenheim, "Studies in the Logic of Explanation," 138.

39. Hempel and Oppenheim, "Studies in the Logic of Explanation," 138.

40. Hempel and Oppenheim, "Studies in the Logic of Explanation," 138.

41. Hempel and Oppenheim, "Studies in the Logic of Explanation," 139.

42. Sami Abuhamdeg and Mihaly Csikszentmihalyi, "The Artistic Personality: A System Perspective," in *The Systems Model of Creativity*, ed. Mihaly Csikszentmihalyi (Dordrecht: Springer, 2014), 227–237.

43. Hempel and Oppenheim, "Studies in the Logic of Explanation," 139. The debate in philosophy of science on the symmetrical link between prediction and explanation is

202   **NOTES TO PAGES 25–29**

a long-standing one. For more, see John Losee, *The Golden Age of the Philosophy of Science* (London: Bloomsbury, 2018).

44. Hempel and Oppenheim, "Studies in the Logic of Explanation," 142.

45. Hempel and Oppenheim, "Studies in the Logic of Explanation," 143.

46. Hempel and Oppenheim, "Studies in the Logic of Explanation," 143.

47. A popular version was presented in a bestseller, see B. F. Skinner, *Beyond Freedom and Dignity* (New York: Pelican, 1971). According to Zuboff, this environmentalist and positivist approach to behavior and cognition informed capitalist practices of digital extraction, which she describes as algorithmically controlled future behavior markets. Shoshanna Zuboff, *The Age of Surveillance Capitalism: The Fight for a Human Future at the New Frontier of Power* (New York: Profile Books, 2019).

48. In the early versions of cybernetics, purposive behavior was conceptualized in such a way that knowing the intention of an animal or a machine was not necessary to predict its behavior. In engineering and management applications, dynamic systems—that is, systems that both change internally and can generate changes in their environment—were designed to be controlled via feedback loops. From a human point of view such systems may appear to "have a purpose," for instance, in a robot vacuum cleaner. However, what appears as "purpose" is in fact just an expression of the system's architecture, its ability to interact with the environment. Similarly, in cybernetically informed approaches in neuroscience and psychiatry, the concept of the intentional decision can also be bypassed at lower levels of organization, where information exchange is seen as part of (subconscious) behavior and adaptation. Note that ability to adapt alone does not guarantee viability: adaptation can be dysfunctional. See, for instance, Gregory Bateson's double bind theory of schizophrenia. Andrew Pickering, *The Cybernetic Brain: Sketches of Another Future* (Chicago: University of Chicago Press, 2010), 173–175.

49. Zygmunt Bauman, *Legislators and Interpreters: Of Modernity, Post-Modernity and Intellectuals* (London: Polity, 1989).

50. See, for instance, Donald McCloskey, "The Art of Forecasting: From Ancient to Modern Times," *Cato Journal* 12, no. 1 (1992): 23–48.

51. Douglas, "Reintroducing Prediction to Explanation," 454.

52. Robert Northcott, "When Are Purely Predictive Models Best?" *Disputatio* 9, no. 47 (2017): 631–656.

53. Wesley C. Salmon, "Rational Prediction," *British Journal for the Philosophy of Science* 32, no. 2 (1981): 115–125.

54. Stuart Russell, *Human Compatible: Artificial Intelligence and the Problem of Control* (London: Viking, 2019).

55. Poovey, *A History of the Modern Fact*, 282.

56. The meaning of prediction in statistics has been changing, just like the very meaning of statistics itself; for a useful review see Bertrand S. Clarke and Jennifer L. Clarke, *Predictive Statistics: Analysis and Inference Beyond Models* (Cambridge: Cambridge University Press, 2018).

57. For a revisionist history of inference in statistics as a shift from detecting "probable errors" to "probable data," see Jeff Bidel and Marcel Boumans, "Exploring the History of Statistical Inference in Economics: Introduction," *History of Political Economy* 53S (2021): 1–24.

58. Ronald A. Fischer, "The Logic of Inductive Inference," *Journal of the Royal Statistical Society* 98, no. 1 (1935): 39–82.

59. John Norton, *The Material Theory of Induction* (Calgary, AB: University of Calgary Press, 2021), 202.

60. A. S. C. Ehrenberg and J. A. Bound, "Predictability and Prediction," *Journal of the Royal Statistical Society, Series A (Statistics in Society)* 156, no. 2 (1993): 167–206, 167–168.

61. Ehrenberg and Bound, "Predictability and Prediction," 168. Here the term prediction is used to describe a situation where the result in question will hold for some other, different data (e.g., for a sample from another population). "Predictability" means that it will hold routinely, within a relevant range of conditions.

62. Goffman, Erving. *Encounters* (New York: Bobbs-Merrill, 1961).

63. Andrew *The Mangle of Practice: Time, Agency, Science* (Chicago: University of Chicago Press, 1995).

64. Ian Hacking, *The Taming of Chance* (Cambridge: Cambridge University Press, 1990); Alain Desrosières, *The Politics of Large Numbers: A History of Statistical Reasoning* (Cambridge, MA: Harvard University Press, 2002).

65. Matthias Heymann, Gabriele Gramelsberger, and Martin Mahony, "Key Characteristics of Cultures of Prediction," in *Cultures of Prediction in Atmospheric and Climate Science*, eds. Matthias Heymann, Gabriele Gramelsberger, and Martin Mahony (London: Routledge, 2015), 26–27.

66. Frank H. Knight, *Risk, Uncertainty and Profit* (Boston: Riverside Press, 1921), 200.

67. Knight, *Risk*, 201–202.

68. The idea of circular causality was central for the understanding of behavior beyond mechanical determinism and the traditional teleology that attributed the source of behavior to human intentions.

69. Ronald Kline, *The Cybernetics Moment: Or Why We Call Our Age the Information Age* (Baltimore: Johns Hopkins University Press, 2015), 47.

70. Kline, *The Cybernetics Moment*, 57.

71. Kline, *The Cybernetics Moment*, 71–72.

72. Slava Gerovitch, *From Newspeak to Cyberspeak: A History of Soviet Cybernetics* (Cambridge, MA: MIT Press, 2002).

73. Seb Franklin, *Control* (Cambridge, MA: MIT Press, 2015); Zuboff, *The Age of Surveillance Capitalism*.

74. Kline, *The Cybernetics Moment*, 83.

75. Kline, *The Cybernetics Moment*, 136.

76. Kline, *The Cybernetics Moment*, 153–1954.

77. W. Ross Ashby, cited in Pickering, *The Cybernetic Brain*, 6.

78. Anil K. Seth, "The Cybernetic Bayesian Brain: From Interoceptive Inference to Sensorimotor Contingencies," in *Open MIND*, eds. T. Metzinger and J. M. Windt (Frankfurt am Main: MIND Group, 2020), 1–24, doi:10.15502/9783958570108.

79. I thank Dr Giulia Gallia for advising me on neuroscientific approaches to prediction and for reading this chapter. Any views and errors are mine only.

80. Moshe Bar, "The Proactive Brain: Memory for Predictions." *Philosophical Transactions of the Royal Society of London, Series B, Biological Sciences* 364, no. 1521 (2009): 1235–1243.

81. Andy Clark, *Surfing Uncertainty: Prediction, Action and the Embodied Mind* (Oxford: Oxford University Press, 2016); see also Andy Clark, "Whatever Next? Predictive Brains, Situated Agents, and the Future of Cognitive Science," *Behavioral and Brain Sciences* 36 (2013): 181–253.

82. Clark, "Whatever Next?" 183.

83. Moshe Bar, "Visual Objects in Context," *Nature Reviews Neuroscience* 5 (2004): 617–629.

84. Clark, "Whatever Next?" 185.

85. Clark, "Whatever Next?" 187.

86. Clark, "Whatever Next?" 194.

87. Clark, "Whatever Next?" 199.

88. Clark, "Whatever Next?" 200.

204   NOTES TO PAGES 36–40

89. The notion of cybernetic prediction as pattern recognition can be found in the influential writings of Luciana Parisi, *Contagious Architecture: Computation, Aesthetics and Space* (Cambridge, MA: MIT Press, 2013); Mario Carpo, *The Second Digital Turn: Design Beyond Intelligence* (Cambridge, MA: MIT Press, 2017).

90. Pickering, *The Cybernetic Brain*, 18–19.

91. Donella Meadows, John Richardson, and Gerhart Bruckman, *Groping in the Dark: The First Decade of Global Modelling* (Chichester: John Wiley & Sons, 1982).

2. VISIBILITY, TRANSPARENCY, AND PREDICTION

1. Robert Collis, "'Stars Rule Over People, but God Rules Over the Stars': The Astrological World View of Boris Ivanovich Kurakin (1676–1727)," *Jahrbücher für Geschichte Osteuropas* 59, no. 2 (2011): 196.

2. The link between the state and different regimes of visibility has been explored by scholars and fiction writers in too many works to list here. My argument in this chapter is that scientific prediction constituted a novel resource for the political optics of visibility, which, in the Soviet context, had the potential to empower marginalized, nonparty actors (scholars and experts). As in the cases of environmental monitoring, computer technology and citizen science, analyzed by Jennifer Gabrys, the strive for scientific prediction pluralized the Soviet regime of visibility, serving, however, sometimes top-down and other times bottom-up governance. For representative studies on liberal and democratic technologies of visibility see Chris Otter, *The Victorian Eye: A Political History of Light and Vision in Britain, 1800–1910* (Chicago: University of Chicago Press, 2008); Jennifer Gabrys, *Program Earth: Environmental Sensing Technology and the Making of a Computational Planet* (Minneapolis: University of Minnesota Press, 2016).

3. According to Vaclav Smil, growth measurement comes in three forms: linear, exponential, and finite growth patterns. Linear growth occurs when an identical quantity is added during a specified period (p. 876). In statistics, the most common are S-shaped patterns of growth consisting of peak and decline (p. 883). As Smil noted, "growth is always a function of time," where the change of "physical or immaterial phenomena" can be measured against the change of other variables. Vaclav Smil, *Growth: From Microorganisms to Megacities* (Cambridge, MA: MIT Press, 2019), Kindle location 820.

4. For the technicalities of different forms of scientific forecasting see Tuomo Kuosa, *The Evolution of Strategic Foresight: Navigating Public Policy Making* (London: Routledge, 2016).

5. Elena Aronova, *Scientific History: Experiments in History and Politics from the Bolshevik Revolution to the End of the Cold War* (Chicago: University of Chicago Press, 2021), 35.

6. Corinne Bara, "Forecasting Civil War and Political Violence," in *The Politics and Science of Prevision: Governing and Probing the Future*, eds. Andreas Wenger, Ursula Jasper, and Myriam Dunn Cavelty (London: Routledge, 2020), 183.

7. Note that the KGB used the term *glasnost'* to describe what they presented as their new normative orientation, seeking to distance themselves from the Stalinist repressions and rehabilitate their public status in the late 1950s. Julie Elkner, "The Changing Face of Repression under Khrushchev," in *Soviet State and Society Under Nikita Khrushchev*, eds. Melanie Ilic and Jeremy Smith (London: Routledge, 2009), 149.

8. Vladislav Zubok, *Zhivago's Children: The Last Russian Intelligentsia* (Cambridge, MA: Harvard University Press, 2011), 271–272.

9. Zubok, *Zhivago's Children*, 273.

10. Theodore Porter, *Trust in Numbers: The Pursuit of Objectivity in Science and Public Life* (Princeton, NJ: Princeton University Press, 1996).

NOTES TO PAGES 40–44 205

11. I draw on Stefanos Geroulanos's discussion of the utopian expectation of "transparency" in the French context: "To make the world transparent had meant knowing it without illusion and without intermediary. To make the social and political realms transparent had meant cleansing them of injustice, corruption, superstition, and oppression from authority and capital. To make the visible transparent had meant purging it of false images and reaching to its supposed essence." These expectations, however, were never fulfilled: the attempts to introduce greater transparency resulted in the reorganization of opacity. Stefanos Geroulanos, *Transparency in Postwar France: A Critical History of the Present* (Stanford, CA: Stanford University Press, 2017), 8.

12. Francis Dodsworth, *The Security Society: History, Patriarchy, Protection* (Cham: Palgrave Macmillan, 2019).

13. Mary Poovey, *Making a Social Body: British Cultural Formation, 1830–1864* (Chicago: University of Chicago Press, 1995).

14. Smil, *Growth*. See a useful discussion of the epistemology of curves by John Norton, *The Material Theory of Induction* (Calgary: University of Calgary Press, 2021). Both Smil and Norton emphasize that the choice of fitting a particular curve to data is ultimately pragmatic.

15. Smil, *Growth*.

16. Matthias Schmelzer, *The Hegemony of Growth: The OECD and the Making of the Economic Growth Paradigm* (Cambridge: Cambridge University Press, 2016), 75–78.

17. According to Seneta, O. S. Pavlovsky's work *On Probability* (1821) was possibly directly inspired by Laplace (1812), as Pavlovsky was trained in Paris. Eugene Seneta, "Early Influences on Probability and Statistics in the Russian Empire," *Archive for History of Exact Sciences* 53 (1998): 201–213.

18. Alexander Vucinich, *Science in Russian Culture, 1861–1917* (Stanford, CA: Stanford University Press, 1970), 167; Nikolai Krementsov, *With or Without Galton: Vasilii Florinskii and the Fate of Eugenics in Russia* (Cambridge, UK: Open Book Publishers, 2018), 5206. In the UK, the first study of mortality was done by John Graunt in 1662. A century later, the methods for demographic studies, driven by public health and taxation concerns, were launched by the Paris school of medicine.

19. Seneta, "Early Influences on Probability," 203.

20. Larissa Titarenko and Elena Zdravomyslova, *Sociology in Russia: A Brief History* (Cham: Palgrave, 2017).

21. Yuri Slezkine, *The House of Government: A Saga of the Russian Revolution* (Princeton, NJ: Princeton University Press, 2017), 18, 103–104.

22. Joseph Bradley, "Patterns of Peasant Migration to Late Nineteenth Century Moscow: How Much Should We Read into Literacy Rates?" *Russian History* 6, no. 1 (1979): 25.

23. For an excellent study of the tax regimes and politics of visibility in imperial and Soviet Russia, see Yanni Kotsonis, *States of Obligation: Taxes and Citizenship in the Russian Empire and Early Soviet Republic* (Toronto: University of Toronto Press, 2014).

24. Eugene Seneta, "A Sketch of the History of Survey Sampling in Russia," *Journal of the Royal Statistical Society* 148, no. 2 (1985): 118–125; see also Alain Blum and Martine Mespoulet, *L'anarchie bureaucratic: statistique et pouvoir sous Staline* (Paris: La Découverte, 2003).

25. Krementsov, *With or Without Galton*, Kindle location 5206. For the importance of military medicine see Suman Seth, *Difference and Disease: Medicine, Race, and Locality in the Eighteenth-Century British Empire* (Cambridge: Cambridge University Press, 2018). More than a century later, a famous study led by Tiana Zaslavskaya, a Novosibirsk sociologist, would use the clustering method to reveal the pervasive social underdevelopment of Soviet village population. This study would spearhead the revival of quantitative sociology and, eventually, the economic reform movement in the 1980s. See Olesia Kirtchik, "From

Pattern Recognition to Economic Disequilibrium: Emmanuil Braverman's Theory of Control of the Soviet Economy," *History of Political Economy* 51, no. S1 (2019): 190.

26. Vytautas Petronis, "Mapping Lithuanians: The Development of Russian Imperial Ethnic Cartography, 1840s–1860s," *Imago Mundi* 63, no. 1 (2011): 62–75; Juliette Cadiot, "Searching for Nationality: Statistics and National Categories at the End of the Russian Empire (1897–1917)," *Russian Review* 64, no. 3 (2005): 440–455.

27. Simon Naylor and Simon Schaffer, "Nineteenth-Century Survey Sciences: Enterprises, Expeditions and Exhibitions," *Notes and Records* 73, no. 2 (2019): 135–147; Dmitry V. Arzyutov, *Reassembling the Environmental Archives of the Cold War: Perspectives from the Russian North* (Stockholm: KTH Royal Institute of Technology, 2021).

28. Joseph Bradley, *Voluntary Associations in Tsarist Russia: Science, Patriotism, and Civil Society* (Cambridge, MA: Harvard University Press, 2009).

29. Krementsov, *With or Without Galton.*

30. Alexander Vucinich, *Social Thought in Tsarist Russia: The Quest for a General Science of Society, 1861–1917* (Chicago: University of Chicago Press, 1976).

31. Darwin's *On the Origin of Species* reached Russia in a German translation in 1860; a Russian version appeared in 1864. Krementsov, *With or Without Galton.* The theory of ethnogenesis was established in the 1930s, influenced by Marr's paleontology of language and Vladimir Vernadskii's ideas on the cumulative eco-evolution of culture and biosphere. Mark Bassin, *The Gumilev Mystique: Biopolitics, Eurasianism, and the Construction of Community in Modern Russia* (Ithaca, NY: Cornell University Press, 2016); Arzyutov, *Reassembling the Environmental Archives.*

32. Nikolai Shelgunov, "Ubytochnost neznaniia," *Russkoe slovo* 4, no. 1 (1863): 5, cited in Krementsov, *With or Without Galton*, Kindle location 2371.

33. Robert Collis, "Stars Rule Over People."

34. See Pietruska's study of the rise of statistical forecasting in the United States in the 1860s and 1870s. Jamie Pietruska, *Looking Forward: Prediction in America* (Chicago: University of Chicago Press, 2017).

35. Pietruska, *Looking Forward.*

36. David Moon, "Estimating the Peasant Population of Late Imperial Russia from the 1897 Census: A Research Note," *Europe-Asia Studies* 48, no. 1 (1996): 141–153.

37. For a discussion of the concept of the culture of prediction, see Pietruska, *Looking Forward*, and Matthias Heymann, Gabriele Gramelsberger, and Martin Mahony, eds., *Cultures of Prediction in Atmospheric and Climate Science: Epistemic and Cultural Shifts in Computer-based Modelling and Simulation* (London: Routledge, 2017).

38. Slezkine, *The House of Government*, 72–73.

39. Slezkine, *The House of Government*, 36–37.

40. Richard Stites, *The Revolutionary Dreams: Utopian Vision and Experimental Life in the Russian Revolution* (Oxford: Oxford University Press, 1989), 108. Stites, however, does not expand on these "godless" scientific predictions and their reception.

41. Mark Harrison, "Chayanov and the Economics of the Russian Peasantry," *Journal of Peasant Studies* 2, no. 4 (1975): 389–417. See also work by Teodor Shanin, ed., *Peasants and Peasant Societies* (Oxford: Blackwell, 1987).

42. Jens Beckert, *Imagined Futures: Fictional Expectations and Capitalist Dynamics* (Cambridge, MA: Harvard University Press, 2016), 24.

43. It is important to note that different explorations of the social body were informed by different scientific epistemologies. In the eighteenth and nineteenth centuries, which represent the exploratory stage of the documentation and classification of social malaises, as shown by Poovey, social reformers relied on the visual nomenclature of anatomy. The notions of light, vision, hygiene, and self-regulation informed the assessment and transformation of urban spaces, as shown in many works of Foucaultian historians and sociolo-

NOTES TO PAGES 46–48

gists, such as, for instance, Chris Otter and Tony Bennett. As Poovey noted, the anatomic perspective on the social resulted in static pictures that were compatible with the early positivist epistemology. However, at the same time, there were other forms of understanding emerging, which drew on biology and physiology to conceptualize the social body and looked for rhythms, cycles, and cumulative development of changes. Krementsov, *With or Without Galton*, Kindle location 2854; Alexander Vucinich, *Darwin in Russian Thought* (Berkeley: University of California Press, 1989); Tony Bennett, Fiona Cameron, Nélia Dias, Ben Dibley, Rodney Harrison, Ira Jacknis, and Conal McCarthy, *Collecting, Ordering, Governing: Anthropology, Museums, and Liberal Government* (Durham, NC: Duke University Press, 2017).

44. Tony Bennett, *Pasts Beyond Memory: Evolution, Museums, Colonialism* (London: Routledge, 1994).

45. Slezkine, *The House of Government*, 105.

46. Alexander Gofman, "The Russian Career of Durkheim's Sociology of Religion and 'Les Formes Élémentaires': Contribution to a Study," *Durkheimian Studies / Études Durkheimiennes* 19 (2013): 101–124

47. Tomila V. Lankina, *The Estate Origins of Democracy in Russia: From Imperial Bourgeoisie to Post-Communist Middle Class* (Cambridge: Cambridge University Press, 2021).

48. Martine Mespoulet, *Construire le socialisme par les chiffres: enquetes et recensements en URSS de 1917 a 1991* (Paris: Institute National d'Etudes Demographiques, 2008).

49. Blum and Mespoulet, *L'anarchie bureaucratique*.

50. V. M. Bautin, "Nikolai Dmitrievich Kondrat'ev i ego rol' v stanovlenii agroekonomicheskoi nauki i obrazovaniia v Rossii," *Izvestiia TSKhA* 2 (2017): 134–153. See also Vincent Barnett, *Kondratiev and the Dynamics of Economic Development: Long Cycles and Industrial Growth in Historical Context* (Basingstoke, UK: Macmillan, 1998).

51. Eli Cook, *The Pricing of Progress: Economic Indicators and the Capitalization of American Life* (Cambridge, MA: Harvard University Press, 2017), 255–261; Pietruska, *Looking Forward*.

52. Beckert, *Imagined Futures*, 309. The Russian émigré and economic modeler Wasily Leontieff started his career at the Kiel Institute for World Economy, where business cycles were modeled in the 1920s. At Kiel, according to Bockman, economists were interested in discerning particular development paths, which could be evolutionary (understood as linear at that time) or cyclic. Their research agenda was later expanded to include the idea of a world economy, global structure, and development. Johanna Bockman, "The Struggle Over Structural Adjustment: Socialist Revolution Versus Capitalist Counterrevolution in Yugoslavia and the World," *History of Political Economy* 51, no. S1 (2019): 256.

53. This model of growth that split the economy into two sectors of goods of uneven priority was proposed by Grigorii Feldman in 1928 and adopted widely in state socialist planning of public policy, for instance, influencing the hierarchy of priorities in cultural policy. See Eglė Rindzevičiūtė, *Constructing Soviet Cultural Policy: Cybernetics and Governance in Lithuania after World War II* (Linköping, Sweden: Linköping University, 2008). On how Russian economic work on growth interacted with Western economic thought, see Schmelzer, *The Hegemony of Growth*, 78–80. See also Michael Ellman, *Socialist Planning* (Cambridge: Cambridge University Press, 2008); Adam Leeds, "Administrative Monsters: Yurii Yaremenko's Critique of the Late Soviet State," *History of Political Economy* 51 (2019): 139.

54. Titarenko and Zdravomyslova, *Sociology in Russia*, Kindle location 829.

55. See the extensive work by Natalia Makasheva who situated Kondrat'ev's empiricist and data driven approach in the wider economic debates on equilibrium. Natalia Makasheva, "Zagadka N.D. Kondrat'eva: neokonchennaia teoriia dinamiki i metodologicheskie problemy ekonomicheskoi nauki," *Voprosy ekonomiki* (2002): 4–16. There is a growing

208   NOTES TO PAGES 48–49

body of work in economic history exploring Kondrat'ev's intellectual legacy, although a full history of the East–West transfer of his ideas remains to be written. Kondrat'ev's early work on long waves was translated into German in 1926 and English in 1935. Although the four volumes of translation of Kondrat'ev's work into English were published only in 1998, Kondrat'ev's long wave cycle theory was very widely discussed in the 1980s. See Mary S. Morgan, "Narrative Inference with and without Statistics: Making Sense of Economic Cycles with Malthus and Kondratiev," *History of Political Economy* 53S (2021): 113–138.

56. Walt Friedman, *Fortune Tellers: The Story of America's First Forecasters* (Princeton, NJ: Princeton University Press, 2014); Pietruska, *Looking Forward*. See also Laetitia Lenel, "Searching for a Tide Table Business: Interwar Conceptions of Statistical Inference in Forecasting," *History of Political Economy* 53S (2021): 139–174.

57. Among other Russian scholars who worked on business cycles was Viktor Novozhilov, who later supported the future Nobel prize winner, Leonid Kantorovich, an operations researcher and key figure in the Soviet optimal planning after the Second World War.

58. Vucinich, *Science in Russian Culture*, 466–469; Dmitrij Gutnov, "L'École russe des hautes études sociales de Paris (1901–1906)," *Cahiers du monde Russe* 43, nos. 2–3 (2002): 375–410.

59. Titarenko and Zdravomyslova, *Sociology in Russia*.

60. Kondrat'ev read Grimanelli's lecture on the uses of Comte's theory of prediction in social research. Grimanelli's argument went as follows: in order to be scientific, sociology must be able to predict social facts. However, because sociology is a young science, its predictive capacity is low. It does not help that social phenomena are complex and interrelated. Grimanelli argued that it would be impossible to calculate the evolution of the economy without factoring in social conflict, population movements, and political events. In contrast, astronomical prevision is more accurate because it is easier to abstract the qualities of astronomical phenomena, whereas the observed phenomena, albeit interacting with each other, are fairly independent. Given the lack of social facts, argued Grimanelli, sociological prediction should aim to establish the general and average direction of evolution and avoid seeking to predict individual events. This, according to Grimanelli, was much more important for "social arts and political practice". Pericles Grimanelli, "La prévision en sociologie," *Revue internationale de sociologie* 12 (1911): 861–879, 875.

61. N. D. Kondrat'ev, *Bol'shie tsikly, kon"iunktury i teoriia predvideniia* (Moscow: Akademicheskii proekt, 2015), 473. He sets out the scope for prediction with the examples of astronomy (Halley's Comet) and mathematics (Laplace's demon), which is a classic approach to the historiography of modern science used also by Norbert Wiener in 1948: see the next chapter.

62. Kondrat'ev, *Bol'shie tsikly*, 474, 476–477. Kondrat'ev argued that prediction of the "facts which are not known yet" is part of a constructionist science, one that reconstructs the unknown, reserving the notion of foresight (*predvidenie*) as a prediction of what has not happened yet. He added though that the discovery of the facts that are simply not known and are situated in the past can be regarded as a "retrospective prognosis." Heather Douglas would have called this conceptual operation "accommodation." Kondrat'ev, *Bol'shie tsikly*, 477.

63. Kondrat'ev, *Bol'shie tsikly*, 477.

64. Emile Durkheim, *The Rules of Sociological Method*, trans. W. D. Halls (1895; New York: Free Press, 1982), 139.

65. Durkheim, *The Rules of Sociological Method*, 140.

66. Other scholars, such as, for instance the Dutchman Jan Tinbergen, worked on economic barometers for business cycles and were greatly bothered by the difficulty of making logical inferences from incomplete economic statistics. They resorted to narrative as an aid to make sense of the transitions between events. See Morgan, "Narrative Inference."

NOTES TO PAGES 49–52 209

67. As Mirowski summarized helpfully, "In the Laplacian Dream, science aspired to discover the single mathematical formula that described the entire world. . . . The only real difficulty with the use of such a formula would be the required collection of the staggering number of facts that characterize the system at a given point in time. It is of profound importance to note that the world, the subject of prediction, is assumed to be fully captured by the equation at any point of time, and therefore must be indifferent to the passage of historical time." Philip Mirowski, *More Heat Than Light. Economics as Social Physics: Physics as Nature's Economics* (Cambridge: Cambridge University Press, 1999), 28.

68. See Stefanos Geroulanos and Todd Meyers, *The Human Body in the Age of Catastrophe: Brittleness, Integration, Science and the Great War* (Chicago: University of Chicago Press, 2018); Eugene Raikhel, *Governing Habits: Treating Alcoholism in Post-Soviet Clinic* (Ithaca, NY: Cornell University Press, 2016).

69. Kondrat'ev, *Bol'shie tsikly*, 477. According to the traditional view, Comte did not approve of hypothesizing (a theoretical induction) as a proper scientific method, although some historians of science offer an alternative interpretation suggesting that Comte's writing contained elements of predictive hypothesis, for instance, expressed in his idea of "logical artifice," which Comte considered different from a physical discovery of a fact. See Larry Laudan, "Towards a Reassessment of Comte's 'Méthod Positive,'" *Philosophy of Science* 38, no. 1 (1971): 50–51.

70. Kondrat'ev, *Bol'shie tsikly*, 481–482, 490–493, 496–497.

71. Kondrat'ev, *Bol'shie tsikly*, 497.

72. Kondrat'ev, *Bol'shie tsikly*, 504.

73. Pitirim Sorokin, "A Survey of the Cyclical Conceptions of Social and Historical Process," *Social Forces* 6, no. 1 (1927): 28–40.

74. Kondrat'ev, *Bol'shie tsikly*.

75. As I show in chapter 6, Nikita Moiseev powerfully reintroduced the awareness of uncertainties in prediction methods to criticize not only the existing practice of Soviet planning and governance, but also the emergent framework of global government in the 1970s -1990s. The intellectual trajectory of Russian predictive thought tracks the development of the Western debate about the limits of statistical scientific prediction. As Slobodian shows, in the 1930s Hayek argued that it was common to misunderstand measurement as prediction. For instance, a barometer can be considered as a predictor of the weather, although it just measures the pressure. This critique was developed by Hayek, Oskar Morgenstern, and Alfred Cowles in the 1930s and expanded by Karl Popper after the Second World War. See Beckert, *Imagined Futures*, 227–228; Quinn Slobodian, *The Globalists: The End of Empire and the Birth of Neoliberalism* (Cambridge, MA: Harvard University Press, 2018), Kindle location 1196. See also Alfred Cowles, "Can Stock Markets Forecast?" *Econometrica* 1, no. 3 (1933): 309–324.

76. Joan Valsiner, "From Energy to Collectivity: A Commentary on the Development of Bekhterev's Theoretical Views," in *Collective Reflexology* by V. M. Bekhterev, ed. Lloyd H. Strickland (Abingdon, UK: Routledge, 2017), 1–12.

77. Alexander Luria, *The Nature of Human Conflicts, of Emotion, Conflict, and Will* (New York: Liveright Publishers, 1932); cf. Geroulanos and Meyers, *The Human Body*, 23.

78. For Luria, see Geroulanos and Meyers, *The Human Body*, 196.

79. Otter, *The Victorian Eye*, 14.

80. Stephen Collier, *Post-Soviet Social: Neoliberalism, Social Modernity, Biopolitics* (Princeton, NJ: Princeton University Press, 2011).

81. This was suggested by Boris Kuznetsov, who chaired the research unit for energy and electrification at GOELRO and later pioneered the Soviet history of science. Kuznetsov was a member and later the head of the Institute of History of Natural Sciences and

210 NOTES TO PAGES 52–56

Technology, established in 1932 and first headed by Nikolai Bukharin. The institute was shut down in 1938, when Bukharin was executed. However, the institute was revived in 1944 and became a key platform for the development of Soviet theories of scientific and technical revolution. On Kuznetsov, see Boris Doktorov, *Sovremennaia Rossiiskaia sotsiologiia: Tom 9, Istoriko-biograficheskoe i avtobiograficheskoe* (Moscow: TsSPim, 2016), 30–32; on the intellectual origins of the scientific-technical revolution theory and its deployment to counter Talcott Parson's and Will Rostow's modernization theory in the Cold War competition, see Eglė Rindzevičiūtė, *The Power of Systems: How Policy Sciences Opened Up the Cold War World* (Ithaca, NY: Cornell University Press, 2016), chap. 2. On the notion of "scientific history" as a source for developmental models of growth, see Aronova, *Scientific History*.

82. V. S. Klebaner, "V.A. Bazarov: Myslitel', uchenyi, grazhdanin," *Problemy prognozirovaniia* 6 (2004): 150–156, 153–154.

83. Nikolai D. Kondrat'ev, "Plan i predvidenie," in Nikolai D. Kondrat'ev, *Bol'shie tsikly kon'iunktury i teoriia predvideniia. Izbrannye Trudy* (Moscow: Akademicheskii proekt, 2015), 542, 554, 555.

84. Kondrat'ev, "Plan i predvidenie," 519.

85. Kondrat'ev, "Plan i predvidenie," 519.

86. Kondrat'ev, "Plan i predvidenie," 529.

87. Kondrat'ev, "Plan i predvidenie," 536. He focused on two examples of such unnecessarily detailed, flawed, and failed plans: the Siberian agricultural plan to introduce a soil management system known as "travopol'e" (1926) and Strumilin's "Perspective orientation of Gosplan" (1926). Kondrat'ev, "Plan i predvidenie," 536–538.

88. Kondrat'ev, "Plan i predvidenie," 542–543.

89. Kondrat'ev, "Plan i predvidenie," 556.

90. I thank Ivan Boldyrev for pointing out the importance of this confrontation. For more on Strumilin's approach to teleological planning, see Collier, *Post-Soviet Social*.

91. Nikolai Krementsov, *A Martian Stranded on Earth: Alexander Bogdanov, Blood Transfusion and the Proletarian Science* (Chicago: University of Chicago Press, 2011). Note that Bogdanov's writings contained little engagement with the theoretical sophistication presented in the work of neurophysiologists or even Kondrat'ev. Bogdanov's take on order and the system were closer in its spirit to Comtean positivism and Laplacean mechanics.

92. For an excellent revisionist criticism of the historiography of Western management as excessively focused on efficiency see Stephen Cummings, Todd Bridgman, John Hassard, and Michael Rowlinson, *A New History of Management* (Cambridge: Cambridge University Press, 2017).

93. I thank Oleg Genisaretskii for drawing my attention to Murav'ev.

94. Valerian Murav'ev, *Ovladenie vremenem kak osnovnaia zadacha truda* (Moscow: Mospoligraf, 1924).

95. Platon Kerzhentsev, "Bor'ba za vremia (1923)," in *Printsipy organizatsii* (Moscow: Ekonomika, 1968), 376.

96. Kerzhentsev, "Bor'ba za vremia (1923)," 338.

97. Elsewhere in Europe, scientific management was criticized, most influentially in the French school of European Science of Work. In the Soviet Union, a more nuanced, feedback-based approach to management was developed in response to the cybernetic breakthrough in the 1960s. Christopher O'Neill, "Taylorism, the European Science of Work, and the Quantified Self at Work," *Science, Technology and Human Values* 42, no. 4 (2017): 600–621.

98. Slava Gerovitch, *From Newspeak to Cyberspeak: A History of Soviet Cybernetics* (Cambridge, MA: MIT Press, 2002), 44–45.

99. Theories that brought together individual physical bodies, social groups, and the natural environment as interrelated systems were articulated in the works on biosphere

by Vladimir Vernadsky (1863–1945) and general organization by Aleksander Bogdanov (Malinovsky) (1873–1928).

100. Schmelzer, *The Hegemony of Growth*, 75, 86.

101. Smil, *Growth*, Kindle location 8181.

102. Judy L. Klein, *Statistical Visions in Time: A History of Time Series Analysis, 1662–1938* (Cambridge: Cambridge University Press, 2008), 278.

103. Peter Rutland, *The Myth of the Plan: Lessons of Soviet Planning Experience* (London: Open Court, 1985). Gregory suggested that the Soviet economy was in fact guided by short term operational plans, five-year plans being only "propaganda instruments" for focusing "the population on the bright future." Gregory does not, however, discuss the role of longer term, fifteen- to twenty-year plans. Paul R. Gregory, *The Political Economy of Stalinism: Evidence from the Soviet Secret Archives* (Cambridge: Cambridge University Press, 2004), 118–120, 124. For a brief discussion of forecasting see Pekka Sutela, *Economic Thought and Economic Reform in the Soviet Union* (Cambridge: Cambridge University Press, 1991).

104. Loren Graham, *The Ghost of the Executed Engineer: Technology and the Fall of the Soviet Union* (Cambridge, MA: Harvard University Press, 1996).

105. Daniel A. Wren, "Scientific Management in the U.S.S.R., with Particular Reference to the Contribution of Walter N. Polakov," *Academy of Management Review* 5, no. 1 (1980): 1–11.

106. At IIASA, Kondrat'ev's ideas informed the work on innovation cycles; Dennis Meadows developed a STRATAGEM decision training tool on the basis of Kondrat'ev's cycle theory. Several IIASA papers drew on presentations of Kondrat'ev's ideas found in secondary sources, such as work by Joseph Schumpeter, computer modeler Jay Forrester, and the US–German economist of innovation Gerhard Mensch. See Rindzevičiūtė, *The Power of Systems*; Makasheva, "Zagadka N.D. Kondrat'eva."

3. CYBERNETIC PREDICTION AND THE LATE MODERN GOVERNANCE

1. Elena Aronova, *Scientific History: Experiments in History and Politics from the Bolshevik Revolution to the End of the Cold War* (Chicago: University of Chicago Press, 2021), 19.

2. Danielle Judith Zola Carr, "'Ghastly Marionettes' and the Political Metaphysics of Cognitive Liberalism: Anti-behaviourism, Language, and the Origins of Totalitarianism," *History of the Human Sciences* 33, no. 1 (2020): 147–174; M. Susan Lindee, *Rational Fog* (Cambridge, MA: Harvard University Press, 2020).

3. Norbert Wiener, *The Human Use of Human Beings: Cybernetics and Society* (Boston: Da Capo, 1954), 15.

4. For an example of the use of Wiener's concept of prediction in the context of AI see Stuart Russell, *Human Compatible: Artificial Intelligence and the Problem of Control* (London: Viking, 2019).

5. Karl W. Deutsch, *The Nerves of Government: Models of Political Communication and Control* (New York: Free Press, 1963); Stafford Beer, *Decision and Control: The Meaning of Operational Research and Management Cybernetics* (London: Wiley, 1966); Niklas Luhmann, *Social Systems* (1984; Stanford, CA: Stanford University Press, 1995).

6. Stefanos Geroulanos, *Transparency in Postwar France: A Critical History of the Present* (Stanford, CA: Stanford University Press, 2017), 318. For the influence of Wiener's concepts in French theory, particularly Gilbert Simondon, Jean-François Lyotard, Deleuze, and Guattari, see Céline Lafontaine, *L'empire cybernétique: Des machines à penser à la pensée machine* (Paris: Le Seuil, 2004); Bernard Dionysius Geoghegan, "From Information Theory to French Theory: Jakobson, Lévi-Strauss, and the Cybernetic Apparatus," *Critical Inquiry* 38, no. 1 (2011): 96–111.

7. Martin Heidegger, "Nur noch ein Gott kann uns retten," *Der Spiegel* 23 (31 May 1976): 193–219; cf. Brian Simbirski, "Cybernetic Muse: Hannah Arendt on Automation, 1951–1958," *Journal of the History of Ideas* 77, no. 4 (October 2016): 589–613, 595, 597. See also Geroulanos, *Transparency in Postwar France*, 327.

8. Simbirski, "Cybernetic Muse," 597.

9. Debora Hammond, *The Science of Synthesis: Exploring the Social Implications of General Systems Theory* (Boulder: University Press of Colorado, 2003), 64.

10. John Johnston, *The Allure of Machinic Life: Cybernetics, Artificial Life, and the New AI* (Cambridge, MA: MIT Press, 2008), 25.

11. See Slava Gerovitch, *From Newspeak to Cyberspeak: A History of Soviet Cybernetics* (Cambridge, MA: MIT Press, 2002); Eden Medina, *Cybernetic Revolutionaries: Technology and Politics in Allende's Chile* (Cambridge, MA: MIT Press, 2011); Benjamin Peters, *How Not to Network a Nation: The Uneasy History of the Soviet Internet* (Cambridge, MA: MIT Press, 2016), Thomas Rid, *Rise of the Machines: The Lost History of Cybernetics* (London: Scribe, 2016); Alcibiades Malapi-Nelson, *The Nature of the Machine and the Collapse of Cybernetics: A Transhumanist Lesson for Emerging Technologies* (Basingstoke, UK: Palgrave Macmillan, 2017). The scholarship exploring the complexity of Soviet cybernetics has been growing and is covering increasingly wide ground. The key impetus for these studies was Slava Gerovitch's study of Soviet cybernetics as a component of social and political reform, followed by Benjamin Peter's history of cybernetics and the Soviet internet, my own work on cybernetics and systems analysis in cultural policy and global governance, Aro Velmet's ongoing work on the legacy of Soviet cybernetics in the Estonian e-state, the work on cybernetics and economic thought by Ivan Boldyrev, Yakov Feygin, Adam Leeds, and Olessia Kirtchik, as well as the growing body of interdisciplinary scholarship on Soviet urban planning, architecture, design, and art with key works by David Crowley, Andres Kurg, Diana Kurkovsky-West, and Yanina Prudenko.

12. Eglė Rindzevičiūtė, *The Power of Systems: How Policy Sciences Opened Up the Cold War World* (Ithaca, NY: Cornell University Press, 2016).

13. Leone Montagnini, *Harmonies of Disorder: Norbert Wiener, a Mathematician-Philosopher of Our Time* (Berlin: Springer, 2017); Rid, *Rise of the Machines*; Ronald Kline, *The Cybernetics Moment: Or Why We Call Our Age the Information Age* (Baltimore: Johns Hopkins University Press, 2015), 19–21; Flo Conway and Jim Siegelman, *Dark Hero of the Information Age: In Search of Norbert Wiener, the Father of Cybernetics* (New York: Basic Books, 2009); Lars Ingelstam, *System: Att tänka över samhälle och teknik* (Eskilstuna, Sweden: Energimyndighetens förlag, 2012); Pesi Masani, *Norbert Wiener, 1894–1964* (Basel, Switzerland: Birkauser, 1990); Steve J. Heims, *John Von Neumann and Norbert Wiener: From Mathematics to the Technologies of Life and Death* (Cambridge, MA: MIT Press, 1980).

14. Wiener, *The Human Use of Human Beings*, 12.

15. Wiener, *The Human Use of Human Beings*, 153.

16. For a helpful discussion of how prediction operates in statistical theory, see A. S. C. Ehrenberg and J. A. Bound, "Predictability and Prediction," *Journal of the Royal Statistical Society, Series A* 156, no. 2 (1993): 167–206.

17. Wiener, *The Human Use of Human Beings*, 24.

18. Wiener, *The Human Use of Human Beings*, 61.

19. Wiener, *The Human Use of Human Beings*, 61–62.

20. Norbert Wiener, *Cybernetics: Or Control and Communication in the Animal and the Machine* (1948; Cambridge, MA: MIT Press, 1965), 8–9.

21. Arturo Rosenblueth, Norbert Wiener, and Julian Bigelow, "Behavior, Purpose and Teleology," *Philosophy of Science* 10, no. 1 (1943): 18–24, 18.

22. Rosenblueth et al., "Behavior, Purpose and Teleology," 20–21.

NOTES TO PAGES 63–69 213

23. Johnston, *The Allure of Machinic Life*, 29.

24. Rosenblueth et al., "Behavior, Purpose and Teleology," 24.

25. Wiener, *The Human Use of Human Beings*, 180–181.

26. Wiener, *The Human Use of Human Beings*, 180–181.

27. Wiener, *Cybernetics*, 9.

28. Rosenblueth et al., "Behavior, Purpose and Teleology."

29. See, for instance, Aksel I. Berg, *Cybernetics in the Service of Communism* (Washington DC: U.S. Army Foreign Science and Technology Center, 1969).

30. Norbert Wiener, *God and Golem, Inc.: A Comment on Certain Points Where Cybernetics Impinges on Religion* (Cambridge, MA: MIT Press, 1964), 92.

31. Eric Wolf, *The People Without History* (Berkeley: University of California Press, 1982).

32. Wiener, *God and Golem, Inc.*, 91.

33. Wiener, *Cybernetics*, 25; Wiener, *God and Golem, Inc.*, 94.

34. Matthias Heymann, Gabriele Gramelsberger, and Martin Mahony, eds., *Cultures of Prediction in Atmospheric and Climate Science: Epistemic and Cultural Shifts in Computer-based Modelling and Simulation* (London: Routledge, 2017); Jennifer Gabrys, *Program Earth: Environmental Sensing Technology and the Making of a Computational Planet* (Minneapolis: University of Minnesota Press, 2016); Paul Edwards, *The Closed World: Computers and the Politics of Discourse in Cold War America* (Cambridge, MA: MIT Press, 1996).

35. Wiener, *Cybernetics*, 32.

36. Wiener, *Cybernetics*, 33.

37. Wiener, *Cybernetics*, 33.

38. Wiener, *Cybernetics*, 33.

39. Seb Franklin, *Control: Digitality as Cultural Logic* (Cambridge, MA: MIT Press, 2015).

40. Wiener, *Cybernetics*, 132.

41. Katherine Hayles, *How We Became Posthuman: Virtual Bodies in Cybernetics, Literature, and Informatics* (Chicago: University of Chicago Press, 1999), 54–57.

42. Nick Bostrom, *Superintelligence: Paths, Dangers, Strategies* (Oxford: Oxford University Press, 2014), 14.

43. Kline, *The Cybernetics Moment*, chap. 4. See also Mara Mills, "On Disability and Cybernetics: Helen Keller, Norbert Wiener, and the Hearing Glove," *Differences* 22, nos. 2–3 (2011): 74–111.

44. Wiener, *Cybernetics*, 33–34.

45. Wiener, *Cybernetics*, 35.

46. Wiener, *The Human Use of Human Beings*, 183.

47. Henning Schmidgen, "Cybernetic Times: Norbert Wiener, John Stroud, and the 'Brain Clock' Hypothesis," *History of Human Sciences* 33, no. 1 (2020): 81.

48. Craik (1947), 59, quoted in Schmidgen, "Cybernetic Times," 88.

49. Michael Power, *Organized Uncertainty: Designing a World of Risk Management* (Oxford: Oxford University Press, 2007).

50. Peter Galison, "The Ontology of the Enemy: Norbert Wiener and the Cybernetic Vision," *Critical Inquiry* 21, no. 1 (1994): 228–266; Paul Edwards, *A Vast Machine: Computer Models, Climate Data and the Politics of Global Warming* (Cambridge, MA: MIT Press, 2010); Hunter Heyck, *Age of System: Understanding the Development of Modern Social Science* (Baltimore: Johns Hopkins University Press, 2015).

51. In the early 1950s Wiener cut off his relations with McCulloch, Wiesner, and Pitts, whom he regarded as being too closely involved in the military-industrial complex (Kline, *The Cybernetics Moment*, 65, 85–87). For the argument that system-cybernetic

214   NOTES TO PAGES 70–73

epistemology enabled liberal forms of social order, see also Fred Turner, *From Counter-culture to Cyberculture: Stewart Brand, the Whole Earth Network, and the Rise of Digital Utopianism* (Chicago: University of Chicago Press, 2006); Andrew Pickering, *The Cybernetic Brain: Sketches of Another Future* (Chicago: University of Chicago Press, 2008); Kline, *The Cybernetics Moment*; Rindzevičiūtė, *The Power of Systems*; Clifford Siskin, *System: The Shaping of Modern Knowledge* (Cambridge, MA: MIT Press, 2016).

52. The classical work here is Otto Mayr, *Authority, Liberty and Automatic Machinery in Early Modern Europe* (Baltimore: Johns Hopkins University Press, 1986).

53. Peter Galison, *Einstein's Clocks, Poincare's Maps* (London: Sceptre, 2003), chap. 5.

54. Paul Erickson, Judy L. Klein, Lorraine Daston, Rebecca Lemov, Thomas Sturm, and Michael D. Gordin, *How Reason Almost Lost Its Mind: The Strange Career of Cold War Rationality* (Chicago: University of Chicago Press, 2013).

55. Ariel Colonomos, *Selling the Future: The Perils of Predicting Global Politics* (London: Hurst, 2016).

56. Franklin, *Control*, 47–48, 54.

57. Louise Amoore, *The Politics of Possibility: Risk and Security Beyond Probability* (Durham, NC: Duke University Press, 2013), 11.

58. C. P. Snow, *The Two Cultures and the Scientific Revolution* (New York: Cambridge University Press, 1961).

59. Wiener, *God and Golem, Inc.*, 68.

60. For examples of deterministic uses of predictive technology in security and risk assessment see Amoore, *The Politics of Possibility*, chap. 2.

61. Naomi Oreskes, "The Fact of Uncertainty, the Uncertainty of Facts and the Cultural Resonance of Doubt," *Philosophical Transactions of the Royal Society Series A* 373, no. 2055 (2015): 1–21.

4. FORECASTING AND THE CYBERNETIC SENSIBILITY

1. Slava Gerovitch, *From Newspeak to Cyberspeak: A History of Soviet Cybernetics* (Cambridge, MA: MIT Press, 2002).

2. For the systems-cybernetic approach in social information management in communist China, see Angela Xiao Wu, "Journalism via Systems Cybernetics: The Birth of Chinese Communication Discipline and Post-Mao Press Reforms," *History of Media Studies* 2 (2022). doi:10.32376/d895a0ea.182c7595.

3. I argued this first in my doctoral dissertation, *Constructing Soviet Cultural Policy: Cybernetics and Governance in Lithuania after World War II* (Linköping, Sweden: Linköping University, 2008), where I showed that cybernetics influenced epistemologies in many fields of knowledge because separate elements of cybernetics, such as concepts, models and principles, could be bricolaged and adapted depending on the context.

4. Gerovitch, *From Newspeak to Cyberspeak*.

5. Gerovitch, *From Newspeak to Cyberspeak*; for cybernetics and the Soviet internet, Benjamin Peters, *How Not to Network a Nation: The Uneasy History of the Soviet Internet* (Cambridge, MA: MIT Press, 2016); for cybernetics, culture and design, see David Crowley and Jane Pavitt, eds. *Cold War Modern 1945–1970* (London: V&A, 2010); Andres Kurg, "Feedback Environment: Rethinking Art and Design Practices in Tallinn During the Early 1970s," *Kunstiteaduslikke Uurimusi* nos.1–2 (2011): 26–50; Ianina Prudenko, *Kibernetika v gumanitarnykh naukakh i iskusstve v SSSR: Analiz bol'shikh baz dannykh i komp'iuternoe tvorchestvo* (Moscow: Garazh, 2018).

6. The relay development of governance by numbers was picked up in the 1930s and 1940s by applied mathematicians, who developed methods for logistics and linear planning, as well as for electronics, and automatic engineering. In the Soviet Union, thought-

ful and extensive reflections about scientific prediction and governance, as in Kondrat'ev's writings, disappeared and resumed only in the 1970s in writings about the global biosphere and the long-term future. Aspects of the epistemology of scientific prediction were examined mainly in niche scientific publications. Interest in statistical forecasting, however, returned as part of economic and administrative reforms in the 1960s.

7. For a link between Soviet economic thought and theoretical and applied strands of cybernetics, mathematics, and computer science, see Adam Leeds, "Dreams in Cybernetic Fugue: Cold War Technoscience, the Intelligentsia, and the Birth of Soviet Mathematical Economics," *Historical Studies in the Natural Sciences*, 46, no. 5 (2016): 633–668. For the cybernetic logic of informational organization of the economy in Soviet territorial administrations, see Diana Kurkovsky, "Cybernetics for the Command Economy: Foregrounding Entropy in Late Soviet Planning," *History of the Human Sciences* 33, no. 1 (2020): 36–51.

8. The Archives of the Russian Academy of Science (henceforth ARAN), f. 1977, op. 2, d. 5, l. 2.

9. Lennart Samuelson, *Tankograd: The Formation of a Soviet Company Town: Cheliabinsk, 1900s–1950s* (Basingstoke, UK: Palgrave Macmillan, 2011), 15.

10. For technology assessment in the Red Army, see Ian Johnson, "Technology's Cutting Edge: Futurism and Research in the Red Army, 1917–1973," *Technology and Culture* 59 (2018): 689–718.

11. Judy L. Klein, *Statistical Visions in Time: A History of Time Series Analysis, 1662–1938* (Cambridge: University of Cambridge Press, 1997).

12. Ivan Boldyrev and Till Duppe, "Programming the USSR: Leonid V. Kantorovich in Context," *British Journal of History of Science* (2020): 1–24, 5.

13. Boldyrev and Duppe, "Programming the USSR," 7–9, 11.

14. Hunter Heyck, *The Age of System: Understanding the Development of Modern Social Science* (Baltimore: Johns Hopkins University Press, 2015).

15. See the excellent studies on postwar planning in Michel Christian, Sandrine Kott, and Ondřej Matějka, eds., *Planning in Cold War Europe: Competition, Cooperation, Circulations (1950s–1970s)* (Berlin: de Gruyter, 2018) and Quinn Slobodian's *Globalists: The End of Empire and the Birth of Neoliberalism* (Cambridge, MA: Harvard University Press, 2018).

16. Matthias Schmelzer, *The Hegemony of Growth: The OECD and the Making of the Economic Growth Paradigm* (Cambridge: Cambridge University Press, 2016), 96.

17. Paul R. Gregory, *The Political Economy of Stalinism: Evidence from the Soviet Secret Archives* (Cambridge: Cambridge University Press, 2004). In 1954, Soviet economists began lobbying to reintroduce training in statistical methods in universities. Yakov Feygin, "Reforming the Cold War State: Economic Thought, Internationalization, and the Politics of Soviet Reform, 1955–1985" (unpublished doctoral dissertation, University of Pennsylvania, 2017), 57–58.

18. The Russian State Archives of Economics (henceforth RGAE), f. 99, op. 1, l. 1–4. From 1960 to 1964, the NIEI was under the State Economic Council.

19. Polish planners also travelled to meet French planning specialists in 1956. Lukas Becht, "From Euphoria to Frustration: Institutionalizing Prognostic Research in the Polish People's Republic, 1969–76," *Acta Poloniae Historica* 116 (2017): 283.

20. For more on the French trip to the Soviet Union and the exchange between the French and Soviet economists, see Isabelle Gouarné, "Mandatory Planning Versus Indicative Planning? The Eastern Itinerary of French Planners (1960s–1970s)," in *Planning in Cold War Europe: Competition, Cooperation, Circulations (1950s–1970s)*, eds. Michel Christian, Sandrine Kott, and Ondřej Matějka (Berlin: De Gruyter, 2018), 71–77.

21. "Otchet" (November 1958), RGAE, f. 99, op. 1, d. 858, l. 5–6.

22. "Otchet" (November 1958), RGAE, f. 99, op. 1, d. 858, l. 5–6.

216   NOTES TO PAGES 76–78

23. For instance, a scheme for continuous planning (1957) included general perspective plans (fifteen to twenty years), five-year plans, and annual plans. RGAE, f. 99, op. 1, d. 862, l. 21–22. A French planner noted that Gosplan's perspective planning was based on calculations of the optimal development of existing trends. The French also stated that their prospective planning that examined several alternative futures alongside each other was "not thinkable" for Soviet economists. Robert Fraisse, "Notes sur planification a long terme en Union Sovietique" (December 1966), *BR 4/513/8*, Sciences Po, p. 11. See also Pekka Sutela, *Socialism, Planning and Optimality: A Study in Soviet Economic Thought* (Helsinki: Finnish Society of Science and Letters, 1984).

24. Grigorii Sapov, "Tri interv'iu s E.B. Ershovym" (February to March 1999), http://www.sapov.ru/staroe/si06.html.

25. "Stenograma" (Moscow, 14 December 1966), RGAE, f. 99, op. 1, d. 869; Bernard Rosier, ed., *Wassily Leontief: textes et itinéraire* (Paris: La Découverte, 1986).

26. I base this statement on the memoir by Nikita Moiseev, *Kak daleko do zavtreshnego dnia . . . Svobodnye razmyshleniia 1917–1993* (Moscow: Taideks, 1997).

27. Iu. V. Ershov and A. S. Popovich, "Propushchennaia vozmozhnost' obognat Ameriku, ili k chemu provodit ignorirovanie prognoz," *Top Club Journal* 3, no. 21 (2012): 8–17. For more on the intellectual legacy of Dobrov as a theorist of the history of science and technology, see Elena Aronova, *Scientific History: Experiments in History and Politics from the Bolshevik Revolution to the End of the Cold War* (Chicago: University of Chicago Press, 2021).

28. The historiography of the Soviet military-industrial complex is still limited due to the lack of access to archival sources, although as Vladislav Zubok noted in his *Collapse: The Fall of the Soviet Union* (New Haven, CT: Yale University Press, 2021) some archives of individual institutes and enterprises that were part of the military-industrial complex are becoming available. Many historians continue using memoirs as key sources, because they capture informal social interaction that was key for the industry. Key work on the Cold War military-industrial complex and public policy expertise includes Slava Gerovitch, *Soviet Space Mythologies: Public Images, Private Memories, and the Making of a Cultural Identity* (Pittsburgh: Pittsburgh University Press, 2015); John Barber and Mark Harrison, eds., *The Soviet Defence Industry Complex from Stalin to Khrushchev* (Basingstoke, UK: Macmillan, 2000). For RAND, see Daniel Bessner, *Democracy in Exile: Hans Speier and the Rise of the Defense Intellectual* (Ithaca, NY: Cornell University Press, 2018); Paul Rubinson, *Redefining Science: Scientists, the National Security State, and Nuclear Weapons in Cold War America* (Amherst: University of Massachusetts Press, 2016); Joy Rohde, *Armed with Expertise: The Militarization of American Social Research during the Cold War* (Ithaca, NY: Cornell University Press, 2013); Nils Gilman, *The Mandarins of the Future: Modernization Theory in Cold War America* (Baltimore: Johns Hopkins University Press, 2007); Jennifer S. Light, *From Warfare to Welfare: Defense Intellectuals and Urban Problems in Cold War America* (Baltimore: Johns Hopkins University Press, 2003); Fred Kaplan, *The Wizards of Armageddon* (Stanford, CA: Stanford University Press, 1991).

29. Dmitry Travin and Otar Marganiya, "Resource Curse: Rethinking the Soviet Experience," in *Resource Curse and Post-Soviet Eurasia: Oil, Gas and Modernization*, eds. Vladimir Gel'man and Otar Marganiya (New York: Lexington Books, 2010), 31–32; Dmitry Efremenko, *Vvedenie v otsenku tehniki* (Moscow: MNEPU, 2002), 59.

30. Dzhermen Gvishiani, "Upravlenie: prezhde vsego nauka," *Izvestiia* no. 118 (1963): 2.

31. For Kosygin, see Aappo Kähönen, "Optimal Planning, Optimal Economy, Optimal Life? The Kosygin Reforms, 1965–72," in *Competition in Socialist Society*, eds. Katalin Miklossy and Melanie Ilic (London: Routledge, 2014), 23–40.

NOTES TO PAGES 78–82   217

32. In 1964, the academician Vadim Trapeznikov published an article in *Pravda*, where he criticized the blind use of numbers in true Kondrat'ev's spirit. For Trapeznikov and the economic reform, see Feygin, "Reforming the Cold War State," 148–150.

33. Aleksei Kosygin, "Povyshenie nauchnoi obosnovannosti planov-vazhneishaia zadacha planovykh organov," *Planovoe khoziaistvo* 4 (1965): 4–5.

34. Kosygin, "Povyshenie," 4. See alsoA. N. Klepach and G. O. Kuranov, "Razvitie sotsial'no-ekonomicheskogo prognozirovaniia i idei A.I.Anchishkina," *Voprosy ekonomiki* 8 (2013): 143–155.

35. Stephen Collier, *Post-Soviet Social: Neoliberalism, Social Modernity, Biopolitics* (Princeton, NJ: Princeton University Press, 2011), 62–64.

36. RGAE, f. 4372, op. 65, l. 3; RGAE, f. 99, op. 1, d. 869, l. 3.

37. The most influential were the institutes of the all-union Academy of Sciences, Gosplan, and the State Committee for Science and Technology (GKNT) under the Council of Ministers. The Central Institute for Mathematical Economics calculated economic and demographic forecasts; the academy's Computer Center did forecasts on oil and gas procurement, and environmental and climate change; labor markets were forecasted by the Institute of International Labor Movement; and the way of life and the attitudes of youth were explored at the Institute for Concrete Social Research.

38. "Stenograma" (Moscow, 14 December 1966), RGAE, f. 99, op. 1, d. 869, l. 115.

39. RGAE, f. 99, op. 1, d. 869, l. 15.

40. RGAE, f. 99, op. 1, d. 869, l. 15, 97–105.

41. RGAE, f. 99, op. 1, d. 869, l. 15, 43–46, 52.

42. RGAE, f. 99, op. 1, d. 869, l. 15, 27.

43. RGAE, f. 99, op. 1, d. 869, l. 15, 13.

44. Klepach and Kuranov, "Razvitie sotsial'no-ekonomicheskogo prognozirovanie."

45. "Stenograma" (Moscow, 14 December 1966), RGAE, f. 99, op. 1, d. 869, l. 17.

46. "Stenograma" (Moscow, 14 December 1966), RGAE, f. 99, op. 1, d. 869, l. 17, 32–33.

47. RGAE, f. 99, op. 1, d. 870, l.7. See also Klepach and Kuranov, "Razvitie sotsial'no-ekonomicheskogo prognozirovanie."

48. This was a limited and modest pluralism referring to different pathways leading to different levels of achievement, such as maximum, minimum, and average. RGAE, f. 99, op. 1, d. 869, l. 7–9.

49. RGAE, f. 99, op. 1, d. 869, l. 7–9, 64–68.

50. Sapov, "Tri interv'iu s E.B. Ershovym."

51. ARAN, f. 2, op. 1, d. 858, l. 172–173.

52. ARAN, f. 2, op. 1, d. 858, l. 172–173, 26.

53. "Stenograma" (Moscow, 14 December 1966), RGAE, f. 99, op. 1, d. 869, l. 2.

54. ARAN, f. 2, op. 1, d. 858, l. 76.

55. For scientific patronage and clientelism in Soviet policymaking see Alexei Kojevnikov, *Stalin's Great Science: The Times and Adventures of Soviet Physicists* (London: Imperial College Press, 2004); Stephen Fortescue, ed., *Russian Politics: From Lenin to Putin* (Basingstoke, UK: Palgrave Macmillan, 2010).

56. Lee Schwartz, "A History of Russian and Soviet Censuses," in *Research Guide to the Russian and Soviet Censuses*, ed. Ralph Clem (Ithaca, NY: Cornell University Press, 1986), 48–69. In the 1920s and 1930s, Stanislav Strumilin, another student of Kovalevskii, amassed the data on labor for economic sociology studies. However, from 1929 the very term "sociology" was not used anymore. The only legitimate social theory was Marxist philosophy and historical materialism. Larissa Titarenko and Elena Zdravomyslova, *Sociology in Russia: A Brief History* (Cham: Palgrave, 2017), Kindle location 844.

218   NOTES TO PAGES 82–85

57. Rindzevičiūtė, *Constructing Soviet Cultural Policy.*

58. The first Soviet institute to conduct demographic research was established in the Ukrainian Academy of Science in 1919 (closed in 1938). In Russia, the first such academic institution was founded at the Leningrad branch of the Academy of Science in the 1930s (closed in 1934). Thereafter population data was collected only by the Central Statistical Agency. Population data was published until the 1930s, although even then it was edited to emphasize population growth and hide the deaths caused by the communist terror. There was a weak link between demography and sociology, however. The first sociologists hailed from philosophy and economics departments; in the summer of 1968, the Institute of Concrete Social Research (IKSI) was established as a separate institute, on the basis of the Department of Social Research (established February 1966) at the Institute of Philosophy. ARAN, f. 1977, op. 1, d. 2, l. 1–2. See Elisabeth Weinberg, *Sociology in the Soviet Union and Beyond: Social Enquiry and Social Change* (Farnham, UK: Ashgate: 2004).

59. Wolfgang Lutz, Sergei Scherbov, and Andrei Volkov, "Introduction: Past and Present Studies of the Soviet Population," in *Demographic Trends and Patterns in the Soviet Union Before 1991*, eds. Wolfgang Lutz, Sergei Scherbov, and Andrei Volkov, xxxi–xl (London: Routledge, 1994).

60. For a detailed discussion of the genealogy of the term "scientific-technical revolution" as it was used in both the Soviet Union and the West, see chapter 1 in my *The Power of Systems: How Policy Sciences Opened Up the Cold War World* (Ithaca, NY: Cornell University Press, 2016).

61. Titarenko and Zdravomyslova, *Sociology in Russia*, Kindle location 1021.

62. "Ustav" (1968), ARAN, f. 2, op. 6m, d. 437, l. 137.

63. Margaret J. Osler, *Rethinking the Scientific Revolution* (Cambridge: Cambridge University Press, 2000).

64. Michael Ellman, *Socialist Planning* (Cambridge: Cambridge University Press, 2008).

65. Papers of John F. Kennedy, Presidential Papers, National Security Files, Meetings and Memoranda, Staff memoranda: Rostow, Walt W., December 1960 to June 1961, JFKNSF-323-006, John F. Kennedy Presidential Library and Museum, Boston, MA.

66. Aronova, *Scientific History*, 126.

67. I have detailed on this in Rindzevičiūtė, *The Power of Systems*, 27–32.

68. "Spravka," ARAN, f. 1977, op. 1, d. 40, l. 14–15.

69. Titarenko and Zdravomyslova, *Sociology in Russia*, Kindle location 1096.

70. This is based on the very useful description of the official Soviet sociological framework proposed in 1971 that is offered in Titarenko and Zdravomyslova, *Sociology in Russia*, Kindle location 1341.

71. Titarenko and Zdravomyslova, *Sociology in Russia*, Kindle location 1313.

72. The reports were sent to Gosplan, GKNT, and the Foreign Ministry. ARAN, f. 1977, op. 1, d. 40, l. 4.

73. Liah Greenfeld, "Soviet Sociology and Sociology in the Soviet Union," *Annual Review of Sociology* 14 (1988): 99, 113.

74. Titarenko and Zdravomyslova, *Sociology in Russia*, Kindle location 1406.

75. "Sotsialnyi progress v SSSR" (1973), ARAN, f. 1977, op. 2, d. 66, l. 52.

76. IKSI's research plan (1969), ARAN, f. 1977, op. 1, d. 7, l. 3.

77. "Sotsialnye aspekty prognozirovaniia urovnia zhizni" (1966), RGAE, f. 99, op. 1, d. 879, l. 2.

78. RGAE, f. 99, op. 1, d. 882, l. 2.

79. RGAE, f. 99, op. 1, d. 869, l. 47; ARAN, f. 1977, op. 1, d. 42, l. 6.

80. ARAN, f. 1977, op. 1, d. 59, l. 12.

81. ARAN, f. 1977, op. 1, d. 59, l. 12, 77.

NOTES TO PAGES 86–87   219

82. As in the Soviet Union, public opinion surveys were launched in Poland in the 1960s. Becht, "From Euphoria to Frustration."

83. In 1960, only 17.5 percent of Soviet sociologists had degrees in economics, natural science, and psychology and none was trained in sociology. Titarenko and Zdravomyslova, *Sociology in Russia*, Kindle location, 1268–1275.

84. IKSI staff grew from about one hundred in 1968 to almost three hundred in the mid-1970s, and Bestuzhev-Lada's unit grew to fifteen staff. A year after its establishment IKSI lacked basic equipment, such as desks and typewriters. Scholars complained about having to work in insufficiently lit basement offices. IKSI's first computer, a standard machine used in universities and research institutes, Minsk-32, arrived only in 1971. ARAN, f. 1977, op. 1, d. 42, l. 1–2; ARAN, f. 1977, op. 1, d. 7, l. 114; ARAN, f. 1977, op. 1, d. 38, l. 16; ARAN, f. 1977, op. 1, d. 59, l. 12; ARAN, f. 1977, op. 1, d. 59, l. 12, 48–49; ARAN, f. 1977, op. 1, d. 203, l. 78.

85. At the end of the 1960s two publications attracted harsh ideological criticism: a humble print run of lecture notes on Western sociological theories by Iurii Levada and an edited collection *The Mathematical Modeling of Social Processes*, edited by Osipov, Aganbegian, and Moiseev. See Boris Firsov, *Istoriia sovetskoi sotsiologii 1950–1980 gg* (St Petersburg: Izd. Evropeiskogo universiteta v Sankt Peterburge, 2012).

86. Bestuzhev-Lada did not hesitate to present himself as "the leading Soviet forecaster," which in turn was echoed in the Western historiography on Soviet future studies. See, for instance, Gordon Rocca, "'A Second Party in Our Midst': The History of the Soviet Scientific Forecasting Association," *Social Studies of Science* 11, no. 2 (1981): 199–247. For Bestuzhev-Lada's early involvement in the emerging futurist networks, see Wendell Bell, *Foundations of Futures Studies: History, Purposes, and Knowledge*, vol. 1 of *Human Science for a New Era* (London: Routledge, 2009), 36. For Bestuzhev-Lada as an internationalizer see Jenny Andersson, *The Future of the World: Futurology, Futurists, and the Struggle for the Post-Cold War Imagination* (Oxford: Oxford University Press, 2018).

87. Igor' Bestuzhev-Lada, "Prognozirovanie bylo iznachal'no oberecheno na pogrom," in *Rosiiskaia sotsiologiia shestidesiatykh godov v vospominaniakh i dokumantakh*, edited by G. Batygin, M.G. Pugacheva, S. F. Iarmoliuk, 404–427 (Saint Petersburg: Izdatel'stvo Russkogo Khristianskogo gumanitarnogo universiteta, 1999).

88. The Western term "futurology," coined by the German scholar Ossip Flechtheim in 1943, was not well received in the Soviet Union: like cybernetics, futurology was derided as a bourgeois science although, unlike cybernetics or genetics in the 1950s, futurology was never completely rejected. The Soviet ideologues did not like the emancipatory touch with which Flechtheim imbued his version of future studies. The purpose of future studies, for Flechtheim, was to liberate the future from technocrats, be they state socialist or capitalist.

89. Bestuzhev-Lada, "Prognozirovanie bylo iznachal'no."

90. The 1967 paper was intended for the First Future Studies conference organized by Johan Galtung in Oslo. Bestuzhev-Lada was invited alongside the leading figure of technical assessment and history of science and technology, Genadii Dobrov, but due to bureaucratic delays neither could attend. Their papers were published in the conference proceedings *Mankind 2000*. ARAN, f. 1977, op. 2, d. 60, l. 4. Bestuzhev-Lada's first publications in the field of scientific forecasting included a report *Problemy obshchei i sotsialnoi prognostiki* (Moscow: USSR Academy of Sciences, 1968), and lecture notes on social forecasting, published in 1969.

91. Geroulanos, *Transparency in Postwar France: A Critical History of the Present* (Stanford, CA: Stanford University Press, 2017).

92. Andersson, *The Future of the World*; Ariel Colonomos, *Selling the Future: The Perils of Predicting Global Politics* (London: Hurst, 2016), but see also the internalist perspective by Tuomo Kuosa, *The Evolution of Strategic Foresight: Navigating Public Policy Making* (Farnham, UK: Ashgate, 2012).

220   NOTES TO PAGES 88–91

93. Jens Beckert, *Imagined Futures: Fictional Expectations and Capitalist Dynamics* (Cambridge, MA: Harvard University Press, 2016); Andersson, *The Future of the World*; Christian Dayé, *Experts, Social Scientists and Techniques of Prognosis in Cold War America* (Cham: Palgrave, 2019).

94. Christian et al., *Planning in Cold War Europe*.

95. On the Delphi method, see Dayé, *Experts, Social Scientists*. See also Philip Tetlock and Dan Gardner, *Superforecasting: The Art and Science of Prediction* (New York: Random House, 2016).

96. ARAN, f. 1957, op. 1, d. 29, l. 16.

97. See, for example, a nostalgic tale about the intellectual circles at IMRD in the documentary *Otdel* by Aleksandr Arkhangel'skii (2010). Note that Bestuzhev-Lada did not feature in this documentary.

98. Arab-Ogly actively networked with Western thinkers: in 1959 he met Daniel Bell, and at the ISA Congress in Italy, he met Raymond Aron and Robert Merton. Starting in the late 1950s he corresponded with a French Christian Marxist, Roger Garaudy, who would later be the first to publish Bestuzhev-Lada's writings in the West in 1968. Arab-Ogly, *Demograficheskie i ekologicheskie prognozy* (Moscow: Statistika, 1978); Arab-Ogly, "Togda kazalos',chto koe-to udavalos'," in *Rossiiskaia sotsiologiia shestidesiatykh godov v vospominaniiakh i dokumentakh*, edited by G. Batygin, M.G. Pugacheva, S. F. Iarmoliuk, 358-370. St Petersburg: Izdatel'stvo Russkogo Khristianskogo gumanitarnogo universiteta, 1999).

99. Bestuzhev-Lada, "Prognozirovanie bylo iznachal'no."

100. Author's interview with a Russian scientist Sergei, Moscow, April 2013.

101. Bestuzhev-Lada, "Prognozirovanie bylo iznachal'no."

102. Bestuzhev-Lada, "Prognozirovanie bylo iznachal'no"; Arab-Ogly, "Togda kazalos', chto koe-to udavalos'."

103. ARAN, f. 1977, op. 1, d. 31, l. 26–76.

104. A. A. Zvorykin, *Cultural Policy in the Union of Soviet Socialist Republics* (Paris: UNESCO, 1970), 32. For more, see Rindzevičiūtė, *Constructing Soviet Cultural Policy*. On the significance of Zvorykin for Soviet cultural planning, see Vitaly Kurennoy, "Contemporary State Cultural Policy in Russia: Organization, Political Discourse and Ceremonial Behavior," *International Journal of Cultural Policy* 27, no. 2 (2021): 163–176.

105. Zvorykin, *Cultural Policy*, 32–35; cf. Rindzevičiūtė, *Constructing Soviet Cultural Policy*.

106. Rindzevičiūtė, *Constructing Soviet Cultural Policy*.

107. ARAN, f. 1977, op. 1, d. 42, l. 1–5.

108. In his memoir Bestuzhev-Lada wrote that he hated mathematics almost as much as homosexuality, Igor' Bestuzhev-Lada, *Svozhu schety s zhizn'iu: zapisi futurologa o proshedshem i prikhodiashchem* (Moscow: Algoritm, 2004), 289–290.

109. This is suggested by the speed at which Zvorykin completed his research projects at IKSI. Although Bestuzhev-Lada began his work in winter 1969, his first research project, a forecast of young people's future values, was not launched before 1972. During this time Zvorykin delivered several research reports to the Academy and the Central Committee.

110. In 1969, Bestuzhev-Lada spoke at several of the Academy institutes and delivered a course on the history of forecasting at the philosophy department of Moscow State University. ARAN, f. 1977, op. 1, d. 7, l. 86.

111. Due to a lack of space, the connections between scientific forecasting and science-fiction writing could not be addressed in this chapter; this subject, indeed, merits a study of its own. I will only note that Efremov's biographers appear to have overlooked his international connections with Western futurologists, something that might have ex-

NOTES TO PAGES 91–92 221

plained the KGB's suspicion of Efremov after his death. Ol'ga Erelina and Nikolai Smirnov, *Ivan Efremov* (Moscow: Molodaia gvardiia, 2013).

112. Dmitri N. Shalin, "The Development of Soviet Sociology, 1956–1976," *Annual Review of Sociology* 4 (1978), 171; Bestuzhev-Lada, "Prognozirovanie bylo iznachal'no."

113. ARAN, f. 1977, op. 2, d. 60.

114. Bestuzhev-Lada was instructed to strictly focus on the socioeconomic aspects of disarmament in his Oslo talk. IKSI (September 1970), ARAN, f. 1977, op. 1, d. 52, l. 70–72; "Direktivnye ukazaniia" (IMRD, 30 October 1968), ARAN, f. 1957, op. 1, d. 39, l. 38. I could not locate his report on this visit; Rocca indicated that Bestuzhev-Lada indeed travelled to Oslo.

115. Bestuzhev-Lada, "Prognozirovanie bylo iznachal'no."

116. In the 1980s Rocca, "A Second Party in Our Midst," painstakingly tried to trace the organization of the SSF, but with little success due to the lack of reliable sources and conflicting narrative accounts. Some more reliable information about the SSF can be found in Firsov, *Istoriia sovetskoi.* It is still not clear just how significant was this movement to establish a cross-disciplinary community around the idea of predictive social science.

117. In his autobiography, Bestuzhev-Lada claimed that these spontaneous conferences on forecasting stemmed from his seminar at IMRD in 1967. In May 1968 the SSF committee organized a Public Institute for Social Prognosis with Bestuzhev-Lada named as director (although he denied this). Bestuzhev-Lada was tasked to organize of the second congress on scientific prognosis, and Tardov took over the organization of the third congress. Bestuzhev Lada, "Prognozirovanie bylo iznachal'no."

118. Maria Rogacheva, *The Private World of Soviet Scientists: From Stalin to Gorbachev* (Cambridge: Cambridge University Press, 2017); Eglė Rindzevičiūtė, "When Formal Organisations Meet Informal Relations in Soviet Lithuania: Action Nets, Networks and Boundary Objects in the Construction of the Lithuanian Sea Museum," *Lithuanian Historical Studies* 15 (2011): 107–134.

119. Vasilii Parin, "Nauchnye trudy za 1935–71," ARAN, f. 1640, op. 1.

120. Mitrokhin, 536–537. One document noted that Dobrov and Bestuzhev-Lada refused to join this initiative to reform the committee into an association. "Zapiska otdela," in S. F. Iarmoliuk, ed., *Rossiiskaia sotsiologiia shestidesiatykh godov v vospominaniiakh i dokumentakh* (St Petersburg: Izdatel'stvo Russkogo Khristianskogo gumanitarnogo universiteta, , 1999).

121. "Dopolnenie k zapiske," in S. F. Iarmoliuk, ed., *Rossiiskaia sotsiologiia shestidesiatykh godov v vospominaniiakh i dokumentakh* (St Petersburg: Izdatel'stvo Russkogo Khristianskogo gumanitarnogo universiteta; Firsov, *Istoriia sovetskoi*, 31.

122. Bestuzhev-Lada, "Prognozirovanie bylo iznachal'no"; "Prikaz no.14–104" (Moscow 23 June 1972), ARAN, f. 1977, op. 1, d. 59, l. 17–18. In July Bestuzhev-Lada was appointed as the head of the unit for the methodological problems of forecasting social needs. Iarmoliuk, *Rossiiskaia sotsiologiia shestidesiatykh.*

123. ARAN, f. 1977, op. 2, d. 60.

124. This was some achievement because B. M. Kedrov spoke vehemently against participating in such conferences. ARAN f. 1731, op. 1, d. 160, l. 127–136. Another issue was that the famous Western futurologist Jungk pressurized the Soviet Union to permit the emigration of Jewish scientists at the Bucharest conference.

125. The common denominator for these purges is probably the attack against Rumiantsev. For instance, a letter to the Central Committee which listed the ideological errors committed at IKSI did not mention either Bestuzhev-Lada or forecasting. TsKhSD, f. 4, op. 20, d. 770, l. 41–42, in Iarmoliuk, *Rossiiskaia sotsiologiia shestidesiatykh.*

126. Nikolai Krementsov, *Stalinist Science* (Princeton, NJ: Princeton University Press, 1996).

222 **NOTES TO PAGES 92–96**

127. ARAN, f. 2, op. 6m, d. 500, l. 180–181.

128. Starting in 1975 the commission organized annual conferences and summer schools in forecasting. Igor' Bestuzhev-Lada, ed., *Rabochiaia kniga po prognozirovaniiu* (Moscow: Mysl', 1982), 69.

129. In his interview, Bestuzhev-Lada mentioned regular meetings with assistants of Politburo members in 1967 to 1969; he wrote, "in my thoughts I was far away from IKSI and close to the Politburo." Bestuzhev-Lada, "Prognozirovanie bylo iznachal'no."

130. On the high modernist plans for large-scale industrialization with catastrophic effects on the natural environment, see Paul R. Josephson, *Industrialized Nature: Brute Force Technology and the Transformation of the Natural World* (Washington, DC: Island Press, 2002).

131. Igor' Bestuzhev-Lada, *Esli mir*, 6, 18, 43–44.

132. Jonathan Oldfield, *The Soviet Union and Global Environmental Change: Modifying the Biosphere and Conceptualizing Society–Nature Interaction* (London: Routledge, 2021).

133. Bestuzhev-Lada *Esli mir*, 63. A revised version was entitled *The Contours of the Future*: Igor' Bestuzhev Lada and Oleg Pisarzhevski, *Kontury griadushchego* (Moscow: Znanie, 1965).

134. "Otchet," RGAE, f. 99, op. 1, d. 890, l. 111.

135. Igor' Bestuzhev Lada, *Okno v budushchee: Sovremennye problemy sotsialnogo prognozirovaniia* (Moscow: Mysl, 1970), 14–15.

136. BestuzhevLada, *Okno v budushchee*, 62.

137. Bestuzhev-Lada, *Okno v budushchee*, 63.

138. Aro Velmet, "The Blank Slate E-State: Estonian Information Society and the Politics of Novelty in the 1990s," *Engaging Science, Technology, and Society* 6 (2020): 162–184.

139. Protocols (1969), ARAN, f. 1977, op. 1, d. 8, l. 35–36.

140. The term Delphi method was originally created by Kaplan in 1950, and was developed by Olaf Helmer, Norman Dalkey, and T. J. Gordon at RAND. See G. S. Pospelov and V. I. Maksimenko, "Predislovie," in *Gorizonty nauki i tekhniki*, eds. I. V. Bestuzhev-Lada and R. A. Fesenko (Moscow: Mir, 1969), 8–9; Andersson, *The Future of the World*.

141. Extending the NKVD (People's Commissariat for Internal Affairs) practice where special gulag camps were created for secret research, the KGB gathered economic information via expert opinion surveys in factories and its own hospitals and medical research agencies; see Asif Siddiqi, "Scientists and Specialists in the Gulag: Life and Death in Stalin's Sharashka," *Kritika* 16, no. 3 (2015): 557–588; Kate Brown, *Manual for Survival: A Chernobyl Guide for the Future* (London: Penguin, 2019); Feygin, *Reforming the Cold War State*, 202–203. These KGB information and surveillance systems were incrementally computerized in the late 1980s, Rindzevičiūtė, *Constructing Soviet Cultural Policy*.

142. IKSI (3 March 1972), ARAN, f. 1977, op. 1, d. 61, l.11.

143. ARAN, f. 1977, op. 1, d. 91, l. 8–9.

144. "Pilot fieldwork, 1973," ARAN, f. 1977, op. 1, d. 91, l. 2–3.

145. ARAN, f. 1977, op. 1, d. 91, l. 8–9.

146. IKSI protocols (6 February 1973, 6–15 March 1973), ARAN, f. 1977, op. 1, d. 91, l. 6–9.

147. His published work also contained hardly any empirical information. See Igor' Bestuzhev-Lada, *Poiskovoe sotsial'noe prognozirovanie: perspektivnye problem obshchestva* (Moscow: Nauka, 1984), 81–84.

148. Although domestic social research into existing patterns of addiction and deviance was done in psychology research institutes. These patterns, to my knowledge, were not projected into the future. See Eugene Raikhel, *Governing Habits: Treating Alcoholism*

NOTES TO PAGES 96–100   223

in Post-Soviet Clinic (Ithaca, NY: Cornell University Press, 2016). However, demographic studies of mortality and addictions were pursued in Soviet collaboration with international partners, such as the IIASA. Rindzevičiūtė, *The Power of Systems*.

149. Klein, *Statistical Visions in Time*.

150. Eglė Rindzevičiūtė, "The Unlikely Revolutionaries: Decision Sciences in the Soviet Government," In *The Decisionist Imagination: Sovereignty, Social Science and Democracy in the 20th Century*, eds. Daniel Bessner and Nicolas Guilhot (Oxford: Berghahn Books, 2019), 217–249.

151. Rindzevičiūtė, *The Power of Systems*, chap. 5.

152. Rindzevičiūtė, *The Power of Systems*, chap. 5; "Academician S. Shatalin," *Options* (September 1989), 10–11.

153. Zubok, *Collapse*.

154. Rudolf G. Pikhoia, unpublished paper presented in workshop "Reevaluating the Soviet Collapse: Domestic and International Frameworks of Politics and Economics" (London School of Economics, London, UK, 23 March 2018).

155. Zubok, *Collapse*.

156. Leeds, "Dreams in Cybernetic Fugue."

157. For an overview, see Jane Cave, "Political Reform and Scientific Freedom Under Gorbachev," *Technology in Society* 13 (1991): 69–89.

158. In 2014, Glazyev was placed on the UK's sanctions list in response to Russia's invasion of Ukraine, https://assets.publishing.service.gov.uk/government/uploads /system/uploads/attachment_data/file/957466/Russia.pdf.

159. Boris Doktorov, "Interv'iu s I.V. Zadorinym: 'V otnoshenie k rabote moia professional'naia pozitsiia vsegda byla sil'nee grazhdanskoi . . .'." *Monitoring obshchest-vennogo mneniia: ekonomicheskie i sotsialnye peremeny* 1 (2016): 363-380.

160. TsIRKON employs about ten staff. The company is presented as independent, not involved in either direct consultancy of political parties or "social engineering" of public opinion. Boris Doktorov, *Sovremennaia Rossiiskaia sotsiologiia: istoriko biogra-ficheskie poiski*, vol. 8.1 (Moscow: TsPIM, 2016), 127; A. A. Iakovlev's interview with Igor' Zadorin, "V professionalnom sotsiologicheskom soobshchestve ne khvataet nezavisi-mykh ekspertov," *Ekonomicheskaia sotsiologiia* 14, no. 1 (2013): 10–26.

161. Vaclav Smil, *Growth: From Microorganisms to Megacities* (Cambridge, MA: MIT Press, 2019), Kindle location 1689.

162. Smil, *Growth*, Kindle location xx.

163. Northcott, "When Are Purely Predictive Models Best?" *Disputatio* 9, no. 47 (2017): 631–656.

164. Gregory, *The Political Economy of Stalinism*.

165. For example, in 1969 Rumiantsev complained to Suslov that much social research was unnecessarily classified in the Soviet Union, indicating that similar studies were publicly available in the United States. This secrecy, argued Rumiantsev, was an obstacle to both Soviet science and governance. "Zapiska A.M. Rumiantseva M.A. Suslovu o poez-dke v SShA" (22 January 1969), *Rossiiskaia sotsiologiia shestidesiatykh godov v vospomi-naniiakh i dokumentakh*, edited by G. Batygin, M.G. Pugacheva, S. F. Iarmoliuk, 473–475 (St Petersburg: Izdatel'stvo Russkogo Khristianskogo gumanitarnogo universiteta, 1999).

166. Although there was an underground movement of Soviet astrology that started in the 1970s. Joseph Kellner, "As Above, So Below: Astrology and the Fate of Soviet Scientism," *Kritika* 20, no. 4 (2019): 783–812.

167. "Otchet" (Geneva, 2–7 October 1967), RGAE, f. 99, op. 1, d. 890, l. 54.

168. "Stenograma" (28 April 1983), ARAN, f. 2, op. 1, d. 585, l. 169.

169. "Stenograma" (28 April 1983), ARAN, f. 2, op. 1, d. 585, l. 91–177.

224   NOTES TO PAGES 100–104

170. In May 1972 GKNT warned the Central Committee that coal, oil, and gas resources would be exhausted within the next 150 years. RGAE, f. 9480, op. 9, d. 1566 (1), l. 69.

5. PREDICTION AND THE OPAQUE

1. For key studies on utopian, modernist projects in the arts, architecture and design, society and industry, see Boris Groys, *The Total Art of Stalinism: Avant-garde, Aesthetic Dictatorship and Beyond* (Princeton, NJ: Princeton University Press, 1992); David Crowley and Jane Pavitt, eds., *Cold War Modern 1945–1970* (London: V&A, 2010); Richard Stites, *The Revolutionary Dreams: Utopian Vision and Experimental Life in the Russian Revolution* (Oxford: Oxford University Press, 1989); Edith Cloves, *Russian Experimental Fiction: Resisting Ideology After Utopia* (Princeton, NJ: Princeton University Press, 1993); Paul Josephson, "'Projects of the Century' in Soviet History: Large-Scale Technologies from Stalin to Gorbachev," *Technology and Culture* 36, no. 3 (1995): 519–559.

2. James C. Scott, *Seeing Like a State: How Certain Schemes to Improve the Human Condition Have Failed* (New Haven, CT: Yale University Press, 1999).

3. Hannah Arendt, *The Origins of Totalitarianism* (1951; London: Penguin, 2017). See also Katherine Verdery, *Secrets and Truths: Ethnography in the Archive of Romania's Secret Police* (Budapest: Central European University Press, 2014)

4. Alena Ledeneva, *Can Russia Modernise? Sistema, Power Networks and Informal Governance* (Cambridge: Cambridge University Press, 2013); Alena Ledeneva, ed., *The Global Encyclopaedia of Informality: Understanding Social and Cultural Complexity*, vols. 1–2 (London: UCL Press, 2020).

5. Il'ia Kukulin criticized Shchedrovitskii's method as a distinctly illiberal alternative to state socialist control. Il'ia Kukulin, "Alternative Social Blueprinting in Soviet Society of the 1960s and the 1970s, or Why Left-Wing Political Practices Have Not Caught on in Contemporary Russia," *Russian Studies in History* 49, no. 4 (2011): 51–92.

6. Alena Ledeneva, *How Russia Really Works: The Informal Practices That Shaped Post-Soviet Politics and Business* (Ithaca, NY: Cornell University Press, 2006); Carole Sigman, "Les clubs politiques informels acteurs du basculement de la perestroïka," *Revue française de science politique* 5, no. 58 (2008): 617–642; Alena Ledeneva, *Russia's Economy of Favours: Blat, Networking and Informal Exchange* (Cambridge: Cambridge University Press, 1998).

7. Vladislav Zubok, *Collapse: The Fall of the Soviet Union* (New Haven, CT: Yale University Press, 2021).

8. Georgii Shchedrovitskii, "Sistemnoe dvizhenie i perspektivy razvitiia sistemno-strukturnoi metodologii," in *Izbrannye Trudy* by Georgii Shchedrovitskii (Moscow: Shkola kul´turnoi politiki, 1995), 57–87.

9. Tatiana Osintseva, "Novaia utka," accessed 10 April 2015, http://www.Prometa.ru.

10. This is evidenced in several documentary films that were produced to demonstrate the link between the intellectual avant-garde of the 1960s and 1970s and the post-Soviet intellectual elites in the capital. See films by Grigorii Kakovkin, *Shchedrovitskii: v poiskakh elity* (2004), Aleksandr Arkhangel'skii, *Otdel* (2010), Elena Laskari, *Kto esli ne ia?* (2019).

11. For instance, the catalogue of the National Library of Russia lists over 1,700 doctoral dissertations dating from the 1990s that contain references to Georgii Shchedrovitskii's work.

12. Earlier studies on Soviet management distinguished a group of "Americanizers" who directly borrowed US ideas of leadership and human interaction. Focusing on the formalization of governance through institutional design, new technologies of data processing and control, such as computers and computer networks, and planning techniques, these studies overlooked the important role of the Russian intellectual tradition

of conceptualizing management. They also missed the cross-fertilization of Soviet management thinking and Soviet physiology, biology, cognitive science, and operations research. Semi-underground approaches to management and those which were not institutionalized, like Shchedrovitskii's, also escaped the attention. Richard Vidmer, "Management Science in the USSR: The Role of 'Americanizers'," *International Studies Quarterly* 24, no. 3 (1980): 392–414, 402. This said, Shchedrovitskii is not always acknowledged in the Russian historiography of management thought, probably because he is considered a philosopher. For instance, Shchedrovitskii is missing from N. V. Ovchinnikova, ed., *Istoriia upravlencheskoi mysli* (Moscow: RGGU, 2013), but is featured prominently in Vladislav A. Lektorsky and Marina F. Bykova, eds., *Philosophical Thought in Russia in the Second Half of the Twentieth Century: A Contemporary View from Russia and Abroad* (London: Bloomsbury, 2019). The only extensive historical account on Georgii Shchedrovitskii is published by his former student in French, where Shchedrovitskii's thought and practice are explored in relation to Marxist philosophy, social theory, and social psychology, but not management. Svetlana Tabatchnikova, *Le cercle de méthodologie de Moscou (1954–1988): Une pensée, une pratique* (Paris: EHESS, 2007).

13. Both Khristenko and Reus hail from Cheliabinsk in Siberia because their parents were deported to the Gulag. Khristenko and Reus published a sizeable collection on Shchedrovitskii's and their own writing, not only in Russian, but also in English with Bloomsbury in 2014. The UK publication was shortlisted for the Chartered Management Institute's Management Book of the Year. Shchedrovitskii's thought had traveled on quite a journey, from semi-underground discussion clubs of the 1950s to the boardrooms of Rosatom and the pages of an officially endorsed publication with a major London-based press. See V. B. Khristenko, A. G. Reus, A. P. Zinchenko et al., *Methodological School of Management* (London: Bloomsbury, 2014).

14. For a comparative analysis of high modernism see Scott, *Seeing Like a State*.

15. For a well-structured overview of different methods of forecasting, see J. Scott Armstrong, *Long-Range Forecasting: From Crystal Ball to Computer* (New York: Wiley, 1985); for governmental uses of statistics, Alain Desrosières, *The Politics of Large Numbers: A History of Statistical Reasoning* (Cambridge, MA: Harvard University Press, 1998). For predictive technologies in the high modernist state, see Jenny Andersson, "Governing Futures: States and the Management of Expectations," in *Reconfiguring European States in Crisis*, eds. Patrick Le Gales and Desmond King (Oxford: Oxford University Press, 2017), 298–312.

16. For a useful discussion of different notions of technocracy, see Frank Fischer, *Technocracy and the Politics of Expertise* (Newbury Park, CA: Sage, 1990); see also Peter Galison and Bruce William Hevly, eds., *Big Science: The Growth of Large Scale Research* (Stanford, CA: Stanford University Press, 1992).

17. Georgii Shchedrovitskii, *Orgupravlencheskoe myshlenie: ideologiia, metodologiia, tekhnologiia* (Moscow: Studia Artemeva Lebedeva, 2013).

18. Arturo Rosenblueth, Norbert Wiener, and Julian Bigelow, "Behavior, Purpose and Teleology," *Philosophy of Science*, 10 (1943): 18–24.

19. See a summary of the cybernetic approach to goal-seeking behavior by the cybernetician Bernard Scott, "The Sociocybernetics of Observation and Reflexivity," *Current Sociology* 67, no. 4 (2019): 495–510.

20. See Ledeneva's work on informality and Stephen Fortescue, ed., *Russian Politics: From Lenin to Putin* (Basingstoke, UK: Palgrave Macmillan, 2010).

21. This led some scholars to propose that it was the KGB and not scientific experts that played the central role of information processing in Soviet governance. Scott Shane, *Dismantling Utopia: How Information Ended the Soviet Union* (Chicago: Ivan R. Dee, 1994). See also Michael Ellman and Vladimir Kantorovich, eds., *The Destruction of the Soviet Economic System: An Insider's History* (London: Routledge, 1988).

226   **NOTES TO PAGES 107–109**

22. Georgii Shchedrovitskii, *Ia vsegda byl idealistom . . .* (Moscow: NNF Institut razvitiia im. G.P. Shchedrovitskogo, 2001).

23. Shchedrovitskii, *Ia vsegda byl idealistom*; Elena Laskari, *Kto, esli ne ia* (2019).

24. Laskari, *Kto, esli ne ia.*

25. One of the first Russian philosophers of logic was Pavel Florensky, a trained mathematician and an Orthodox priest, who proposed a formal method to systematize Orthodox theology. Florensky was invited to participate in the first large-scale infrastructural planning effort, the GOELRO. He was killed in Stalin's purges in 1937. Kirill Sokolov and Avril Pyman, "Father Pavel Florensky and Vladimir Favorsky: Mutual Insights into the Perception of Space," *Leonardo* 22, no. 2 (1989): 237–244.

26. A. M. Anisov, O. V. Maliukova, and L. A. Demina, *Stanovlenie otechestvennoi logiki: diskursy i sudby* (Moscow: Prospekt, 2019); Valentin Bazhanov, *Istoriia logiki v Rossii i SSSR: kontseptual'nyĭ kontekst universitetskoĭ filosofii* (Moscow: Kanon, 2007); Georgii Shchedrovitskii, "Lektsiia 1: 18 fevralia 1988," in *Zapisi Rizhskogo metodologicheskogo seminara*, vol. 1 (Riga: BISI, 2010), 27–28.

27. For the links between philosophy and history, see Elena Aronova, *Scientific History: Experiments in History and Politics from the Bolshevik Revolution to the End of the Cold War* (Chicago: University of Chicago Press, 2021).

28. Shchedrovitskii, "Lektsiia 1," 17, 52.

29. Ianina Prudenko, *Kibernetika v gumanitarnykh naukakh i iskusstve v SSSR: Analiz bol'shikh baz dannykh i komp'iuternoe tvorchestvo* (Moscow: Garazh, 2018), 168.

30. Vladislav Zubok, *Zhivago's Children: The Last Russian Intelligentsia* (Cambridge, MA: Harvard University Press, 2011), 90–93. For the Soviet aid programs and exchanges with the developing countries, see James Mark, Artemy M. Kalinovsky and Steffi Marung, eds., *Alternative Globalizations: Eastern Europe and the Postcolonial World* (Bloomington: Indiana University Press, 2020).

31. Zubok, *Zhivago's Children*, 126; Asif Siddiqi, "Atomized Urbanism: Secrecy and Security from the Gulag to the Closed City," *Urban History* (2021): 1–21.

32. Some historians suggested that Shchedrovitskii's group launched "a seminar movement" in Soviet humanities and social sciences. See Larissa Titarenko and Elena Zdravomyslova, *Sociology in Russia: A Brief History* (Cham: Palgrave, 2017), Kindle location 1291. However, such meetings were fairly common, they expressed the spirit of the times: the mid-1950s, at least in Moscow, saw a spontaneous rise in informal group activities among cultural intelligentsia. These meetings were clamped down on, starting in 1956 and 1957. See Vladislav Zubok, *Zhivago's Children*, 81–82. The sociologist Tomila Lankina links this form of carefully cultivated informal intellectual sociability to the habitus of the Russian middle class as it resisted the fragmenting and disruptive forces of the communist repression and bureaucracy. Shchedrovitskii—as well as other key thinkers discussed in this book—were certainly representatives of the middle and upper classes. Tomila Lankina, *The Estate Origins of Democracy in Russia: From Imperial Bourgeoisie to Post-Communist Middle Class* (Cambridge: Cambridge University Press, 2021).

33. Slava Gerovitch, *From Newspeak to Cyberspeak: A History of Soviet Cybernetics* (Cambridge, MA: MIT Press, 2002); Prudenko, *Kibernetika*, 70.

34. Gerovitch, *From Newspeak to Cyberspeak*, 219–220.

35. Vesa Oittinen, ed., *Evald Ilyenkov's Philosophy Revisited* (Helsinki: Kikimora, 2000).

36. This seminar was criticized by some influential hardliners, such as philosopher and academician Todor Pavlov. Georgii Shchedrovitskii, "Problemy metodologii sistemnogo issledovaniia (1964)," in *Izbrannye Trudy* by Georgii Shchedrovitskii (Moscow: Shkola kul′turnoi politiki, 1995), 155–196; also Anatolii Piskoppel′, "K tvorcheskoi bio-

grafii G.P. Shchedrovitskogo (1929–1994)," in *Izbrannye Trudy* by Georgii Shchedrovitskii (Moscow: Shkola kul´turnoi politiki, 1995), xxiii–xxiv.

37. Georgii Shchedrovitskii, "Problemy metodologii sistemnogo issledovaniia."

38. Shchedrovitskii situated his approach in the context of the East–West transfer of management sciences, such as systems analysis and operations research. Shchedrovitskii's thought was inspired by the interwar study of linguistics and pedagogy. Yet due to space limitation, in this chapter I focus my discussion on the postwar development of cybernetics and systems analysis, the fields that gave legitimacy to Shchedrovitskii's work during the Soviet period. See Vladislav A. Lektorsky, "The Activity Approach in Soviet Philosophy and Contemporary Cognitive Studies," in *Philosophical Thought in Russia in the Second Half of the Twentieth Century: A Contemporary View from Russia and Abroad*, eds. Vladislav Lektorsky and Marina Bykova (London: Bloomsbury, 2019), 137–153.

39. Ekaterina Babintseva, "'Overtake and Surpass': Soviet Algorithmic Thinking as a Revinvention of Western Theories during the Cold War," in *Cold War Social Science: Transnational Entanglements*, eds. Mark Solovey and Christian Daye (Cham: Springer, 2021), 45–72; Matvei Solomonovich Khromchenko, *Letopis'* (Moscow: Studia Korolovae, 2019), 27, https://conflictmanagement.ru/wp-content/uploads/2016/02/letopis_MKh03.pdf.

40. See the biography on www.fondgp.org.

41. Vladimir Lefebvre, *Konfliktuiushchie struktury* (Moscow: Vysh.shkola, 1967).

42. Timothy L. Thomas, "Russia's Reflexive Control Theory and the Military," *Journal of Slavic Military Studies* 17 (2004): 237–256.

43. Some criticized Shchedrovitskii's "totalitarian attitude"; see the memoir by his colleague at VINITE. Igor Golomstock, *A Ransomed Dissident: A Life in Art Under the Soviets* (London: I.B. Tauris, 2019).

44. Laskari, *Kto, esli ne ia.*

45. Shchedrovitskii often cited academic works published in English. He read the principal works in systems analysis by Edward Quade, Stanford Optner, Russell Ackoff, Ludwig von Bertalanffy, Anatolii Rapoport, and Herbert Simon, many of which were both translated into Russian and available in the original languages at Moscow libraries. Shchedrovitskii often referred to structuralists, such as Saussure and Parsons. It is curious, however, that he did not refer to any Western works on business games or strategy simulation games, although publications on these methods were available, for instance, published by Voenizdat (a publishing house specializing in military defense). See Shchedrovitskii, *Izbrannye Trudy* (Moscow: Shkola kul´turnoi politiki, 1995).

46. For Soviet artists and intelligentsia pushing the limits of the freedom of expression in the 1960s, see Zubok, *Zhivago's Children*, 140–200.

47. Dmitry Azrikan, "VNIITE, Dinosaur of Totalitarianism or Plato's Academy of Design?" *Design Issues* 15, no. 3 (1999): 45–77.

48. Zubok, *Zhivago's Children*, 277.

49. This became known as the Trial of the Four. It led to a protest and a petition campaign. In all, about ninety individuals signed the letters, including the designer of the first Soviet thermonuclear bomb, Andrei Sakharov. Robert Horvath, *The Legacy of Soviet Dissent: Dissidents, Democratisation and Radical Nationalism in Russia* (London: Routledge, 2005).

50. Reportedly, all the signatories of this letter lost their jobs. Shchedrovitskii began to publish again a few years after the repression: in addition to many articles, he coauthored a monograph on automated systems in design, together with Oleg Genisaretskii and Anatolii Rapaport, among others, published in 1975. Piskoppel´, "K tvorcheskoi," xxxii–xxxiii.

51. Piskoppel´, "K tvorcheskoi," xxxii–xxxiii.

228   NOTES TO PAGES 111–113

52. Biographers note that several colleagues of Shchedrovitskii left his circle in the mid-1970s fearing that their participation in this informal collective could obstruct their careers. Piskoppel', "K tvorcheskoi," xxxiii.

53. Andrew Schumann, "Rationality in Belarusian Thinking," *Studies in Logic, Grammar and Rhetoric* 13, no. 26 (2008): 7–26, 19.

54. Nikolai Lapin and Boris Sazonov, "The Activity-Systems Approach to Development of the Human Factor in Innovation," in *A Science of Goal Formulation: American and Soviet Discussions of Cybernetics and Systems Theory*, eds. Stuart A. Umpleby and Vadim N. Sadovsky (New York: Hemisphere, 1991), 195–206.

55. Georgii Shchedrovitskii, "Printsipy i obshchaia schema metodologicheskoi organizatsii sistemno-strukturnykh issledovanii i razrabotok (1981)," in *Izbrannye Trudy* by Georgii Shchedrovitskii (Moscow: Shkola kul'turnoi politiki, 1995), 95.

56. Shchedrovitskii, "Printsipy."

57. See the entry in the Oxford English Dictionary, www.oed.com, accessed 10 April 2015.

58. Georgii Shchedrovitskii, "Mental Activity and Pure Thought," in *Methodological School of Management*, eds. V. B. Khristenko, A. G. Reus, A. P. Zinchenko, et al. (London: Bloomsbury, 2014), 33–50, 38.

59. Namely, the work of Lefebvre, see Georgii Shchedrovitskii, "Refleksiia (1974)," in *Izbrannye Trudy* (Moscow: Shkola kul'turnoi politiki, 1995), 485–495.

60. For a discussion of different modes and historical development of reflexivity, see Margaret Archer, *The Reflexive Imperative in Late Modernity* (Cambridge: Cambridge University Press, 2012); Roger Smith, "Does Reflexivity Separate the Human Sciences from the Natural Sciences?" *History of the Human Sciences* 18, no. 4 (2005): 1–25. I return to the question of reflexivity in chapter 6.

61. George Dantzig and Jay Forrester were among the first to develop computer applications for group decisions. For RAND and planning, see Jennifer S. Light, *From Warfare to Welfare: Defense Intellectuals and Urban Problems in Cold War America* (Baltimore: Johns Hopkins University Press, 2003); Jennifer S. Light, "Taking Games Seriously," *Technology and Culture* 49, no. 2 (2008): 347–375. For an overview of business games, see Joseph Wolfe, "A History of Business Teaching Games in English-Speaking and Post-Socialist Countries: The Origination and Diffusion of a Management Education and Development Technology," *Simulation and Gaming* 24, no. 4 (1993): 445–463; D. J. Power, *A Brief History of Decision Support Systems*, DSSResources.com, version 4.0 (10 March 2007).

62. On *la prospective* as a form of social engineering, see Jenny Andersson, *The Future of the World: Futurology, Futurists, and the Struggle for the Post-Cold War Imagination* (Oxford: Oxford University Press, 2018), 65–70. For examples of normativity asserted by the representatives of *la prospective*, see Michel Godet, "From Forecasting to *la prospective*: A New Way of Looking at Futures," *Journal of Forecasting* 1 (1982): 293–301; Tuomo Kuosa, *The Evolution of Strategic Foresight: Navigating Public Policy Making* (Farnham, UK: Ashgate, 2012).

63. Shchedrovitskii, "Printsipy," 112.

64. John H. Gagnon, "Mary M. Birshtein: The Mother of Soviet Simulation Gaming," *Simulation Gaming* 18, no. 3 (1987): 3–12; M. Belchikov and M. M. Birshtein, *Delovye igry* (Riga, Latvia: AVOTS, 1989).

65. V. N. Makarevich, "Igropraktiki, metodologi: 'Nezrimoe soobshchestvo' vykhodit iz podpol'ia," *SOTSIS* 7 (1992): 50–56.

66. A. J. Faria, David Hutchinson, William Wellington, and Steven Gold, "Developments in Business Gaming: A Review of the Past 40 Years," *Simulation and Gaming* 40, no. 4 (2009): 464–487.

67. Stephen Cummings, Todd Bridgman, John Hassard, and Michael Rowlinson, *A New History of Management* (Cambridge: Cambridge University Press, 2017), 65–174.

68. Georgii Shchedrovitskii and S. I. Kotel′nikov, "Organizatsionno-deiatel′nostnaia igra kak novaia forma organizatsii i metod razvitiia kollektivnoi mysledeiatel′nosti (1983)," in G. P. Shchedrovitskii, *Izbrannye Trudy* (Moscow: Shkola kul′turnoi politiki, 1995), 115–142.

69. Gregory Bedny, Mark Seglin, and David Meister, "Activity Theory: History, Research and Application," *Theoretical Issues in Ergonomics Science* 1, no. 2 (2000): 168–206.

70. Georgii Shchedrovitskii, "Lektsiia 2: 19 fevralia 1988," *Zapisi Rizhskogo metodologicheskogo seminara*, vol. 1 (Riga, Latvia: BISI, 2010), 65.

71. Katherine Hayles, *How We Became Posthuman: Virtual Bodies in Cybernetics, Literature, and Informatics* (Chicago: University of Chicago Press, 1999), 136.

72. Titarenko and Zdravomyslova, *Sociology in Russia*, Kindle location 1060.

73. Shchedrovitskii and Kotel′nikov, "Organizatsionno-deiatel′nostnaia igra," 121, 124–125.

74. Osintseva, "Novaia Utka."

75. Shchedrovitskii and Kotel′nikov, "Organizatsionno-deiatel′nostnaia igra," 127–128.

76. Shchedrovitskii and Kotel′nikov, "Organizatsionno-deiatel′nostnaia igra," 113–142.

77. Shchedrovitskii and Kotel′nikov, "Organizatsionno-deiatel′nostnaia igra," 118.

78. Petr Shchedrovitskii, "Predislovie," in Georgii Shchedrovitskii, *Orgupravlencheskoe myshlenie: ideologiia, metodologiia, tekhnologiia* (Moscow: Izdatel'stvo Studii Artemiia Lebedeva, 2014).

79. I thank Tatiana Kasperski for the information on the Beloiarsk nuclear power plant.

80. Petr Shchedrovitskii, "Predislovie."

81. Petr Shchedrovitskii, "Predislovie," 140.

82. See the story narrated by Georgii Shchedrovitskii, "Perspektivy i programmy razvitiia SMD-metodologii," www.bdn-steiner.ru, accessed 10 April 2015, http://bdn-steiner.ru/modules.php?name=Archives&l_op=visit&lid=31.

83. Shchedrovitskii and Kotel'nikov, "Organizatsionno-deiatel′nostnaia igra," 138.

84. Shchedrovitskii and Kotel'nikov, "Organizatsionno-deiatel′nostnaia igra," 138.

85. Erving Goffman, *Encounters* (New York: Bobbs-Merrill, 1961); cf. Light, "Taking Games Seriously," 372.

86. Boris Iudin, "Ot gumanitarnogo znaniia k gumanitarnym tekhnologiiam," *Gumanitarnye nauki: teoriia i metodologiia* 4 (2005): 104–107. Stephen Collier and Anke Gruendel, "Design and Government: City Planning, Space-Making, and Urban Politics," *Political Geography* 97 (2022): 1–13.

87. Shchedrovitskii and Kotel'nikov, "Organizatsionno-deiatel′nostnaia igra," 141.

88. Shchedrovitskii refers to the Russian translation (1962) of the work of US scholars Harry Good and Robert Machol, *Systems Engineering: An Introduction to the Design of Large-Scale Systems* (New York: McGraw Hill, 1957).

89. Georgii Shchedrovitskii, "Budushchee est′ rabota myshleniia i deistviia," *Voprosy metodologii*, 3–4 (1994). Available at fondgp.ru/publications/.

90. Shchedrovitskii and Kotel'nikov, "Organizatsionno-deiatel′nostnaia igra."

91. Shchedrovitskii, "Lektsiia 2," 71.

92. Shchedrovitskii, "Lektsiia 2."

93. This was perceived as transgressive by some Party ideologues. For instance, at a game on free elections, a high official in the Riga city government warned the participants to "behave themselves," something which game technologist Sergei Popov refused to do.

230 NOTES TO PAGES 118–124

Georgii Shchedrovitskii, *Organizatsiia, rukovodstvo, upravlenie II* (Moscow: Put', 2003), 36–37.

94. Shchedrovitskii, "Budushchee est´ rabota myshleniia i deistviia."

95. For more on "Russian world," see Michael Gorham, "Virtual Rusophonia: Language Policy as 'Soft Power' in the New Media Age," *Digital Icons* 5 (2011): 23–48; Andis Kudors, "'Russian World': Russia's Soft Power Approach to Compatriots Policy," *Russian Analytical Digest* 81 (16 June 2010): 2–4.

96. Violetta Volkova, *Iz istorii teorii sistem i sistemnogo analiza* (St Petersburg: SPbGPU, 2004); also Tabatchnikova, *Le cercle*; Khristenko et al., *Methodological School of Management*.

97. Aaron Wildawsky, *Speaking Truth to Power: The Art and Craft of Policy Analysis* (London: Macmillan, 1980).

6. REFLEXIVE CONTROL

1. Reflexive control appears in many papers written to alert Western governments to the Russian threat. Timothy Thomas, "Russia's Military Strategy and Ukraine: Indirect, Asymmetric, and Putin-Led," *Journal of Slavic Military Studies* 28, no. 3 (2015): 445–461; Kan Casapoglu, "Russia's Renewed Military Thinking: Non-Linear Warfare and Reflexive Control," *NATO Defence College Research Paper* 121 (2015): 1–12; Michał Wojnowski, "'Zarządzanie refleksyjne' jako paradygmat rosyjskich operacji informacyjno-psychologicznych w XXI w.," *Przegląd Bezpieczeństwa Wewnętrznego* 12 (2015): 11–36; Han Bowmeester, "Lo and Behold: Let the Truth Be Told—Russian Deception Warfare in Crimea and Ukraine and the Return of 'Maskirovka' and 'Reflexive Control Theory,'" in *Netherlands Annual Review of Military Studies 2017*, eds. Paul A. L. Ducheine and Frans P. B. Osinga (The Hague: Springer, 2017), 140–142; Hakan Gunneriusson and Sascha Dov Bachmann, "Western Denial and Russian Control: How Russia's National Security Strategy Threatens a Western-Based Approach to Global Security, the Rule of Law and Globalization," *Polish Political Science Yearbook* 46, no. 1 (2017): 9–29; Nicolás de Pedro, Panagiota Manoli, Sergey Sukhankin, and Theodoros Tsakiris, *Facing Russia's Strategic Challenge: Security Developments from the Baltic Sea to the Black Sea* (Brussels: European Parliament Policy Department, Directorate General for External Policies, 2017).

2. Vladimir Lefebvre, "Elementy logiki refleksivnykh igr," *Problemy inzhinernoi psikhologii* 4 (1966): 273–299. Although Lefebvre himself wrote that reflexive control theory is not about strategy if "strategy" is defined in a narrow way as the most efficient means to the achievement of particular ends. For Lefebvre, reflexive control theory is rather a wider governmental technique that can contain a strategic component but is not reduced to it.

3. Robert Seely, "Defining Contemporary Russian Warfare: Beyond the Hybrid Headline," *RUSI Journal* 162, no. 1 (April 3, 2017): 50–59.

4. Vladimir Lefebvre, *Lektsii po teorii refleksivnykh igr* (Moscow: Kogito-Tsentr, 2009), 7.

5. Robert Merton, *The Sociology of Science: Theoretical and Empirical Investigations* (Chicago: University of Chicago Press, 1972), 265–278.

6. Nikolai Gogol, *The Gamblers and Marriage*, trans. Alexander Berkman (Digireads, Kindle edition, 2014), Kindle location 256–257.

7. Diego A. Ruiz Palmer, "Back to the Future: Russia's Hybrid Warfare, Revolutions in Military Affairs, and Cold War Comparisons," *NATO Defence College Research Paper* 120 (2015): 1–12.

8. For the changing direction of Putin's geopolitics see Iver B. Neumann, "Russia's Europe, 1991–2016: Inferiority to Superiority," *International Affairs* 92, no. 6 (2016): 1381–1399; Maria Snegovaya, *Putin's Information Warfare in Ukraine: Soviet Origins of Russian*

Hybrid Warfare, Russia Report I (Washington, DC: NATO STRATCOM, September 2015). For Cold War analyses of Soviet reflexive control see Diane Chotikul, "The Soviet Theory of Reflexive Control in Historical and Psychocultural Perspective: Preliminary Study," (unpublished thesis, Naval Postgraduate School, Monterey, CA, 1986); Brian D. Dailey and Patrick J. Parker, eds., *Soviet Strategic Deception* (Lanham, MD: Lexington, 1987); E. Boginskii, *Refleksivnoe upravlenie pri doprose* (Kharkiv: KhIuI, 1983). Note that these authors share an assumption that reflexive control is "realist," that is, rational, instrumental and directly implemented in practice.

9. For background, see Katri Pynnöniemi, "Russia's National Security Strategy: Analysis of Conceptual Evolution," *Journal of Slavic Military Studies* 31, no. 2 (2018): 240–256.

10. In 2004, there was an attempt to create a Club of the Strategic Elite, gathering scholars and leaders to shape the domestic and international strategy for Russia's development. Moscow-based reflexive control scholars kept close links with key corporations such as Rosatom and the presidential administration. For instance, as pointed out by Snegovaya, Aleksandr Beritskii, an influential strategy consultant and now the director of Tavricheskii Informational-Analytical Center, wrote a doctoral dissertation on reflexive control. See Mark Galeotti, *Russian Political War: Moving Beyond the Hybrid* (London: Routledge, 2019); Aki-Mauri Huhtinen, Noora Kotilainen, Saara Särmä, and Mikko Streng, "Information Influence in Hybrid Environment: Reflexive Control as an Analytical Tool for Understanding Warfare in Social Media," *International Journal of Cyber Warfare and Terrorism* 9, no. 3 (2019): 1–20.

11. In addition to Georgii Shchedrovitskii, see, for instance, Aleksandr Avilov, *Refleksivnoe upravlenie: metodologicheskie osnovanie* (Moscow: GUU, 2003); Vladimir Usov, *Refleksivnoe upravlenie: filosofsko-metodologicheskii aspect* (Cheliabinsk: Iurgu, 2010); and the many works by Vladimir Lepskii, the key promoter of reflexive control theory in Russia at this moment of writing.

12. B. F. Skinner, *Beyond Freedom and Dignity* (New York: Pelican, 1971). Skinnerian behaviorism, according to Shoshanna Zuboff, informed the practice of "cybernetic behaviorism" where digital technology companies seek to make user behavior predictable, although as I show in this book, the concept of prediction is much more complicated than the one presented in Zuboff's account. Shoshanna Zuboff, *The Age of Surveillance Capitalism: The Fight for a Human Future at the New Frontier of Power* (New York: Profile Books, 2019).

13. Stuart Russell, *Human Compatible: Artificial Intelligence and the Problem of Control* (London: Viking, 2019).

14. Il'ia Kriger, "Vladimir Lefevr: Ideologiiu nel'zia sozdat'—ona vozniknet nezametno samo soboi," *Novaia gazeta* 84 (1 November 2007).

15. Some of Lefebvre's writings were discussed by Karl Popper and there is an attempt to situate Lefebvre's ideas in the history of second-order cybernetics. Vladimir Lefebvre, *Research on Bipolarity and Reflexivity* (New York: Edwin Mellen, 2006); Alexander Riegler, Karl Muller, and Stuart Umpleby, eds., *New Horizons for Second Order Cybernetics* (Hackensack, NJ: World Scientific, 2017).

15. For instance, Lefebvre's former graduate student Vladimir Lepskii made sure that from the 1990s, the Academy of Sciences' Institute of Philosophy published a number of volumes dedicated to Lefebvre. In the United States, Stuart Umpleby facilitated links between Russian and US systems thinkers from the 1980s. See Stuart Umpleby, "From Complexity to Reflexivity: Underlying Logics Used in Science," *Journal of the Washington Academy of Sciences* 96, no. 1 (2010): 15–26.

16. Georgii Smolian, "Refleksivnoe upravlenie: tekhnologiia priniatiia manipulativnykh reshenii," *Trudy instituta sistemnogo analiza RAN* 63, no. 2 (2013): 54–61. Reflexive control entered popular culture through the fiction writer Viktor Pelevin. In his many

NOTES TO PAGES 125–128

bestsellers, such as *Chapaev and the Void* (originally published in Moscow in 1996, translated into English and published as *Buddha's Little Finger* by Penguin in 2001), Pelevin depicted social relations in Russian society as subject to extreme semiotic manipulation that undermines the stability of social and physical reality. Pelevin combined references to Buddhism and reflexive control to narrate the post-Soviet transition from central planning to a marketing-based business model as a semiotic construct. The free choice, wrote Pelevin, was a necessary illusion, although the actual mechanism of choosing could be better captured in the phrase "coercive orientation." Indeed, this translation of reflexive control into popular fiction was explored by Smolian, Lefebvre's close intellectual collaborator. See Georgii Smolian and Galina Solntseva, "Vladimir Lefevr i Viktor Pelevin ob upravlenie vyborom resheniia" (unpublished paper presented at "Reflexive Processes and Governance," RAN Institute of Philosophy, Moscow, October 2013), 1–18.

17. Hilary Lawson, *Reflexivity: The Post-Modern Predicament* (London: Hutchinson, 1985).

18. Michel Foucault, *The Order of Things: An Archaeology of the Human Sciences* (New York: Vintage Books, 1970), 6.

19. Foucault, *The Order of Things*, 327.

20. Joel Snyder, "'Las Meninas' and the Mirror of the Prince." *Critical Inquiry* 11, no. 4 (1983): 539–572.

21. Snyder, "Las Meninas."

22. Owen Flanagan, "Psychology, Progress, and the Problem of Reflexivity: A Study in the Epistemological Foundations of Psychology," *Journal of the History of Behavioral Sciences* 17, no. 3 (1981): 375.

23. Tony Bennett, Francis Dodsworth, Greg Noble, Mary Poovey, and Megan Watkins, "Introduction," *Body and Society* 19, nos. 2&3 (2013): 3–29. For the affinity between Michel Foucault's notion of the reflexive self and neoliberal subjectivity see Mitchell Dean and Daniel Zamora, *The Last Man Takes LSD: Foucault and the End of Revolution* (London: Verso, 2021).

24. Pierre Bourdieu and Loic Wacquant, *An Invitation to Reflexive Sociology* (Cambridge, UK: Polity Press, 1992). From the mid-1970s, Giddens developed an approach to reflexivity as social self-regulation at the individual and institutional levels, where the circulation of social scientific knowledge as a reflexive device plays a constitutive role. See Christopher G. A. Bryant, "George Soros's Theory of Reflexivity: A Comparison with the Theories of Giddens and Beck and a Consideration of Its Practical Value," *Economy and Society* 31, no. 1 (2002): 112–131; Anthony Giddens, *New Rules of Sociological Method* (Stanford, CA: Stanford University Press, 1976).

25. Steve Woolgar, ed. *Knowledge and Reflexivity: New Frontiers in the Sociology of Knowledge* (London: Sage, 1988).

26. Dick Pels, "Reflexivity: One Step Up," *Theory, Culture and Society* 17, no. 3 (2000): 1–25.

27. Michael Werner and Benedicte Zimmerman, "*Histoire Croisée*: Between the Empirical and Reflexivity," *Annales: Histoire, science sociales* 1 (2003): 7–36.

28. See a special issue examining the use of habit as a stratifying and discriminatory concept in the early sociological accounts of human behavior, Bennett et al., "Introduction."

29. Tony Bennett, "Habit: Time, Freedom, Governance." *Body and Society* 19, nos. 2&3 (2013): 107–135, 108.

30. Although see Richard Staley's argument that the uses of the machine as a metaphor for the social addressed complexity and synchronization in early twentieth century discourses. Richard Staley, "The Interwar Period as a Machine Age: Mechanics, the Machine, Mechanisms and the Market in Discourse," *Science in Context* 31, no. 3 (2018): 263–292.

31. Eugene Raikhel, "Reflex/Рефлекс," *Somatosphere* (November 2014), http://somatosphere.net/2014/reflex%D1%80%D0%B5%D1%84%D0%BB%D0%B5%D0%BA%D1%81.html/.

32. As the medical historian Eugene Raikhel has shown, following Georges Canguilhem, in biology, reflex was not limited to "an isolated organ's mechanical response to a stimulus." On the contrary, biologists understood reflex as "an already coordinated movement determined in part by stimuli in a certain part of the organism and in part by the organism's global state." Raikhel, "Reflex/Рефлекс."

33. The principal studies draw mainly on US, UK, and French intellectual developments and oscillate between the political critique of cybernetic models of decisions and control as a form of (neoliberal) authoritarianism and genealogical analysis of its hybrid roots in different disciplines. Nicolas Guilhot and Daniel Bessner, eds., *Decisionist Imagination: Sovereignty, Social Science and Democracy in the 20th Century* (Oxford: Berghahn Books, 2018); Ron Robin, *The Cold World They Made: The Strategic Legacy of Roberta and Albert Wohlstetter* (Cambridge, MA: Harvard University Press, 2016); S. M. Amadae, *Prisoners of Reason: Game Theory and Neoliberal Political Economy* (Cambridge: Cambridge University Press, 2015); Daniel Bessner, "Organizing Complexity: The Hopeful Dreams and Harsh Realities of Interdisciplinary Collaboration at the Rand Corporation in the Early Cold War," *Journal of the History of the Behavioral Sciences* 51, no. 1 (2015): 31–53; Paul Erickson, *The World the Game Theorists Made* (Chicago: University of Chicago Press, 2015); Roger Backhouse and Philippe Fontaine, eds., *A Historiography of the Modern Social Sciences* (Cambridge: Cambridge University Press, 2014); Rebecca Slayton, *Arguments That Count: Physics, Computing, and Missile Defense, 1949–2012* (Cambridge, MA: MIT Press, 2013); Mark Solovey and Hamilton Cravens, eds., *Cold War Social Science: Knowledge Production, Liberal Democracy, and Human Nature* (Basingstoke, UK: Macmillan, 2012); Nicolas Guilhot, "Cybernetic Pantocrator: International Relations Theory from Decisionism to Rational Choice," *Journal of the History of the Behavioral Sciences* 47, no. 3 (2011): 279–301; Paul Edwards, *Vast Machine: Computer Models, Climate Data and the Politics of Global Warming* (Cambridge, MA: MIT Press, 2010); John Agar, *The Government Machine: A Revolutionary History of the Computer* (Cambridge: MIT Press, 2003); S. M. Amadae, *Rationalizing Capitalist Democracy: The Cold War Origins of Rational Choice Liberalism* (Chicago: University of Chicago Press, 2003).

34. See also Bernard Scott, "The Sociocybernetics of Observation and Reflexivity," *Current Sociology* 67, no. 4 (2019): 495–510.

35. Gregory Bateson, *Steps to an Ecology of Mind: Collected Essays in Anthropology, Psychiatry, Evolution, and Epistemology* (Chicago: University of Chicago Press, 2000); Peter Harries-Jones, *A Recursive Vision: Ecological Understanding and Gregory Bateson* (Toronto: University of Toronto Press, 1995), 111–112. Harries-Jones refers to Bateson's model of the self as a reflexive loop, "which somehow acquires a contrast of self, in relation to system, as it spirals towards its own origin" (*A Recursive Vision*, 180). For Lefebvre this trajectory of the self would describe only one dimension of reflexivity, where the projection of the self seeks to be identical with the self that is projected by others. Bateson's influential idea of the "double bind" described a type of dysfunctional communication where the individual sends contradicting signals to another, for instance, a mother says that she loves her child but at the same time pushes the child away. In Russian reflexive control, this Batesonian "double bind" was adopted as a cognitive resource to confuse and paralyze the opponent. See V. E. Lepskii, *Tekhnologii upravleniia v informatsionnykh voinakh (ot klassiki do postneklassiki)* (Moscow: Kogito-Tsentr, 2016), 76.

36. Xenia Kramer, Tim Kaiser, Stefan Schmidt, Jim Davidson, and Vladimir Lefebvre, "Ot predskazanii k refleksivnomu upravleniiu," *Refleksivnye protsessy i upravlenie* 2, no. 3 (2003): 35–52.

234   **NOTES TO PAGES 131–134**

37. Aleksandr G. Rappaport, "V.A. Lefevr—20 (50) let spustia," *Refleksivnye protsessy i upravlenie* 16, nos. 1–2 (2016): 85–91.

38. A. E. Levintov, "Proiskhozhdenie i priroda refleksii," *Refleksivnye protsessy i upravlenie* 16, nos. 1–2 (2016): 82–85.

39. Irina Sandomirskaja, *Blokada v slove: Ocherki kriticheskoi teorii i biopolitiki iazyka* (Moscow: NLO, 2013).

40. Vladimir Lefebvre, "Vozvrashchenie," in Vladimir Lefevr, *Refleksiia* (Moscow: Kogito-Tsentr, 2003), 436; Vladimir Lefevr, "Rasskazy o Zinchenko," *Refleksivnye protsessy i upravlenie* 11, nos. 1–2 (2011): 93–98, 95.

41. The first publication about reflexive control theory, "The Elements of the Logic of Reflexive Games," appeared in the journal *Problems of Engineering Psychology*, published by Leningrad University, in 1966. Georgii Smolian, "Sub'ektivnye zametki k iubileiu V.A. Lefevra," *Refleksivnye protsessy i upravlenie* 6, no. 1 (2006): 14–26.

42. A small detour. In 1967, the design of the third generation of the ICBM missile landed on Lefebvre's and Zinchenko's desk: but what their boss wanted to know was their opinion on why the Americans had made public the materials on this strategic weapon. At that time, wrote Lefebvre, they considered this publication was a message to the Soviets, demonstrating the procedure preventing an uncoordinated or accidental launch (two buttons had to be pressed synchronously to launch the missile). However, writing in retrospect, Lefebvre noted that making the secret designs public was probably destined for internal communication with American taxpayers to reassure them that the military-industrial complex was delivering. Lefebvre, "Vozvrashchenie," 96.

43. The NIIAA (nauchnoe-issledovatel'skii institute avtomaticheskoi apparatury), located in the southwest of Moscow.

44. V. P. Isaev, "Pervyi v SSSR podvizhnyi vychislitel'nyi tsentr voennogo naznacheniia (1963–1968 gg)," *Virtualnyi komp'iuternyi muzei* (26 January 2011), http://www.computer-museum.ru/histussr/pvp_platforma.htm.

45. Lefebvre, "Vozvrashchenie," 437.

46. Lefebvre, "Vozvrashchenie," 436.

47. Tara Abraham, *Rebel Genius: Warren S. McCulloch's Transdisciplinary Life in Science* (Cambridge, MA: MIT Press, 2016). See the seminal article by Warren McCulloch and Walter Pitts, "A Logical Calculus of the Ideas Immanent in Nervous Activity," *Bulletin of Mathematical Biophysics* 5 (1943): 115–133.

48. Lefebvre, "Vozvrashchenie," 436.

49. See Elena Aronova's work on scientific information in the Soviet Union as East–West exchange, for instance, Elena Aronova, "The Politics and Contexts of Soviet Science Studies (*Naukovedenie*): Soviet Philosophy of Science at the Crossroads," *Studies in East European Thought* 63, no. 3 (2011): 175–202; and Elena Aronova, *Scientific History: Experiments in History and Politics from the Bolshevik Revolution to the End of the Cold War* (Chicago: University of Chicago Press, 2021).

50. Vladimir Lefebvre, "Konfliktuiushchie struktury (1967)," in Vladimir Lefevr, *Refleksiia* (Moscow: Kogito-Tsentr, 2003), 132–133.

51. Lefebvre, "Vozvrashchenie," 438.

52. Cecily Deegan and Stephen Latham, "The B-School vs the Wall Street Journal: Who Is Misrepresenting Whom," *Harvard Crimson* (1 March 1979), https://www.thecrimson.com/article/1979/3/1/the-b-school-vs-the-wall-street/.

53. Bessner, "Organizing Complexity."

54. Vladimir Lefebvre and Georgii Smolian, *Algebra konflikta* (Moscow: Librokom, 2013), 3. Not only Russian decision scholars resorted to literature: fiction was held in high regard by RAND's Social Science Division scientists as well. See Daniel Bessner, *Democ-*

NOTES TO PAGES 134–137 235

racy in Exile: Hans Speier and the Rise of the Defense Intellectual (Ithaca, NY: Cornell University Press, 2018).

55. Lefebvre, "Vozvrashchenie," 436. See also Roman Khandozhko, *Vzaimodeistvie neofitsial'noi filosofii i nauchno-tekhnicheskogo soobshchestva v pozdnem SSSR: sluchai Obninska* (Moscow: Ranepa, 2016); Vladimir Lepskii, "Lefevre i refleksiia," *Refleksivnye protsessy i upravlenie* 6, no. 1 (2006): 28.

56. Slava Gerovitch, "'We Teach Them to Be Free': Specialized Math Schools and the Cultivation of the Soviet Technical Intelligentsia," *Kritika: Explorations in Russian and Eurasian History* 20, no. 4 (2019): 717–754.

57. Rappaport, "V.A. Lefevr—20 (50) let spustia," 86.

58. F. I. Ereshko, "Ravnovesie na mnozhestve refleksivnykh strategii," *Refleksivnye protsessy i upravlenie* 16, nos. 1–2 (2016): 59–64; I. N. Semenov, "Personologiia zhiznet-vorchestva V.A. Lefevra i razvitie refleksivnykh nauk (ot logiki i psikhologii cherez kiber-netiku i etiku k kosmologii," *Refleksivnye protsesy i upravlenie* 16, nos. 1–2 (2016): 100–106. A circle of Lefebvre's followers continued the institutionalization of the interdisciplinary study of reflexivity: research centers and education departments were established at the Russian Academy of Sciences and the National Research University—Higher School of Economics in Moscow. The RAN center is a member of the World Organization of Systems and Cybernetics.

59. Vitalii Tsygichko, "Predislovie ko vtorumu izdaniiu," in Vladimir Lefebvre and Georgii Smolian, *Algebra konflikta* (Moscow: Librokom, 2013), 1.

60. For instance, Lepskii presented his work on reflexive control at the fourth all-union congress of psychologists in Tbilisi, 1971. Research into behavioral prediction was developed by S. L. Rubinshtein and his students, such as Andrei Brushlinskii (1933–2002), who directed the Institute of Psychology at the Russian Academy of Science from 1989 to 2002.

61. For more on TsEMI's role in the development of Soviet economic cybernetics, see Ivan Boldyrev and Olessia Kirtchik, "The Cultures of Mathematical Economics in the Postwar Soviet Union: More Than a Method, Less Than a Discipline," *Studies in History and Philosophy of Science Part A* 63 (2017): 1–10.

62. Semenov, *Personologiia*, 100–101.

63. Jack Murphy, "Russian Reflexive Control Is Subverting the American Political Landscape," *Sofrep* (26 September 2018), https://sofrep.com/news/russian-reflexive-control-is-subverting-the-american-political-landscape/.

64. David Priestland, *Merchant, Soldier, Sage: A New History of Power* (London: Allen, 2012), 126–132.

65. Will Thomas, *The Rational Action: The Sciences of Policy in Britain and America, 1940-1960* (Cambridge, MA: MIT Press, 2015), 84.

66. Pavel Podvig, "History and the Current Status of the Russian Early Warning System," *Science and Global Security* 10 (2002): 21–60; V. G. Repin, "Sobytie i liudi," in *Rubezhy oborony: v kosmose i na zemle. Ocherki istorii rakteno-kosmicheskoi oborony*, ed. N. G. Zavalin (Moscow: Veche, 2003), 433–472.

67. Thomas, *Rational Action*, 139, 145, 179; Condoleezza Rice, "The Party, the Military, and Decision Authority in the Soviet Union," *World Politics* 40, no. 1 (October 1987): 55–81.

68. Correspondence between Vladimir Lefebvre and Anatol Rapoport, reproduced in a magazine published by the Russian Academy of Sciences, Anatol Rapoport and Vladimir Lefebvre, "Vozmozhno li samoosvobozhdenie?" *Chelovek* 5 (1991): 79–85.

69. Petrus Buwalda, *They Did Not Dwell Alone: Jewish Emigration from the Soviet Union, 1967-1990* (Baltimore: Johns Hopkins University Press, 1997), xv.

236   **NOTES TO PAGES 137–142**

70. Jim Washburn, "The Human Equation: UC Irvine Theoretical Psychologist Vladimir Lefebvre Uses Mathematics to Show Us Who We Are," *Los Angeles Times* (31 March 1993). For the emigration of scholars and intelligentsia, see Slava Gerovitch, *From Newspeak to Cyberspeak: A History of Soviet Cybernetics* (Cambridge, MA: MIT Press, 2002), 290–291; and particularly Vladislav Zubok, *Zhivago's Children: The Last Russian Intelligentsia* (Cambridge, MA: Harvard University Press, 2011).

71. The Russian mathematician and game theorist Andrei Toom defected in 1989. Loren Graham and Irina Dezhina, *Science in the New Russia: Crisis, Aid, Reform* (Bloomington: Indiana University Press, 2008).

72. Vladimir Lefebvre, "Algebra sovesti: vospominanie avtora," *Znanie i sila* 3 (2002).

73. Jack Matlock to Robert Mcfarlane, National Security Council, 3 August 1984; Jack Matlock to Robert McFarlane, National Security Council, 7 June 1984. Ronald Reagan Presidential Library Digital Library Collections, Collection: Matlock, Jack F.: Files Folder Title: Matlock Chron June 1984 [06/01/1984-06/07/1984] Box: 5.

74. Iuliia Netesova, "Upravliaiushchie katastrofoi: refleksivnye modeli sovetskogo i amerikanskogo obshchestv," *Ruskii zhurnal* (Summer 2008): 129–130.

75. Jack Matlock to Vladimir Lefebvre, 8 October 1986. Copy supplied by Lefebvre to the journal. Ronald Reagan Presidential Library Digital Library Collections, Collection: Matlock, Jack.

76. Anatol Rapoport personal records, B2005–0018, University of Toronto Archives.

77. Lefebvre's session was also attended by Ernst von Glasersfeld, Francesco Maturana, and Stuart Umpleby. EMCSR meetings were organized by the Austrian Society of Cybernetics and chaired by Robert Trappl; the first meeting was organized in Vienna, in 1972. Robert Trappl, ed., *Power, Autonomy, Utopia: New Approaches toward Complex Systems* (New York: Plenum Press, 1986).

78. Vladimir Lefebvre interviewed by N. Kuznetsova, "Vozvraschenie," *Voprosy filosofii* 7 (1990): 51–58. For Lefebvre's engagement with the international community of cybernetics and systems thinkers, see Vladimir Lefebvre, "Second Order Cybernetics in the Soviet Union and the West," in *Power, Autonomy, Utopia: New Approaches toward Complex Systems*, ed. Robert Trappl (New York: Plenum Press, 1986), 123.

79. Raikhel, "Reflex/Рефлекс"; Eglė Rindzevičiūtė, *The Power of Systems: How Policy Sciences Opened Up the Cold War World* (Ithaca, NY: Cornell University Press, 2016).

80. Isaac Joel, "Strategy as Intellectual History," *Modern Intellectual History* (2018): 1–15, 4.

81. Joel, "Strategy," 7.

82. For reflexivity as a difficult and therefore ignored problem in social science, see Steve Woolgar and Malcolm Ashmore, "The Next Step: Introduction to the Reflexive Project," in Steve Woolgar ed., *Knowledge and Reflexivity: New Frontiers in the Sociology of Knowledge* (London: Sage, 1988), 1–13.

83. Lefebvre and Smolian, *Algebra konflikta*, 8.

84. Lefebvre and Smolian, *Algebra konflikta*, 12, 14.

85. Lefebvre and Smolian, *Algebra konflikta*, 20.

86. Lefebvre and Smolian, *Algebra konflikta*, 18.

87. Lefebvre and Smolian, *Algebra konflikta*, 18.

88. Lefebvre and Smolian, *Algebra konflikta*, 18–19.

89. Anatol Rapoport, "Foreword," in Vladimir Lefebvre, *Algebra of Conscience: A Comparative Analysis of Western and Soviet Ethical Systems* (Dordrecht, Holland: D. Reidel, 1982), vii–xii, ix.

90. Bessner, "Organizing Complexity."

91. Lefebvre and Smolian, *Algebra konflikta*, 20.

92. For Lefebvre reflexive control theory is not necessarily about individual human beings, but rather about "macro individuals," that is, actors whose minds are inevitably tapped into the environments of meaning.

93. Lefebvre and Smolian, *Algebra konflikta*, 30–31.

94. The strategy of disguise "aims to supply the opponent with fairly concrete information, rather than blocking any flow of information," seeking to convince the opponent that "there is nothing here" or to create "false objects," such as the presence of troops that actually are not there. Lefebvre and Smolian, *Algebra konflikta*, 36–37.

95. Lefebvre and Smolian, *Algebra konflikta*, 37.

96. Lefebvre and Smolian, *Algebra konflikta*, 43.

97. Lefebvre and Smolian, *Algebra konflikta*, 45.

98. Lefebvre and Smolian, *Algebra konflikta*, 50.

99. Christopher G. A. Bryant, "George Soros's Theory," 118.

100. Daniel Bessner, "The Globalist: George Soros After the Open Society," *N + 1* (18 June 2018).

101. For Soros, see Bryant, "George Soros's Theory," 121.

102. George Soros, "Fallibility, Reflexivity, and the Human Uncertainty Principle," *Journal of Economic Methodology* 20, no. 4 (2014): 309–329, 312.

103. George Soros, *The Crisis of Global Capitalism: Open Society Endangered* (London: Little, 1998), 22, cited from Bryant, "George Soros's Theory," 127.

104. Soros, "Fallibility."

105. Alex Rosenberg, "From Rational Choice to Reflexivity: Learning from Sen, Keynes, Hayek, Soros, and Most of All, from Darwin," *Economic Thought* 3, no. 1 (2014): 21–41, 35.

106. For an example, see Robert Jervis, *Perception and Misperception in International Politics* (Princeton, NJ: Princeton University Press, 1976), for a practice-oriented analysis, see Gregoire Mallard and Andrew Lakoff, "How Claims to Know the Future Are Used to Understand the Present: Techniques of Prospection in the Field of National Security," in *Social Knowledge in the Making*, eds. Charles Camic, Michele Lamont, and Neil Gross (Chicago: University of Chicago Press, 2010), 339–379.

107. Luca Zan, "Complexity, Anachronism and Time-Parochialism: Historicising Strategy While Strategising History," *Business History* 58, no. 4 (2016): 571–596. This divide is also acknowledged in histories of strategic thought based on case studies. For instance, in his magisterial work, Lawrence Freedman demonstrated that although strategy thinking is enjoying high status in political circles, historically it has been difficult, or even impossible, to "implement" strategy in tactics, particularly in complex and messy battlefield situations. Lawrence Freedman, *Strategy: A History* (Oxford: Oxford University Press, 2013).

108. Chris Carter, Stewart Clegg, and Martin Kornberger, "Strategy as Practice?" *Strategic Organization* 6, no. 1 (2008): 83–99.

109. Chris Carter, Stewart Clegg, and Martin Kornberger, "Re-framing Strategy: Power, Politics and Accounting," *Accounting, Auditing and Accountability Journal* 23, no. 5 (2010): 573–594, 574.

110. Carter et al., "Strategy as Practice?" 83.

111. Strategic discourse as an organizational mediator is a modern phenomenon, descriptions of which can be found in treatises from the eighteenth and nineteenth centuries. Freedman, *Strategy*.

112. Mark Solovey and Hamilton Cravens, *Cold War Social Science*.

113. Carter et al., "Re-framing Strategy," 574–575.

114. John W. Meyer and Brian Rowan, "Institutionalized Organizations: Formal Structure as Myth and Ceremony," *American Journal of Sociology* 83, no. 2 (1977): 340–363; Carter et al. "Re-framing Strategy," 580.

238 NOTES TO PAGES 146-152

115. Timothy L. Thomas, "Russian Military Thought: Concepts and Elements," MITRE Corporation (August 2019), 44–46.

116. Thomas, "Russian Military Thought," 47–48; M. Hammond-Errey, "Understanding and Assessing Information Influence and Foreign Interference," *Journal of Information Warfare* 18, no. 1 (2019): 1–22.

117. Brandon Valeriano and Ryan Maness, "Fancy Bears and Digital Trolls: Cyber Strategy with a Russian Twist," *Journal of Strategic Studies* (ahead of print, 2019): 14.

118. Ronald W. Sprang, "The Development of Operational Art and CEMA in Multi-Domain Battle during the Guadalcanal Campaign 1942–1943 and Russia in the Ukraine 2013–2016," School of Advanced Military Studies, US Army Command and General Staff College, Fort Leavenworth, 2018; T. S. Allen and A. J. Moore, "Victory without Casualties: Russia's Information Operations," *Parameters* 48, no. 1 (2018): 64.

119. Valeriano and Maness, "Fancy Bears," 9–10.

120. Lord Jopling, *Countering Russia's Hybrid Threats: An Update* (Committee of the Civil Dimension of Security, NATO Parliamentary Assembly, 1 October 2018), 2.

121. Valeriano and Maness, "Fancy Bears," 14. Ido Kilovaty, "Doxfare: Politically Motivated Leaks and the Future of the Norm on Non-Intervention in the Era of Weaponized Information," *Harvard National Security Journal* 9, no. 1 (2018): 146–179.

122. Carter et al., "Strategy as Practice?" 92.

123. Carter et al., "Strategy as Practice?" 93.

124. Lefebvre and Smolian, *Algebra konflikta*, 61.

125. Bruno Latour, "The Politics of Explanation: An Alternative," in *Knowledge and Reflexivity: New Frontiers in the Sociology of Knowledge*, ed. Steve Woolgar (London: Sage, 1988), 155–176, 159.

126. Hammond-Errey, "Understanding and Assessing," 11,

127. Soros, "Fallibility," 326.

128. Xenia Kramer et al., "Ot predskazanii," 49.

7. GLOBAL PREDICTION

1. Michael Mahony and Martin Hulme, "Epistemic Geographies of Climate Change: Science, Space and Politics," *Progress in Human Geography* (2016): 1–30. For antecedents of the Anthropocene concept, see Christophe Bonneuil and Jean-Baptiste Fressoz, *The Shock of the Anthropocene: The Earth, History and Us* (London: Verso, 2016); Libby Robin, Sverker Sörlin, and Paul Warde, eds., *The Future of Nature: The Documents of Global Change* (New Haven, CT: Yale University Press, 2013).

2. These were not only the emerging global climate scientists, but also vulcanologists, who were expected to deliver policy-relevant information about the highly uncertain movement of tectonic plates. For an East–West study, see Elena Aronova, "Earthquake Prediction, Biological Clocks, and the Cold War Psy-ops: Using Animals as Seismic Sensors in the 1970s California," *Studies in History and Philosophy of Science, Part A* 70 (2018): 50–57; Elena Aronova, "Citizen Seismology, Stalinist Science, and Vladimir Mannar's Cold Wars," *Science, Technology, & Human Values* 42, no. 2 (2017): 226–256.

3. The work on the social and political history of cybernetic feedback was pioneered by James Beniger, *The Control Revolution: Technological and Economic Origins of the Informational Society* (Cambridge, MA: Harvard University Press, 1989) and continued in Peter Galison, "The Ontology of the Enemy: Norbert Wiener and the Cybernetic Vision," *Critical Inquiry* 21, no. 1 (1994): 228–266; Slava Gerovitch, *From Newspeak to Cyberspeak: A History of Soviet Cybernetics* (Cambridge, MA: MIT Press, 2002); David Mindell, *Between Human and Machine: Feedback, Control, and Computing Before Cybernetics* (Baltimore: Johns Hopkins University Press, 2002); John Agar, *The Government Machine: A*

Revolutionary History of the Computer (Cambridge, MA: MIT Press, 2003); Andrew Pickering, *The Cybernetic Brain: Sketches of Another Future* (Chicago: University of Chicago Press, 2009); Eglė Rindzevičiūtė, "Purification and Hybridisation of Soviet Cybernetics: The Politics of Scientific Governance in an Authoritarian Regime," *Archiv fur sozialgeschichte* 50 (2010): 289–309; Eden Medina, *Cybernetic Revolutionaries: Technology and Politics in Allende's Chile* (Cambridge, MA: MIT Press, 2011); Ronald Kline, *The Cybernetics Moment: Or Why We Call Our Age the Information Age* (Baltimore: Johns Hopkins University Press, 2015); Benjamin Peters, *How Not to Network a Nation: The Uneasy History of the Soviet Internet* (Cambridge, MA: MIT Press, 2016); Clifford Siskin, *System: The Shaping of Modern Knowledge* (Cambridge, MA: MIT Press, 2016).

4. Eldar Shafir, ed., *The Behavioral Foundations of Public Policy* (Princeton, NJ: Princeton University Press, 2013); for the epistemological analysis of behavioral policy see Magdalena Małecka, "Knowledge, Behaviour, and Policy: Questioning the Epistemic Presuppositions of Applying Behavioural Science in Public Policymaking," *Synthese* 199 (2021): 5311–5338.

5. Michel Foucault, *Security, Territory, Population: Lectures at the Collège de France 1978–1979* (Basingstoke, UK: Palgrave, 2009), 20–21, 23.

6. For Canguilhem's influence see Jennifer Gabrys, *Program Earth: Environmental Sensing Technology and the Making of a Computational Planet* (Minneapolis: University of Minnesota Press, 2016); Stuart Elden, *Canguilhem* (Cambridge: Polity, 2019).

7. Georges Canguilhem, "The Living and Its Milieu," trans. from French, originally published 1952, *Grey Room* 3 (2001): 7–31.

8. Stefanos Geroulanos and Todd Meyers, *The Human Body in the Age of Catastrophe: Brittleness, Integration, Science, and the Great War* (Chicago: University of Chicago Press, 2018). For Skinner see Roy Moxley, "Ernst Mach and B. F Skinner: Their Similarities with Two Traditions for Verbal Behavior," *The Behavior Analyst* 28, no. 1 (2005): 29–48.

9. Very interesting articulations of governance through milieu, materiality, and behavior have been offered in museum and heritage studies. See Haidy Geismar, *Museum Object: Lessons for the Digital Age* (London: UCL Press, 2018); and Rodney Harrison and Colin Sterling, eds., *Deterritorializing the Future: Heritage In, Of and After the Anthropocene* (London: Open Humanities Press, 2020).

10. Tony Bennett, *Making Culture, Changing Society* (London: Routledge, 2013); Tony Bennett, Fiona Cameron, Nélia Dias, Ben Dibley, Rodney Harrison, Ira Jacknis, and Conal McCarthy, *Collecting, Ordering, Governing: Anthropology, Museums, and Liberal Government* (Durham, NC: Duke University Press, 2017).

11. Gabrys, *Program Earth*.

12. Timothy W. Luke, "On Environmentality: Geo-Power and Eco-Knowledge in the Discourses of Contemporary Environmentalism," *Cultural Critique* 31 (1995): 57–81; Arun Agrawal, *Environmentality: Technologies of Government and the Making of Subjects* (Durham, NC: Duke University Press, 2005).

13. For the overlap between Foucault's own and the neoliberal thinking about indirect governance through milieu see Dean and Zamora, *The Last Man Takes LSD: Foucault and the End of Revolution* (London: Verso, 2021).

14. Paul Crutzen, "Geology of Mankind," *Nature* 415, no. 3 (2002): 23.

15. Will Steffen, Katherine Richardson, Johan Rockstrom, Sarah E. Cornell, Ingo Fetzer, Elena M. Bennett, Reinette Biggs, et al., "Planetary Boundaries: Guiding Human Development on a Changing Planet," *Science* 347 (2015): 736.

16. Jonathan Oldfield and Denis Shaw, eds., *The Development of Russian Environmental Thought: Scientific and Geographical Perspectives on the Natural Environment* (London: Routledge, 2016); Jonathan Oldfield, *The Soviet Union and Global Environmental*

240   NOTES TO PAGES 155–157

Change: Modifying the Biosphere and Conceptualizing Society–Nature Interaction (London: Routledge, 2021).

17. Although Vernadskii's biosphere theory is familiar to environmental historians, the Russian version of noosphere theory is little known in the West. Key works are Jonathan Oldfield and Denis Shaw, "V.I. Vernadskii and the Development of Biogeochemical Understandings of the Biosphere, c.1880s–1968," *British Journal for the History of Science* 46, no. 2 (2013): 287–310; Stanislav Shmelev, *Ecological Economics: Sustainability in Practice* (Berlin: Springer, 2012); Rafal Serafin, "Noosphere, Gaia and the Science of the Biosphere," *Environmental Ethics* 10, no. 2 (1988): 121–137. Also see Nikita Moiseev, "Reflection on Noosphere: Humanism in Our Time," in *The Biosphere and Noosphere Reader: Global Environment, Society and Change*, eds. David Pitt and Paul Samson (London: Routledge, 1999), 167–179.

18. See the volume comprising statements on Vernadskii's influence by scientists representing different disciplines: Andrei Lapo and Aleksandr Ianshin, eds., *V.I.Vernadskii: Pro et Contra* (Saint Petersburg: Izdatelstvo Russkogo Khristianskogo gumanitarnogo universiteta, 2000); Giulia Rispoli, "Between 'Biosphere' and 'Gaia': Earth as a Living Organism in Soviet Geo-ecology," *Cosmos and History: The Journal of Natural and Social Philosophy* 10, no. 2 (2014): 78–91; Jonathan Oldfield, "Russia, Systemic Transformation and the Concept of Sustainable Development," *Environmental Politics* 10, no. 3 (2001): 94–110. For important studies on the Soviet environmental movements and scientific expertise see Douglas R. Weiner, *A Little Corner of Freedom: Russian Nature Protection from Stalin to Gorbachev* (Berkeley: University of California Press, 1999); Paul Josephson, Nicolai Dronin, Ruben Mnatsakanian, Aleh Cherp, Dmitry Efremenko, and Vladislav Larin, *An Environmental History of Russia* (Cambridge: Cambridge University Press, 2013); Andy Bruno, *The Nature of Soviet Power: An Arctic Environmental History* (Cambridge: Cambridge University Press, 2016).

19. Vladislav Zubok, *Collapse: The Fall of the Soviet Union* (New Haven, CT: Yale University Press, 2021).

20. This is based on Moiseev's contemporaries' memoirs; a study of archival materials is necessary to further detail his influence on Gorbachev. Aleksandr A. Petrov, *Nikita Nikolaevich Moiseev: Sud'ba strany v sud'be uchenogo* (Moscow: Ekologiia i zhizn, 2011), 106–107.

21. Petrov, *Nikita Nikolaevich Moiseev*, 107–109. This agricultural decision-making model was developed by Feliks Ereshko, V. Y. Lebedev, and Kirit Parikh in 1983, see I. V. Iakimets, "Background and Requirements for the SOVAM: Soviet Agricultural Model" (IIASA Working Paper, WP-84-097, IIASA, Austria, 1984).

22. Zubok, *Collapse*.

23. Moiseev's biographies and volumes engaging with his work were published shortly after his death in 2000. See Ivan Larin, *On uchil berech zemliu* (Moscow: Rosekopress, 2002); *Myslitel' planetarnogo mashtaba: materialy 'kruglogo stola' po kn. N.N.Moiseeva 'Byt' ili ne byt' chelovechestvu?'* (Moscow: MNEPU, 2000). Prominent politicians such as former Prime Minister Evgenii Primakov endorsed Moiseev's contributions, see Evgenii Primakov, "Nikita Moiseev: vydaiushchii'sia uchenyi' i grazhdanin," *Alma Mater* 6 (2007): 43. Many contemporary Russian scholars draw on Moiseev's work to rethink Russia's development, see Elena Glushenkova, *Ekopolitologiia N. N. Moiseeva i ustoichivoe razvitie Rossii* (Moscow: MNEPU, 2015). Major memorial conferences marking anniversaries of Moiseev's birth were convened by the Moscow State University (2007) and the Trapeznikov Institute of Control Problems at the Russian Academy of Sciences (2017), not to mention the many events organized by the International Independent Ecological-Political University in Moscow, which was cofounded by Moiseev and Nikolai Reimers in 1992.

NOTES TO PAGES 157–161   241

24. Quinn Slobodian, *Globalists: The End of Empire and the Birth of Neoliberalism* (Cambridge, MA: Harvard University Press, 2018).

25. Nikita N. Moiseev, *Kak daleko do zavtrashnego dnia . . . Svobodnye razmyshleniia 1917–1993* (Moscow: Taideks, 1993/2002), 148, 331, 339; Petrov, *Nikita Nikolaevich Moiseev.*

26. Tomila V. Lankina, *The Estate Origins of Democracy in Russia: From Imperial Bourgeoisie to Post-Communist Middle Class* (Cambridge: Cambridge University Press, 2021).

27. Moiseev, *Kak daleko*, 22, 111.

28. For more on the Soviet space program, see Asif Sidiqqi, *The Red Rocket's Glare: Spaceflight and the Russian Imagination, 1857–1957* (Cambridge: Cambridge University Press, 2010); Slava Gerovitch, *Voices of the Space Program: Cosmonauts, Soldiers, and Engineers Who Took the USSR into Space* (London: Palgrave, 2014); Slava Gerovitch, *Soviet Space Mythologies.*

29. Moiseev, *Kak daleko*, 25–28; Nikita N. Moiseev, *Izbrannye trudy* (Moscow: Taideks, 2003), 261. Moiseev retired from the Computer Center in 1987 but served as a member of the center's directors' board until 2000.

30. For Moiseev's links with mathematical economists see Ivan Boldyrev and Olessia Kirtchik, "The Cultures of Mathematical Economics in the Postwar Soviet Union: More Than a Method, Less Than a Discipline," *Studies in History and Philosophy of Science Part A* 63 (2017): 1–10. For Lavrent'ev's role in the modernization of Soviet science, see Ksenia Tatarchenko, "Calculating a Showcase: Mikhail Lavrentiev, the Politics of Expertise, and the International Life of the Siberian Science-City," *Historical Studies in the Natural Sciences* 46, no. 5 (2016): 592–632. For Moiseev's correspondence with Lyapunov, see the Open Archive of the Siberian Branch of the Russian Academy of Sciences, fund of A. A. Lyapunov, http://odasib.ru/OpenArchive/Portrait.cshtml?id=Xu1_pavl_6352123351357812 50_4042. For Gluskhov, see Peters, *How Not to Network a Nation.*

31. Vladislav Zubok, *A Failed Empire: The Soviet Union in the Cold War from Stalin to Gorbachev* (Chapel Hill: North Carolina University Press, 2009); Charles Ziegler, *Environmental Policy in the USSR* (Amherst: University of Massachusetts Press, 1987).

32. Paul Warde and Sverker Sörlin, "Expertise for the Future: The Emergence of 'Relevant Knowledge' in Environmental Predictions and Global Change, c.1920–1970," in *The Struggle for the Long Term in Transnational Science and Politics during the Cold War*, eds. Jenny Andersson and Eglė Rindzevičiūtė (New York: Routledge, 2015), 39–62.

33. Warde and Sörlin, "Expertise for the Future."

34. Warde and Sörlin, "Expertise for the Future."

35. Oldfield, *The Soviet Union and Global Environmental Change*, 42–65.

36. Joan DeBardeleben, *The Environment and Marxism–Leninism: The Soviet and East German Experience* (Boulder, CO: Westview Press, 1985); Oleg Ianitskii, "Environmental Sociology Yesterday and Today," *Sociological Research* 33, no. 1 (1994): 7–32, 9.

37. For the rituals of scientific expertise in Soviet planning see Peter Rutland, *The Myth of the Plan: Lessons of Soviet Planning Experience* (London: Open Court, 1985).

38. Slobodian, *Globalists*, Kindle location 4514.

39. On Koopman's links with Soviet science see Till Düppe, "Koopmans in the Soviet Union: A Travel Report of the Summer of 1965," *Journal of the History of Economic Thought* 38, no. 1 (2016): 81–104.

40. Norbert Wiener, *Cybernetics: Or Control and Communication in the Animal and in the Machine* (Cambridge, MA: MIT Press, 1965), 25.

41. Moiseev, *Kak daleko*, 193–195.

42. Boldyrev and Kirtchik, "Cultures of Mathematical Economics," 7; Nikita Moiseev, *Prosteishie matematicheskie modeli ekonomicheskogo prognozirovaniia* (Moscow: Znanie, 1975).

242   NOTES TO PAGES 161–164

43. Eglė Rindzevičiūtė, "The Unlikely Revolutionaries: Decision Sciences in the Soviet Government," in *The Decisionist Imagination: Sovereignty, Social Science and Democracy in the 20th Century*, eds. Daniel Bessner and Nicolas Guilhot (Oxford: Berghahn Books, 2019), 217–249.

44. Moiseev, *Kak daleko*, 230; Nikita Moiseev, *Chelovek i noosfera* (Moscow: Molodaia gvardiia, 1990), 269–270.

45. In his memoir, Moiseev dates this trip 1959, although he mentions meeting the prominent, US-based mathematician and engineer Rudolf Kalman, who established a systems automation research unit at the École des Mines in Fontainebleau, which makes it more likely to be the late 1960s. Although Moiseev noted reading Hayek as a significant event, he did not engage with Hayek's idea of the failure of any centers to govern complex, large scale economy. Instead, Moiseev often referred to the Russian organization theorist Aleksandr Bogdanov, who proposed that any governmental apparatus must be regularly decentralized. It is clear, though, that Hayek's neoliberal ideas had appeal to Moiseev as a policy scientist interested in complexity. For Hayek's intellectual affinity with the resilience approach see David Chandler, *Resilience: The Governance of Complexity* (London: Routledge, 2014).

46. Moiseev had close links with some of the leading cyberneticians: he co-published with Alexei Rumiantsev and Sergei Sobolev, who was the opponent of Moiseev's doctoral dissertation. Moiseev's key publications from this period are concise volumes *On the Theory of Optimal Systems* (1975), *Methods of Optimization* (1978), and *Mathematics, Governance and Economics* (1970).

47. Many of Moiseev's books remain in print, the most recent editions dating to 2020.

48. Mikhail Budyko, *Global Ecology* (Moscow: Progress Publishers, 1977); Jonathan Oldfield, "Mikhail Budyko's (1920–2001) Contributions to Global Climate Science: From Heat Balances to Climate Change and Global Ecology," *WIREs Climate Change* 7, no. 5 (2016): 682–692.

49. Evgenii Fedorov, *Vzaimodeistvie obshchestva i prirody* (Leningrad: Gidrometeoizdat, 1972); Evgenii Fedorov, *Ecological Crisis and Social Progress* (Moscow: Progress, 1977); Julia Lajus, "Soviet Official Critiques of the Resource Scarcity Prediction by *Limits to Growth* Report: The Case of Evgenii Fedorov's Ecological Crisis Rhetoric," *European Review of History* 27, no. 3 (2020): 321–341.

50. For an overview of Soviet scientific ecology's shift toward mathematization, see Weiner, *A Little Corner of Freedom*, 384–389.

51. Moiseev, *Kak daleko.*

52. Lawrence Badash, *A Nuclear Winter's Tale: Science and Politics in the 1980s* (Cambridge, MA: MIT Press, 2009); Joseph Masco, "Bad Weather: On Planetary Crisis," *Social Studies of Science* 40, no. 1 (2010): 7–40; Paul Rubinson, "The Global Effects of Nuclear Winter: Science and Antinuclear Protest in the United States and the Soviet Union During the 1980s," *Cold War History* 14 (2014): 47–69; Eglė Rindzevičiūtė, *The Power of Systems: How Policy Sciences Opened Up the Cold War World* (Ithaca, NY: Cornell University Press, 2016).

53. Crutzen, "Geology of Mankind," 23.

54. Rindzevičiūtė, "The Unlikely Revolutionaries."

55. Nikita Moiseev and Ivan T. Frolov, "Vysokoe soprikosnovenie: obshchesto, chelovek, i priroda v vek mikroelektroniki, informatiki i biotekhnologii," *Voprosy filosofii* 9 (1984): 24–41.

56. Zubok, *Collapse.*

57. For scientific and civic activism in the late Soviet Union, see Weiner, *A Little Corner of Freedom*, 12–14; David Priestland, *Merchant, Soldier, Sage: A New History of Power* (London: Allen, 2012).

NOTES TO PAGES 164–169   243

58. The first explicit presentation of this idea can be found in Moiseev's short book *Mathematics, Government and Economics*, published in 1970, translated into German in 1973. Those few of Moiseev's publications that are available in English lack the lucidity of argument and engaging style that characterize his writings in Russian. Nikita Moiseev, "A New Look at Evolution: Marx, Teilhard de Chardin, Vernadsky," *World Futures* 36, no. 1 (1993): 1–19.

59. Oldfield and Shaw, "V.I. Vernadskii," 299.

60. Beryl Radin, *Beyond Machiavelli: Policy Analysis Comes of Age* (Washington, DC: Georgetown University Press, 2000); Hunter Heyck, *Age of System: Understanding the Development of Modern Social Science* (Baltimore: Johns Hopkins University Press, 2015); Rindzevičiūtė, *The Power of Systems*.

61. Mark Bassin, *The Gumilev Mystique: Biopolitics, Eurasianism, and the Construction of Community in Modern Russia* (Ithaca, NY: Cornell University Press, 2016).

62. Gerovitch, *From Newspeak to Cyberspeak*, 215–216; Oldfield, *The Soviet Union and Global Environmental Change*.

63. Marc Elie, "Formulating the Global Environment: Soviet Soil Scientists and the International Desertification Discussion, 1968–91," *Slavonic and East European Review* 93, no. 1 (2015): 181–204.

64. Such afterword essays played an important role in intellectual agenda setting in the Soviet scientific culture and were widely understood as such. For instance, the influential geophysicist and climatologist Fedorov wrote an afterword to the first translation of Barry Commoner's *The Closing Circle* (published in Russian in 1974), thus spearheading the globally oriented environmental policy. Nikita Moiseev, "'Mirovaia dinamika' Forrestera i aktual'nye voprosy mirovoi evoliutsii," in *Mirovaia dinamika*, ed. Jay Forrester (Moscow: Nauka, 1978), 264–290; also Lajus, "Soviet Official Critiques of the Resource Scarcity."

65. Moiseev's afterword inspired the prominent dissident Viacheslav Igrunov to organize an alternative department of the Club of Rome in Russia. Viacheslav Igrunov, "O Nikite Nikolaiche Moiseeve i o tom, kak nesostoialsia Moskovskii Rimskii klub," http://www.igrunov.ru/cv/vchk-cv-memotalks/talks/vchk-cv-memotalks-talks-moiseev.html.

66. Moiseev, *Chelovek i noosfera*.

67. Nikita Moiseev, Vladimir Aleksandrov, and Aleksandr Tarko, *Chelovek i biosfera* (Moscow: Mysl', 1985), 5; Moiseev, *Chelovek i noosfera*, 235.

68. Thomas Robertson, "Revisiting the Early 1970s Commoner–Erlich Debate About Population and Environment: Dueling Critiques of Production and Consumption in the Global Age," in *A World of Populations: Transnational Perspectives on Demography*, eds. Heinrich Hartmann and Corinna Unger (New York: Berghahn, 2014), 108–215, 109.

69. Paul Erlich and Peter Raven, "Butterflies and Plants: A Study in Coevolution," *Evolution* 18, no. 4 (1967): 586–608, 606; Andrei Lapenis, "Directed Evolution of the Biosphere: Biogeochemical Selection or Gaia?" *Professional Geographer* 54, no. 3 (2002): 379–391, 380.

70. Moiseev, *Matematika, Upravlienie, Ekonomika* (Moscow: Znanie, 1970), 15.

71. Slobodian, *Globalists*.

72. See my argument in "The Unlikely Revolutionaries."

73. Moiseev, *Chelovek i noosfera*, 10–11.

74. Moiseev, *Chelovek i noosfera*, 55.

75. Moiseev, *Chelovek i noosfera*, 141.

76. Moiseev, *Chelovek i noosfera*, 61.

77. Moiseev et al., *Chelovek i biosfera*, 11.

78. Stephen Cummings, Todd Bridgman, John Hassard, and Michael Rowlinson, *A New History of Management* (Cambridge: Cambridge University Press, 2017), 99–103.

NOTES TO PAGES 169–174

79. Moiseev, *Chelovek i noosfera*, 7.

80. Moiseev, *Chelovek i noosfera*, 72, 84–85.

81. James E. Lovelock and Lynn Margulis, "Atmospheric Homeostasis By and For the Biosphere: The Gaia Hypothesis," *Telus* 26, nos. 1–2 (1974): 2–10.

82. Moiseev, *Chelovek i noosfera*.

83. Moiseev, *Chelovek i noosfera*, 85.

84. Evgenii Fedorov, *Man and Nature: The Ecological Crisis and Social Progress* (New York: Progress, 1981), 88–99, 164.

85. Rindzevičiūtė, *The Power of Systems*; Adam Leeds, "Dreams in Cybernetic Fugue: Cold War Technoscience, the Intelligentsia, and the Birth of Soviet Mathematical Economics," *Historical Studies in the Natural Sciences* 46, no. 5 (2016): 633–668.

86. For OGAS, see Peters, *How Not to Network a Nation*.

87. To this list of problems we can add synchronization, which Moiseev did not consider extensively, because he was more interested in destabilizing the link between what was presumed to be certain scientific knowledge about the evolution of the biosphere. The problem of implementation and action was secondary for him. But at the same time, in the 1970s, synchronization, which is an important part of predictive governance, was explored by organizational scholars like Michael Cohen, James March, and Johan Olsen, who proposed the famous garbage can model to explain decisions in organizations. In the garbage can model, decisions are taken on the basis of the synchronization and timing that allows problems and actions to converge. It is because of what is perceived as good timing and less structural or logical reasons that certain problems and actions are prioritized in organizations. To improve an ineffective organization, therefore, means to fix the problem of synchronization. Michael Cohen, James March, and Johan P. Olsen, "A Garbage Can Model of Organizational Choice," *Administrative Science Quarterly* 17, no. 1 (1972): 1–25.

88. Moiseev, *Chelovek i noosfera*, 319.

89. Moiseev, *Chelovek i noosfera*, 319.

90. In this respect Moiseev's model of planetary governance resembles what Mitchell Dean described as the hidden authoritarianism of Western liberal governmentality. Mitchell Dean, *Governmentality: Power and Rule in Modern Society* (London: Sage, 2009).

91. Moiseev, *Chelovek i noosfera*, 316–319. Moiseev noted that his concept of guided development was in principle similar to prominent geographer Lev Berg's concept of "guided evolution," although Berg based his theory on completely different argumentation. Moiseev, *Izbrannye Trudy*, 111.

92. Slobodian, *Globalists*, Kindle location 4590.

93. Stefanos Geroulanos, *Transparency in Postwar France: A Critical History of the Present* (Stanford, CA: Stanford University Press, 2017).

94. Angela Oels, "Climate Security as Governmentality: From Precaution to Preparedness," in *Governing the Climate: New Approaches to Rationality, Power and Politics*, eds. Johannes Stripple and Harriet Bulkeley (Cambridge: Cambridge University Press, 2013), 197–216, 205–206.

95. Timothy O'Riordan and Steve Rayner, "Risk Management for Global Environmental Change," *Global Environmental Change* 1, no. 2 (1991): 91–108, 103–104.

96. Stephen Collier, *Post-Soviet Social: Neoliberalism, Social Modernity, Biopolitics* (Princeton, NJ: Princeton University Press, 2011); Claudia Aradau and Rens van Munster, *Politics of Catastrophe: Genealogies of the Unknown* (London: Routledge, 2011).

97. Oels, "Climate Security," 208; Isabell Schrickel, "Von Schmetterlingen und Atomreaktoren: Medien und Politiken der Resilienz am IIASA," *Behemoth* 7, no. 2 (2014): 5–25; Jeremy Walker and Melinda Cooper, "Genealogies of Resilience: From Systems Ecology to the Political Economy of Crisis Adaptation," *Security Dialogue* 42, no. 2 (2011): 143–160.

98. Slobodian, *Globalists*, Kindle location 1128–1136.

99. Slobodian, *Globalists*, Kindle location 1236.

100. Slobodian, *Globalists*, Kindle location 1144.

101. Slobodian, *Globalists*, Kindle location 1220.

102. Slobodian, *Globalists*, Kindle location 1152.

103. Slobodian, *Globalists*, Kindle location 1152.

104. In 1938, Lippmann, as Slobodian argued, signaled a move "from the economic to the legal," to bypass the "problem of knowledge" of the volatile workings of national and world economies. Slobodian, *Globalists*, Kindle location 1582.

105. Moiseev, *Chelovek i noosfera*, 275.

106. Slobodian, *Globalists*, Kindle location 1693. In the 1930s, neoliberals rejected the nineteenth century's model of governance by numbers; as Slobodian put it, for them a proper governmental intervention "was not in measurement, observation, or surveillance but in the establishment of a common, enforceable law and a means of accounting for the vital needs of humanity not provided by the market." Slobodian, *Globalists*, Kindle location 1700.

107. Slobodian, *Globalists*, Kindle location 4672. As Slobodian suggested, for Hayek the concept of order did not entail prescription of goals and targets, but rather, as for Moiseev, it posited a need to "defer to the wisdom of the system" (Kindle location 4743).

108. Slobodian, *Globalists*, Kindle location 4548.

109. Zygmunt Bauman, *Modernity and the Holocaust* (Cambridge: Polity Press, 1989).

110. Michael Hviid Jacobsen and Sophia Marshman, "Bauman on Metaphors: A Harbinger of Humanistic Hybrid Sociology," in *The Sociology of Zygmunt Bauman: Challenges and Critique*, eds. Michael Hviid Jacobsen and Paul Poder (London: Routledge, 2008), 19–40.

111. Slobodian, *Globalists*, Kindle location 4556.

112. Moiseev, *Chelovek i noosfera*.

113. Moiseev, *Chelovek i noosfera*, 305.

114. Moiseev, *Chelovek i noosfera*, 331–336.

115. Zubok, *Collapse*.

116. Moiseev, *Chelovek i noosfera*, 340–342.

117. Thomas Hughes, *Networks of Power: Electrification in Western Society, 1880–1930* (Baltimore: Johns Hopkins University Press, 1993); Gabriella Hecht, *The Radiance of France: Nuclear Power and National Identity After World War II* (Cambridge, MA: MIT Press, 1998); Andrew Barry, *Political Machines: Governing a Technological Society* (London: Routledge, 2001); Paul Edwards, *A Vast Machine: Computer Models, Climate Data and the Politics of Global Warming* (Cambridge, MA: MIT Press, 2010).

118. Theodore Porter, "Thin Description: Surface and Depth in Science and Science Studies," *Osiris* 27, no. 1 (2012): 209–226.

119. Moiseev et al., *Chelovek i biosfera*, 34.

120. O'Riordan and Rayner, "Risk Management," 91.

121. Rens van Munster and Casper Sylvester, eds., *The Politics of Globality Since 1945: Assembling the Planet* (London: Routledge, 2016), 25–27.

122. Bennett, *Making Culture*, 37.

123. Bennett, *Making Culture*. See also Tony Bennett, "Habit: Time, Freedom, Governance," *Body and Society* 19, nos. 2 & 3 (2013): 107–135.

124. Eglė Rindzevičiūtė, "Toward a Joint Future Beyond the Iron Curtain: East–West Politics of Global Modelling," in *The Struggle for the Long-Term in Transnational Science and Politics: Forging the Future*, eds. Jenny Andersson and Eglė Rindzevičiūtė (London: Routledge, 2015), 115–143.

125. Brian Wynne, "Strange Weather, Again: Climate Science as Political Art," *Theory, Culture and Society* 27, nos. 2–3 (2013): 289–305, 295.

246 NOTES TO PAGES 180–187

126. Ingrid Visseren-Hamakers, "Integrative Environmental Governance: Enhancing Governance in the Era of Synergies," *Current Opinion in Environmental Sustainability* 14 (2015): 136–143; Hans Joachim Schellnhuber and Volker Wenzel, eds., *Earth System Analysis: Integrating Science for Sustainability* (Berlin: Springer, 2013).

127. Pierre Teilhard de Chardin, *The Phenomenon of Man* (New York: Harper, 1959); Kenneth Boulding, *Ecodynamics: A New Theory of Societal Evolution* (London: Sage, 1978).

128. The noosphere is often invoked in contemporary political discourses in Russia. One example is the theory of a Eurasian civilization, developed by anthropologist Lev Gumilev (1912–1992), which incorporated some mystical aspects of Vernadskii's noosphere theory. From the 1990s Gumilev's Eurasianism inspired a new era of Russian geopolitical thinking, according to which Russia is the crucible of a spiritual civilization, different from the rationalist West and therefore destined to become a world leader. The most disturbing version of this sort of radicalized Eurasianism is Aleksandr Dugin's vision of Russia's future. Furthermore, a peculiar version of Vernadskii's noosphere theory attracted international attention when it transpired that Vladimir Putin's chief of staff, Anton Vaino, published several fairly senseless articles on government of the global noosphere, claiming to have developed a global predictive control machine, the nooscope. Anton Vaino, "Kapitalizatsiia budushchego," *Voprosy ekonomiki i prava* 4 (2012): 42–57. In the 1990s Moiseev, too, became attracted to Eurasianist ideas, writing that the North Eurasia continent is the geopolitical future of Russia, but it is difficult to imagine Moiseev endorsing an antagonistic foreign policy for Russia.

129. Johan Rockstrom, Will Steffen, Kevin Noone, Åsa Persson, F. Stuart III Chapin, Eric Lambin, Timothy M. Lenton, et al., "Planetary Boundaries: Exploring the Safe Operating Space for Humanity," *Ecology and Society* 14, no. 2 (2009): 32.

130. Frank Biermann, *Earth System Governance: World Politics in the Anthropocene* (Cambridge, MA: MIT Press, 2014).

CONCLUSION

1. This resonates with the work of Philip Tetlock and Dan Gardner, who searched not for a magical formula of prediction, but rather a form of a collective orchestration of prediction-making that can perform best in a changing context. Philip Tetlock and Dan Gardner, *Superforecasting: The Art and Science of Prediction* (New York: Crown Publishing, 2015).

2. It is argued that the idea of rationality as rule-based decision-making that can be divorced from its context became a sort of myth in the Cold War, leading to blunders in both science and politics. See Paul Erickson, Judy L. Klein, Lorraine Daston, Rebecca Lemov, Thomas Sturm, and Michael D. Gordin, *How Reason Almost Lost Its Mind: The Strange Career of Cold War Rationality* (Chicago: University of Chicago Press, 2013).

3. A good example is the treatment of the findings of the Soviet population census of 1937, which revealed not only a disastrous demographic situation, but also the failure to enhance the social mobility of workers and peasants. See Tomila V. Lankina, *The Estate Origins of Democracy: From Imperial Bourgeoisie to Post-Communist Middle Class* (Cambridge: Cambridge University Press, 2021).

4. Katri Pynnöniemi, "Russia's War against Ukraine: Wider Implications" (presentation, discussion panel, Aleksanteri Institute, 4 March 2022).

5. As Thomas noted, the increasingly mechanical and applied character of military operations research frustrated the founders of the field, such as Russell Ackoff and C. West Churchman, who thought that the OR was no longer intellectually stimulating in the 1970s. Will Thomas, *The Rational Action: The Sciences of Policy in Britain and America, 1940-1960* (Cambridge, MA: MIT Press, 2015), 276–277.

NOTES TO PAGES 188–191   247

6. Bilel Benbouzid, "Values and Consequences in Predictive Machine Evaluation: A Sociology of Predictive Policing," *Science and Technology Studies* (2020): 119–136; Angèle Christin, "Predictive Algorithms and Criminal Sentencing," in *The Decisionist Imagination: Sovereignty, Social Science and Democracy in the 20th Century*, eds. Daniel Bessner and Nicolas Guilhot, 272–294 (New York: Berghahn, 2018).

7. Matthias Lesse, "'We Do That Once per Day': Cyclical Futures and Institutional Ponderousness in Predictive Policing," in *The Politics and Science of Prevision: Governing and Probing the Future*, eds. Andreas Wenger, Ursula Jasper, and Myrian Dunn Cavelty (London: Routledge, 2020), 213–226.

8. Louise Amoore, *The Politics of Possibility: Risk and Security Beyond Probability* (Durham, NC: Duke University Press, 2013); Claudia Aradau and Tobias Lemke, *Algorithmic Reason* (Oxford: Oxford University Press, 2022).

9. See also the argument about opacity as a form of civic resistance to algorithmic surveillance in Engin Isin and Evelyn Ruppert, "The Birth of Sensory Power: How a Pandemic Made It Visible?" *Big Data and Society* (2020): 1–15.

10. See Frank Biermann, *Earth System Governance: World Politics in the Anthropocene* (Cambridge, MA: MIT Press, 2014); as well as Oran Young, *Governing Complex Systems: Social Capital for the Anthropocene* (Cambridge, MA: MIT Press, 2017).

11. The work by Adriana Petryna on horizoning as orchestrating scientific predictive statements is a good example of this evolving approach. Adriana Petryna, *Horizon Work: At the Edges of Knowledge in an Age of Runaway Climate Change* (Princeton, NJ: Princeton University Press, 2022).

12. Adam Kucharski, "How Modelling Covid Has Changed the Way We Think About Epidemics," *Guardian* (UK edition), 4 January 2021; Isin and Ruppert, "The Birth of Sensory Power."

13. Shoshana Zuboff, *The Age of Surveillance Capitalism: The Fight for a Human Future at the New Frontier of Power* (New York: Profile Books, 2019).

14. Christophe Bonneuil and Jean Baptiste Fressoz, *The Shock of the Anthropocene: The Earth, History and Us* (London: Verso, 2016).

15. Julia Ioffe, "'Before, Putin Was Unpredictable; Now It's Trump': Moscow Grapples with a Strange Week in Washington," *Atlantic*, 18 February 2017, https://www.theatlantic.com/international/archive/2017/02/putin-trump-flynn/517224/.

16. Peter Pomerantsev, *This Is Not Propaganda: Adventures in the War Against Reality* (London: Faber & Faber, 2019).

17. Michael Ellman and Vladimir Kantorovich, eds. *The Destruction of the Soviet Economic System: An Insider's History* (London: Routledge, 1988).

18. Michael Ellman, "Was the Collapse of the USSR Entirely Unforeseen?" *Perspectives on Political Science* 31, no. 3 (2002): 132–135.

19. Leonidas Donskis, "Aleksandras Shtromas: The Lithuanian Prophet of Postcommunism," *Journal of Interdisciplinary Studies* 18, nos. 1–2 (2006): 76.

20. Randall Collins, "Prediction in Macrosociology: The Case of the Soviet Collapse," *American Journal of Sociology* 100, no. 6 (1995): 1552–1593.

21. Later, Taagepera argued for the need to embrace statistical modeling in social and historical sciences, equating "scientificity" with prediction. Rein Taagepera, *Making Social Science More Scientific: The Need for Predictive Models* (Oxford: Oxford University Press, 2008).

22. Jack Goldstone, "Predicting Revolutions: Why We Could (and Should) Have Foreseen the Revolutions of 1989–1991 in the U.S.S.R. and Eastern Europe," *Contention* 2, no. 2 (1993): 127–152.

23. For a good overview, see Richard Sakwa, "The Soviet Collapse: Contradictions and Neo-Modernisation," *Journal of Eurasian Studies* 4 (2013): 65–77; the review essay

248   NOTES TO PAGES 191–192

by Manfred Zeller, "Before and After the End of the World: Rethinking the Soviet Collapse," *Kritika* 18, no. 3 (2017): 591–601; and, for the reconstruction of the political process leading to the Soviet collapse, see Vladislav Zubok, *Collapse: The Fall of the Soviet Union* (New Haven, CT: Yale University Press, 2021); Chris Miller, *The Struggle to Save the Soviet Economy: Mikhail Gorbachev and the Collapse of the USSR* (Chapel Hill: University of North Carolina Press, 2016).

24. Zubok, *Collapse*.

25. Karl E. Weick, *Making Sense of the Organization* (Oxford: Blackwell, 2001), 74–77, 159–164.

26. For instance, in post-Soviet Lithuania, politicians' reliance on clairvoyants was widely debated in relation to the impeachment of President Paksas, bringing back the debate about the status of expertise and the political legacies of astrology. See S. C. Rowell, "The Jagellonians and the Stars: Dynasty-Sponsored Astrology in the Fifteenth Century," *Lithuanian Historical Studies* 7 (2002): 23–42; Algis Krupavicius, "Lithuania's President: A Formal and Informal Power," in *Presidents Above Parties? Presidents in Central and Eastern Europe, Their Formal Competencies and Informal Power*, eds. Vít Hloušek et al. (Prague: Masaryk University, 2013), 205–232. There is vast research on witchcraft and magical practice in African politics and business: James Howard Smith, *Bewitching Development: Witchcraft and Reinvention of Development in Neoliberal Kenya* (Chicago: University of Chicago Press, 2008).

27. See Donald McCloskey, "The Art of Forecasting: From Ancient to Modern Times," *Cato Journal* 12, no. 1 (1992): 23–48; and the ongoing work by Caley Horan, as well as Matthew Connelly, "Future Shock: The End of the World as They Knew It," *The Shock of the Global: The 1970s in Perspective*, eds. Niall Ferguson, Charles S. Maier, Erez Manela, and Daniel J. Sargent (Cambridge, MA: Harvard University Press, 2011), 337–356.

Bibliography

ARCHIVES

Archives of the International Institute of Applied Systems Analysis, Laxenburg, Austria
Archives of the Russian Academy of Sciences (ARAN)
John F. Kennedy Presidential Library and Museum
Ronald Reagan Presidential Library Digital Library Collections
Russian State Archives of the Economy (RGAE)
University of Toronto Archives

Abbott, Kenneth W., Philipp Genschel, Duncan Snidal, and Bernhard Zangl, eds. *International Organizations as Orchestrators*. Cambridge: Cambridge University Press, 2015.

Abbott, Kenneth Wayne, Philipp Genschel, Duncan Snidal, and Bernhard Zangl. "Orchestration: Global Governance through Intermediaries" (6 August 2012). doi:10.2139/ssrn.2125452.

Abbott, Kenneth W., Philipp Genschel, Duncan Snidal, and Bernhard Zangl. "Two Logics of Indirect Governance: Delegation and Orchestration." *British Journal of Political Science* FirstView (2015): 1–11.

Abraham, Tara. *Rebel Genius: Warren S. McCulloch's Transdisciplinary Life in Science*. Cambridge, MA: MIT Press, 2016.

Abuhamdeg, Sami, and Mihaly Csikszentmihalyi. "The Artistic Personality: A System Perspective." In *The Systems Model of Creativity*, edited by Mihaly Csikszentmihalyi, 227–237. Dordrecht: Springer, 2014.

Adam, Barbara, and Chris Groves. *Future Matters: Action, Knowledge, Ethics*. Leiden: Brill, 2007.

Agar, John. *The Government Machine: A Revolutionary History of the Computer*. Cambridge, MA: MIT Press, 2003.

Agrawal, Arun. *Environmentality: Technologies of Government and the Making of Subjects*. Durham, NC: Duke University Press, 2005.

Åkerstrøm Andersen, Nielsen, and Justin Grønbaek Pors. *Public Management in Transition: The Orchestration of Potentiality*. Bristol: Policy Press, 2016.

Allen, T. S., and A. J. Moore. "Victory Without Casualties: Russia's Information Operations." *Parameters* 48, no. 1 (2018): 59–71.

Amadae, S. M. *Prisoners of Reason: Game Theory and Neoliberal Political Economy*. Cambridge: Cambridge University Press, 2015.

Amadae, S. M. *Rationalizing Capitalist Democracy: The Cold War Origins of Rational Choice Liberalism*. Chicago: University of Chicago Press, 2003.

Amoore, Louise. *The Politics of Possibility: Risk and Security Beyond Probability*. Durham, NC: Duke University Press, 2013.

Andersson, Jenny. *The Future of the World: Futurology, Futurists, and the Struggle for the Post-Cold War Imagination*. Oxford: Oxford University Press, 2018.

Andersson, Jenny. "Governing Futures: States and the Management of Expectations." In *Reconfiguring European States in Crisis*, edited by Patrick Le Gales and Desmond King, 298–312. Oxford: Oxford University Press, 2017.

250 BIBLIOGRAPHY

Andersson, Jenny, and Eglė Rindzevičiūtė, eds. *The Struggle for the Long Term in Transnational Science and Politics: Forging the Future*. New York: Routledge, 2015.

Anisov, A. M., O. V. Maliukova, and L. A. Demina. *Stanovlenie otechestvennoi logiki: diskursy i sudby*. Moscow: Prospekt, 2019.

Arab-Ogly, Edvard. *Demograficheskie i ekologicheskie prognozy: kritika sovremennykh burzhuaznykh kontseptsii*. Moscow: Statistika, 1978.

Arab-Ogly, Edvard. "Togda kazalos', chto koe-to udavalos'." In *Rossiiskaia sotsiologiia shestidesiatykh godov v vospominaniiakh i dokumentakh*, edited by G. Batygin, M.G. Pugacheva, S. F. Iarmoliuk, 358–370. St Petersburg: Izdatel'stvo Russkogo Khristianskogo gumanitarnogo universiteta, 1999.

Aradau, Claudia, and Tobias Blanke. "Politics of Prediction: Security and the Time/Space of Governmentality in the Age of Big Data." *European Journal of Social Theory* 20, no. 3 (2017): 373–391.

Aradau, Claudia, and Tobias Lemke, *Algorithmic Reason*. Oxford: Oxford University Press, 2022.

Aradau, Claudia, and Rens van Munster. *Politics of Catastrophe: Genealogies of the Unknown*. London: Routledge, 2011.

Archer, Margaret. *The Reflexive Imperative in Late Modernity*. Cambridge: Cambridge University, 2012.

Arendt, Hannah. *The Origins of Totalitarianism*. London: Penguin, 2017 [1951].

Ariely, Dan. *Predictably Irrational: The Hidden Forces That Shape Our Decisions*. New York: HarperCollins, 2008.

Armstrong, J. Scott. *Long-Range Forecasting: From Crystal Ball to Computer*. New York: Wiley, 1985.

Aronova, Elena. "Citizen Seismology, Stalinist Science, and Vladimir Mannar's Cold Wars." *Science, Technology, & Human Values* 42, no. 2 (2017): 226–256.

Aronova, Elena. "Earthquake Prediction, Biological Clocks, and the Cold War Psy-ops: Using Animals as Seismic Sensors in the 1970s California." *Studies in History and Philosophy of Science, Part A* 70 (2018): 50–57.

Aronova, Elena. "The Politics and Contexts of Soviet Science Studies (*Naukovedenie*): Soviet Philosophy of Science at the Crossroads." *Studies in East European Thought* 63, no. 3 (2011): 175–202.

Aronova, Elena. *Scientific History: Experiments in History and Politics from the Bolshevik Revolution to the End of the Cold War*. Chicago: University of Chicago Press, 2021.

Arrow, Kenneth. *Social Choice and Individual Values*. New York: Wiley, 1951.

Arzyutov, Dmitry V. *Reassembling the Environmental Archives of the Cold War: Perspectives from the Russian North*. Stockholm: KTH Royal Institute of Technology, 2021.

Avilov, Aleksandr. *Refleksivnoe upravlenie: metodologicheskie osnovanie*. Moscow: GUU, 2003.

Aykut, Stefan C., David Demortain, and Bilel Benbouzid. "The Politics of Anticipatory Expertise: Plurality and Contestation of Futures Knowledge in Governance—Introduction to the Special Issue." *Science & Technology Studies, Finnish Association for Science and Technology Studies* 32, no. 4 (2019): 2–12.

Azrikan, Dmitry. "VNIITE, Dinosaur of Totalitarianism or Plato's Academy of Design?" *Design Issues* 15, no. 3 (1999): 45–77.

Babintseva, Ekaterina. "'Overtake and Surpass': Soviet Algorithmic Thinking as a Revinvention of Western Theories during the Cold War." In *Cold War Social Science: Transnational Entanglements*, edited by Mark Solovey and Christian Daye, 45–72. Cham, Switzerland: Springer, 2021.

Backhouse, Roger, and Philippe Fontaine, eds. *A Historiography of the Modern Social Sciences*. Cambridge: Cambridge University Press, 2014.

Badash, Lawrence. *A Nuclear Winter's Tale: Science and Politics in the 1980s*. Cambridge, MA: MIT Press, 2009.

Bandura, Albert. "Human Agency in Social Cognitive Theory." *American Psychologist* 9 (1989): 1175–1184.

Bar, Moshe. "The Proactive Brain: Memory for Predictions." *Philosophical Transactions of the Royal Society of London. Series B, Biological Sciences* 364, no. 1521 (2009): 1235–1243.

Bar, Moshe. "Visual Objects in Context." *Nature Reviews Neuroscience* 5 (2004): 617–629.

Bara, Corinne. "Forecasting Civil War and Political Violence." In *The Politics and Science of Prevision: Governing and Probing the Future*, edited by Andreas Wenger, Ursula Jasper, and Myriam Dunn Cavelty, 177–193. London: Routledge, 2020.

Barber, John, and Mark Harrison, eds. *The Soviet Defence Industry Complex from Stalin to Khrushchev*. Basingstoke, UK: Macmillan, 2000.

Barnett, Vincent. *Kondratiev and the Dynamics of Economic Development: Long Cycles and Industrial Growth in Historical Context*. Basingstoke, UK: Macmillan, 1998.

Barry, Andrew. *Political Machines: Governing a Technological Society*. London: Routledge, 2001.

Bassin, Mark. *The Gumilev Mystique: Biopolitics, Eurasianism, and the Construction of Community in Modern Russia*. Ithaca, NY: Cornell University Press, 2016.

Bateson, Gregory. *Steps to an Ecology of Mind: Collected Essays in Anthropology, Psychiatry, Evolution, and Epistemology*. Chicago: University of Chicago Press, 2000.

Bauman, Zygmunt. *Legislators and Interpreters: Of Modernity, Post-Modernity and Intellectuals*. London: Polity, 1989.

Bauman, Zygmunt. *Modernity and the Holocaust*. Cambridge, UK: Polity Press, 1989.

Bautin, V. M. "Nikolai Dmitrievich Kondrat'ev i ego rol' v stanovlenii agroekonomicheskoi nauki i obrazovaniia v Rossii." *Izvestiia TSKhA* 2 (2017): 134–153.

Bazhanov, Valentin. *Istoriia logiki v Rossii i SSSR: kontseptual'nyĭ kontekst universitetskoĭ filosofii*. Moscow: Kanon, 2007.

Becht, Lukas. "From Euphoria to Frustration: Institutionalizing Prognostic Research in the Polish People's Republic, 1969–76." *Acta Poloniae Historica* 116 (2017): 277–299.

Beck, Silke. "Moving Beyond the Linear Model of Expertise? IPCC and the Test of Adaptation." *Regional Environmental Change* 11 (2011): 297–306.

Beck, Ulrich. *Risk Society: Towards a New Modernity*. Thousand Oaks, CA: Sage, 1993.

Beckert, Jens. *Imagined Futures: Fictional Expectations and Capitalist Dynamics*. Cambridge, MA: Harvard University Press, 2016.

Bedny, Gregory, Mark Seglin, and David Meister. "Activity Theory: History, Research and Application." *Theoretical Issues in Ergonomics Science* 1, no. 2 (2000): 168–206.

Beer, Stafford. *Decision and Control: The Meaning of Operational Research and Management Cybernetics*. London: Wiley, 1966.

Belchikov, M., and M. M. Birshtein. *Delovye igry*. Riga: AVOTS, 1989.

Bell, Wendell. *Foundations of Futures Studies: History, Purposes, and Knowledge*. Vol. 1 of *Human Science for a New Era*. London: Routledge, 2009.

Benbouzid, Bilel. "Values and Consequences in Predictive Machine Evaluation: A Sociology of Predictive Policing." *Science and Technology Studies* (2020): 119–136.

Bendlin, Lena. *Orchestrating Local Climate Policy in the European Union: Inter-Municipal Coordination and the Covenant of Mayors in Germany and France*. London: Springer, 2020.

Beniger, James. *The Control Revolution: Technological and Economic Origins of the Informational Society*. Cambridge, MA: Harvard University Press, 1989.

Bennett, Tony. "Habit: Time, Freedom, Governance." *Body and Society* 19, nos. 2–3 (2013): 107–135.

BIBLIOGRAPHY

Bennett, Tony. *Making Culture, Changing Society.* London: Routledge, 2013.

Bennett, Tony. *Pasts Beyond Memory: Evolution, Museums, Colonialism.* London: Routledge, 1994.

Bennett, Tony, Fiona Cameron, Nélia Dias, Ben Dibley, Rodney Harrison, Ira Jacknis, and Conal McCarthy. *Collecting, Ordering, Governing: Anthropology, Museums, and Liberal Government.* Durham, NC: Duke University Press, 2017.

Bennett, Tony, Francis Dodsworth, Greg Noble, Mary Poovey, and Megan Watkins. "Introduction." *Body and Society* 19, nos. 2–3 (2013): 3–29.

Berg, Aksel I. *Cybernetics in the Service of Communism.* Washington D.C.: U.S. Army Foreign Science and Technology Center, 1969.

Bessner, Daniel. *Democracy in Exile: Hans Speier and the Rise of the Defense Intellectual.* Ithaca, NY: Cornell University Press, 2018.

Bessner, Daniel. "The Globalist: George Soros after the Open Society." *N + 1* (18 June 2018).

Bessner, Daniel. "Organizing Complexity: The Hopeful Dreams and Harsh Realities of Interdisciplinary Collaboration at the Rand Corporation in the Early Cold War." *Journal of the History of the Behavioral Sciences* 51, no. 1 (2015): 31–53.

Bestuzhev-Lada, Igor', ed. *Malaia rosiiskaia entsiklopedia prognostiki.* Moscow: Institut ekonomicheskikh strategii, 2007.

Bestuzhev-Lada, Igor. *Okno v budushchee: Sovremennye problemy sotsialnogo prognozirovaniia.* Moscow: Mysl, 1970.

Bestuzhev-Lada, Igor'. *Poiskovoe sotsial'noe prognozirovanie: perspektivnye problem obshchestva.* Moscow: Nauka, 1984.

Bestuzhev-Lada, Igor. "Prognozirovanie bylo iznachal'no oberecheno na pogrom." In *Rosiiskaia sotsiologiia shestidesiatykh godov v vospominaniakh i dokumantakh*, edited by G. Batygin, M.G. Pugacheva, S. F. Iarmoliuk, 404–427. St Petersburg: Izdatel'stvo Russkogo Khristianskogo gumanitarnogo instituta, 1999.

Bestuzhev-Lada, Igor'. *Svozhu schety s zhizn'iu: zapisi futurologa o proshedshem i prikhodiashchem.* Moscow: Algoritm, 2004.

Bidel, Jeff, and Marcel Boumans. "Exploring the History of Statistical Inference in Economics: Introduction." *History of Political Economy* 53S (2021): 1–24.

Biermann, Frank. *Earth System Governance: World Politics in the Anthropocene.* Cambridge, MA: MIT Press, 2014.

Blum, Alain, and Martine Mespoulet. *L'anarchie bureaucratic: statistique et pouvoir sous Staline.* Paris: La Découverte, 2003.

Bockman, Johanna. "The Struggle over Structural Adjustment: Socialist Revolution Versus Capitalist Counterrevolution in Yugoslavia and the World." *History of Political Economy* 51, no. S1 (2019).

Boginskii, E. *Refleksivnoe upravlenie pri doprose.* Kharkiv: KhIuI, 1983.

Boldyrev, Ivan, and Till Duppe. "Programming the USSR: Leonid V. Kantorovich in Context." *British Journal of History of Science* (2020): 1–24.

Boldyrev, Ivan, and Olessia Kirtchik. "The Cultures of Mathematical Economics in the Postwar Soviet Union: More Than a Method, Less Than a Discipline." *Studies in History and Philosophy of Science Part A* 63 (2017): 1–10.

Bonneuil, Christophe, and Jean Baptiste Fressoz. *The Shock of the Anthropocene: The Earth, History and Us.* London: Verso, 2016.

Bostrom, Nick. *Superintelligence: Paths, Dangers, Strategies.* Oxford: Oxford University Press, 2014.

Boulding, Kenneth. *Ecodynamics: A New Theory of Societal Evolution.* London: Sage, 1978.

Bourdieu, Pierre, and Loic Wacquant. *An Invitation to Reflexive Sociology.* Cambridge, UK: Polity Press, 1992.

Bowler, P. J. *A History of the Future: Prophets of Progress from H.G. Wells to Isaac Asimov.* Cambridge: Cambridge University Press, 2017.

Bowmeester, Han. "Lo and Behold: Let the Truth Be Told—Russian Deception Warfare in Crimea and Ukraine and the Return of 'Maskirovka' and 'Reflexive Control Theory.'" In *Netherlands Annual Review of Military Studies 2017*, edited by Paul A. L. Ducheine and Frans P. B. Osinga. The Hague: Springer, 2017.

Boy, Guy A. *Orchestrating Human-Centred Design.* London: Springer, 2013.

Bradley, Joseph. "Patterns of Peasant Migration to Late Nineteenth Century Moscow: How Much Should We Read into Literacy Rates?" *Russian History* 6, no. 1 (1979): 22–38.

Bradley, Joseph. *Voluntary Associations in Tsarist Russia: Science, Patriotism, and Civil Society.* Cambridge, MA: Harvard University Press, 2009.

Brown, Kate. *Manual for Survival: A Chernobyl Guide for the Future.* London: Penguin, 2019.

Bruno, Andy. *The Nature of Soviet Power: An Arctic Environmental History.* Cambridge, UK: Cambridge University Press, 2016.

Bryant, Christopher G. A. "George Soros's Theory of Reflexivity: A Comparison with the Theories of Giddens and Beck and a Consideration of Its Practical Value." *Economy and Society* 31, no. 1 (2002): 112–131.

Budyko, Mikhail. *Global Ecology.* Moscow: Progress Publishers, 1977.

Buwalda, Petrus. *They Did Not Dwell Alone: Jewish Emigration from the Soviet Union, 1967–1990.* Baltimore: Johns Hopkins University Press, 1997.

Cadiot, Juliette. "Searching for Nationality: Statistics and National Categories at the End of the Russian Empire (1897–1917)." *Russian Review* 64, no. 3 (2005): 440–455.

Callon, Michel. "Some Elements of a Sociology of Translation: Domestication of the Scallops and the Fishermen of St Brieuc Bay." *Sociological Review* 32, no. 1 (1984): 196–233.

Canguilhem, Georges. "The Living and Its Milieu." Translated from French, originally published in 1952. *Grey Room* 3 (2001): 7–31.

Carpo, Mario. *The Second Digital Turn: Design Beyond Intelligence.* Cambridge, MA: MIT Press, 2017.

Carr, Danielle Judith Zola. "'Ghastly Marionettes' and the Political Metaphysics of Cognitive Liberalism: Anti-behaviourism, Language, and the Origins of Totalitarianism." *History of the Human Sciences* 33, no. 1 (2020): 147–174.

Carrier, Martin. "Prediction in Context: On the Comparative Epistemic Merit of Predictive Success." *Studies in History and Philosophy of Science* 45 (2014): 97–102.

Carter, Chris, Stewart Clegg, and Martin Kornberger. "Re-framing Strategy: Power, Politics and Accounting." *Accounting, Auditing and Accountability Journal* 23, no. 5 (2010): 573–594.

Carter, Chris, Stewart Clegg, and Martin Kornberger. "Strategy as Practice?" *Strategic Organization* 6, no. 1 (2008): 83–99.

Casapoglu, Kan. "Russia's Renewed Military Thinking: Non-Linear Warfare and Reflexive Control." *NATO Defence College Research Paper* 121 (2015): 1–12.

Cave, Jane. "Political Reform and Scientific Freedom Under Gorbachev." *Technology in Society* 13 (1991): 69–89.

Chandler, David. *Resilience: The Governance of Complexity.* London: Routledge, 2014.

Chotikul, Diane. "The Soviet Theory of Reflexive Control in Historical and Psychocultural Perspective: Preliminary Study." Unpublished thesis, Naval Postgraduate School, Monterey, CA, 1986.

Christian, Michel, Sandrine Kott, and Ondřej Matějka, eds. *Planning in Cold War Europe: Competition, Cooperation, Circulations (1950s–1970s).* Berlin: de Gruyter, 2018.

254   BIBLIOGRAPHY

Christin, Angèle. "Predictive Algorithms and Criminal Sentencing." In *The Decisionist Imagination*, edited by Daniel Bessner and Nicolas Guilhot, 272–294. New York: Berghahn, 2018.

Clark, Andy. *Surfing Uncertainty: Prediction, Action and the Embodied Mind.* Oxford: Oxford University Press, 2016.

Clark, Andy. "Whatever Next? Predictive Brains, Situated Agents, and the Future of Cognitive Science." *Behavioral and Brain Sciences* 36 (2013): 181–253.

Clarke, Bertrand S., and Jennifer L. Clarke. *Predictive Statistics: Analysis and Inference Beyond Models.* Cambridge: Cambridge University, 2018.

Cloves, Edith. *Russian Experimental Fiction: Resisting Ideology After Utopia.* Princeton, NJ: Princeton University Press, 1993.

Cohen, Michael D., James G. March, and Johan P. Olsen. "A Garbage Can Model of Organizational Choice." *Administrative Science Quarterly* 17, no. 1 (1972): 1–25.

Collier, Stephen. *Post-Soviet Social: Neoliberalism, Social Modernity, Biopolitics.* Princeton, NJ: Princeton University Press, 2011.

Collier, Stephen and Anke Gruendel. "Design and Government: City Planning, Space-Making, and Urban Politics." *Political Geography* 97 (2022): 1-13.

Collins, Randall. "Prediction in Macrosociology: The Case of the Soviet Collapse." *American Journal of Sociology* 100, no. 6 (1995): 1552–1593.

Collis, Robert. "'Stars Rule Over People, but God Rules Over the Stars': The Astrological World View of Boris Ivanovich Kurakin (1676–1727)." *Jahrbücher für Geschichte Osteuropas* 59, no. 2 (2011): 195–216.

Colonomos, Ariel. *Selling the Future: The Perils of Predicting Global Politics.* London: Hurst, 2016.

Comte, Auguste. *The Positive Philosophy* (1830–1842), translated by Harriet Martineau [1896]. Kitchener, ON: Batocher Books, 2000.

Connelly, Matthew. "Future Shock: The End of the World as They Knew It." In *The Shock of the Global: The 1970s in Perspective*, edited by Niall Ferguson, Charles S. Maier, Erez Manela, and Daniel J. Sargent, 337–356. Cambridge, MA: Harvard University Press, 2011.

Conway, Flo, and Jim Siegelman. *Dark Hero of the Information Age: In Search of Norbert Wiener, the Father of Cybernetics.* New York: Basic Books, 2009.

Cook, Eli. *The Pricing of Progress: Economic Indicators and the Capitalization of American Life.* Cambridge, MA: Harvard University Press, 2017.

Cowles, Alfred. "Can Stock Markets Forecast?" *Econometrica* 1, no. 3 (1933): 309–324.

Crowley, David, and Jane Pavitt, eds. *Cold War Modern 1945–1970.* London: V&A, 2010.

Crutzen, Paul. "Geology of Mankind." *Nature* 415, no. 3 (2002): 23.

Cummings, Stephen, Todd Bridgman, John Hassard, and Michael Rowlinson. *A New History of Management.* Cambridge: Cambridge University Press, 2017.

Czarniawska, Barbara, and Guje Sevón, eds. *Translating Organizational Change.* Berlin: De Gruyter, 1996.

Dahl, Matilda. *States Under Scrutiny: International Organizations, Transformation and the Construction of Progress.* Stockholm: Stockholm University Dissertations, 2007.

Dailey, Brian D., and Patrick J. Parker, eds. *Soviet Strategic Deception.* Lanham, MD: Lexington, 1987.

Dayé, Christian. *Experts, Social Scientists and Techniques of Prognosis in Cold War America.* Cham, Switzerland: Palgrave, 2019.

Daye, Christian. "How to Train Your Oracle: The Delphi Method and Its Turbulent Youth in Operations Research and the Policy Sciences." *Social Studies of Science* 48, no. 6 (2018).

de Pedro, Nicolás, Panagiota Manoli, Sergey Sukhankin, and Theodoros Tsakiris. *Facing Russia's Strategic Challenge: Security Developments from the Baltic Sea to the Black Sea*. Brussels: European Parliament Policy Department, Directorate General for External Policies, 2017.

Dean, Mitchell. *Governmentality: Power and Rule in Modern Society*. London: Sage, 2009.

Dean, Mitchell, and Daniel Zamora, *The Last Man Takes LSD: Foucault and the End of Revolution*. London: Verso, 2021.

DeBardeleben, Joan. *The Environment and Marxism-Leninism: The Soviet and East German Experience*. Boulder, CO: Westview Press, 1985.

Deegan, Cecily, and Stephen Latham. "The B-School vs the Wall Street Journal: Who Is Misrepresenting Whom?" *Harvard Crimson*, 1 March 1979, https://www.thecrimson .com/article/1979/3/1/the-b-school-vs-the-wall-street/.

Denyer, Nicholas. "The Case Against Divination: An Examination of Cicero's De Divinatione." *Cambridge Classical Journal* 31 (1985): 1–10.

Desrosières, Alain. *The Politics of Large Numbers: A History of Statistical Reasoning*. Cambridge, MA: Harvard University Press, 2002.

Deutsch, Karl W. *The Nerves of Government: Models of Political Communication and Control*. New York: Free Press, 1963.

Dodsworth, Francis. *The Security Society: History, Patriarchy, Protection*. Cham, Switzerland: Palgrave Macmillan, 2019.

Doktorov, Boris. *Sovremennaia Rossiiskaia sotsiologiia: istoriko biograficheskie poiski*. Vol. 8.1. Moscow: TsPIM, 2016.

Doktorov, Boris. *Sovremennaia Rossiiskaia sotsiologiia: istoriko-biograficheskoe i avtobiograficheskoe*. Vol. 9. Moscow: TsSPim, 2016.

Doktorov, Boris. "Interv'iu s I.V. Zadorinym: 'V otnoshenie k rabote moia professional'naia pozitsiia vsegda byla sil'nee grazhdanskoi . . .'." *Monitoring obshchestvennogo mneniia: ekonomicheskie i sotsialnye peremeny* 1 (2016): 363–380.

Dolan, Emily. *The Orchestral Revolution: Haydn and the Technologies of Timbre*. Cambridge, UK: Cambridge University Press, 2013.

Donskis, Leonidas. "Aleksandras Shtromas: The Lithuanian Prophet of Postcommunism." *Journal of Interdisciplinary Studies* 18, nos. 1–2 (2006): 75–92.

Douglas, Heather. "Reintroducing Prediction to Explanation." *Philosophy of Science* 76 (2009): 444–463.

Douglas, Mary, and Aaron Wildavsky. *Risk and Culture: An Essay on the Selection of Technological and Environmental Dangers*. Berkeley: University of California Press, 1983.

du Gay, Paul. *In Praise of Bureaucracy: Weber–Organization–Ethics*. London: Sage, 2000.

Düppe, Till. "Koopmans in the Soviet Union: A Travel Report of the Summer of 1965." *Journal of the History of Economic Thought* 38, no. 1 (2016): 81–104.

Durkheim, Emile. *The Rules of Sociological Method*, translated by W. D. Halls [1895]. New York: Free Press, 1982.

Edwards, Paul. *The Closed World: Computers and the Politics of Discourse in Cold War America*. Cambridge, MA: MIT Press, 1996.

Edwards, Paul. *A Vast Machine: Computer Models, Climate Data and the Politics of Global Warming*. Cambridge, MA: MIT Press, 2010.

Efremenko, Dmitry. *Vvedenie v otsenku tekhniki*. Moscow: MNEPU, 2002.

Ehrenberg, A. S. C., and J. A. Bound. "Predictability and Prediction." *Journal of the Royal Statistical Society, Series A (Statistics in Society)* 156, no. 2 (1993): 167–206.

Elden, Stuart. *Canguilhem*. Cambridge: Polity, 2019.

Eliade, Mircea. *The Myth of Eternal Return: Cosmos and History*. Oxford: Blackwell, 2018 [1949].

Elie, Marc. "Formulating the Global Environment: Soviet Soil Scientists and the International Desertification Discussion, 1968–91." *Slavonic and East European Review* 93, no. 1 (2015): 181–204.

Elie, Marc. "Governing by Hazard: Controlling Mudslides and Promoting Tourism in the Mountains Above Alma-Ata (Kazakhstan), 1966–1977." In *Governing Disasters: Beyond Risk Culture*, edited by Sandrine Revet and Julien Langumier, 23–57. Cham, Switzerland: Palgrave, 2015.

Elie, Marc. "Late Soviet Responses to Disasters, 1989–1991: A New Approach to Crisis Management or the Acme of Soviet Technocratic Thinking?" *Soviet and Post-Soviet Review* 40, no. 2 (2013): 214–238.

Elkner, Julie. "The Changing Face of Repression under Khrushchev." In *Soviet State and Society Under Nikita Khrushchev*, edited by Melanie Ilic and Jeremy Smith, 142–161 (London: Routledge, 2009).

Ellman, Michael. *Socialist Planning*. Cambridge: Cambridge University Press, 2008.

Ellman, Michael. "Was the Collapse of the USSR Entirely Unforeseen?" *Perspectives on Political Science* 31, no. 3 (2002): 132–135.

Ellman, Michael, and Vladimir Kantorovich, eds. *The Destruction of the Soviet Economic System: An Insider's History*. London: Routledge, 1988.

Erelina, Ol'ga, and Nikolai Smirnov. *Ivan Efremov*. Moscow: Molodaia gvardiia, 2013.

Ereshko, F. I. "Ravnovesie na mnozhestve refleksivnykh strategii." *Refleksivnye protsessy i upravlenie* 16, nos. 1–2 (2016): 59–64.

Erickson, Paul. *The World the Game Theorists Made*. Chicago: University of Chicago Press, 2015.

Erickson, Paul, Judy L. Klein, Lorraine Daston, Rebecca Lemov, Thomas Sturm, and Michael D. Gordin. *How Reason Almost Lost Its Mind: The Strange Career of Cold War Rationality*. Chicago: University of Chicago Press, 2013.

Erlich, Paul, and Peter Raven. "Butterflies and Plants: A Study in Coevolution." *Evolution* 18, no. 4 (1967): 586–608.

Ershov, Iu. V. and A. S. Popovich. "Propushchennaia vozmozhnost' obognat Ameriku, ili k chemu provodit ignorirovanie prognoz." *Top Club Journal* 3, no. 21 (2012): 8–17.

Faria, A. J., David Hutchinson, William Wellington, and Steven Gold. "Developments in Business Gaming: A Review of the Past 40 Years." *Simulation and Gaming* 40, no. 4 (2009): 464–487.

Fedorov, Evgenii. *Ecological Crisis and Social Progress*. Moscow: Progress, 1977.

Fedorov, Evgenii. *Man and Nature: The Ecological Crisis and Social Progress*. New York: Progress, 1981.

Fedorov, Evgenii. *Vzaimodeistvie obshchestva i prirody*. Leningrad: Gidrometeoizdat, 1972.

Feygin, Yakov. "Reforming the Cold War State: Economic Thought, Internationalization, and the Politics of Soviet Reform, 1955–1985." Unpublished doctoral dissertation, University of Pennsylvania, 2017.

Fidora, Alexander. "Divination and Scientific Prediction: The Epistemology of Prognostic Sciences in Medieval Europe." *Early Science and Medicine* 18 (2013): 517–535.

Firsov, Boris. *Istoriia sovetskoi sotsiologii 1950–1980 gg.* St Petersburg: Izd. Evropeiskogo universiteta v Sankt Peterburge, 2012.

Fischer, Frank. *Technocracy and the Politics of Expertise*. Newbury Park, CA: Sage, 1990.

Fischer, Ronald A. "The Logic of Inductive Inference." *Journal of the Royal Statistical Society* 98, no. 1 (1935): 39–82.

Flanagan, Owen. "Psychology, Progress, and the Problem of Reflexivity: A Study in the Epistemological Foundations of Psychology." *Journal of the History of Behavioral Sciences* 17, no. 3 (1981): 375–386.

Fortescue, Stephen, ed. *Russian Politics: From Lenin to Putin*. Basingstoke, UK: Palgrave, 2010.

Foucault, Michel. *The Order of Things: An Archaeology of the Human Sciences*. New York: Vintage Books, 1970.

Foucault, Michel. *Security, Territory, Population: Lectures at the Collège de France 1978–1979*. Basingstoke, UK: Palgrave, 2009.

Fraisse, Robert. "Notes sur planification a long terme en Union Sovietique." December 1966, *BR 4/513/8*, Sciences Po.

Franklin, Seb. *Control: Digitality as Cultural Logic*. Cambridge, MA: MIT Press, 2015.

Freedman, Lawrence. *Strategy: A History*. Oxford: Oxford University Press, 2013.

Friedman, Walt. *Fortune Tellers: The Story of America's First Forecasters*. Princeton, NJ: Princeton University Press, 2014.

Fuller, Jonathan, Alex Broadbent, and Luis J. Flores. "Prediction in Epidemiology and Medicine." *Studies in History and Philosophy of Biological and Biomedical Sciences* (2015): 1–4.

Gabrys, Jennifer. *Program Earth: Environmental Sensing Technology and the Making of a Computational Planet*. Minneapolis: University of Minnesota Press, 2016.

Gagnon, John H. "Mary M. Birshtein: The Mother of Soviet Simulation Gaming." *Simulation Gaming* 18, no. 3 (1987): 3–12.

Galeotti, Mark. *Russian Political War: Moving Beyond the Hybrid*. London: Routledge, 2019.

Galison, Peter. *Einstein's Clocks, Poincare's Maps*. London: Sceptre, 2003.

Galison, Peter. "The Ontology of the Enemy: Norbert Wiener and the Cybernetic Vision." *Critical Inquiry* 21, no. 1 (1994): 228–266.

Galison, Peter, and Bruce William Hevly, eds. *Big Science: The Growth of Large Scale Research*. Stanford, CA: Stanford University Press, 1992.

Geismar, Haidy. *Museum Object: Lessons for the Digital Age*. London: UCL Press, 2018.

Geoghegan, Bernard Dionysius. "From Information Theory to French Theory: Jakobson, Lévi-Strauss, and the Cybernetic Apparatus." *Critical Inquiry* 38, no. 1 (2011): 96–111.

Geroulanos, Stefanos. *Transparency in Postwar France: A Critical History of the Present*. Stanford, CA: Stanford University Press, 2017.

Geroulanos, Stefanos, and Todd Meyers. *The Human Body in the Age of Catastrophe: Brittleness, Integration, Science and the Great War*. Chicago: University of Chicago Press, 2018.

Gerovitch, Slava. *From Newspeak to Cyberspeak: A History of Soviet Cybernetics*. Cambridge, MA: MIT Press, 2002.

Gerovitch, Slava. *Soviet Space Mythologies: Public Images, Private Memories, and the Making of a Cultural Identity*. Pittsburgh: Pittsburgh University Press, 2015.

Gerovitch, Slava. *Voices of the Space Program: Cosmonauts, Soldiers, and Engineers Who Took the USSR into Space*. London: Palgrave, 2014.

Gerovitch, Slava. "'We Teach Them to Be Free': Specialized Math Schools and the Cultivation of the Soviet Technical Intelligentsia." *Kritika: Explorations in Russian and Eurasian History* 20, no. 4 (2019): 717–754.

Giddens, Anthony. *New Rules of Sociological Method*. Stanford, CA: Stanford University Press, 1976.

Gilman, Nils. *The Mandarins of the Future: Modernization Theory in Cold War America*. Baltimore: Johns Hopkins University Press, 2007.

Gjaltema, Jonna, Robbert Biesbroek, and Katrien Termeer. "From Government to Governance: A Systematic Literature Review." *Public Management Review* 22, no. 12 (2020): 1760–1780.

BIBLIOGRAPHY

Glushenkova, Elena. *Ekopolitologiia N. N. Moiseeva i ustoichivoe razvitie Rossii*. Moscow: MNEPU, 2015.

Godet, Michel. "From Forecasting to *la prospective*: A New Way of Looking at Futures." *Journal of Forecasting* 1 (1982): 293–301.

Godin, Benoît. "The Linear Model of Innovation: The Historical Construction of an Analytical Framework." *Science, Technology and Human Values* 31, no. 6 (2006): 639–667.

Gofman, Alexander. "The Russian Career of Durkheim's Sociology of Religion and 'Les Formes Élémentaires': Contribution to a Study." *Durkheimian Studies / Études Durkheimiennes* 19 (2013): 101–124

Goffman, Erving. *Encounters*. New York: Bobbs-Merrill, 1961.

Gogol, Nikolai. *The Gamblers and Marriage*, translated by Alexander Berkman. Digireads, Kindle edition, 2014.

Goldstone, Jack. "Predicting Revolutions: Why We Could (and Should) Have Foreseen the Revolutions of 1989–1991 in the U.S.S.R. and Eastern Europe." *Contention* 2, no. 2 (1993): 127–152.

Golomstock, Igor. *A Ransomed Dissident: A Life in Art Under the Soviets*. London: I. B. Tauris, 2019.

Good, Harry, and Robert Machol. *Systems Engineering: An Introduction to the Design of Large-Scale Systems*. New York: McGraw Hill, 1957.

Gorham, Michael. "Virtual Rusophonia: Language Policy as 'Soft Power' in the New Media Age." *Digital Icons* 5 (2011): 23–48.

Gouarné, Isabelle. "Mandatory Planning Versus Indicative Planning? The Eastern Itinerary of French Planners (1960s–1970s)." In *Planning in Cold War Europe: Competition, Cooperation, Circulations (1950s–1970s)*, edited by Michel Christian, Sandrine Kott, and Ondřej Matějka, 71–77. Berlin: De Gruyter, 2018.

Graham, Loren. *The Ghost of the Executed Engineer: Technology and the Fall of the Soviet Union*. Cambridge, MA: Harvard University Press, 1996.

Graham, Loren, and Irina Dezhina. *Science in the New Russia: Crisis, Aid, Reform*. Bloomington: Indiana University Press, 2008.

Greenfeld, Liah. "Soviet Sociology and Sociology in the Soviet Union." *Annual Review of Sociology* 14 (1988): 99–123.

Gregory, Paul R. *The Political Economy of Stalinism: Evidence from the Soviet Secret Archives*. Cambridge: Cambridge University Press, 2004.

Grimanelli, Pericles. "La prévision en sociologie." *Revue internationale de sociologie* 12 (1911): 861–879.

Groys, Boris. *The Total Art of Stalinism: Avant-garde, Aesthetic Dictatorship and Beyond*. Princeton, NJ: Princeton University Press, 1992.

Guilhot, Nicolas. "Cybernetic Pantocrator: International Relations Theory from Decisionism to Rational Choice." *Journal of the History of the Behavioral Sciences* 47, no. 3 (2011): 279–301.

Guilhot, Nicolas, and Daniel Bessner, eds. *Decisionist Imagination: Sovereignty, Social Science and Democracy in the 20th Century*. Oxford: Berghahn Books, 2018.

Gunneriusson, Hakan, and Sascha Dov Bachmann. "Western Denial and Russian Control: How Russia's National Security Strategy Threatens a Western-based Approach to Global Security, the Rule of Law and Globalization." *Polish Political Science Yearbook* 46, no. 1 (2017): 9–29.

Gutnov, Dmitrij. "L'École russe des hautes études sociales de Paris (1901–1906)." *Cahiers du monde Russe* 43, nos. 2–3 (2002): 375–410.

Gvishiani, Dzhermen. "Upravlenie—prezhde vsego nauka." *Izvestiia* no. 118 (1963): 2.

Hacking, Ian. *The Taming of Chance*. Cambridge: Cambridge University Press, 1990.

Hale, Thomas, and Charles Roger. "Orchestration and Transnational Climate Governance." *Review International Organization* 9 (2014): 59–82.

Hammond, Debora. *The Science of Synthesis: Exploring the Social Implications of General Systems Theory.* Boulder: University Press of Colorado, 2003.

Hammond-Errey, M. "Understanding and Assessing Information Influence and Foreign Interference." *Journal of Information Warfare* 18, no. 1 (2019): 1–22.

Harries-Jones, Peter. *A Recursive Vision: Ecological Understanding and Gregory Bateson.* Toronto: University of Toronto Press, 1995.

Harrison, Mark. "Chayanov and the Economics of the Russian Peasantry." *Journal of Peasant Studies* 2, no. 4 (1975): 389–417.

Harrison, Rodney, and Colin Sterling, eds. *Deterritorializing the Future: Heritage In, Of and After the Anthropocene.* London: Open Humanities Press, 2020.

Hayles, Katherine. *How We Became Posthuman: Virtual Bodies in Cybernetics, Literature, and Informatics.* Chicago: University of Chicago Press, 1999.

Hecht, Gabriella. *The Radiance of France: Nuclear Power and National Identity After World War II.* Cambridge, MA: MIT Press, 1998.

Heidegger, Martin. "Nur noch ein Gott kann uns retten." *Der Spiegel* 23 (31 May 1976): 193–219.

Heims, Steve J. *John Von Neumann and Norbert Wiener: From Mathematics to the Technologies of Life and Death.* Cambridge, MA: MIT Press, 1980.

Hempel, Carl G., and Paul Oppenheim. "Studies in the Logic of Explanation." *Philosophy of Science* 15, no. 2 (1948): 135–175.

Heyck, Hunter. *Age of System: Understanding the Development of Modern Social Science.* Baltimore: Johns Hopkins University Press, 2015.

Heymann, Matthias, Gabriele Gramelsberger, and Martin Mahony, eds. *Cultures of Prediction in Atmospheric and Climate Science: Epistemic and Cultural Shifts in Computer-based Modelling and Simulation.* London: Routledge, 2017.

Heymann, Matthias, Gabriele Gramelsberger, and Martin Mahony. "Key Characteristics of Cultures of Prediction." In *Cultures of Prediction in Atmospheric and Climate Science*, edited by Matthias Heymann, Gabriele Gramelsberger, and Martin Mahony, 18–42. London: Routledge, 2015.

Horan, Caley. "Investing in the Stars: The Astrology of Money and Markets in the Modern United States." Unpublished presentation, STS Circle at Harvard, 19 November 2018.

Horvath, Robert. *The Legacy of Soviet Dissent: Dissidents, Democratisation and Radical Nationalism in Russia.* London: Routledge, 2005.

Howe, Leo, and Alan Wain, eds. *Predicting the Future.* Cambridge: Cambridge University Press, 1993.

Hughes, Thomas. *Networks of Power: Electrification in Western Society, 1880–1930.* Baltimore: Johns Hopkins University Press, 1993.

Huhtinen, Aki-Mauri, Noora Kotilainen, Saara Särmä, and Mikko Streng, "Information Influence in Hybrid Environment: Reflexive Control as an Analytical Tool for Understanding Warfare in Social Media." *International Journal of Cyber Warfare and Terrorism* 9, no. 3 (2019): 1–20.

Hviid Jacobsen, Michael, and Sophia Marshman. "Bauman on Metaphors: A Harbinger of Humanistic Hybrid Sociology." In *The Sociology of Zygmunt Bauman: Challenges and Critique*, edited by Michael Hviid Jacobsen and Paul Poder, 19–40. London: Routledge, 2008.

Iakimets, I. V. "Background and Requirements for the SOVAM: Soviet Agricultural Model." IIASA Working Paper, WP-84-097, IIASA, Austria, 1984.

BIBLIOGRAPHY

Iakovlev, A.A. Interview with Igor' Zadorin, "v professionalnom sotsiologicheskom soobshchestve ne khvataet nezavisimykh ekspertov." *Ekonomicheskaia sotsiologiia* 14, no. 1 (2013): 10–26.

Ianitskii, Oleg. "Environmental Sociology Yesterday and Today." *Sociological Research* 33, no. 1 (1994): 7–32.

Iarmoliuk, S. F., ed. *Rossiiskaia sotsiologiia shestidesiatykh godov v vospominaniiakh i dokumentakh*. St Petersburg: Izdatel'stvo Russkogo Khristianskogo gumanitarnogo universiteta, 1999.

Igrunov, Viacheslav. "O Nikite Nikolaiche Moiseeve i o tom, kak nesostoialsia Moskovskii Rimskii klub." http://www.igrunov.ru/cv/vchk-cv-memotalks/talks/vchk-cv-memo talks-talks-moiseev.html.

Ingelstam, Lars. *System: Att tänka över samhälle och teknik*. Eskilstuna: Energimyndighetens förlag, 2012.

Ioffe, Julia. "'Before, Putin Was Unpredictable; Now It's Trump': Moscow Grapples with a Strange Week in Washington." *Atlantic*, 18 February 2017, https://www.theatlantic.com/international/archive/2017/02/putin-trump-flynn/517224/.

Isaev, V. P. "Pervyi v SSSR podvizhnyi vychislitel'nyi tsentr voennogo naznacheniia (1963–1968 gg)." *Virtualnyi komp'iuternyi muzei*, 26 January 2011, http://www.computer-museum.ru/histussr/pvp_platforma.htm.

Isin, Engin, and Evelyn Ruppert. "The Birth of Sensory Power: How a Pandemic Made It Visible." *Big Data & Society* (2020): 1–15.

Iudin, Boris. "Ot gumanitarnogo znaniia k gumanitarnym tekhnologiiam." *Gumanitarnye nauki: teoriia i metodologiia* 4 (2005): 104–107.

Jameson, Frederic. *Archaeologies of the Future: The Desire of Utopia and Other Science Fictions*. London: Verso, 2005.

Jervis, Robert. *Perception and Misperception in International Politics*. Princeton, NJ: Princeton University Press, 1976.

Joel, Isaac. "Strategy as Intellectual History." *Modern Intellectual History* (2018): 1–15.

Johnson, Ann. "Rational and Empirical Cultures of Prediction." In *Mathematics as a Tool*, edited by Johannes Lenhard and Martin Carrier, 23–35. Cham, Switzerland: Springer, 2017.

Johnson, Ian. "Technology's Cutting Edge: Futurism and Research in the Red Army, 1917–1973." *Technology and Culture* 59 (2018): 689–718.

Johnston, John. *The Allure of Machinic Life: Cybernetics, Artificial Life, and the New AI*. Cambridge, MA: MIT Press, 2008.

Jopling, Lord. *Countering Russia's Hybrid Threats: An Update*. Committee of the Civil Dimension of Security, NATO Parliamentary Assembly, 1 October 2018.

Josephson, Paul R. *Industrialized Nature: Brute Force Technology and the Transformation of the Natural World*. Washington, DC: Island Press, 2002.

Josephson, Paul R. "'Projects of the Century' in Soviet History: Large-Scale Technologies from Stalin to Gorbachev." *Technology and Culture* 36, no. 3 (1995): 519–559.

Josephson, Paul, Nicolai Dronin, Ruben Mnatsakanian, Aleh Cherp, Dmitry Efremenko, and Vladislav Larin. *An Environmental History of Russia*. Cambridge: Cambridge University Press, 2013.

Kahneman, Daniel, and Amos Tversky. "On the Psychology of Prediction." *Psychological Review* 80, no. 4 (1973): 237–251.

Kähönen, Aappo. "Optimal Planning, Optimal Economy, Optimal Life? The Kosygin Reforms, 1965–72." In *Competition in Socialist Society*, edited by Katalin Miklossy and Melanie Ilic, 23–40. London: Routledge, 2014.

Kantola, Ilkka. *Probability and Moral Uncertainty in Late Medieval and Early Modern Times*. Helsinki, Finland: Luther-Agricola Society, 1994.

BIBLIOGRAPHY

Kaplan, Fred. *The Wizards of Armageddon*. Stanford, CA: Stanford University Press, 1991.

Kellner, Joseph. "As Above, So Below: Astrology and the Fate of Soviet Scientism." *Kritika* 20, no. 4 (2019): 783–812.

Kemp, Sandra, and Jenny Andersson, eds. *Futures*. Oxford: Oxford University Press, 2021.

Kerzhentsev, Platon. "Bor'ba za vremia (1923)." In *Printsipy organizatsii* by Platon Kerzhentsev, 335–384. Moscow: Ekonomika, 1968.

Khandozhko, Roman. *Vzaimodeistvie neofitsial'noi filosofii i nauchno-tekhnicheskogo soobshchestva v pozdnem SSSR: sluchai Obninska*. Moscow: Ranepa, 2016.

Khristenko, V. B., A. G. Reus, A. P. Zinchenko., *Methodological School of Management*. London: Bloomsbury, 2014.

Khromchenko, Matvei Solomonovich. *Letopis'*. Moscow: Studia Korolovae, 2019, https://conflictmanagement.ru/wp-content/uploads/2016/02/letopis_MKh03.pdf.

Kilovaty, Ido. "Doxfare: Politically Motivated Leaks and the Future of the Norm on Non-Intervention in the Era of Weaponized Information." *Harvard National Security Journal* 9, no. 1 (2018): 146–179.

Kirchhof, Astrid, and John Robert McNeill, eds. *Nature and the Iron Curtain: Environmental Policy and Social Movements in Communist and Capitalist Countries, 1945–1990*. Pittsburgh: University of Pittsburgh Press, 2019.

Kirtchik, Olesia. "From Pattern Recognition to Economic Disequilibrium: Emmanuil Braverman's Theory of Control of the Soviet Economy." *History of Political Economy* 51, no. S1 (2019): 180–203.

Klebaner, V. S. "V.A. Bazarov: Myslitel', uchenyi, grazhdanin." *Problemy prognozirovaniia* 6 (2004):150–154.

Klein, Judy L. *Statistical Visions in Time: A History of Time Series Analysis, 1662–1938*. Cambridge: Cambridge University Press, 1997.

Klepach, A. N., and G. O. Kuranov. "Razvitie sotsial'no-ekonomicheskogo prognozirovanie i idei A. I. Anchishkina." *Voprosy ekonomiki* 8 (2013): 143–155.

Kline, Ronald. *The Cybernetics Moment: Or Why We Call Our Age the Information Age*. Baltimore: Johns Hopkins University Press, 2015.

Knight, Frank H. *Risk, Uncertainty and Profit*. Boston: Riverside Press, 1921.

Knutti, Retto. "Should We Believe Model Predictions of Future Climate Change?" *Philosophical Transactions of the Royal Society Series A* 366 (2008): 4647–4664.

Kojevnikov, Alexei. *Stalin's Great Science: The Times and Adventures of Soviet Physicists*. London: Imperial College Press, 2004.

Kondrat'ev, N. D. *Bol'shie tsikly, kon"iunktury i teoriia predvideniia*. Moscow: Akademicheskii proekt, 2015.

Kornai, Janos. *The Socialist System: The Political Economics of Communism*. Princeton, NJ: Princeton University Press, 1992.

Koselleck, Reinhart. *Futures Past: On the Semantics of Historical Time*. New York: Columbia University Press, 2004 [1979].

Kosygin, Aleksei. "Povyshenie nauchnoi obosnovannosti planov-vazhneishaia zadacha planovykh organov." *Planovoe khoziaistvo* 4 (1965): 4–5.

Kotsonis, Yanni. *States of Obligation: Taxes and Citizenship in the Russian Empire and Early Soviet Republic*. Toronto: University of Toronto Press, 2014.

Kramer, Xenia, Tim Kaiser, Stefan Schmidt, Jim Davidson, and Vladimir Lefebvre. "Ot predskazanii k refleksivnomu upravleniiu." *Refleksivnye protsessy i upravlenie* 2, no. 3 (2003): 35–52.

Krementsov, Nikolai. *A Martian Stranded on Earth: Alexander Bogdanov, Blood Transfusion and the Proletarian Science*. Chicago: University of Chicago Press, 2011.

Krementsov, Nikolai. *Stalinist Science*. Princeton, NJ: Princeton University Press, 1996.

262   **BIBLIOGRAPHY**

Krementsov, Nikolai. *With or Without Galton: Vasilii Florinskii and the Fate of Eugenics in Russia*. Cambridge, UK: Open Book Publishers, 2018.

Kriger, Il'ia. "Vladimir Lefevr: Ideologiiu nel'zia sozdat'—ona vozniknet nezametno samo soboi." *Novaia gazeta* 84 (1 November 2007), https://novayagazeta.ru/articles /2007/11/01/31285-vladimir-lefevr-ideologiyu-nelzya-sozdat-ona-vozniknet -nezametno-sama-soboy.

Krupavicius, Algis. "Lithuania's President: A Formal and Informal Power." In *Presidents above Parties? Presidents in Central and Eastern Europe, Their Formal Competencies and Informal Power*, edited by Vít Hloušek et al., 205–232. Prague: Masaryk University, 2013.

Kucharski, Adam. "How Modelling Covid Has Changed the Way We Think About Epidemics." *Guardian* (UK edition), 4 January 2021.

Kudors, Andis. "'Russian World': Russia's Soft Power Approach to Compatriots Policy." *Russian Analytical Digest* 81 (16 June 2010): 2–4.

Kukulin, Il'ia. "Alternative Social Blueprinting in Soviet Society of the 1960s and the 1970s, or Why Left-Wing Political Practices Have Not Caught on in Contemporary Russia." *Russian Studies in History* 49, no. 4 (2011): 51–92.

Kuosa, Tuomo. *The Evolution of Strategic Foresight: Navigating Public Policy Making*. Farnham, UK: Ashgate, 2012.

Kurennoy, Vitaly. "Contemporary State Cultural Policy in Russia: Organization, Political Discourse and Ceremonial Behavior." *International Journal of Cultural Policy* 27, no. 2 (2021): 163–176.

Kurg, Andres. "Feedback Environment: Rethinking Art and Design Practices in Tallinn During the Early 1970s." *Kunstiteaduslikke Uurimusi*, nos.1–2 (2011): 26–50.

Kurkovsky, Diana. "Cybernetics for the Command Economy: Foregrounding Entropy in Late Soviet Planning." *History of the Human Sciences* 33, no. 1 (2020): 36–51.

Kuznetsova, N. "Vozvraschenie." *Voprosy filosofii* 7 (1990): 51–58.

Lackner, Michael, ed. *Coping with the Future: Theories and Practices of Divination in East Asia*. Leiden: Brill, 2018.

Lafontaine, Céline. *L'empire cybernétique: Des machines à penser à la pensée machine*. Paris: Le Seuil, 2004.

Lajus, Julia. "Soviet Official Critiques of the Resource Scarcity Prediction by *Limits to Growth* Report: The Case of Evgenii Fedorov's Ecological Crisis Rhetoric." *European Review of History* 27, no. 3 (2020): 321–341.

Lankina, Tomila V. *The Estate Origins of Democracy in Russia: From Imperial Bourgeoisie to Post-Communist Middle Class*. Cambridge: Cambridge University Press, 2021.

Lapenis, Andrei. "Directed Evolution of the Biosphere: Biogeochemical Selection or Gaia?" *Professional Geographer* 54, no. 3 (2002): 379–391.

Lapin, Nikolai, and Boris Sazonov. "The Activity-Systems Approach to Development of the Human Factor in Innovation." In *A Science of Goal Formulation: American and Soviet Discussions of Cybernetics and Systems Theory*, edited by Stuart A. Umpleby, and Vadim N. Sadovsky, 195–206. New York: Hemisphere, 1991.

Lapo, Andrei, and Aleksandr Ianshin, ed. *V.I.Vernadskii: Pro et Contra*. Saint Petersburg: Izdatelstvo Russkogo khristianskogo gumanitarnogo instituta, 2000.

Larin, Ivan. *On uchil berech zemliu*. Moscow: Rosekopress, 2002.

Latour, Bruno. "The Politics of Explanation: An Alternative." In *Knowledge and Reflexivity: New Frontiers in the Sociology of Knowledge*, edited by Steve Woolgar, 155–176. London: Sage, 1988.

Latour, Bruno. *Reassembling the Social: An Introduction to Actor Network Theory*. Oxford: Oxford University Press, 2005.

Laudan, Larry. "Towards a Reassessment of Comte's 'Méthod Positive.'" *Philosophy of Science* 38, no. 1 (1971): 35–53.

Law, John. *After Method: Mess in Social Science Research*. London: Routledge, 2004.

Law, John. "Notes on the Theory of the Actor-Network: Ordering, Strategy and Heterogeneity." *Systems Practice* 5 (1992): 379–393.

Lawson, Hilary. *Reflexivity: The Post-Modern Predicament*. London: Hutchinson, 1985.

Ledeneva, Alena. *Can Russia Modernise? Sistema, Power Networks and Informal Governance*. Cambridge: Cambridge University Press, 2013.

Ledeneva, Alena, ed. *The Global Encyclopaedia of Informality: Understanding Social and Cultural Complexity, Vols. 1–2*. London: UCL Press, 2020.

Ledeneva, Alena. *How Russia Really Works: The Informal Practices That Shaped Post-Soviet Politics and Business*. Ithaca, NY: Cornell University Press, 2006.

Ledeneva, Alena. *Russia's Economy of Favours: Blat, Networking and Informal Exchange*. Cambridge: Cambridge University Press, 1998.

Leeds, Adam. "Administrative Monsters: Yurii Yaremenko's Critique of the Late Soviet State." *History of Political Economy* 51 (2019): 127–151.

Leeds, Adam. "Dreams in Cybernetic Fugue: Cold War Technoscience, the Intelligentsia, and the Birth of Soviet Mathematical Economics." *Historical Studies in the Natural Sciences* 46, no. 5 (2016): 633–668.

Lefebvre, Vladimir. "Algebra sovesti: vospominanie avtora." *Znanie i sila* 3 (2002). Available online http://www.reflexion.ru/Library/Lefebvre_2002_a.htm

Lefebvre, Vladimir. "Elementy logiki refleksivnykh igr." *Problemy inzhinernoi psikhologii* 4 (1966): 273–299.

Lefebvre, Vladimir. "Formal'nyi metod issledovaniia refleksivnykh protsessov." *Voprosy filosofii* 9 (1971): 103–115.

Lefebvre, Vladimir. "Konfliktuiushchie struktury (1967)." In Vladimir Lefebvre, *Refleksiia*, 132–133. Moscow: Kogito-Tsentr, 2003.

Lefebvre, Vladimir. *Lektsii po teorii refleksivnykh igr*. Moscow: Kogito-Tsentr, 2009.

Lefebvre, Vladimir. *Research on Bipolarity and Reflexivity*. New York: Edwin Mellen, 2006.

Lefebvre, Vladimir. "Second Order Cybernetics in the Soviet Union and the West." In *Power, Autonomy, Utopia: New Approaches Toward Complex Systems*, edited by Robert Trappl, 123–132. New York: Plenum Press, 1986.

Lefebvre, Vladimir. "Vozvrashchenie." In *Refleksiia*. Moscow: Kogito-Tsentr, 2003.

Lefebvre, Vladimir, and Georgii Smolian. *Algebra konflikta*. Moscow: Librokom, 2013 [1967].

Lefevr, Vladimir. *Konfliktuiushchie struktury*. Moscow: Vysh.shkola, 1967.

Lefevr, Vladimir. "Rasskazy o Zinchenko." *Refleksivnye protsessy i upravlenie* 11, nos. 1–2 (2011): 93–98.

Lektorsky, Vladislav A. "The Activity Approach in Soviet Philosophy and Contemporary Cognitive Studies." in *Philosophical Thought in Russia in the Second Half of the Twentieth Century: A Contemporary View from Russia and Abroad*, edited by Vladislav Lektorsky and Marina Bykova, 137–153. London: Bloomsbury, 2019.

Lektorsky, Vladislav A., and Marina F. Bykova, eds. *Philosophical Thought in Russia in the Second Half of the Twentieth Century: A Contemporary View from Russia and Abroad*. London: Bloomsbury, 2019.

Lenel, Laetitia. "Searching for a Tide Table Business: Interwar Conceptions of Statistical Inference in Forecasting." *History of Political Economy* 53S (2021): 139–174.

Lenzer, Gertrude, ed. *Auguste Comte and Positivism: The Essential Writings*. London: Routledge, 1998.

264 BIBLIOGRAPHY

Lepskii, Vladimir. "Lefevre i refleksiia." *Refleksivnye protsessy i upravlenie* 6, no. 1 (2006): 26–37.

Lepskii, Vladimir. *Tekhnologii upravleniia v informatsionnykh voinakh (ot klassiki do postneklassiki)*. Moscow: Kogito-Tsentr, 2016.

Lesse, Matthias. "'We Do That Once per Day': Cyclical Futures and Institutional Ponderousness in Predictive Policing." In *The Politics and Science of Prevision: Governing and Probing the Future*, edited by Andreas Wenger, Ursula Jasper, and Myrian Dunn Cavelty, 213–226. London: Routledge, 2020.

Levintov, A. E. "Proiskhozhdenie i priroda refleksii." *Refleksivnye protsessy i upravlenie* 16, nos. 1–2 (2016): 82–85.

Light, Jennifer S. *From Warfare to Welfare: Defense Intellectuals and Urban Problems in Cold War America*. Baltimore: Johns Hopkins University Press, 2003.

Light, Jennifer. "Taking Games Seriously." *Technology and Culture* 49, no. 2 (2008): 347–375.

Lindee, M. Susan. *Rational Fog*. Cambridge, MA: Harvard University Press, 2020.

Losee, John. *The Golden Age of the Philosophy of Science*. London: Bloomsbury, 2018.

Lovelock, James E., and Lyn Margulis. "Atmospheric Homeostasis By and For the Biosphere: The Gaia Hypothesis." *Telus* 26, nos. 1–2 (1974): 2–10.

Luhmann, Niklas. *Social Systems*. Stanford, CA: Stanford University Press, 1995 [1984].

Luke, Timothy W. "On Environmentality: Geo-Power and Eco-Knowledge in the Discourses of Contemporary Environmentalism." *Cultural Critique* 31 (1995): 57–81.

Luria, Alexander. *The Nature of Human Conflicts, of Emotion, Conflict, and Will*. New York: Liveright Publishers, 1932.

Lutz, Wolfgang, Sergei Scherbov, and Andrei Volkov. "Introduction: Past and Present Studies of the Soviet Population." In *Demographic Trends and Patterns in the Soviet Union Before 1991*, edited by Wolfgang Lutz, Sergei Scherbov, and Andrei Volkov, xxxi–xl. London: Routledge, 1994.

Mahony, Michael, and Martin Hulme. "Epistemic Geographies of Climate Change: Science, Space and Politics." *Progress in Human Geography* (2016): 1–30.

Makarevich, V. N. "Igropraktiki, metodologi: 'Nezrimoe soobshchestvo' vykhodit iz podpol'ia." *SOTSIS* 7 (1992): 50–56.

Makasheva, Natalia. "Zagadka N.D. Kondrat'eva: neokonchennaia teoriia dinamiki i metodologicheskie problemy ekonomicheskoi nauki." *Voprosy ekonomiki* (2002): 4–16.

Malapi-Nelson, Alcibiades. *The Nature of the Machine and the Collapse of Cybernetics: A Transhumanist Lesson for Emerging Technologies*. Basingstoke, UK: Palgrave Macmillan, 2017.

Małecka, Magdalena. "Knowledge, Behaviour, and Policy: Questioning the Epistemic Presuppositions of Applying Behavioural Science in Public Policymaking." *Synthese* 199 (2021): 5311–5338.

Mallard, Gregoire, and Andrew Lakoff, "How Claims to Know the Future Are Used to Understand the Present: Techniques of Prospection in the Field of National Security." In *Social Knowledge in the Making*, edited by Charles Camic, Michele Lamont, and Neil Gross, 339–379. Chicago: University of Chicago Press, 2010.

Mark, James, Artemy M. Kalinovsky, and Steffi Marung, eds. *Alternative Globalizations: Eastern Europe and the Postcolonial World*. Bloomington: Indiana University Press, 2020.

Masani, Pesi. *Norbert Wiener, 1894–1964*. Basel, Switzerland: Birkauser, 1990.

Masco, Joseph. "Bad Weather: On Planetary Crisis." *Social Studies of Science* 40, no. 1 (2010): 7–40.

Mayr, Otto. *Authority, Liberty and Automatic Machinery in Early Modern Europe.* Baltimore: Johns Hopkins University Press, 1986.

McCloskey, Donald. "The Art of Forecasting: From Ancient to Modern Times." *Cato Journal* 12, no. 1 (1992): 23–48.

McCulloch, Warren, and Walter Pitts. "A Logical Calculus of the Ideas Immanent in Nervous Activity." *Bulletin of Mathematical Biophysics* 5 (1943): 115–133.

Meadows, Donella, John Richardson, and Gerhart Bruckman. *Groping in the Dark: The First Decade of Global Modelling.* Chichester, UK: John Wiley & Sons, 1982.

Medina, Eden. *Cybernetic Revolutionaries: Technology and Politics in Allende's Chile.* Cambridge, MA: MIT Press, 2011.

Merton, Robert. *The Sociology of Science: Theoretical and Empirical Investigations.* Chicago: University of Chicago Press, 1972.

Mespoulet, Martine. *Construire le socialisme par les chiffres: enquetes et recensements en URSS de 1917 a 1991.* Paris: Institute National d'Etudes Demographiques, 2008.

Meyer, John W., and Brian Rowan. "Institutionalized Organizations: Formal Structure as Myth and Ceremony." *American Journal of Sociology* 83, no. 2 (1977): 340–363.

Miller, Chris. *The Struggle to Save the Soviet Economy: Mikhail Gorbachev and the Collapse of the USSR.* Chapel Hill: University of North Carolina Press, 2016.

Mills, Mara. "On Disability and Cybernetics: Helen Keller, Norbert Wiener, and the Hearing Glove." *Differences* 22, nos. 2–3 (2011): 74–111.

Mindell, David. *Between Human and Machine: Feedback, Control, and Computing Before Cybernetics.* Baltimore: Johns Hopkins University Press, 2002.

Mirowski, Philip. *Machine Dreams: Economics Becomes a Cyborg Science.* Cambridge: Cambridge University Press, 2002.

Mirowski, Philip. *More Heat Than Light. Economics as Social Physics: Physics as Nature's Economics.* Cambridge: Cambridge University Press, 1999.

Moiseev, Nikita. *Chelovek i noosfera.* Moscow: Molodaia gvardiia, 1990.

Moiseev, Nikita N. *Izbrannye Trudy.* Moscow: Taideks, 2003.

Moiseev, Nikita. *Kak daleko do zavtreshnego dnia . . . Svobodnye razmyshleniia 1917–1993.* Moscow: Taideks, 1997.

Moiseev, Nikita. *Matematika, Upravlienie, Ekonomika.* Moscow: Znanie, 1970.

Moiseev, Nikita. "'Mirovaia dinamika' Forrestera i aktual'nye voprosy mirovoi evoliutsii." In *Mirovaia dinamika*, Jay Forrester, 264–290. Moscow: Nauka, 1978.

Moiseev, Nikita. "A New Look at Evolution: Marx, Teilhard de Chardin, Vernadsky." *World Futures* 36, no. 1 (1993): 1–19.

Moiseev, Nikita. *Prosteishiie matematicheskie modeli ekonomicheskogo prognozirovaniia.* Moscow: Znanie, 1975.

Moiseev, Nikita. *Chelovek, sreda, obshchestvo: problemy formalizovannogo opisaniia.* Moscow: Nauka, 1982.

Moiseev, Nikita. *Algoritmy razvitiia.* Moscow: Nauka, 1987.

Moiseev, Nikita. "Reflection on Noosphere: Humanism in Our Time." In *The Biosphere and Noosphere Reader: Global Environment, Society and Change*, edited by David Pitt and Paul Samson, 167–179. London: Routledge, 1999.

Moiseev, Nikita, and Ivan T. Frolov. "Vysokoe soprikosnovenie: obshchesto, chelovek, i priroda v vek mikroelektroniki, informatiki i biotekhnologii." *Voprosy filosofii* 9 (1984): 24–41.

Moiseev, Nikita, Vladimir Aleksandrov, and Aleksandr Tarko. *Chelovek i biosfera.* Moscow: Mysl', 1985.

Montagnini, Leone. *Harmonies of Disorder: Norbert Wiener, a Mathematician-Philosopher of Our Time.* Berlin: Springer, 2017.

BIBLIOGRAPHY

Moon, David. "Estimating the Peasant Population of Late Imperial Russia from the 1897 Census: A Research Note." *Europe-Asia Studies* 48, no. 1 (1996): 141–153.

Morgan, Mary S. "Narrative Inference with and without Statistics: Making Sense of Economic Cycles with Malthus and Kondratiev." *History of Political Economy* 53S (2021): 113–138.

Moxley, Roy. "Ernst Mach and B. F Skinner: Their Similarities with Two Traditions for Verbal Behavior." *Behavior Analyst* 28, no. 1 (2005): 29–48.

Murav'ev, Valerian. *Ovladenie vremenem kak osnovnaia zadacha truda.* Moscow: Mospoligraf, 1924.

Murphy, Jack. "Russian Reflexive Control Is Subverting the American Political Landscape." *Sofrep* (26 September 2018), https://sofrep.com/news/russian-reflexive-control-is-subverting-the-american-political-landscape/.

Naylor, Simon, and Simon Schaffer. "Nineteenth-century Survey Sciences: Enterprises, Expeditions and Exhibitions." *Notes and Records* 73, no. 2 (2019): 135–147.

Netesova, Iuliia. "Upravliaiushchie katastrofoi: refleksivnye modeli sovetskogo i amerikanskogo obshchestv." *Ruskii zhurnal* (Summer 2008): 129–130.

Neumann, Iver B. "Russia's Europe, 1991–2016: Inferiority to Superiority." *International Affairs* 92, no. 6 (2016): 1381–1399.

Northcott, Robert. "When Are Purely Predictive Models Best?" *Disputatio* 9, no. 47 (2017): 631–656.

Norton, John. *The Material Theory of Induction.* Calgary, AB: University of Calgary Press, 2021.

Nowotny, Helga. *The Cunning of Uncertainty.* Cambridge, UK: Polity Press, 2016.

Oatley, Keith. *Our Minds, Our Selves.* Princeton, NJ: Princeton University Press, 2018.

Odum, Eugene. *Fundamentals of Ecology.* Philadelphia: W. B. Saunders Co, 1959

Oels, Angela. "Climate Security as Governmentality: From Precaution to Preparedness." In *Governing the Climate: New Approaches to Rationality, Power and Politics,* edited by Johannes Stripple and Harriet Bulkeley, 197–216. Cambridge: Cambridge University Press, 2013.

Oittinen, Vesa, ed. *Evald Ilyenkov's Philosophy Revisited.* Helsinki, Finland: Kikimora, 2000.

Oldfield, Jonathan. "Mikhail Budyko's (1920–2001) Contributions to Global Climate Science: From Heat Balances to Climate Change and Global Ecology." *WIREs Climate Change* 7, no. 5 (2016): 682–692.

Oldfield, Jonathan. "Russia, Systemic Transformation and the Concept of Sustainable Development." *Environmental Politics* 10, no. 3 (2001): 94–110.

Oldfield, Jonathan. *The Soviet Union and Global Environmental Change: Modifying the Biosphere and Conceptualizing Society–Nature Interaction.* London: Routledge, 2021.

Oldfield, Jonathan, and Denis Shaw, eds. *The Development of Russian Environmental Thought: Scientific and Geographical Perspectives on the Natural Environment.* London: Routledge, 2016.

Oldfield, Jonathan, and Denis Shaw. "V. I. Vernadskii and the Development of Biogeochemical Understandings of the Biosphere, *c.*1880s–1968." *British Journal for the History of Science* 46, no. 2 (2013): 287–310.

O'Neill, Christopher. "Taylorism, the European Science of Work, and the Quantified Self at Work." *Science, Technology and Human Values* 42, no. 4 (2017): 600–621.

O'Rand, Angela, and Robert A. Ellis. "Social Class and Social Time Perspective." *Social Forces* 53, no. 1 (1974): 53–62.

Oreskes, Naomi. "The Fact of Uncertainty, the Uncertainty of Facts and the Cultural Resonance of Doubt." *Philosophical Transactions of the Royal Society Series A Mathematical Physical and Engineering Sciences* 373, no. 2055 (2015): 1–21.

Oreskes, Naomi, and Erik M. Conway. *Merchants of Doubt: How a Handful of Scientists Obscured the Truth on Issues from Tobacco Smoke to Climate Change*. London: Bloomsbury, 2011.

O'Riordan, Timothy, and Steve Rayner. "Risk Management for Global Environmental Change." *Global Environmental Change* 1, no. 2 (1991): 91–108.

Osintseva, Tatiana. "Novaia utka," http://prometa.ru, accessed 10 April 2015.

Osler, Margaret J. *Rethinking the Scientific Revolution*. Cambridge: Cambridge University Press, 2000.

Otter, Chris. *The Victorian Eye: A Political History of Light and Vision in Britain, 1800–1910*. Chicago: University of Chicago Press, 2008.

Ovchinnikova, N. V., ed. *Istoriia upravlencheskoi mysli*. Moscow: RGGU, 2013.

Parisi, Luciano. *Contagious Architecture: Computation, Aesthetics and Space*. Cambridge, MA: MIT Press, 2013.

Pels, Dick. "Reflexivity: One Step Up." *Theory, Culture and Society* 17, no. 3 (2000): 1–25.

Pestre, Dominique. "Complex Systems and Total War: British Operational Research and the PM Statistical Branch at the Beginning of World War II." In *Nature Engaged: Science in Practice from the Renaissance to the Present*, edited by N. Biagoli and J. Riskin, 83–100. New York: Palgrave Macmillan, 2012.

Peters, Benjamin. *How Not to Network a Nation: The Uneasy History of the Soviet Internet*. Cambridge, MA: MIT Press, 2016.

Petronis, Vytautas. "Mapping Lithuanians: The Development of Russian Imperial Ethnic Cartography, 1840s–1860s." *Imago Mundi* 63, no. 1 (2011): 62–75.

Petrov, Aleksandr A. *Nikita Nikolaevich Moiseev: Sud'ba strany v sud'be uchenogo*. Moscow: Ekologiia i zhizn, 2011.

Petryna, Adriana. *Horizon Work: At the Edges of Knowledge in an Age of Runaway Climate Change*. Princeton, NJ: Princeton University Press, 2022.

Pickering, Andrew. *The Mangle of Practice: Time, Agency, Science*. Chicago: University of Chicago Press, 1995.

Pickering, Andrew. *The Cybernetic Brain: Sketches of Another Future*. Chicago: University of Chicago Press, 2010.

Pietruska, Jamie. *Looking Forward: Prediction in America*. Chicago: University of Chicago Press, 2017.

Piskoppel´, Anatolii. "K tvorcheskoi biografii G.P. Shchedrovitskogo (1929–1994)." In *Izbrannye Trudy*, edited by G. P. Shchedrovitskii, xxxii–xxxiii. Moscow: Shkola kul´turnoi politiki, 1995.

Podvig, Pavel. "History and the Current Status of the Russian Early Warning System." *Science and Global Security* 10 (2002): 21–60.

Pomerantsev, Peter. *This Is Not Propaganda: Adventures in the War Against Reality*. London: Faber & Faber, 2019.

Poovey, Mary. *A History of the Modern Fact: Problems of Knowledge in the Sciences of Wealth and Society*. Chicago: University of Chicago Press, 1998.

Poovey, Mary. *Making a Social Body: British Cultural Formation, 1830–1864*. Chicago: University of Chicago Press, 1995.

Porter, Theodore. "Thin Description: Surface and Depth in Science and Science Studies." *Osiris* 27, no. 1 (2012): 209–226.

Porter, Theodore. *Trust in Numbers: The Pursuit of Objectivity in Science and Public Life*. Princeton, NJ: Princeton University Press, 1995.

Pospelov, G. S., and V. I. Maksimenko. "Predislovie." In *Gorizonty nauki i tekhniki*, edited by I. V. Bestuzhev-Lada and R. A. Fesenko, 5–17. Moscow: Mir, 1969.

Power, D. J. *A Brief History of Decision Support Systems*. DSSResources.com, version 4.0 (10 March 2007).

268 BIBLIOGRAPHY

Power, Michael. *The Audit Society: Rituals of Verification.* Oxford: Oxford University Press, 1997.

Power, Michael. *Organized Uncertainty: Designing a World of Risk Management.* Oxford: Oxford University Press, 2007.

Priestland, David. *Merchant, Soldier, Sage: A New History of Power.* London: Allen, 2012.

Primakov, Evgenii. "Nikita Moiseev—vydaiushchii'sia uchenyi' i grazhdanin." *Alma Mater* 6 (2007): 43.

Prpic, Martina. "The Open Method of Coordination." European Parliamentary Research Service, PE 542.142 (2014), 1–2.

Prudenko, Ianina. *Kibernetika v gumanitarnykh naukakh i iskusstve v SSSR: Analiz bol'shikh baz dannykh i komp'iuternoe tvorchestvo.* Moscow: Garazh, 2018.

Pynnöniemi, Katri. "Russia's National Security Strategy: Analysis of Conceptual Evolution." *Journal of Slavic Military Studies* 31, no. 2 (2018): 240–256.

Pynnöniemi, Katri. "Russia's War against Ukraine: Wider Implications." Paper presented at discussion panel, Aleksanteri Institute, 4 March 2022.

Radin, Beryl. *Beyond Machiavelli: Policy Analysis Comes of Age.* Washington, DC: Georgetown University Press, 2000.

Raikhel, Eugene. *Governing Habits: Treating Alcoholism in Post-Soviet Clinic.* Ithaca, NY: Cornell University Press, 2016.

Raikhel, Eugene. "Reflex/Рефлекс." *Somatosphere* (November 2014). http://somatosphere .net/2014/reflex%D1%80%D0%B5%D1%84%D0%BB%D0%B5%D0%BA%D1%81 .html/

Raphals, Lisa. *Divination and Prediction in Early China and Ancient Greece.* Cambridge: Cambridge University Press, 2013.

Raphals, Lisa. "The Ethics of Prediction." In *How Should One Live? Comparing Ethics in Ancient China and Greco-Roman Antiquity,* edited by R. A. H. King and Dennis Schilling, 278–303. Berlin: De Gruyter, 2011.

Rapoport, Anatol. "Foreword." In *Algebra of Conscience: A Comparative Analysis of Western and Soviet Ethical Systems,* edited by Vladimir Lefebvre, vii–xii. Dordrecht, Holland: D. Reidel, 1982.

Rapoport, Anatol and Vladimir Lefebvre. "Vozmozhno li samoosvobozhdenie?" *Chelovek* 5 (1991): 79–85.

Rappaport, A. G. "V.A. Lefevr—20 (50) let spustia." *Refleksivnye protsessy i upravlenie* 16, nos. 1–2 (2016): 85–91.

Rayner, Steve. "Uncomfortable Knowledge: The Social Construction of Ignorance in Science and Environmental Policy Discourses." *Economy and Society* 41, no. 1 (2012): 107–125.

Repin, V. G. "Sobytie i liudi." In *Rubezhi oborony: v kosmose i na zemle. Ocherki istorii rakteno-kosmicheskoi oborony,* edited by N. G. Zavalin, 433–472. Moscow: Veche, 2003.

Rice, Condoleezza. "The Party, the Military, and Decision Authority in the Soviet Union." *World Politics* 40, no. 1 (October 1987): 55–81.

Rich, Nathaniel. "The New Science of Disaster Prediction." *New Yorker,* 19 November 2013, https://www.newyorker.com/news/news-desk/the-new-science-of-disaster -prediction.

Rid, Thomas. *Rise of the Machines: The Lost History of Cybernetics.* London: Scribe, 2016.

Riegler, Alexander, Karl Muller, and Stuart Umpleby, eds. *New Horizons for Second Order Cybernetics.* Hackensack, NJ: World Scientific, 2017.

Rindzevičiūtė, Eglė. *Constructing Soviet Cultural Policy: Cybernetics and Governance in Lithuania after World War II.* Linköping, Sweden: Linköping University, 2008.

Rindzevičiūtė, Eglė. *The Power of Systems: How Policy Sciences Opened Up the Cold War World*. Ithaca, NY: Cornell University Press, 2016.

Rindzevičiūtė, Eglė. "Purification and Hybridisation of Soviet Cybernetics: The Politics of Scientific Governance in an Authoritarian Regime." *Archiv fur sozialgeschichte* 50 (2010): 289–309.

Rindzevičiūtė, Eglė. "Toward a Joint Future Beyond the Iron Curtain: East–West Politics of Global Modelling." In *The Struggle for the Long-Term in Transnational Science and Politics: Forging the Future*, edited by Jenny Andersson and Eglė Rindzevičiūtė, 115–143. London: Routledge, 2015.

Rindzevičiūtė, Eglė. "The Unlikely Revolutionaries: Decision Sciences in the Soviet Government." In *The Decisionist Imagination: Sovereignty, Social Science and Democracy in the 20th Century*, edited by Daniel Bessner and Nicolas Guilhot, 217–249. Oxford: Berghahn Books, 2019.

Rindzevičiūtė, Eglė. "When Formal Organisations Meet Informal Relations in Soviet Lithuania: Action Nets, Networks and Boundary Objects in the Construction of the Lithuanian Sea Museum." *Lithuanian Historical Studies* 15 (2011): 107–134.

Rispoli, Giulia. "Between 'Biosphere' and 'Gaia': Earth as a Living Organism in Soviet Geo-ecology." *Cosmos and History: The Journal of Natural and Social Philosophy* 10, no. 2 (2014): 78–91.

Robertson, Thomas. "Revisiting the Early 1970s Commoner–Erlich Debate About Population and Environment: Dueling Critiques of Production and Consumption in the Global Age." In *A World of Populations: Transnational Perspectives on Demography*, edited by Heinrich Hartmann and Corinna Unger, 108–125. New York: Berghahn, 2014.

Robin, Libby, Sverker Sörlin, and Paul Warde, eds. *The Future of Nature: The Documents of Global Change*. New Haven, CT: Yale University Press, 2013.

Robin, Ron. *The Cold World They Made: The Strategic Legacy of Roberta and Albert Wohlstetter*. Cambridge, MA: Harvard University Press, 2016.

Rocca, Gordon. "'A Second Party in Our Midst': The History of the Soviet Scientific Forecasting Association." *Social Studies of Science* 11, no. 2 (1981): 199–247.

Rockström, Johan, Will Steffen, Kevin Noone, Åsa Persson, F. Stuart III Chapin, Eric Lambin, Timothy M. Lenton, et al. "Planetary Boundaries: Exploring the Safe Operating Space for Humanity." *Ecology and Society* 14, no. 2 (2009), https://www.ecologyandsociety.org/vol14/iss2/art32/.

Rogacheva, Maria. *The Private World of Soviet Scientists: From Stalin to Gorbachev*. Cambridge: Cambridge University Press, 2017.

Rohde, Joy. *Armed with Expertise: The Militarization of American Social Research during the Cold War*. Ithaca, NY: Cornell University Press, 2013.

Rose, Nikolas. *The Powers of Freedom: Reframing Political Thought*. Cambridge: Cambridge University Press, 1999.

Rosenberg, Alex. "From Rational Choice to Reflexivity: Learning from Sen, Keynes, Hayek, Soros, and Most of All, from Darwin." *Economic Thought* 3, no. 1 (2014): 21–41.

Rosenblueth, Arturo, Norbert Wiener, and Julian Bigelow. "Behavior, Purpose and Teleology." *Philosophy of Science* 10, no. 1 (1943): 18–24.

Rosier, Bernard, ed. *Wassily Leontief: textes et itinéraire*. Paris: La Découverte, 1986.

Rowell, S. C. "The Jagellonians and the Stars: Dynasty-Sponsored Astrology in the Fifteenth Century." *Lithuanian Historical Studies* 7 (2002): 23–42.

Rubinson, Paul. "The Global Effects of Nuclear Winter: Science and Antinuclear Protest in the United States and the Soviet Union During the 1980s." *Cold War History* 14 (2014): 47–69.

270 BIBLIOGRAPHY

Rubinson, Paul. *Redefining Science: Scientists, the National Security State, and Nuclear Weapons in Cold War America*. Amherst: University of Massachusetts Press, 2016.

Ruiz Palmer, Diego A. "Back to the Future: Russia's Hybrid Warfare, Revolutions in Military Affairs, and Cold War Comparisons." *NATO Defence College Research Paper* 120 (2015): 1–12.

Ruppert, Evelyn, Engin Isin, and Dider Bigo. "Data Politics." *Big Data & Society* 4, no. 2 (2017): 1–7.

Russell, Stuart. *Human Compatible: Artificial Intelligence and the Problem of Control*. London: Viking, 2019.

Rutland, Peter. *The Myth of the Plan: Lessons of Soviet Planning Experience*. London: Open Court, 1985.

Sakwa, Richard. "The Soviet Collapse: Contradictions and Neo-Modernisation." *Journal of Eurasian Studies* 4 (2013): 65–77.

Salmon, Wesley C. "Rational Prediction." *British Journal for the Philosophy of Science* 32, no. 2 (1981): 115–125.

Samuelson, Lennart. *Tankograd: The Formation of a Soviet Company Town: Cheliabinsk, 1900s–1950s*. Basingstoke, UK: Palgrave Macmillan, 2011.

Sandomirskaja, Irina. *Blokada v slove: Ocherki kriticheskoi teorii i biopolitiki iazyka*. Moscow: NLO, 2013.

Santangelo, Federico. *Divination, Prediction and the End of the Roman Republic*. Cambridge: Cambridge University Press, 2013.

Sapov, Grigorii. "Tri interv'iu s E.B. Ershovym" (February to March 1999), http://www.sapov.ru/staroe/si06.html.

Saunders, Max. *Imagined Futures: Writing, Science and Modernity in the To-Day and To-Morrow Book Series, 1923–31*. Oxford: Oxford University Press, 2019.

Schellnhuber, Hans Joachim, and Volker Wenzel, eds. *Earth System Analysis: Integrating Science for Sustainability*. Berlin: Springer, 2013.

Schmelzer, Matthias. *The Hegemony of Growth: The OECD and the Making of the Economic Growth Paradigm*. Cambridge: Cambridge University Press, 2016.

Schmid, Sonja. "Chernobyl: Data Wars and Disaster Politics." *Nature* 566, no. 7745 (2019): 450.

Schmidgen, Henning. "Cybernetic Times: Norbert Wiener, John Stroud, and the 'Brain Clock' Hypothesis." *History of Human Sciences* 33, no. 1 (2020): 80–108.

Schrickel, Isabell. "Von Schmetterlingen und Atomreaktoren: Medien und Politiken der Resilienz am IIASA." *Behemoth* 7, no. 2 (2014): 5–25.

Schumann, Andrew. "Rationality in Belarusian Thinking." *Studies in Logic, Grammar and Rhetoric* 13, no. 26 (2008): 7–26.

Schwartz, Lee. "A History of Russian and Soviet Censuses." In *Research Guide to the Russian and Soviet Censuses*, edited by Ralph Clem, 48–69. Ithaca, NY: Cornell University Press, 1986.

Scott, Bernard. "The Sociocybernetics of Observation and Reflexivity." *Current Sociology* 67, no. 4 (2019): 495–510.

Scott, James C. *Seeing Like a State: How Certain Schemes to Improve the Human Condition Have Failed*. New Haven, CT: Yale University Press, 1999.

Sebastián-Enesco, Carla, and Felix Warneken. "The Shadow of the Future: 5-Year-Olds, but Not 3-Year-Olds, Adjust Their Sharing in Anticipation of Reciprocation." *Journal of Experimental Child Psychology* 129 (2015): 40–54.

Seefried, Elke. "Globalized Science: The 1970s Futures Field." *Centaurus: An International Journal of History of Science and Its Cultural Aspects* 59, nos. 1–2 (2017): 40–57.

Seefried, Elke. "Steering the Future: The Emergence of 'Western' Futures Research and Its Production of Expertise, 1950s to Early 1970s." *European Journal of Futures Research* 2, no. 29 (2014), doi:10.1007/s40309-013-0029-y.

Seely, Robert. "Defining Contemporary Russian Warfare: Beyond the Hybrid Headline." *RUSI Journal* 162, no. 1 (2017): 50–59.

Semenov, I. N. "Personologiia zhiznetvorchestva V.A. Lefevra i razvitie refleksivnykh nauk (ot logiki i psikhologii cherez kibernetiku i etiku k kosmologii)." *Refleksivnye protsesy i upravlenie* 16, nos. 1–2 (2016): 100–106.

Seneta, E. "Early Influences on Probability and Statistics in the Russian Empire." *Archive for History of Exact Sciences* 53 (1998): 201–213.

Seneta, Eugene. "A Sketch of the History of Survey Sampling in Russia." *Journal of the Royal Statistical Society* 148, no.2 (1985): 118–125.

Serafin, Rafal. "Noosphere, Gaia and the Science of the Biosphere." *Environmental Ethics* 10, no. 2 (1988): 121–137.

Seth, Anil K. "The Cybernetic Bayesian Brain: From Interoceptive Inference to Sensorimotor Contingencies." In *Open MIND*, edited by T. Metzinger and J. M. Windt, 1–24. Frankfurt am Main: MIND Group, 2020, doi:10.15502/9783958570108.

Seth, Suman. *Difference and Disease: Medicine, Race, and Locality in the Eighteenth-Century British Empire*. Cambridge: Cambridge University Press, 2018.

Shafir, Eldar, ed. *The Behavioral Foundations of Public Policy*. Princeton, NJ: Princeton University Press, 2013.

Shalin, Dmitri N. "The Development of Soviet Sociology, 1956–1976," *Annual Review of Sociology* 4 (1978): 171–191.

Shane, Scott. *Dismantling Utopia: How Information Ended the Soviet Union*. Chicago: Ivan R. Dee, 1994.

Shanin, Teodor, ed. *Peasants and Peasant Societies*. Oxford: Blackwell, 1987.

Shchedrovitskii, Georgii. "Budushchee est´ rabota myshleniia i deistviia." *Voprosy metodologii* 3–4 (1994), https://www.fondgp.ru/publications/.

Shchedrovitskii, Georgii. *Ia vsegda byl idealistom . . .* Moscow: NNF Institut razvitiia im. G.P. Shchedrovitskogo, 2001.

Shchedrovitskii, Georgii. *Izbrannye Trudy*. Moscow: Shkola kul´turnoi politiki, 1995.

Shchedrovitskii, Georgii. "Lektsiia 1: 18 fevralia 1988." In *Zapisi Rizhskogo metodologicheskogo seminara*, vol. 1, 27–28. Riga, Latvia: BISI, 2010.

Shchedrovitskii, Georgii. "Lektsiia 2: 19 fevralia 1988." In *Zapisi Rizhskogo metodologicheskogo seminara*, vol. 1, 65. Riga, Latvia: BISI, 2010.

Shchedrovitskii, Georgii. "Mental Activity and Pure Thought." In *Methodological School of Management*, edited by V. B. Khristenko, A. G. Reus, and A. P. Zinchenko, 33–50. London: Bloomsbury, 2014.

Shchedrovitskii, Georgii. *Organizatsiia, rukovodstvo, upravlenie II*. Moscow: Put´, 2003.

Shchedrovitskii, Georgii. "Organizatsionno-deiatel´nostnaia igra kak novaia forma organizatsii i metod razvitiia kollektivnoi mysledeiatel´nosti (1983)." In *Izbrannye Trudy* by Georgii Shchedrovitskii, 115–142. Moscow: Shkola kul´turnoi politiki, 1995.

Shchedrovitskii, Georgii. *Orgupravlencheskoe myshlenie: ideologiia, metodologiia, tekhnologiia*. Moscow: Studia Artemeva Lebedeva, 2013.

Shchedrovitskii, Georgii. "Perspektivy i programmy razvitiia SMD-metodologii," http://bdn-steiner.ru/modules.php?name=Archives&l_op=visit&lid=31.

Shchedrovitskii, Georgii. "Printsipy i obshchaia skhema metodologicheskoi organizatsii sistemno-strukturnykh issledovanii i razrabotok (1981)." In *Izbrannye Trudy* by Georgii Shchedrovitskii, 88–114. Moscow: Shkola kul´turnoi politiki, 1995.

Shchedrovitskii, Georgii. "Problemy metodologii sistemnogo issledovaniia (1964)." In *Izbrannye Trudy* by Georgii Shchedrovitskii, 155–196. Moscow: Shkola kul'turnoi politiki, 1995.

Shchedrovitskii, Georgii. "Refleksiia" (1974). In *Izbrannye Trudy* by Georgii Shchedrovitskii, 485–495. Moscow: Shkola kul'turnoi politiki, 1995.

Shchedrovitskii, Georgii. "Sistemnoe dvizhenie i perspektivy razvitiia sistemnostrukturnoi metodologii." In *Izbrannye Trudy*, 57–87. Moscow: Shkola kul'turnoi politiki, 1995.

Shchedrovitskii, Georgii, and S. I. Kotel'nikov. "Organizatsionno-deiatel'nostnaia igra kak novaia forma organizatsii i metod razvitiia kollektivnoi mysledeiatel'nosti (1983)." In *Izbrannye Trudy* by Georgii Shchedrovitskii, 113–142. Moscow: Shkola kul'turnoi politiki, 1995.

Shchedrovitskii, Petr. "Predislovie." In *Orgupravlencheskoe myshlenie: ideologiia, metodologiia, tekhnologiia* by Georgii Shchedrovitskii, 9–21. Moscow: Izdatel'stvo Studii Artemiia Lebedeva, 2014.

Shmelev, Stanislav. *Ecological Economics: Sustainability in Practice*. Berlin: Springer, 2012.

Siddiqi, Asif. "Atomized Urbanism: Secrecy and Security from the Gulag to the Closed City." *Urban History* (2021): 1–21.

Siddiqqi, Asif. *The Red Rocket's Glare: Spaceflight and the Russian Imagination, 1857–1957*. Cambridge: Cambridge University Press, 2010.

Siddiqi, Asif. "Scientists and Specialists in the Gulag: Life and Death in Stalin's Sharashka." *Kritika* 16, no. 3 (2015): 557–588.

Siegmund, David O. "Probability Theory." *Encyclopaedia Britannica* (2018), https://www.britannica.com/science/probability-theory/Conditional-expectation-and-least-squares-prediction#ref407444.

Sigman, Carole. "Les clubs politiques informels acteurs du basculement de la perestroika." *Revue française de science politique* 5, no. 58 (2008): 617–642.

Simandan, Dragos. "Wisdom and Foresight in Chinese Thought: Sensing the Immediate Future." *Journal of Future Studies* 22, no. 3 (2018): 35–50.

Simbirski, Brian. "Cybernetic Muse: Hannah Arendt on Automation, 1951–1958." *Journal of the History of Ideas* 77, no. 4 (2016): 589–613.

Sirmon, David G., Michael A. Hitt, R. Duane Ireland, and Brett Anitra Gilbert. "Resource Orchestration to Create Competitive Advantage: Breadth, Depth, and Life Cycle Effects." *Journal of Management* 37, no. 5 (2011): 1390–1412.

Siskin, Clifford. *System: The Shaping of Modern Knowledge*. Cambridge, MA: MIT Press, 2016.

Skinner, B. F. *Beyond Freedom and Dignity*. New York: Pelican, 1971.

Slayton, Rebecca. *Arguments That Count: Physics, Computing, and Missile Defense, 1949–2012*. Cambridge, MA: MIT Press, 2013.

Slezkine, Yuri. *The House of Government: A Saga of the Russian Revolution*. Princeton, NJ: Princeton University Press, 2017.

Slobodian, Quinn. *Globalists: The End of Empire and the Birth of Neoliberalism*. Cambridge, MA: Harvard University Press, 2018.

Smil, Vaclav. *Growth: From Microorganisms to Megacities*. Cambridge, MA: MIT Press, 2019.

Smith, James Howard. *Bewitching Development: Witchcraft and Reinvention of Development in Neoliberal Kenya*. Chicago: University of Chicago Press, 2008.

Smith, Roger. "Does Reflexivity Separate the Human Sciences from the Natural Sciences?" *History of the Human Sciences* 18, no. 4 (2005): 1–25.

Smolian, Georgii. "Refleksivnoe upravlenie: tekhnologiia priniatiia manipuliativnykh reshenii." *Trudy instituta sistemnogo analiza RAN* 63, no. 2 (2013): 54–61.

Smolian, Georgii. "Sub'ektivnye zametki k iubileiu V.A. Lefevra." *Refleksivnye protsessy i upravlenie* 6, no. 1 (2006): 14–26.

Smolian, Georgii, and Galina Solntseva. "Vladimir Lefevr i Viktor Pelevin ob upravlenie vyborom resheniia." Unpublished paper presented at "Reflexive Processes and Governance," RAN Institute of Philosophy, Moscow, 1–18 October 2013.

Snegovaya, Maria. *Putin's Information Warfare in Ukraine: Soviet Origins of Russian Hybrid Warfare, Russia Report I.* Washington, DC: NATO STRATCOM, 2015.

Snow, C. P. *The Two Cultures and the Scientific Revolution.* New York: Cambridge University Press, 1961.

Snyder, Joel. "'Las Meninas' and the Mirror of the Prince." *Critical Inquiry* 11, no. 4 (1983): 539–572.

Sokolov, Kirill, and Avril Pyman. "Father Pavel Florensky and Vladimir Favorsky: Mutual Insights into the Perception of Space." *Leonardo* 22, no. 2 (1989): 237–244.

Solovey, Mark, and Hamilton Cravens, eds. *Cold War Social Science: Knowledge Production, Liberal Democracy, and Human Nature.* Basingstoke, UK: Macmillan, 2012.

Sommer, Vítězslav. "Forecasting the Post-Socialist Future: Prognostika in Late Socialist Czechoslovakia, 1970–1989." In *The Struggle for the Long Term in Transnational Science and Politics during the Cold War,* edited by Jenny Andersson and Eglė Rindzevičiūtė, 144–168. New York: Routledge, 2015.

Sorokin, Pitirim. "A Survey of the Cyclical Conceptions of Social and Historical Process." *Social Forces* 6, no. 1 (1927): 28–40.

Soros, George. *The Crisis of Global Capitalism: Open Society Endangered.* London: Little, 1998.

Soros, George. "Fallibility, Reflexivity, and the Human Uncertainty Principle." *Journal of Economic Methodology* 20, no. 4 (2014): 309–329.

Sprang, Ronald W. "The Development of Operational Art and CEMA in Multi-Domain Battle during the Guadalcanal Campaign 1942–1943 and Russia in the Ukraine 2013–2016." School of Advanced Military Studies, US Army Command and General Staff College, Fort Leavenworth, 2018.

Staley, Richard. "The Interwar Period as a Machine Age: Mechanics, the Machine, Mechanisms and the Market in Discourse." *Science in Context* 31, no. 3 (2018): 263–292.

Steffen, Will, Katherine Richardson, Johan Rockström, Sarah E. Cornell, Ingo Fetzer, Elena M. Bennett, Reinette Biggs, et al. "Planetary Boundaries: Guiding Human Development on a Changing Planet." *Science* 347, 1259855 (2015), 736–746.

Stites, Richard. *The Revolutionary Dreams: Utopian Vision and Experimental Life in the Russian Revolution.* Oxford: Oxford University Press, 1989.

Stockdale, Liam P. D. *Taming an Uncertain Future: Temporality, Sovereignty, and the Politics of Anticipatory Governance.* London: Rowman & Littlefield, 2016.

Sutela, Pekka. *Economic Thought and Economic Reform in the Soviet Union.* Cambridge: Cambridge University Press, 1991.

Sutela, Pekka. *Socialism, Planning and Optimality: A Study in Soviet Economic Thought.* Helsinki, Finland: Finnish Society of Science and Letters, 1984.

Taagepera, Rein. *Making Social Science More Scientific: The Need for Predictive Models.* Oxford: Oxford University Press, 2008.

Tabatchnikova, Svetlana. *Le cercle de méthodologie de Moscou (1954–1988): Une pensée, une pratique.* Paris: EHESS, 2007.

Tatarchenko, Ksenia. "Calculating a Showcase: Mikhail Lavrentiev, the Politics of Expertise, and the International Life of the Siberian Science-City." *Historical Studies in the Natural Sciences* 46, no. 5 (2016): 592–632.

Teilhard de Chardin, Pierre. *The Phenomenon of Man.* New York: Harper, 1959.

Tetlock, Philip, and Dan Gardner. *Superforecasting: The Art and Science of Prediction.* New York: Random House, 2016.

Thomas, Timothy L. "Russian Military Thought: Concepts and Elements." MITRE Corporation, August 2019, 44–46.

Thomas, Timothy. "Russia's Military Strategy and Ukraine: Indirect, Asymmetric, and Putin-Led." *Journal of Slavic Military Studies* 28, no. 3 (2015): 445–461.

Thomas, Timothy L. "Russia's Reflexive Control Theory and the Military." *Journal of Slavic Military Studies* 17 (2004): 237–256.

Thomas, Will. *The Rational Action: The Sciences of Policy in Britain and America, 1940-1960.* Cambridge, MA: MIT Press, 2015.

Titarenko, Larissa, and Elena Zdravomyslova. *Sociology in Russia: A Brief History.* Cham, Switzerland: Palgrave, 2017.

Trappl, Robert, ed. *Power, Autonomy, Utopia: New Approaches toward Complex Systems.* New York: Plenum Press, 1986.

Travin, Dmitry, and Otar Marganiya. "Resource Curse: Rethinking the Soviet Experience." In *Resource Curse and Post-Soviet Eurasia: Oil, Gas and Modernization,* edited by Vladimir Gel'man and Otar Marganiya, 23–38. New York: Lexington Books, 2010.

Tsygichko, Vitalii. "Predislovie ko vtorumu izdaniiu." In *Algebra konflikta,* Vladimir Lefebvre and Georgii Smolian, 1–2. Moscow: Librokom, 2013.

Turner, Fred. *From Counterculture to Cyberculture: Stewart Brand, the Whole Earth Network, and the Rise of Digital Utopianism.* Chicago: University of Chicago Press, 2006.

Umpleby, Stuart. "From Complexity to Reflexivity: Underlying Logics Used in Science." *Journal of the Washington Academy of Sciences* 96, no. 1 (2010): 15–26.

Usov, Vladimir. *Refleksivnoe upravlenie: filosofsko-metodologicheskii aspect.* Cheliabinsk: Iurgu, 2010.

Vaino, Anton. "Kapitalizatsiia budushchego." *Voprosy ekonomiki i prava* 4 (2012): 42–57.

Valeriano, Brandon, and Ryan Maness. "Fancy Bears and Digital Trolls: Cyber Strategy with a Russian Twist." *Journal of Strategic Studies* 42, no. 2 (2019): 212–234.

Valsiner, Joan. "From Energy to Collectivity: A Commentary on the Development of Bekhterev's Theoretical Views." In *Collective Reflexology,* V. M. Bekhterev, 1–12. Abingdon: Routledge, 2017.

van Munster, Rens, and Casper Sylvester, eds. *The Politics of Globality Since 1945: Assembling the Planet.* London: Routledge, 2016.

Velmet, Aro. "The Blank Slate E-State: Estonian Information Society and the Politics of Novelty in the 1990s." *Engaging Science, Technology, and Society* 6 (2020): 162–184.

Verdery, Katherine. *Secrets and Truths: Ethnography in the Archive of Romania's Secret Police.* Budapest: Central European University Press, 2014.

Vidmer, Richard. "Management Science in the USSR: The Role of 'Americanizers.'" *International Studies Quarterly* 24, no. 3 (1980): 392–414.

Visseren-Hamakers, Ingrid. "Integrative Environmental Governance: Enhancing Governance in the Era of Synergies." *Current Opinion in Environmental Sustainability* 14 (2015): 136–143.

Volkova, Violetta. *Iz istorii teorii sistem i sistemnogo analiza.* St Petersburg.: SPbGPU, 2004.

Vucinich, Alexander. *Science in Russian Culture, 1861-1917.* Stanford, CA: Stanford University Press, 1970.

Vucinich, Alexander. *Social Thought in Tsarist Russia: The Quest for a General Science of Society, 1861-1917.* Chicago: University of Chicago Press, 1976.

Vucinich, Alexander. *Darwin in Russian Thought.* Berkeley: University of California Press, 1989.

Walker, Jeremy, and Melinda Cooper. "Genealogies of Resilience: From Systems Ecology to the Political Economy of Crisis Adaptation." *Security Dialogue* 42, no. 2 (2011): 143–160.

Warde, Paul, and Sverker Sörlin. "Expertise for the Future: The Emergence of 'Relevant Knowledge' in Environmental Predictions and Global Change, c.1920–1970." In *The Struggle for the Long Term in Transnational Science and Politics during the Cold War*, edited by Jenny Andersson and Eglė Rindzevičiūtė, 39–62. New York: Routledge, 2015.

Washburn, Jim. "The Human Equation: UC Irvine Theoretical Psychologist Vladimir Lefebvre Uses Mathematics to Show Us Who We Are." *Los Angeles Times*, 31 March 1993.

Weber, Elke U., and Paul Stern. "Public Understanding of Climate Change in the United States." *American Psychologist* 66, no. 4 (2011): 315–328.

Weick, Karl E. *Making Sense of the Organization*. Oxford: Blackwell, 2001.

Weinberg, Elisabeth. *Sociology in the Soviet Union and Beyond: Social Enquiry and Social Change*. Farnham: Ashgate, 2004.

Weiner, Douglas R. *A Little Corner of Freedom: Russian Nature Protection from Stalin to Gorbachev*. Berkeley: University of California Press, 1999.

Wenger, Andreas, Ursula Jasper, and Myriam Dunn Cavelty, eds. *The Politics and Science of Prevision: Governing and Probing the Future*. London: Routledge, 2020.

Werner, Michael, and Benedicte Zimmerman. "*Histoire Croisée*: Between the Empirical and Reflexivity." *Annales: Histoire, science sociales* 1 (2003): 7–36.

Wiener, Norbert. *Cybernetics: Or Control and Communication in the Animal and the Machine*. Cambridge, MA: MIT Press, 1965 [1948].

Wiener, Norbert. *God and Golem, Inc.: A Comment on Certain Points Where Cybernetics Impinges on Religion*. Cambridge, MA: MIT Press, 1964.

Wiener, Norbert. *The Human Use of Human Beings: Cybernetics and Society*. Boston: Da Capo, 1954.

Wildawsky, Aaron. *Speaking Truth to Power: The Art and Craft of Policy Analysis*. London: Macmillan, 1980.

Williams, Linda L. *Nietzsche's Mirror: The World as Will to Power*. Lanham: Rowan & Littlefield, 2001.

Wojnowski, Michał. "'Zarządzanie refleksyjne' jako paradygmat rosyjskich operacji informacyjno-psychologicznych w XXI w." *Przegląd Bezpieczeństwa Wewnętrznego* 12 (2015): 11–36.

Wolf, Eric. *The People Without History*. Berkeley, CA: University of California Press, 1982.

Wolfe, Joseph. "A History of Business Teaching Games in English-Speaking and Post-Socialist Countries: The Origination and Diffusion of a Management Education and Development Technology." *Simulation and Gaming* 24, no. 4 (1993): 445–463.

Woolgar, Steve, ed. *Knowledge and Reflexivity: New Frontiers in the Sociology of Knowledge*. London: Sage, 1988.

Woolgar, Steve, and Malcolm Ashmore. "The Next Step: Introduction to the Reflexive Project." In *Knowledge and Reflexivity: New Frontiers in the Sociology of Knowledge*, edited by Steve Woolgar, 1–13. London: Sage, 1988.

Wren, Daniel A. "Scientific Management in the U.S.S.R., with Particular Reference to the Contribution of Walter N. Polakov." *Academy of Management Review* 5, no. 1 (1980): 1–11.

Wu, Angela Xiao. "Journalism via Systems Cybernetics: The Birth of Chinese Communication Discipline and Post-Mao Press Reforms." *History of Media Studies*, 2 (2022), doi:10.32376/d895a0ea.182c7595.

276 **BIBLIOGRAPHY**

Wynne, Brian. "Strange Weather, Again: Climate Science as Political Art." *Theory, Culture and Society* 27, nos. 2–3 (2013): 289–305.

Yates, Kit. "Why Mathematicians Sometimes Get Covid Projections Wrong." *Guardian* (UK edition), 26 January 2022.

Young, Oran. *Governing Complex Systems: Social Capital for the Anthropocene*. Cambridge, MA: MIT Press, 2017.

Zan, Luca. "Complexity, Anachronism and Time-Parochialism: Historicising Strategy While Strategising History." *Business History* 58, no. 4 (2016): 571–596.

Zeller, Manfred. "Before and After the End of the World: Rethinking the Soviet Collapse." *Kritika* 18, no. 3 (2017): 591–601.

Ziegler, Charles. *Environmental Policy in the USSR*. Amherst: University of Massachusetts Press, 1987.

Zuboff, Shoshana. *The Age of Surveillance Capitalism: The Fight for a Human Future at the New Frontier of Power*. New York: Profile Books, 2019.

Zubok, Vladislav. *Collapse: The Fall of the Soviet Union*. New Haven, CT: Yale University Press, 2021.

Zubok, Vladislav. *A Failed Empire: The Soviet Union in the Cold War from Stalin to Gorbachev*. Chapel Hill: North Carolina University Press, 2009.

Zubok, Vladislav. *Zhivago's Children: The Last Russian Intelligentsia*. Cambridge, MA: Harvard University Press, 2011.

Zvorykin, A. A. *Cultural Policy in the Union of Soviet Socialist Republics*. Paris: UNESCO, 1970.

Index

Page numbers followed by *f* or n indicate figures or notes.

Abbott, Kenneth, 8
accountability, 100
action-oriented learning, 113
action-oriented prediction processing, 35
actor–network theory, 10, 18
adaptation: "non-modern," 37; reflexive, 129, 151; strategy of nature, 169
adaptive behavior: open-ended, 62; prognosis as component of, 51; role of prediction, 70; supported by information processing, 106
Afanas'ev, Georgii, 131
Aganbegian, Abel, 80, 97
Algebra of Conflict, The (1968), 135, 140
algorithms: of global development, 14; predictions, 12, 27, 188; profiling, 70
All-Union Institute for Systems Research (VNIISI), 93, 97, 111, 135
Anchishkin, Aleksandr, 80, 97
Andersson, Jenny, 3
Andromeda Nebula (1957), 9, 93
antecedent conditions, 24–26, 31
Anthropocene, 14, 155–56, 163–64
antiaircraft systems, 60, 64, 132, 169
Arab-Ogly, Edvard, 88–89, 220n98
Arendt, Hannah, 59, 102
Aronova, Elena, 83
Arrow, Kenneth, 176
artificial intelligence (AI): influence of cybernetics, 32; research, 67, 125; Wiener's impact in field, 59
Ashby, W. Ross, 13, 33, 129
astrology, 20, 38, 45, 99
astronomical vs, meteorological systems, 66
astronomy, 22, 66, 133
authoritarianism: cybernetic, 12, 59; environmental, 13, 189; hidden liberal, 244n90; neoliberal, 233n32; positivist, 26; "scientific", 58; Soviet, 12; technocratic, 3
"autohypnosis" by numbers, 53, 54, 96, 175
automata theory, 15
Automated System of Analysis of Social Information (ASAI), 86

automation: age of, 71; Arendt's critique, 59; technologies, 10
autopoiesis, 32–33, 110, 114

Bacon, Francis, 21
Bateson, Gregory: model of learning, 129; model of self, 233n35
Bauman, Zygmunt, 176–77
Bazarov, Vladimir, 52, 57
Beer, Stafford, 139, 176, 188
behaviorism, 26; cybernetic, 129, 131, 151, 231; methods of time control, 55; neurophysiological, 34–35; Skinnerian, 26, 32, 154, 231n12
Bekhterev, Vladimir, 46, 51
Beloiarsk power plant, 115
Bennett, Tony, 128, 179, 180, 206–7n43
Berg, Axsel, 137
Bernshtein, Nikolai, 55, 109
Bestuzhev-Lada, Igor', 86–96, 98, 219n86, 221n117
Biermann, Frank, 181
Bigelow, Julian, 31, 62, 106
Big Science, 105
biogeocenose, 160
biological determinism, 59
Biosphere, The (1926)
biosphere: governing the, 156, 163; man as manager of, 169; modeling, 161, 164; and noosphere, 165–67; Moiseev's use of idea, 162, 172–73; origin, 155; history of term, 165; theory, 173–76, 178–81, 210n99; Vernadiskii's theory, 159
Birshtein, Maria, 113
blat, 102
Bogdanov, Aleksandr, 167, 242n45
Boolean algebra, 141, 145, 148
bottom-up processing, 33, 106
Bound, John, 29
brain, the: acting machine model, 33; activity, 33; digital model of, 31; predictive, 33–35
brain drain, 137, 164
Breev, Boris, 80

278   INDEX

Brezhnev, Leonid, 78, 110, 136, 137
Bryant, Christopher, 143
Budyko, Mikhail, 93, 131, 165, 166
Buniakovskii, Viktor, 43

Canguilhem, Georges, 59, 154
Carter, Chris, 146, 147
causalities, 50, 66
causal loop, 19, 192
censorship, 85
Central Institute of Mathematical Economics
    at the All-Union Academy of Sciences
    (TsEMI), 77, 100, 135, 137
Central Statistical Agency, 47, 218n58
Centre for Intellectual Resources and
    Cooperation in Societal Sciences
    (TsIRKON), 98, 223n160
Chayanov, Aleksandr, 46
Chernobyl, 164
chronology, problem of, 24, 54
Cicero, 16–17
circular causality, 31, 62, 203n68
Clark, Andy, 34–35
Clegg, Stewart, 146, 147
climate change crisis, 13, 94, 150
climate engineering, 93
"closed worlds", 12
coevolution: conditions for, 169; definitions,
    166; global, 155, 167; organizational forms,
    168, 181
cognition: abstract models, 146; coordinating
    with action, 35; cybernetic approaches, 33;
    form of power, 147; higher levels, 34; part of
    social interaction, 113; self-reflexive model,
    125, 129; Skinner's perspective, 26; special
    form of power, 190
cognitive valuation theory, 138
Cold War: competition, 60, 75, 183; moder-
    nity, 146, 150; politics, 99, 125; strategy, 12,
    13, 139, 140–41, 148; totalitarianism, 12;
    uses of scientific prediction, 5. See also
    Neumann, John von: game theory of
    strategy
collapse of Soviet system, 190–191
collective preferences, 13
Collier, Stephen, 52, 78, 117
commonsense knowledge, 24, 189
commonsense notion of prediction, 192,
    199n4
Communist Party of the Soviet Union
    (CPSU), 5, 12, 110, 156, 164, 191
complexity, levels, 35–36, 50, 153, 168, 172,
    177, 188

Computer Centre, Soviet Academy of
    Sciences, 159, 162, 166, 181
computer modeling: "alternative social
    sciences", 97; global, 156, 166; in policy
    sciences, 33; as social practice, 167, 177–79
Comte, Auguste: influence in Russia, 39, 43,
    49–50, 94; positivist tradition of, 28, 39, 48,
    153, 170, 189; on science and prediction,
    21–22, 150–51
Conflicting Structures (1967), 135
conjectural knowledge(s), 18–21, 175
conjectural science (sciencia coniecturalis), 18
conjectural semiology, 19
conjecture: astrological, 52; Greek tradition of
    conjecture, 16–17; prediction as, 15, 16–20;
    process of, 71; status of, 21
Conjuncture Institute, Moscow, 47, 48, 56
consciousness, 140
control: behavioral, 12, 55, 109, 187; guidance,
    as, 180; problem of, 15, 59; semiotic strategy
    of, 110; revolution, 163; societal, 3, 60, 179;
    Soviet definition, 171; teleological, 169, 170,
    175. See also guided development; reflexive
    control theory: practical of; cybernetic
    control
control science, 60
corruption, 97, 103
Course de philosophie positive (1830–1842),
    21–22
Covid-19, 188
Craik, Kenneth, 68
Crimea: annexation of, 43, 87, 146; War
    (1853–1856), 13
critical thresholds, 173
Crutzen, Paul, 155–56, 163, 164, 173
cultivation, 176–177
cultural sector, 89
culture of forecasting, 12
cultures of prediction, 4, 45, 71, 206n37
cumulative prognosis, 28. See also prognosis
curve fitting, 29
cybernation, 187
cybernetic control, 32, 59, 60, 63, 152, 171–73.
    See also control: teleological
cybernetic engineering systems, 73, 169
cybernetic prediction: critics, 69–71;
    influence, 11; materially mediated, 67;
    misuse for domination, 63; orchestration,
    68, 71, 173; use for social governance, 64;
    Wienerian, 59–62. See also governance
cybernetics: biological, 167; interest in
    goal-oriented processes, 59; history of, 31,
    57–59; institutionalization, 139; "non-modern

INDEX 279

science", 36; posthuman effect, 67; science of
  governance, 72–73, 80; second-order, 9, 32,
  114, 139, 231n15; Soviet, 72, 137, 212n11
*Cybernetics: Or Control and Communication in
  the Animal and the Machine* (1948), 32, 68
cybernetic sensibility, 12, 15, 27–30, 72, 186
cybernetic steering, 9, 171

data collection, 7, 79, 178, 185
Dayé, Christian, 3
deception: activities of, 142, 146–47; "anomic
  behavior", 124; in combat situations, 132;
  legitimatizing, 131; logical machine of, 133;
  making outcomes predictable, 123;
  strategic, 36, 124, 187
decision science, 113, 140, 145
decision trees, 19
deduction: logical, 25f, 123; problem of, 28, 50
Delphi method, 88, 95, 220n94, 222n140
demographic research, 43, 82, 218n58
Denyer, Nicholas, 18
Deutsch, Karl, 107, 187
digital computer(s), 31, 33, 132
digitization of labor, 32
disarmament talks, Reykjavik, 125, 139
divination, 16–18, 200n8
Dobrov, Genadii, 77, 87, 216n27
Douglas, Heather, 26–7
Druzhinin, Valentin V., 136
Durkheim, Émile, 22, 49, 124
dynamic systems, 59, 152, 202n48

Earth system science(s), 12, 163, 175, 181.
  See also governmentality: Earth system
economic forecasting: critical approach, 185;
  demand for, 48; emergence, 184
economic growth: social indicators, 160;
  Soviet, 78, 159; Soviet theory of, 47;
  "problem", 171; statistical modeling, 50
economic indicators, 47
economic planning: models influencing, 15,
  77, 184; reforms, 156; Soviet, 40, 54, 74, 85
economics: capitalist, 2; development of, 76;
  industrial, 145; scientific approaches to, 113;
  ungovernability of, 161
economy: evolution of, 208n60; models of, 51,
  167; "not a mosaic", 51; sectors, 47
economy of favors, 102, 160, 186
Efimov, Anatolii, 76, 79
Efremov, Ivan, 91, 220–21n111
Ehrenberg, Andrew, 29
Ellman, Michael, 190
emergent behavior, 63, 67

empathy, 134
engineering: cybernetic systems in, 73,
  202n48; teleological prediction applied, 106.
  See also systems engineering
*Enquiry Concerning Human Understanding,
  An,* (1748)
environment, the: application of cybernetic
  prediction, 65; hybrid system, 160;
  interactions with, 129; term, 159. *See also*
  environmental governance; global
  environmental change
environmental governance, 155, 162, 167, 171,
  177, 181
environmental systems. *See* Earth system
  science(s)
epistemology: cybernetic, 69, 73; empirical,
  26; of forecasting, 85; of governance, 60,
  160, 173–180; heuristic, 99; medical, 41;
  modern scientific, 36; neoliberal, 174; of
  order, 55; postpositivist, 157; scientific, 3,
  11, 36, 68; of scientific prediction, 19, 50, 51,
  99, 185; social constructivist, 128; of social
  prediction, 93; of transparency, 59
equilibrium: of economy, 48, 207n55; of Earth,
  170
Ereshko, Feliks, 135
ergonomics, 78
Erlich, Paul, 166
Ershov, Emil', 77, 80
ethics: collectives guided by, 68; vanish in
  reflexive control model, 143, 177
ethnic profiling, 188
ethnogenesis, 45, 206n31
Euler, Leonhard, 42
evolution: biosphere, 173, 244n87; brain, 34;
  Darwinian theory, 41, 45; development
  paths, 207n52; economy, 208n60; epistemology of, 69; guided, 244n91; social/human,
  49, 83, 128; of Soviet system, 191; statistical
  measurement of, 186
expert surveys, 90, 95
explanans, 23–25
extrapolatory prediction, 30, 61, 94

failure of prediction, 189–93
falsifiability, 27, 81, 99, 143
Fedorov, Evgenii, 131, 163, 165, 166, 170,
  243n64
feedback loops, 12, 13, 31, 33, 59–62, 152, 187
Feldman, Grigorii, 47, 83
Fidora, Alexander, 18–20
finance, reflexivity in, 143
Five-Year Plan, first, 51–53

280   INDEX

Flanagan, Owen, 127
Flechtheim, Ossip, 87, 219n88
Forecast (1901), 87, 94
forecasting: Soviet scientific, 42, 78, 88, 96,
    99–100, 103, 105, 118; Soviet social, 82–93,
    96, 98. *See also* statistical forecasting
foretelling, 19, 71
formal knowledge, 105
Forrester, Jay, 166, 228n61
forward-prediction model, 35–36
Foucault, Michel, 126–27, 153–54, 197n24
foundations, 41; institutional landscape, 98;
    limits, 39; macroeconomic, 47; in postrevo-
    lutionary Russia, 184. *See also* Soviet
    economy, forecasting
Foundations of the Mathematical Theory of
    Probabilities (1846), 43
French government, 76
Fundamentals of Ecology (1953), 165
future, the: problem of, 23; intrinsic
    association with prediction, 200n10
future-making, 3
Future of Humanity and the Earth, The (1928),
    87
future studies, 3, 86, 87, 91, 196n16
future-telling, 2
futurology, 87, 219n88

Gaia modeling system, 166, 181
Gaia theory, 166, 170
Galanskov, Iurii, 111
Galison, Peter, 60, 70
Gamblers, The (1842), 123
games. *See* Shchedrovitskii, G.P., activity/
    simulation games and Stalin, Joseph: ban on
    activity games
Games and Decisions (1957), 133
game theory, 4, 63, 133–34, 140, 142
Game Theory and Economic Behavior (1944),
    134
"garbage can" model, 8
"gardening state", 176–77
Gastev, Aleksei, 55, 57
general effects, 21
general laws: how formulated, 22–24, 25f, 44,
    50, 64; for populations and societies, 41, 64.
    See also antecedent conditions
General Staff (Genshtab), 136
Geneva school neoliberals, 11, 175
geological force, humanity as, 151, 155,
    162–63, 166, 168
Geroulanos, Stefano, 40, 59, 87, 173, 205n11
Gerovitch, Slava, 72, 212n11

Giddens, Anthony, 128n232
Ginzburg, Aleksander, 111
glasnost', 40–41, 80–81, 93, 164, 191, 204n7
Glazyev, Sergei, 98, 223n158
global climate crisis, 2, 166, 183
global environmental change: due to human
    activities, 168; imagination of, 159; impact
    of nuclear war, 138; limits of, 172, 176
global governance, 36, 154–55, 164, 167–69,
    172–174, 180; as guidance, 171, 178, 179, 181,
    184, 186; nongovernability, 155, 174
globalists, neoliberal, 67, 157, 175–176, 245n106
global modeling, 164, 166, 178–179
Glushkov, Viktor, 77, 159, 171, 176, 188
goal-seeking behavior, 13, 73, 106, 112, 225n19
goal-setting, 12–13, 106–7, 115
Gorbachev, Mikhail: disarmament talks, 125,
    reforms, 97, 104, 139, 164, 177; new
    approaches to governance, 156, 181
Gosplan, 52, 57, 76, 78–81, 90, 160, 171
governance: of complexity, 164, 181, 198n134;
    diverging approaches, 55; embodied, social,
    117; indirect, 8; habit vs. reflexivity in, 128;
    limited/ negative, 154–55; network, 107, 197;
    by numbers, 41–43; purposive control, 15,
    171, 181; "science", 80; Soviet scientific, 105,
    131; technocratic, 117; without reliable data,
    100. *See also* environmental governance;
    global governance; milieu, governance
    through; target-oriented governance
governmentality: Cold War, 70, 189; Earth
    system, 151, 170–71; globally-integrated,
    181; liberal, 129, 244; neoliberal, 153; of
    noosphere, 173; scholarship, 197n24; Soviet,
    81, 154, 175, 179; Soviet Earth system, 154,
    180; system-cybernetic, 9, 173; types of, 78
Gramelsberger, Gabriele, 30
Gregory, Paul, 57, 99, 211n103
Grimanelli, Pericles, 48, 208n60
Grushin, Boris, 84, 92, 93, 108
guidance: negative, 173, 177, 188; through
    milieu, 151, 155, 179, 184, 186
guided development, 173, 244n91
Gumilev, Lev, 165, 246n128
Gvishiani, Dzhermen, 78, 97, 168

habit: cycle of corrections, 129; vs. reflexivity,
    128
Hayek, Friedrich von, 155, 160–61, 167, 173,
    174, 176
Hayles, Katherine, 67
Heidegger, Martin, 59
Helmer, Olaf, 88

INDEX

Hempel, Carl, 23–25, 87, 88, 99
heuristics: character of forecasts, 99; climate science, 180; information processing, 106
Heymann, Matthias, 30
"high modernist state", 105
Hippocrates, 19
homeostasis, 170
human body, 19
Human Condition, The (1958), 59
humans, as prediction machines, 68
Hume, David, 21
Humean gap, 21, 23, 34
hypotheses: incomplete explanations, 25; "five-year", 53; flawed, 144; forecasts as, 54; predictive, 209n69

If the World Disarms (1961), 93
induction, Hume's problem of, 21
informality: in decision-making, 96; importance of, 106; legitimizing, 13, 107; mobilizing, 112; orchestrating, 119; social, 103, 186; sources of corruption, 103
information: conceptual split re matter, 67; quantum theory, 66; Weiner's view, 32, 62, 66
informational warfare, 122, 146–47
information theory, 66, 67, 95, 104
information transmission, "a predictive cascade", 34–35
input–output model, 7, 13, 34, 56, 80, 105, 119, 185
Institute for the International Labor Movement (IMRD), 89, 110
Institute of Concrete Social Research (IKSI/ISI), 83–86, 89–93, 96, 137, 218n58, 219n84
Institute of Future, 88
Institute of Psychoneurology, 46
institutes of agreement, 175, 181
institutional design, 40, 104, 181, 224n12
International Institute of Applied Systems Analysis (IIASA), 57, 97, 138, 156, 174
International Sociology Association (ISA), 83, 89, 91
interpolative prediction, 29
Introduction to Analysis of the Infinite (1748), 42
Isidore of Seville, 18
Ivanov, Viacheslav, 109, 131

Joel, Isaac, 140
Johnson, Ann, 3
Jungk, Robert, 81, 88, 91, 221n124

Kahn, Herman, 88
Kant, Immanuel, 128

Kantorovich, Leonid, 75, 80, 208n57
Kerzhentsev, Platon, 55, 57
KGB (State Security Committee), 85, 95, 109, 135–36, 204n7, 222n141, 225n21
Khristenko, Viktor, 105, 225n13
Khrushchev, Nikita, 75, 78, 83, 109, 110, 158
Kline, Ronald, 31
Knight, Frank. H., 30–31, 33
knowledge of unknowns (premodern), 16, 17
knowledge transfer, 12
known and unknown events, 49
Kondrat'ev, Nikolai: death, 56; and early Soviet planning, 46–52; pioneer of forecasting, 11; prevision idea, 53, 79, 184; value of indicative forecasts, 161; influence of Grimanelli, 208n62
Koopmans, Tjalling, 161
Kornberger, Martin, 146, 147
Kosygin, Aleksei, 77, 78, 97, 159
Kovalevskii, Mikhail, 46, 48
Kovda, Viktor, 165
Krementsov, Nikolai, 44
Kurakin, Boris, 45

Landa, Lev, 110
Landau, Lev
language: cybernetic, 63, 109; of formal logic, 140; mathematical, 178; statistical, 23
Lankina, Tomila, 158, 226n32
Laplace, Pierre-Simon: influence in Russia, 43, 55; Laplacian "Dream", 209n67; model of economy and society, 167; notion of perfect knowledge, 176; simplistic approach, 55; social physics, 49
Latour, Bruno, 148
Lavrent'ev, Mikhail, 158, 159, 241n30
League of Time, the, 55
Ledeneva, Alena, 103, 186
Lefebvre, Viktorina, 137, 138
Lefebvre, Vladimir, 13, 110, 123, 125, 131–48, 184
Leontief, Wassily, 56, 77, 207n52
Lepskii, Vladimir, 131, 231n11, 231n15, 235n60
limits: thinking from, 166, 177; setting, 173; shift from targets, 176; use of prohibitions with, 172; *Limits to Growth, The* (1972), 94, 162, 166
linear causality, 31, 66. *See also* causalities
linear model of prediction → action, 30
living standards forecasts, 85
logical empiricism, 21, 26, 64, 151, 153, 172, 191
logics of prediction: cybernetic, 73; positivist, 73

INDEX

Long Wave Cycle, The (1928), 56
Lovelock, James, 152, 160, 166, 170
Luce, Duncan, 133
Luria, Alexander, 51
Lyapunov, Aleksandr, 159

machine translation, 61, 62, 109
macroeconomics: forecasting, 47; models, 161; problems, 76; statistics, 56
Macy conferences on cybernetics, 61, 129
Mahony, Martin, 30
Maksimenko, Vitalii, 95
Mamardashvili, Merab,89, 108
management: cybernetization of, 73, 78; Moiseev's use of term, 169; professionalization in Russia, 13; reflexive control, 143; as resource orchestration, 8; Soviet, 54, 57, 78, 84, 104, 105, 114, 171; uses of statistical prediction, 6; time in, 55; type of governance, 181. *See also* scientific management; Shchedrovitskii, G. P.; Taylorism
Man and Noosphere (1990), 162
Manichean sciences, 60
manipulation, 36, 123, 124, 144, 147, 149, 232n16
mantic knowledge: Chinese version, 17; declining status, 29; shift to prognosis, 18, 174; transition from, 4
mantic practice: ancient, 19; premodern notions, 6
mantic science: etymology, 16; typologies, 18, 37
mantike, 16–17
Marx, Karl: *Capital*,108, 109; insufficient model of society, 167; producer goods vs. consumer goods, 47
Marxism–Leninism, 109, 134
"Mastery of Time as the Key Task in the Organization of Work, The" (1924)
materiality question, 67
mathematical modeling: of biosphere, 166; Moiseev's competence in, 162, 178; of reflexive processes, 134; for Soviet economy, 80
mathematics: methods, 3, 54; role of, 42
Matlock, Jack, 138, 139
McCulloch, Warren, 31, 133
McLuhan, Marshall, 187
Meadows, Dennis, 160, 166, 211n106
Meadows, Donella, 160
medical prognosis, 19
medicine, 19–20
Meninas o La Familia de Felipe IV, Las (1656), 126f–27, 143

Merton, Robert, 83, 123, 192
Middle Ages, European, 18
milieu(s): concept, 153; Foucault's use of, 154; milieu, governance through, 13, 151, 165, 178–180, 184, 186. *See also* guidance: through milieu
militarism, culture of, 136
military decision-making, 132
military-industrial complex: USA, 88, 145; USSR, 93, 109, 158–59, 216n28
military research, 77
military strategy, 110, 125, 135, 144
military technology, 12, 77
Mirowski, Philip, 49, 209n67
modernity, reflexive, 128. *See also* Cold War: modernity
modernization: Eurocentric narrative of, 4; Soviet, 181, 192; theory, 83; trap, 103
"modern man", the, 41, 44
Moiseev, Nikita: biosphere and noosphere, 165–67; on complexity, uncertainties, 188, 209n75; contribution, 15, 180–82; family background, 157–58; global concerns, 11, 155–56, 168–71, 178–79; governance as guidance approach, 54, 174–78; intellectual biography, 159–64; orchestration in, 173; prescriptive vs prohibitive approaches, 172
Morgenstein, Oskar, 134
Moscow Methodological Circle, 12, 98, 104, 108–9, 111, 134
Murav'ev, Valerian, 55, 57
mutual assured destruction (MAD), 122

natural givens, 180
nauchnaia organizatsiia truda (NOT), 54, 73, 86
negotiation models/strategies, 125, 139
neoliberalism, 174
Nerves of Government, The (1963), 107
Neumann, John von: influence on Lefebvre, 134; game theory of strategy, 63
neural networks, 31, 33, 37, 59, 106, 107
neural systems modes, 133
neurophysiology, 32, 34, 50, 69
neuropsychology, Soviet, 51
neuroscience, 35
New Cold War, 146
New Economic Policy (NEP), 113
Nietzsche, Friedrich, 1
nooscope, 165
noosphere: de Chardin vs. Vernadiskii, 155; governmentality of, 173; Moiseev's work on, 162–64, 166, 172, 179–81; Russian legacy,

180, 240n17, 246n128; Vernadiskii's vision of, 166
Northcott, Robert, 26, 27, 99
now-casting, 29
nuclear disarmament, 163, 177, 181. *See also* disarmament talks
nuclear energy, 115
nuclear war, 88, 93, 138, 181, 191
nuclear winter study, 156, 163, 170, 181
numbers: avalanche, 174; large sets of, 30; reliability, 28; transparency, 39, 101; visibility, 56. *See also* governance: by numbers; "autohypnosis" by numbers; statistical forecasting
numerical representation, 29, 167

observation, continuous, 10, 35, 72, 152
Odum, Eugene, 165
OGAS project, 171
Oldfield, Jonathan, 159
"On the Problem of Foresight", 48
ontology: cybernetic, 63; man/nature distinction, 168; status of ideas, 35
opacity, 103, 149, 187, 189, 191, 205n11, 247n9. *See also* transparency
operational planning, 136–137
operations research (OR), 75, 112, 131, 136, 159, 246n5
Oppenheim, Paul, 23–25, 87, 88, 99
orchestra: etymology of, 10; model of complexity, 198n34
orchestration: case for, 182; democratic, 193; form of governance, 8; of the future, 117, 150; limits to, 68, 117; long-term predictions, 150, 171; of scientific prediction, 7–10, 13, 71; synchronicity, 69; Wiener's description, 67, 201n28. *See also* cybernetic prediction; orchestration; guidance: through milieu
orchestrator, the, 8
Oreskes, Naomi, 266
organization, as fundamental concept, 168
Organisation for Economic Co-operation and Development (OECD), 88
organizations: management of, 8, 12, 184
organization studies, 7
O'Riordan, Timothy, 173, 174, 178

Panov, Dmitry, 131, 135
Parin, Vasilii, 91–92
Pask, Gordon, 33, 129, 130*f*
pattern processing and recognition: cybernetic notion, 12, 204n89; detection, 71; in fast-changing phenomena, 3;

prediction as, 28–29, 34–35, 186; probabilistic, 62
Pelevin, Viktor, 231–232n16
performative methodology, 111
performative nature of prediction, 3, 51, 73, 78, 98, 125, 151–52
performative strive, 19
perspektyvnyi plan, 52
Peter the Great, 38
Phenomenon of Man, The (1955), 166
Pickering, Andrew, 33, 36, 37, 63
Pietruska, Jamie, 4, 45
"Plan and Foresight" (1927), 53
planetary boundaries, 180–181
planning by design, 117
Poe, Edgar Allan, 141
point predictions, 99
policy action, linear model of, 7, 176
policy processes, 7–8
political economy: of cybernetics, 32; debates, 167; global, 14
Poovey, Mary, 20, 21, 28, 200n12
Popper, Karl, 27, 143
Porter, Theodore, 40, 178, 189
positivism: criticism of, 58, 177; French, 11, 21, 43, 48, 181; Laplacian, 176; logical, 23; in Russia, 39, 48; in USSR, 51; technocratic, 65
positivist prediction, 78, 150, 174, 177
Pospelov, Gemogen, 77, 95
Power, Michael, 6, 69, 70
Prague Spring (1968), 110, 137
precision: false, 172; as normative standard, 19, 21, positivist striving for, 55; search for, 71
predictability, 56, 66, 116, 151, 174, 190–92, 203n61
prediction, term, 199n1
predictive control, 60–61, 169
predictive expertise, research into, 2
predictive knowledge: actionable, 150; forms of, 192; internal diversity, 184, performative aspect, 103
predictive power: of brain, 34; and hypotheses, 25; of opinions, 200n12; of social science, 6
predictive processing, 35, 72, 99
predvidenie, 6, 48, 80, 94
prévision, 48
prevision: Comtean, 21–22; economic, 50, 53; Kondrat'ev' and, 49, 184; premodern, 4
prevoyance (prevision), 21
Priestland, David, 136, 164
Prisoner's Dilemma, 122, 123, 140
probabilistic methods, 27, 35, 43, 62
probabilistic thinking, 21, 22, 62, 80

284 **INDEX**

probability theory, 15, 199n3
*Prognstikon (*Book of Prognosis), 19
prognosis, 6, 18–20, 23, 38, 79, 94
prognostication, 19, 38
prognoz, 48, 50
prognozirovanie, 6, 47
prophecy: "supernatural", 49; self-fulfilling, 19, 192
la prospective, 112, 116, 228n62
prospective reflexivity, 13, 103–4, 112, 115–20, 122, 186
psychographics, 135
"Purloined Letter, The" (1844), 141
purposeful behavior, 62, 63f, 64, 71
purposive behavior, 26, 202n48
Putin, Vladimir, 105, 124, 149, 190
Pynnöniemi, Katri, 124

"quantifiable" growth, 43
quantification, 12

radar technology, 61, 64, 106, 132, 136
Raiffa, Howard, 133
RAND Corporation: Delphi method, 88, 95; military studies, 77; and planning, 228n61; simulation games, 113; Social Science division, 133, 141
Rapoport, Anatol, 133, 137, 141
rational choice theory, 133, 140, 145
Raven, Peter, 166
Rayner, Steve, 173, 174, 178
Reagan, Ronald, 138, 163
real-time information, 61, 188
reflexive control theory: ethical justification, 123, 230n1; events as evidence, 146; practice of, 143–49, 172; problem of parity, 142; "science" of decision-making, 124; "scientific status", 148; tactics, 124; Western reporting on, 125
reflexive deception, 13, 122–24, 132–33, 140–43, 155. *See also* deception
reflexive games, 140–43, 148
reflexivity: forward, 172; in finance, 125; informal relations, and, 116; methodology, 115; "mixed blessing", 127; multilevel information processing, 129–30; original meaning, 112; overflow, 140; performative and prospective, 13, 102–5, 112, 116–20, 122, 186–87; strategic applications, 139; in Western philosophy, 125, 128
resilience, 174, 181
Reus, Andrei, 105, 225n13
risk society, 69

risk studies, 6, 183
Roosevelt, Franklin, 169
Rosenberg, Alex, 144
Rosenblueth, Arthur, 62, 63, 106
Rostow, Walt, 83
Rules of Sociological Method (1895), 21, 49
Rumiantsev, Aleksei, 89, 92, 221n125, 223n165
Russia: cognitive operations, 146; ethnography, 46; eugenic thought, 44; information warfare, 148; institutional foundations of forecasting, 46; literacy rates, 43, 47; military hospitals, 44; peasants, 45; population statistics, 47; public health, 44, 189; scientific prediction, 48
Russian empire, 41–45
Russian nationalism, 157, 190
Russian world idea, 119

Sandomirskaja, Irina, 131
Santangelo, Federico, 16–17
Schelling, Thomas, 133, 140
Schmidgen, Henning, 68
science and technology studies (STS), 128, 181
scientific explanation(s): capacity to predict, 24; incomplete, 24; procedure of, 23; structure of, 25f; ultimate test, 39
scientific forecasting: conditions for, 40, 46; criticism of, 30, 81, 118; logics of prediction, 73; Soviet, 76–82, 87, 91, 96, 100, 159
scientific knowledge: approximate certainty, 21; formal, 105; Hempel and Oppenheim's theory, 23, 26; inevitable uncertainty, 174; vs. lay knowledge, 22; orchestration of production, 184; prediction in, 20, 28f, 186
scientific management, 54, 169, 210n97. *See also* Taylorism
scientific prediction: behavioral, 59, 151, 235n60; as explanation, 23–4, 64; Humean gap in, 21; and hypothesis-making, 56; as inference, 31, 33, 174; late modern, 27–30; logistical meaning, 191; mandate, 183; means to maintain opacity, 102; positivist, 21–26, 151; power to predict, 22; premodern, 16–20; probabilistic, 27, 59, 70, 71; relational concept, 12; structure, 25f. *See also* conjecture; epistemology: of scientific prediction; orchestration: of scientific prediction; pattern processing and recognition: prediction as; performative nature of prediction
Scientific Research Institute of Automatic Machinery (NIIAA), 131, 135

INDEX

Scientific Research Institute of Economics (NIEI), 76, 79, 99
scientific-technical progress (STP), 83
scientific-technical revolution theory (STR), 82–84, 86, 89, 209–10n81
s-curves, 42
Seefried, Elke, 3
self-images, 139
self-organization, 139, 161, 163, 168, 173
self-organizing systems, 130f, 139
"self-reference", term, 139, 144
self-reflexivity, 64
self-regulation: absence of, 179; corrective, 69; cybernetic, 161; via feedback, 96; beyond formal structures, 120; governance at a distance, 9; informational, 33; reflexivity as, 232n24; system level, 59, 152
semiotics, 110, 135, 143, 231–32n16
servomechanisms, 12, 15, 58, 63, 72–73, 132, 187
servomechanism theory, 61, 64, 69
Shatalin, Stanislav, 97, 100
Shchedrovitskii, Georgii Petrovich: activity/simulation games, 113–17; first Soviet management guru, 107–11; legacy, 103–106, 134, 120–21; reflexivity methodology, 118; work continued, 119. *See also* reflexivity; prospective reflexivity
Shchedrovitskii, Petr, 118
Shlapentokh, Vladimir, 84, 96
Skinner, B. F., 26, 34, 124, 154
Slobodian, Quinn, 157, 174–76, 245n106
Smil, Vaclav, 38, 98–99, 204n3
Smolian, Georgii, 135, 231–32n16
Snyder, Joel, 127
social behavior, 25, 129, 185
social engineering, 58, 117, 228n62
social hygiene movement, 43, 44
social mobilization model, 107
social research: domestic, 222n148; prediction in, 48; Soviet, 73, 84; transition between events in, 49
social statistical forecasting, 65
social statistics, 43, 65, 86, 184
social values studies, 85, 93, 96
Society for Scientific Forecasting (SSF), 91–92, 221n116
sociological prediction, 208n60
sociology, Soviet, 82–86
sociotechnics (*sotsiotekhnika*), 117
Sorokin, Pitirim, 47
Soros, George, 125, 143–145, 148
Soviet agriculture, 156
Soviet Association of Sociology (SAS), 82–83

Soviet censuses: 1926, 51; 1937 and 1939, 82
Soviet economy, forecasting, 74–82
Soviet planning: 1920s–1930, 53; 1950s, 76–77, 80; 1960s, 79; early, 46–52; Kosygin era, 78; processes, 57; types of plans, 53
Soviet planning practice, 52, 53, 99, 100, 106
Soviet space program, 158, 241n28
stabilization, 168, 184
Stages of Economic Growth, The: A Non-Communist Manifesto (1960), 83
Stalin, Joseph, ban on activity games, 113
State Commission for Electrification of Russia (GOELRO), 52, 77, 79
State Committee for Science and Technology (GKNT), 93, 161, 217n137
State Security Committee (KGB): and studies, 85, 95, 135, 222n141; investigations, 107, 109; policies, 204n7
static vs. dynamic laws, 50
statistical forecasting: input–output method, 13; cybernetic-like functions, 12; debates, 191; with goal-steering, 62; linear, 71; promise of, 38–40; in Russia, 41–47; status, 48; United States, 4, 45. *See also* social statistical forecasting
statistical prediction: types of, 29–30; cultures, 30, 45, 46
steersman processes, 9, 59, 188
strategic deception. *See* deception: strategic
Strategic Defense Initiative, 138
strategic thought, Soviet, 136, 145–47, 237n107
strategy, symbolic power, 145, 147
Strumilin, Stanislav, 54, 217n56
surveillance, Cold War, 12, 58
sustainable development, 175
symmetry, notion of, 25, 30
synchronization: brain as device, 68; of organizational action, 192; problem of, 8, 54, 244n87; of social action
systems approach and analysis, 104, 109, 111, 151, 159, 165, 170
systems engineering, 117

Taagepera, Rein, 191, 247n21
taboos, 173, 176, 177
Tarde, Gabriel, 128–129
Tardov, Boris N., 91, 221n117
target-oriented governance, 154, 172
target-seeking processes, 151
targets: illusion of control, 78; vs. limits, 173, 176
Taylor, Frederic Winslow, 169
Taylorism: American, 54, 169; Soviet version of, 78

286 INDEX

technocracy, 39, 58, 117, 169
technoscience, 8, 82, 157, 187
technoscientific forecasting, 88, 97
Teilhard de Chardin, Pierre, 155, 166, 167, 180
teleological behavior, 106, 107, 114
teleological control. *See* control: teleological
teleological planning approaches, 54, 63, 78
Thermonuclear War, On, (1960), 88
thinking activity, 111–20
Thomas, Timothy, 146
time series: analyses, 60, 88; methods, 56, 74; use in prediction, 199n2; theory, 60
timetables, 19–20
Timofeev-Resovskii, Nikolai, 165
Titarenko, Larissa, 84
transparency: absence of, 102; desire for, 39–40, 101; in economics, 80, 120; history of idea, 59, 69, 87–88, 123, 173. See also *glasnost'*
Trump, Donald, 190
tselevoe planirovanie, 78. *See also* teleological planning approaches
Tukhachevski, Mikhail, 74, 137
Turetskii, Shamai, 79

Ukraine: decision to invade, 192; Donetsk–Luhansk conflict (2014), 146, 190; invasion (2022), 124, 147, 187; reflexive control used in, 13, 122, 149, 187. *See also* reflexive control theory; strategic deception
uncertainty: in cybernetic prediction, 64, 71; epistemology friendly to, 60; governing, 174, 179; instrument of action, 144; in prospective reflexivity, 120; subversive effect, 85
ungovernability: economic, 161; scientific, 156
United Nations Educational, Scientific and Cultural Organization (UNESCO), 83, 89, 162, 165, 166
United Nations Environment Program (UNEP), 164
US National Bureau of Economic Research (NBER), 47, 174
utopianism: in Bestuzhev-Lada's work, 94, 98; modernist projects, 224n1; Soviet ideas of, 185; technocratic, 5, 189; and transparency, 205n11. *See also* cybernetic sensibility

Vaino, Anton, 105, 246n148
Velázquez, Diego, 126–27
Velmet, Aro, 95, 212n11
Verhulst, Pierre Francois, 42
Vernadskii, Vladimir, 155, 159, 162, 165, 172, 240n18
visibility, 11–12, 39–40, 56, 100, 102, 176, 204n2
Vol'pe, Abram, 74
Voprosy filosofii (Issues of Philosophy), 77, 88, 140
Vygotsky, Lev, 110, 114

weather monitoring, 38, 44, 45
Weick, Karl, 19, 106, 191
"Western" scientific tradition, 4, 16, 75, 81, 123
what if reasoning, 30
"what is to come", Russian words, 94
Wiener, Norbert: cybernetic prediction, 11, 12, 59–65, 68, 71; defining of cybernetics, 9, 59; "events" and "messages", 62; goal-steering, 54; information, 32; loops, 13, 66; materiality, 67; teleology, 78
Wildawsky, Aaron, 120
will to power, 1, 193
will to predict: beliefs behind, 46; legitimacy and ethical issues, 186, 189, 191–92; fueled criticism, 97; generates models, 3; integrating force, 6; requires orchestration, 184; Soviet, 15
Window to the Future, A: The Contemporary Problems of Social Prognosis (1970), 94
World Dynamics (1978), 166
World Future Studies Federation, 91–92
world government, 166, 174

Zadorin, Igor', 98
Zan, Luca, 145
Zdravomyslova, Elena, 84
Zinov'ev, Aleksandr, 89, 104, 108
Zuboff, Shoshana, 32, 35, 189
Zubok, Vladislav, 97, 111, 156, 177, 202n47
Zvorykin, Anatolii, 83, 89, 216n28

Milton Keynes UK
Ingram Content Group UK Ltd.
UKHW010900100524
442427UK00008B/87/J